DATE DUE

GAYLORD			PRINTED IN U.S.A.

AFTERLIFE

THE A

Penelope Fitzgerald

THE AFTERLIFE

A good book is the precious life-blood
of a master-spirit, embalmed and treasured up
on purpose to a life beyond life.

John Milton

Edited by TERENCE DOOLEY

with CHRISTOPHER CARDUFF
AND MANDY KIRKBY

Introduction by HERMIONE LEE

COUNTERPOINT
A MEMBER OF THE PERSEUS BOOKS GROUP
NEW YORK

Counterpoint books are available at special discounts for bulk purchases in the
United States by corporations, institutions, and other organizations. For more
information, please contact the Special Markets Department at the Perseus Books
Group, 11 Cambridge Center, Cambridge, MA 02142, or call (617) 252-5298,
(800) 255-1514, or e-mail j.mccrary@perseusbooks.com.

Owing to limitations of space, all permissions to reprint previously
published material may be found on pages xx–xxii.

First Edition

Book design and composition by Jeff Williams
Set in 11-point Simoncini Garamond

Printed in the United States of America on acid-free paper that meets the American
National Standards Institute Z39–48 Standard.

Library of Congress Cataloging-in-Publication Data

Fitzgerald, Penelope.
The afterlife / Penelope Fitzgerald ; edited by Terence Dooley with
Christopher Carduff and Mandy Kirkby ; introduction by Hermione Lee.
p. cm.
ISBN 1-58243-198-1 (alk. paper)
I. Dooley, Terence, 1950- II. Carduff, Christopher. III. Kirkby, Mandy. IV. Title.

PR6056.I86A69 2003
824'.914—DC21

2003012433

COUNTERPOINT
387 Park Avenue South
New York, N.Y. 10016–8810

10 9 8 7 6 5 4 3 2 1

For
VALPY, IINA, AND MARIA
and in memory of
DESMOND, MARY AND EVOE, AND MOPS
—*T D*

Contents

Master-Spirits

Writers and Witnesses 1980–2000

INTRODUCTION

Because Penelope Fitzgerald's genius as a writer of fiction lay so much in reticence, quietness, and self-obliteration, her admirers will come to her posthumously collected nonfiction with intense curiosity, searching for her likes and dislikes, her preferences and opinions and feelings, in these wonderfully sympathetic, curious, and knowledgeable pieces on writing, art, craft, places, history, and biography. And, in a generous selection of twenty years' worth of essays and reviews, we do find (especially in the last section, on "Life and Letters") Fitzgerald's point of view very plainly set out. She believed, as a novelist, that (as she said to me in an interview in 1997) "you should make it clear where you stand." Here, speaking of E. M. Delafield, she asks: "What is the use of an impartial novelist?" She is forthright and candid here about her moral position in her novels: "I have remained true to my deepest convictions—I mean to the courage of those who are born to be defeated, the weaknesses of the strong, and the tragedy of misunderstandings and missed opportunities which I have done my best to treat as comedy, for otherwise how can we manage to bear it?" "Everyone has a point to which the mind reverts naturally when it is left on its own. I recalled closed situations that created their own story out of the twofold need to take refuge and to escape, and which provided their own limitations. These limitations were also mine." Such utterances throw a revealing light on the novels. But they are also rather cryptic: she expects us to understand what she means by the "point" the mind "reverts to naturally"; she doesn't tell us what she thinks her limitations are. She has a way of saying strange, challenging, unsettling things in a matter-of-fact way, as if these were self-evident truths. Her manner is plain and mild; her prose never shows off. She is practical and vivid and clear and exact about her subject, and leads you right to the heart of the matter: the feeling of a novel, the nature of a life, the understanding of how something or someone works, the sense of a place or a time. All the same, when you get there, you may still feel much left unsaid or unexplained.

There is often that sense of something withheld in her novels, as in the mysterious forest encounter in *The Beginning of Spring*, or the meaning of the story of the "blue flower," never completed, never spelled out. As Fritz tells Sophie in that novel: "If a story begins with finding, it must end with searching." At the end of the story "Desideratus" (in her posthumously published collection *The Means of Escape*) the boy who has lost his keepsake and been on a strange journey to recover it, is told: "You have what you came for." But his quest journey remains baffling and mysterious. And she doesn't care much for explanations. In that 1997 interview she told me (as she often told interviewers) that her books were so short because she didn't like to tell her readers too much: she felt it insulted them to over-explain. She says here in an essay on Charlotte Mew (which preceded her moving and eloquent biography of the poet) that she is a writer who "refuses quite to be explained." She is amused by Byron's impatience with Coleridge's metaphysics: "I wish he would explain his explanation." She likes readers to have their wits about them, and she likes exercising her own, as with her pleasure in Beckett's dialogue:

> What a joy it is to laugh from time to time, [Father Ambrose] said. Is it not? I said. It is peculiar to man, he said. So I have noticed, I said. . . . Animals never laugh, he said. It takes us to find that funny, I said. What? he said. It takes us to find that funny, I said loudly. He mused. Christ never laughed either, he said, as far as we know. He looked at me. Can you wonder? I said.

She comments: "This kind of dialogue shows us what we could say if we had our wits about us, and gives us its own peculiar satisfaction."

Beckett's hollow laughter is a surprising preference for Fitzgerald, who is not herself a player with words or a lugubrious comic. And there are other surprises here. There are pieces on writers we might have guessed she would like—Sarah Orne Jewett for her deep, quiet knowledge of a small community, its silences, pride, and cruelties; John McGahern for his poetic realism, his attention to "small acts of ceremony," and his "magnificently courteous attention to English as it is spoken in Ireland"; William Trevor for his empathy with the innocent and the dispossessed; Olive Schreiner for her strangeness, dreaming, and courage. But there are others she champions more unexpectedly: Roddy Doyle, Carol Shields, D. H. Lawrence, Joyce (even *Finnegans Wake*). This is not a narrow, prissy, or parochial critic.

At the heart of her intellectual passions is a political commitment to an English tradition of creative socialism, a vision at once utopian and practical, of art as work and of the usefulness of art to its community. Her English heroes are Blake, Ruskin, Burne-Jones, William Morris, Lutyens. She is inspired by Morris's dedication to "the transformation of human existence throughout the whole social order." (Though, as in *The Beginning of Spring*, she sees the comedy and pathos of Utopianism too, manifested in the early twentieth century in "Tolstoyan settlements, garden cities and vegetarianism tea-rooms, Shelley's Spirit of Delight . . . and the new Rolls-Royce.") She deeply admires Morris's painful mixture of neurosis, work ethic, resolution, and struggle for self-control. But she likes her idealists best at their most down-to-earth: Ruskin on the joy of shelling peas ("the pop which assures one of a successful start, the fresh colour and scent of the juicy row within. . .") or the cunning arrangements at Burne-Jones's studio at The Grange: "the huge canvases could be passed in and through slits in the walls, there were hot-water pipes, and a skylight so that it could be used for painting with scaffolding." The work of Morris that most delights her is the Kelmscott Press and his experiments with typography.

She always pays great attention to serious craftsmanship, practiced skills, and technical mastery. (There is always a job to be done in her novels: running a bookshop or a school, keeping a barge afloat.) The best compliment she can pay to the biographies she often reviews is "calm professionalism." She is just as interested in non-verbal professions; there is a great deal about art in this book. She tells us about Francis Oliphant's failed attempts at glass painting, William de Morgan's luminous tiles, Charles Ashbee's high-minded devotion to handicrafts (all the same, "he was an architect whose houses stood up"), and Edward Lear's heavenly Mediterranean paintings. She has an eye for illustrations—John Minton's decorations for Elizabeth David's first cookery book, "a kind of delicious ballet in and out of the text," or Ernest Shepard (her stepmother's father) and his feeling for line ("You can recognize it in . . . a study of . . . a young man cutting long grass. . . . The braces are only just sketched in, but you can see how they take the strain"). She loves small well-made books, like J. L. Carr's "delightful tiny booklets, *The Little Poets*" ("I only wish I had a complete set now"). One of her favorite quotations is from the socialist woodworker Romney Green, who held that "if you left any man alone with a block of wood and a chisel, he will start rounding off the corners."

Romney Green was a friend of Harold Monro, founder of the Poetry Bookshop, which had a quirky, idealistic, and influential life from the 1910s to the early 1930s. This is Fitzgerald's golden age: she doesn't like "Georgian" to be used as a term of abuse. Born in 1916, she remembered hearing Walter de la Mare reading at the Poetry Bookshop, and many of her best-loved writers are connected to that period and that atmosphere: A. E. Housman, Edward Thomas, Sylvia Townsend Warner, Stevie Smith. Again, one of the things she liked best about the Poetry Bookshop was the look of its rhyme sheets, which, "in the spirit of William Blake," and using some of the best illustrators of the time (including John and Paul Nash, David Jones, and Edward Bawden), were designed for "the verse and the picture to make their impression together." She shared Townsend Warner's enthusiasm. "We tacked them on our walls, above our beds and our baths."

Harold Monro was a lost cause in the end, a pathetic and gloomy alcoholic, and the Bookshop was carried on gallantly for a while, and then wound up, by his passionate Polish widow, Alida. As in her novels, Fitzgerald is drawn to failures, and some of her most vivid characterizations here, in life as in fiction, are of despairing figures whose struggles and defeats are at once funny and terrible. She is drawn to the sad minor characters in minor English novels. There is the poor faded shabby-genteel Mrs. Morgan in Mrs. Oliphant's *The Rector* ("She cannot afford to complain. Time has robbed her of the luxury of ingratitude"). There is the "uncompromisingly plain Anne Yeo" in Ada Leverson's *Love's Shadow*, "hideously dressed in a mackintosh and golf-cap and 'well aware that there were not many people in London at three o'clock on a sunny afternoon who would care to be found dead with her.'" There is the unmarried Monica in E. M. Delafield's *Thank Heaven Fasting*, a prisoner of early-twentieth-century middle-class English domestic servitude: "Heavy meals come up from the basement kitchen, clothes are worn which can't be taken off without the help of a servant, fires blaze, bells are rung, hairdressers arrive by appointment—every morning and evening bring the spoils of a comfortable unearned income. It is the only home Monica has ever known, and we have to see it turn first into a refuge for the unwanted, and then into a prison." You might not call Penelope Fitzgerald, at first glance, a feminist writer, but she is one.

So conscious of how cruel life can be to its victims, she is generally kind herself. However, she should not be mistaken for a pushover, and can be lethal about poor work. One biographer, busy seeing off his predecessor as "conventional," is dealt with thus: "This leads you to expect a bold treatment of some debatable points, but that would be a mistake." Another is described as writing with "flat-footed persever-ance." She is often at her most ironical when writing about biography, a form that fascinates and exasperates her (and that, in her lives of Charlotte Mew and the Knox brothers, she made entirely her own). She always insists on the need for the fullest possible historical context, and she knows all about the problems of the genre: "The years of success are a biographer's nightmare." "The 'middle stretch' is hard for biogra-phers." "Perhaps the worst case of all for a biographer, nothing defin-able happened at all."

In any life-story, she is alert to cruelty, tyranny, or unfairness, and she has no time for horrible behavior—severely recalling Larkin, on an Arts Council Literature Panel, saying (in response to a query about the fund-ing of "ethnic arts centres") that "anyone lucky enough to be allowed to settle here had a duty to forget their own culture and try to understand ours," or summing up the character Evelyn Waugh assumed for visitors and admirers as "the tiny Master threateningly aloof in his study, emerg-ing with the message: I am bored, you are frightened." Like her father, Evoe Knox, as editor of *Punch*, she will always speak out against tyrants. And she has an acute feeling for—and memory of—the vulnerability of children. She responds to writers (like Walter de la Mare, or Blake, or Olive Schreiner) who enter into the child's dreams, or feelings of exile or homesickness; she is very alert to "the bewilderment of children grow-ing up without love." At her memorial service, appropriately, Humper-dinck's ravishing and consolatory lullaby for the two lost children, Hansel and Gretel, was sung.

Hansel and Gretel (whose lullaby is also heard in *The Bookshop*) believe in angels; Penelope Fitzgerald probably did, too. She certainly believes in minor phenomena like ghosts and poltergeists, and she does a great deal of thinking about religion, as is only natural for the grand-daughter of bishops and the niece of a socialist priest, a notable Roman

Catholic convert and translator of the Bible, and a fiercely skeptical cryptographer. Her novels argue, quietly, over belief, and the relation between the soul and the body. "Because I don't believe in this . . . that doesn't mean it's not true," is Frank's position in *The Beginning of Spring*. The Russian priest he is listening to says to his congregation: "You are not only called upon to work together, but to love each other and pity each other." Fitzgerald has described herself as "deeply pessimistic," but she seems to believe in that sort of ideal. Writing here about *Middlemarch* and its hope that "the growing good of the world" may depend on the diffusive effect of obscure acts of courage, heroism, and compassion, Fitzgerald says, not entirely confidently: "We must believe this, if we can." "Pity" is one of the emotions—or qualities—she most values, especially in comedy. She certainly has a lively interest in little-read late-Victorian theological fiction, and a sharp eye for religious patches seeping through into secular-seeming texts, like Jane Austen's Evangelicism leading Emma to weep over "a sin of thought," or Virginia Woolf inheriting from her father "a Victorian nonconformist conscience painfully detached from its God."

But she is extremely reticent about her own beliefs. The people she admires are those who have a habit of "not making too much of things." She takes aesthetic pleasure in control and restraint: writing about Angus Wilson's homosexuality, she says, with a rare touch of primness: "Getting rid of the restraints didn't improve him as a writer—when does it ever?" What autobiography we get here comes in glimpses—she says of her father that "everything that was of real importance to him he said as an aside." At one point in her life she started to write a biography of her friend L. P. Hartley, but stopped when she realized that it would give pain to his surviving relative. She thinks of him as resisting investigation; one of his characters, when unconscious, is subjected to "a complete examination" by a famous specialist, "which in all his waking moments he had so passionately withstood." One of the very few personal details she gives us in these essays—that she once had a miscarriage—is offered only to illustrate the profound reserve of Ernest Shepard, who came to see her and handed her a bunch of flowers "without a word." She has a lot of time for silence: the silence that falls after a life-story like Coleridge's, the world of Jewett's stories "where silence is understood," the reserve which kept James Barrie from telling us what Mrs. Oliphant said on her death-bed. This collection ends with Virginia Woolf's posthumously published description, in her last novel, of a woman writer—a comic failure, of the kind Fitzgerald enjoyed writing about, too—leaving her audience behind ("she took her voyage away from the shore") and taking with her some mysterious unspoken words.

HERMIONE LEE
June 2003

EDITORS' NOTE

In Penelope Fitzgerald's novel *The Bookshop*, Florence Green, while tidying up the shelves of her establishment, finds herself compelled to open a couple of small, jacketless hardbacks—"old Everyman editions in faded olive boards stamped with gold." The Everymans are second-hand stock and not very good sellers, but they are classics, and to Florence's middle-aged eye they have a shabby dignity that the bright young paperbacks cannot match. She has read the Everymans since she was a girl. They are the books of her heart.

Inside the Everymans she finds the familiar elaborate endpapers with their legend from Milton's *Areopagitica*. "A good book is the precious life-blood of a master-spirit, embalmed and treasured up on purpose to a life beyond life." These words, which puzzled her when she was young, now become her touchstone; they go straight to the core of her love for books, and keep her mindful of why books are deserving of love.

In searching for a title for this posthumous collection of Penelope Fitzgerald's occasional prose writings, we thought of this scene from *The Bookshop*, and about the Everyman motto. Except for a few travel pieces, bits of autobiography, and reviews of contemporary novels and memoirs, all of these writings are concerned with the lives of "master-spirits"—the authors of the classics and the books of Penelope Fitzgerald's own heart. They are also concerned with these writers' afterlives, their "life beyond life" not only in the pages of their works but in the minds of their readers, critics, and biographers.

With one exception—a few words about her father's poems, written in 1972—all of the pieces collected here were published during the years of Penelope Fitzgerald's fame, between 1980, the year after she won the Booker Prize for *Offshore*, and 2000, the year of her death at the age of eighty-three. Though *The Afterlife* contains some eighty items, it is by no means The Complete Short Prose of Penelope Fitzgerald. Such a book would also include, among much else, the reviews of horse shows, movies, plays, and art exhibitions she wrote for *Punch*, under her maiden name P. M. Knox, from 1937 to 1944; the dozens of essays on art and literature she wrote for *World Review*, the monthly magazine she edited with her husband, Desmond Fitzgerald, from 1950 to 1953; and the many further notices of books by her contemporaries, English, Irish, American, Italian, German, and Russian. Other editors would have made different choices. In the future they no doubt will.

We are deeply grateful to Jack Shoemaker, the former publisher of Counterpoint, for making this collection possible. Thanks too to our project editor, Kay Mariea, our copy editor, Marco Pavia, the designer Jeff Williams, and the rest of the staff of Perseus Books Group Central Services for the care they took in producing the book.

We should like to thank Houghton Mifflin Company for permission to reprint an excerpt from *The Gate of Angels*, by Penelope Fitzgerald. Copyright © 1990 by Penelope Fitzgerald.

Acknowledgment is also made to the following periodicals and publishers, who first published the pieces specified, sometimes under different titles and in slightly different form:

BOOKS AND COMPANY: "The News from Dunnet Landing."

THE CHARLESTON MAGAZINE: "Breathing Together."

COUNTRY LIVING: "Thinking of Balcombe."

THE DAILY MAIL: "Well Walk."

THE DAILY TELEGRAPH: "The Consolations of Housman" and "Kipper's Line."

THE EVENING STANDARD: "Raging Martyr," "Joy and Fear," and "A Fortunate Man," Part 1.

THE FOLIO SOCIETY: "The Will to Good," an introduction to *Middlemarch*, by George Eliot. Introduction copyright © 1999 by Penelope Fitzgerald. Reprinted by permission of The Folio Society.

GALE RESEARCH COMPANY: "Curriculum Vitae," from *Contemporary Authors Autobiographical Series,* Volume 10. Copyright © 1989 by Penelope Fitzgerald and Gale Research Company. Reprinted by permission of Gale Group, Farmington Hills, Michigan.

THE INDEPENDENT: "An Unforgettable Voice," "The Moors," and "The Holy Land."

INSTITUTE OF CONTEMPORARY ART (LONDON): "Whatever Is Unhappy Is Immoral," a contribution to the catalogue accompanying "William Morris Today," an exhibition on view at the ICA, 1 March–29 April 1984. Essay copyright © 1984 by Penelope Fitzgerald.

THE JOURNAL OF THE WILLIAM MORRIS SOCIETY: "The Grange."

THE JOURNEYMAN PRESS: "Something Sweet to Come," an introduction to *The Novel on Blue Paper*, by William Morris, edited by Penelope Fitzgerald. Introduction copyright © 1982 by Penelope Fitzgerald.

LIBÉRATION: "Why I Write" (a response, in French, to the question "Pourquoi écrivez-vous?"). Translated for the present volume by Terence Dooley. Translation copyright © 2003 by Terence Dooley.

THE LONDON REVIEW OF BOOKS: "Called Against His Will," "Twice-Born," "His Daily Bread," "The Gospel of Joyous Work," "Obstacles," "Miss Lotti's Story," "Dear Sphinx," "Out of the Stream," "Keeping Warm," "The Real Johnny Hall," "Dame Cissie," "What's Happening in the Engine Room," "'Not at All Whimsical,'" "A Secret Richness," "Luck Dispensers," "Watchers and Waiters," "What Daisy Knew," "Grandmother's Footsteps," and "Following the Plot."

THE NEW CRITERION: "Thin, Fat, and Crazy" and "'Really, One Should Burn Everything.'"

THE NEW YORK TIMES: "Canaletto's Venice."

THE NEW YORK TIMES BOOK REVIEW: "The Unfading Vision," "Talking Through the Darkness," "Lasting Impressions," "The Great Encourager," "The Only Member of His Club," "The Man from Narnia," "A Character in One of God's Dreams," and "To Remember Is to Forgive."

THE NEW YORK TIMES MAGAZINE: "The Need For Open Spaces."

THE OBSERVER: "Not Herself," "The Mystery of Mrs. Oliphant" and "Passion, Scholarship, and Influence."

OXFORD UNIVERSITY PRESS: "Emma's Fancy," an introduction to *Emma*, by Jane Austen, in the Oxford World Classics series. Introduction copyright © 1999 by Penelope Fitzgerald. "The Far and the Near," an introduction to *The Root and the Flower*, by L. H. Myers. Introduction copyright © 1985 by Penelope Fitzgerald. Reprinted by permission of Oxford University Press, Oxford and New York.

PENGUIN BOOKS (UK): "Monty and His Ghosts," an introduction to *The Haunted Dolls' House and Other Stories*, by M. R. James, in the Penguin Classics series. Introduction copyright © 2000 by Penelope

Master-Spirits

JANE AUSTEN

Emma's Fancy

An introduction to *Emma*

Emma (1814–15) is the last novel Jane Austen wrote before, at the age of forty, she began to feel the warning symptoms of her last illness. If a writer's career can ever be said to have a high summer, this was hers.

Emma Woodhouse, we are told, is handsome, clever, and rich, and has lived nearly twenty-one years in this world "with very little to disturb or vex her." Feeling the muted irony of this, we know that quite soon something will happen to distress her. It will be due partly to her own temperament—"a disposition to think a little too well of herself"—partly to her upbringing in quiet Highbury.

As in *Pride and Prejudice* and *Mansfield Park*, visitors arrive to unsettle the neighborhood, but, unlike Elizabeth Bennet or Fanny Price, Emma meets them from a position of undisputed authority. Her reckless desire to manage and control is felt as the result of confining a keenly energetic character within a small space. She is, as Jane Austen is careful to show, very well-adapted to her life. She is the capable manager of a not very easy household and estate (which seems to include a piggery). She is generous and realistic toward the poor, a patient visitor to the cottagers, not expecting gratitude. But this strong-minded, affectionate young woman happens also to be an "imaginist," "on fire with speculation and fancy." One might feel, in fact, that she has the potentialities of a best-selling novelist.

To Jane Austen, however, the contemporary of Byron, "that very dear part of Emma, her fancy," represents a danger of a specific kind. It is shown as the enemy not of reason, but of truth. It tempts Emma to see the blooming, commonplace Harriet as the heroine of a romance, and leads her on through absurd schemes—when she pretends, for instance, to lose the lace of her "half-boot" so that Harriet and Mr. Elton can walk on together—to the moment when, overcome with disappointments and disillusions, she cries out, "O God! that I had never seen her!"

Jane Austen's novels are constructed on a delicate system of losses and gains, or retreats and advances. She undertakes, I think, to show that Emma's release of her creative imagination—in spite of her intervals of remorse and repentance—gradually becomes more and more dangerous, not only to others but to her own nature. Undoubtedly she was worried about this new heroine "whom nobody but myself will much like." To Mr. Clarke, the librarian of Canton House, with whom she was corresponding over the question of dedicating *Emma* to the Prince Regent, she wrote: "I am strongly haunted with the idea that to those readers who have preferred 'Pride and Prejudice' it will appear inferior in wit, and to those who have preferred 'Mansfield Park' inferior in good sense."

"Haunted" is a strong word, and she does not sound as though she is making a conventional disclaimer. Rather it is as if she knew she was taking a risk, the risk, that is, of letting Emma go too far. The great Harriet undertaking is, after all, intended for the benefit of Harriet. It has "the real good will of a mind delighted with its own ideas." Robert Martin, Harriet's suitor, must be got rid of and "Mr. Elton was the very person fixed on by Emma for driving the young farmer out of Harriet's head." The very strength of "fixed" and "driving" seem to echo her determination to make the unreal real. But the fact remains that her object was to "better" her unassuming friend, and her regret—while it lasts—is very real, "with every resolution confirmed of repressing imagination all the rest of her life." By the time the second movement of the novel begins, her imagination—unrepressed—has taken a turn for the worse. She is paying a call on the talkative, poor-genteel Miss Bates. Miss Bates is expecting a long visit from her niece, Jane Fairfax, who is leaving her post as governess to the daughter of old friends. This daughter was recently married to a Mr. Dixon. "At this moment, an ingenious and animating suspicion enter[ed] Emma's brain with regard to Jane Fairfax [and] this charming Mr. Dixon." It is the word "animating" that betrays Emma here. The unkind, even heartless, and quite unfounded notion is like a breath of new life to her. How can she go so far as to share it, as an amusing confidence, with Frank Churchill? What has become of her greatest virtues, compassion and generosity? This, unlike her first fantasy, is not intended to benefit anyone. Indeed, it can only cause immeasurable harm, as Emma not only deceives herself but is in turn deceived by Frank, the gleefully mischievous intruder.

Something is painfully wrong. We realize, certainly by the evening of the box-of-letters game at Hartwell, that Emma is hardly herself. This appears during the day's outing to Box Hill, a harmless party of pleasure to which only Jane Austen could have given such chilling significance. When Emma makes her cutting remark, her openly rude put-down, to Miss Bates, it is as though the heavens — ironically clear and fine—might fall. Miss Bates "did not immediately catch her meaning; but when it burst on her, it could not anger, though a slight blush showed that it could pain her." Poor Miss Bates, always to be borne with, like some gentle natural force, is a moral test for the whole of Highbury, who are in a kind of neighborly conspiracy to make her feel wanted. Emma, of all people, fails the test. "It was badly done, indeed!" says Mr. Knightley. And Emma, who has a great capacity for suffering, has to bear not only this reproach, but, later on, Miss Bates's "dreadful gratitude." Her intrigues have led her farther and farther away from "everything that is decided and open." Not one of the heroines of Jane Austen's other novels is so deluded. None of them is so obstinate. None of them, certainly, makes such a brutal remark. And yet Jane Austen is successful. We love Emma, and hate to see her humbled. The very structure of the book asks us to compare her with Jane Fairfax. Jane is faultless, delicate, unfortunate, and mysterious, but we do not, even for a moment, feel for her as we do for Emma. We have to watch her struggle. She has "two spirits," Mr. Knightley reminds her, the vain and the serious. The two spirits are self-will and conscience, and Emma, in the last instance, has to battle it out for herself.

She has, of course, a safe guide in Mr. Knightley. I once asked some students for an alternative title to the novel, and they suggested "Mr. Rightly." He is "a sensible man about seven- or eight-and-thirty" (much more convincing than if we knew exactly which). He has knowledge, experience, and the courage to speak out. He acts, while others talk. At the dinner party at the Westons', when all are discussing the fallen snow and the impossibility of driving back, Mr. Knightley goes out to have a look for himself, and is able to answer "for there not being the smallest difficulty in their getting home, whenever they liked it." Frank Churchill, the weak romantic hero, rescues Harriet from the gypsies, but it is Mr. Knightley, when she has been grossly humiliated by the Eltons, who asks her to dance. And yet he too has something to learn. Even before Frank's long-delayed arrival in Highbury, the sanely judging Mr. Knightley has taken unreasonably against him, or rather against Emma's interest in him. "'He is a person I never think of from one month's end to another,' said Mr. Knightley, with a degree of vexation, which made Emma immediately talk of something else, though she could not comprehend why he should be angry." Nor can he.

Mr. Knightley is pre-eminently the right man in the right place. Highbury, it is true, is less lively than it used to be—its "brilliant days" are past, and the ballroom is used for a whist club—but the village lies in what seems unthreatened prosperity, surrounded by fields of wheat, oats, turnips, and beans and the parkland and strawberry beds of substantial houses. Jane Austen has been careful to make it a haven of only lightly disturbed peace. Since Mr. Knightley himself is the local magistrate, there is nothing to fear. Emma, unlike the heroines of the other novels, makes no journeys, has never even seen the sea, but we come to realize that Donwell and Hartfield, "English verdure, English comfort, seen under a sun bright, without being oppressive," won't, after all, be restrictive to her soaring temperament. Indeed, she accepts it herself as she stands looking out of the door of Ford's, Highbury's one large draper's shop:

> when her eyes fell only on the butcher with his tray, a tidy old woman travelling homewards from shop with her full basket, two curs quarrelling over a dirty bone, and a string of dawdling children round the baker's little bow-window eyeing the gingerbread, she knew she had no reason to complain, and was amused enough; quite enough still to stand at the door. A mind lively and at ease, can do with seeing nothing, and can see nothing that does not answer.

This passage lies at the very heart of the book, an interlude, not of idleness, but of busy tranquility.

In *Northanger Abbey* Jane Austen refers to the "rules of composition" of "my fable." What were her rules of composition? It is sometimes said that in her later novels she shows contempt and even hatred for her wrong-thinkers and wrongdoers. Certainly she was a writer in whom the comic spirit burned very strongly and who felt that some inhumanities are hard to forgive. But although she had the born satirist's opportunity to punish, she surely used it very sparingly in *Emma*. Frank Churchill, in his negligent way, causes more pain than anyone else in the book. He misleads Emma, largely to safeguard himself, and teases the helpless Jane almost to breaking point. What is his reward? In Mr. Knightley's words,

"His aunt is in the way.—His aunt dies.—He has only to speak.—His friends are eager to promote his happiness.—He has used every body ill—and they are all delighted to forgive him.—He is a fortunate man indeed!" Miss Bates, on the other hand, the woman of "universal good-will," might, by any other writer, have been rewarded, but nothing of the kind occurs. "She is poor; she has sunk from the comforts she was born to; and if she live to old age, must probably sink more." Mr. Elton, however, and his insufferable wife both flourish. Their satisfaction in themselves is not disturbed. They are the unteachables of classic comedy.

Beneath the moral structure of Jane Austen's novels lie, not hidden but taken for granted, her religious beliefs. In *Emma* they are openly expressed only once. After Mr. Knightley declares himself Emma finds that "a very short parley with her own heart produced the most solemn resolution of never quitting her father.—She even wept over the idea of it, as a sin of thought." "Sin of thought" is a phrase familiar from the Evangelical examination of the conscience, and the book here is at its most serious. Emma's love for her father has been, from the first, the way of showing the true deep worth of her character.

But Jane Austen gave her family (so her nephew says in his Memoir) "many little particulars about the subsequent careers of her people." She told them that "Mr. Woodhouse survived his daughter's marriage, and kept her and Mr. Knightley from settling at Donwell, about two years." The story ends, then, with a quite unexpected irony: Mr. Woodhouse was right, after all, to fancy that his health was in a dangerous state. It is hard to imagine Highbury without him, as Jane Austen evidently could. But it is a corresponding relief to think of Emma—the warmhearted, headstrong, even dangerous Emma—safe and in "perfect happiness" at Donwell.

1999

WILLIAM BLAKE

The Unfading Vision

Blake, by Peter Ackroyd

Blake was one of those for whom, in William James's definition, "religion exists not as a dull habit, but as an acute fever rather." He spoke with his visions on equal terms, sat down with them and answered them back. They came as welcome visitors: Jesus Christ, the angel Gabriel, Socrates, Michelangelo, his own younger brother Robert, dead at the age of nineteen. What seemed external reality he called a cloud interposed between human beings and the spiritual world, which would otherwise be too bright to bear. He wanted us all to know this. At one point in his biography of Blake, Peter Ackroyd speaks of him as "keeping his own counsel," but, as the book shows, Blake didn't. It was his mission to recall us from materialism to the freedom and joy of the imagination, and it was humanity's duty to listen to his prophecies.

The Blakes were a plain-living London tradesman's family, pious, sober, dissenting, and radical. William (1757–1827), the third child of James and Catherine Blake, was born on Broad Street, a little to the southeast of what is now Oxford Circus. A workhouse and a slaughterhouse were just around the corner, but so too, to the south, was Golden Square, where the gentry lived. William saw the face of God at the window when he was seven or eight years old, wrote poetry as a child, and was apprenticed at fourteen to James Basire, engraver to the Society of Antiquaries. A republican his whole life, he was involved (we don't quite know how) in the riots of 1780, when the London crowds battled the militia and set fire to Newgate prison.

Perhaps on this account, perhaps because of an illness and a disappointment in love, William was sent across the river to recuperate at the house of a market gardener in Battersea. A year or so later he married the gardener's daughter, Catherine Boucher. He started well enough, opening his own print shop and developing what he called "W. Blake's original stereotype." This was a method of relief printing on copper, each impression being hand-tinted, so that no two were alike. In this way the *Songs of Innocence*, *Songs of Experience*, and the great series of prophetic books were offered (quite unsuccessfully) to the public. His work as a jobbing engraver began to run out, and he had to retreat to a cottage at Felpham, on the south coast. But although Felpham was a place of inspiration—it was the first time Blake had ever seen the sea— he was back three years later in the soot-and-dung-laden air of London that suited him and his wife so well.

"In his later life," Mr. Ackroyd writes, "he was known only as an engraver, a journeyman with wild notions and a propensity for writing unintelligible verse. He labored for his bread, eccentric, dirty and obscure." It might be added that he was childless, and there is no way of calculating the pain that caused him. But Blake is also the poet of joy, and it could be argued that he was a fortunate man. Although he created the overwhelming tyrant figure Urizen, or old Nobodaddy, his own father seems to have been mild enough, never sending William to school because "he so hated a blow." Blake's loyal wife, illiterate when they married, was, as he said, "an angel to me." (He had fallen in love with her because she pitied him, which seems to surprise Mr. Ackroyd, but pity was the great eighteenth-century virtue that Blake most earnestly tells us to cherish.)

Although his earnings ran out, he was never without a patron, and although he had always kept radical company, he never got into serious trouble. When he was living in Felpham he was arrested after a row with a drunken soldier who accused him of speaking seditiously against the King—and so he very well may have done—but at the quarter sessions, where poor Catherine deposed that yes, she would be ready to fight for Bonaparte, Blake was miraculously acquitted. And at the end of his life he acquired a new circle of much younger admirers, artists who called themselves Ancients and understood, partly at least, Blake's transcendent view of history and eternity. One of them, George Richmond, closed Blake's eyes when he died in 1827 in his two-room lodgings, and then kissed them "to keep the vision in." "Yet there was really no need to do so," says Mr. Ackroyd, feeling perhaps he has earned the right to a fine phrase. "That vision had not faded in his pilgrimage of seventy years, and it has not faded yet."

Mr. Ackroyd's *Blake* is much more reader-friendly than his *Dickens*. This time he doesn't make what have been called his Hitchcock-like appearances in the text, but he is there at your elbow, a brilliant guide and interpreter. Blake, he says, "is a 'difficult' poet only if we decide to make him so," and he fearlessly expounds the prophetic books and the technique of their illustrations, which conjure up in dazzling orange, green, violet, and crimson "a wholly original religious landscape."

Like all his predecessors, Mr. Ackroyd is left with the (possibly not true) "familiar anecdotes." Did Thomas Butts (a respectable civil servant) really find the Blakes sitting naked, in imitation of Adam and Eve, in their back garden? Did Blake really encounter the Devil on his way down to the coal cellar? Mr. Ackroyd tells the stories as they come. Blake, like Yeats, mythologized (but never falsified) himself, and the best thing is to accept the myth. More important to Mr. Ackroyd is the re-creation of the poet as a great Londoner—part of his long-term biography of his home city. He invites us to accompany Blake, in his knee breeches and wide-brimmed hat, on one of his long walks through the streets. This is not in itself a new idea. Stanley Gardner, in 1968, was one of the first to study the county survey of late-eighteenth-century London inch by inch and to suggest (for example) that Blake's Valley of Innocence must have been the green fields of Wimbledon, where orphans at that time were put out to nurse. Mr. Gardner didn't supply his readers with a map, nor does Mr. Ackroyd, but he is immensely more detailed.

> A woman filling her kettle at the neighborhood pump, the washing hanging out from poles . . . the bird cages and pots of flowers on the windowsills, the shabby man standing on a corner with a sign in his hat saying "Out of Employ," while another sells toy windmills, the dogs, the cripples, the boys with hoops.

These things, of course, aren't what William Blake saw: he saw walls reddened with soldiers' blood or blackened with the soot that killed off young chimney sweeps, while a single bird cage was for him enough to set heaven in a rage.

But this is emphatically not a political biography. Its object isn't to enlist Blake as a primitive Marxist but to show him as an individual of genius, awkward to deal with, sometimes nervous, often contradictory, but incorruptible. Blake himself believed there were eternal "states" of rage and desire, even of selfhood, through which a man passes, keeping his soul intact. "He knew precisely what he saw," says Mr. Ackroyd affectionately, "and with the sturdy obstinacy of his London stock he refused to be bullied or dissuaded."

Blake was unaccountably true, indeed, even to his strangest prophecies. He had promised his wife that he would never leave her, and after his death he came back, she said, for several hours a day, sat down in his usual chair, and talked to her.

1996

SAMUEL TAYLOR COLERIDGE

Talking Through the Darkness

Coleridge: Darker Reflections, 1804–1834,
by Richard Holmes

Ten years ago, in 1989, Richard Holmes left Coleridge under the stars on an April night in Portsmouth, starting out, in one of the many impulsive moves of his life, for Malta. He asked us to imagine how it would have been if the poet had died on the voyage, as he and all his friends clearly expected. He would then have been remembered as the author of *The Rime of the Ancient Mariner*, a brilliant young Romantic early extinguished. But he didn't die, and the next three decades, Holmes told us, would be more fascinating than anything that had gone before. This second volume, he said, would be subtitled "Later Reflections," but it has turned out to be "Darker Reflections." Possibly he himself has changed a little in this time. In any case, "darker" suggests the water imagery that haunted Coleridge even more closely as his life flowed to an end. Holmes hoped to make him "leap out of these pages—brilliant, animated, endlessly provoking—and invade your imagination (as he has done mine)." Certainly, in his superb second volume, he has succeeded in this.

He also has to show his subject as frequently sunk in melancholy, constipated, a heavy drinker, and addicted (as he had been since the winter of 1801) to opium. Coleridge went to Malta in 1804 partly on account of his health, partly to escape from his marriage and perhaps from his long-term infatuation with Wordsworth's sister-in-law Sara Hutchinson, partly—since Malta was a wartime base for the British fleet—in hope of getting some kind of administrative post. He did get employment, as diplomatic secretary to the Governor, for whom he wrote what are now called position papers on Britain's strategic situation in the Mediterranean. As a hardened journalist, quick to seize the main points of any situation, Coleridge, as long as he was sober, had no difficulty with the work.

On his return to England he made it clear that he was not coming back to his wife, although he always did his erratic best to support her and their three children. Lecturing seemed the ideal occupation for the great talker who rarely paused for an answer, and he lectured, on and off, for almost the whole of the rest of his life—at Bristol (where he was an hour late for his first appearance, having been secured by his friends and deposited on the platform), at the Royal Institution (where he collapsed into opium and missed five engagements), at the Philosophical Institution, at the Surrey Institution, at the Crown and Anchor, at the Royal Society of Literature (on Prometheus). Organizers were always ready to book him, audiences almost always ready to hear him. What did he look like? Like a wildly disheveled Dissenting minister. What did he sound like? Sometimes he was unintelligible, but when he caught fire (as for instance in his celebrated lecture on *Hamlet*) it was agreed that he talked as no man had talked before him.

In 1809 he was taken with the idea of writing and publishing his own journal, *The Friend*. This, he thought, could be done from the Lake District. He stayed there at first with Wordsworth, whose household, with its dutiful womenfolk, was always under good control. But *The Friend* lasted for only twenty-seven numbers.

It was at this point, when Wordsworth saw little or no hope of his recovery, that Coleridge absconded to London and began what started as a fortnight's stay (it turned into six years) with the Morgans, whom he had known in Bristol. John Morgan took down whatever Coleridge could be persuaded to dictate; his wife and daughter put in order Coleridge's papers and notebooks. In January 1813 a play, which he had written many years earlier and now renamed *Remorse*, was put on at the Drury Lane Theater. It was an unexpected success, and he received £400 (although in a few months he was penniless). Meanwhile, news came that the Wordsworths' dearly loved little son Tom had died. Coleridge dithered, delayed, and did not go to Grasmere. Can he be forgiven? On the other hand, during one of his worst periods of opium overdose and suicidal depression he rallied himself, Heaven knows how, to write five articles in praise of the paintings of his old friend Washington Allston. His manic energy and generosity have to be set against his recurrent paralysis of the will, when he could be becalmed like the Mariner on his stagnant sea.

Remorse had been put on partly at the request of Lord Byron, who, however impatient he might be with Coleridge's metaphysics ("I wish he would explain his explanation"), shared the impulse felt by so many that he was worth saving at all costs. Charles Lamb, who had been at school with him at Christ's Hospital, continued a faithful friend; so did the publisher Joseph Cottle, who attributed Coleridge's ills not to alcohol and opium but to satanic possession; so did the young De Quincey and Daniel Stuart, the sage editor of *The Courier*. He had, of course, plenty of unsparing enemies who couldn't forgive him for deserting the radical cause. But for forty disorganized years Coleridge was never at a loss for someone to give him a home. Would the twentieth or the twenty-first century take him in so generously?

In his *Notebooks* Coleridge is a witness, often deeply remorseful, to his own life, creating a double viewpoint. Holmes is perfectly attuned to this, and in addition creates what he calls a "downstage voice" in his footnotes, "reflecting on the action as it develops." Anything less than this would not represent the multiplicity of S.T.C. This often unexpected downstage commentary is particularly valuable when Holmes comes to discuss the *Biographia Literaria*, which Coleridge wrote while he was with the Morgans and which he described to Byron as "a general Preface" to his collected poems, "on the Principles of philosophic and genial criticism relative to the Fine Arts in general; but especially to Poetry." In fact, it began as a dialogue, or rather an argument at a distance, with Wordsworth. But that was not enough. He had much more to say on his own personal philosophical journey from the materialism of Locke to the perception that faith in God is not only beyond reason but a continuation of it. He produced forty-five thousand words in six weeks, anxiously watched by the faithful Morgan. Hard pressed, he borrowed passages wholesale from the German philosopher Friedrich Schelling. Holmes admits the plagiarism, but you can rely on him for a spirited defense. The plagiarisms, he claims, "form a kind of psychodrama within the heart of the *Biographia*." We have to wait for the true Coleridge to free himself and emerge.

Coleridge's last years were spent in Highgate, then a hill village just north of London, with the humane Dr. James Gillman and his motherly wife, Ann. Gillman regulated the opium taking, tactfully overlooking the extra supplies secretly bought from the local chemist, and arranged for

Coleridge something quite new, holidays by the seaside. The Gillmans' fine house and garden was a retreat where he could receive visitors— Thomas Carlyle, Ralph Waldo Emerson, James Fenimore Cooper. A familiar figure by now in the village, Coleridge, looking twenty years older than he was, had become a "white-haired, shuffling sage," walking, according to young John Keats, like an after-dinner alderman but, as he talked, casting the same enchantment still.

"At 6:30 A.M. on 25 July 1834 he slipped into the dark." I could wish that Richard Holmes hadn't felt that here, at the very end, "dark" was the right word. But it's impossible to describe the extraordinary quality of this biography, felt on every page. "There is a particular kind of silence which falls after a life like Coleridge's," Holmes says, "and perhaps it should be observed."

1999

SARAH ORNE JEWETT

The News from Dunnet Landing

Sarah Orne Jewett: Novels and Stories,
edited by Michael Davitt Bell

The author of the novel *The Country of the Pointed Firs*, Sarah Orne Jewett, born in 1849, was widely read at the turn of the century, much less after the First World War. Now that a selection of her works is in the Library of America series, perhaps she will be read again.

Sarah Orne Jewett was a New Englander, descended from a well-to-do merchant family in South Berwick, Maine. Her father was a doctor with a local practice (although he later became Professor of Obstetrics at Bowdoin), and she was brought up as one of an extended family in the "great house" of her grandfather Jewett in South Berwick. It was a place of hospitality where she could listen to the stories told at leisure by visitors, among them superannuated sea captains and ship owners and relatives from the lonely inland farms.

As a child she was not a great scholar, preferring hopscotch and skating and her collections of woodchucks, turtles, and insects. "In those days," she wrote, "I was given to long childish illnesses, to instant drooping if ever I were shut up in school," so that her father, trusting in fresh air as a cure, took her with him on his daily rounds, teaching her at the same time to keep her eyes open, and telling her the names of plants and animals. He recommended her to read (in her teens) Sterne's *Sentimental Journey*, Milton's "L'Allegro," and the poetry of Tennyson and Matthew Arnold. Her mother and grandmother advised *Pride and Prejudice*, George Eliot's *Scenes of Clerical Life*, and Harriet Beecher Stowe's *Pearl of Orr's Island*.

In 1867, Jewett graduated from Berwick Academy with serious thoughts of studying medicine. The echo of her debate with herself can he heard in her novel *A Country Doctor* (1884). Nancy Price, "not a commonplace girl," has been left alone in the world. Her guardian is the beloved country practitioner Dr. Leslie, whose principle is "to work with nature and not against it." He believes the wild, reckless little girl is born to be a doctor, and he turns out to be right. Although on a visit away from home she meets a young lawyer to whom she is in every way suited, she gives him up. In the face of criticism from nearly everyone in her small-town community, she goes back to her medical training.

Jewett herself never had to face the test of society's disapproval. She gave up the idea of becoming a doctor simply because she was not well enough. Rheumatism became a familiar enemy, tormenting her all her life long. A legacy from her grandfather meant that she would never have to earn a living, and she decided against marriage, perhaps because she felt she was not likely to meet anyone to match her father. But her writing, which had begun with small things—stories for young people, occasional poems, and so forth—had become by 1873 "my work—my business, perhaps; and it is so much better than making a mere amusement of it, as I used to."

Like so many great invalids of the nineteenth century, Jewett continued, with amazing fortitude, to travel, to make new friends, to move according to the seasons from one house to another. Wherever she went she answered letters in the morning and wrote in the afternoons. For twenty years she spent the summer and winter months with Mrs. Annie Fields (it was one of those close friendships known as "Boston marriages") and spring and autumn in "the great house" in South Berwick, making time, however, for trips to Europe to meet pretty well everyone she admired. In July 1889 she visited Alice Longfellow (the daughter of the poet) at Mouse Island, in Boothbay Harbor, Maine. This was her first visit to the district of the "pointed firs." She made several more before 1896, when her novel *The Country of the Pointed Firs* appeared, first as a serial in *The Atlantic Monthly* and then in November from the publisher Houghton Mifflin.

This short novel is her masterpiece, no doubt about that, but it is difficult to discuss the plot because it can hardly be said to have one. Dunnet Landing is "a salt-aired, white-clapboarded little town" on the central coast of Maine, more attractive than the rest, perhaps, but much like them. "One evening in June, a single passenger landed upon the steamboat wharf." She is a writer who has taken a lodging in the town, in search of peace and quiet. Her landlady, Mrs. Almira Todd, is the local herbalist, being a very large person, majestic almost, living in the last little house on the way inland. In a few pages Jewett establishes forever the substantial reality of Dunnet Landing. We know it, we have been there, we have walked up the steep streets, we taste the sea air. Now we have got to get to know the inhabitants, slowly, as the narrator does herself, and, in good time, to hear their confidences. Jewett knew all about fishing and smallholding and cooking haddock chowder, about birds, weather, tides, and clouds. She had a wonderful ear for the Maine voice, breaking the immense silences. She quotes, more than once, what her father said to her: "Don't write about things and people. Tell them just as they are." And she understood the natural history of small communities, where you will find impoverished, lonely people, often old but proud, self-respecting and respected.

The narrator of *The Country of the Pointed Firs* rents the local schoolhouse, for fifty cents a week, as her study. Here her first visitor, apart from the bees and an occasional sheep pausing to look in at the open door, is Captain Littlepage, an ancient retired shipmaster. His reminiscences are not what we expect: he tells a story of the unseen—a voyage west of Baffin Island which fetched up "on a coast which wasn't laid down or charted" where the crew saw, or half-saw, the shapes of men through the sea-fog "like a place where there was neither living nor dead." These were men waiting between this life and the next. Captain Littlepage offers no further explanation, and, indeed, it's generally felt in Dunnet Landing that he has overset his mind with too much reading, but Mrs. Todd, with a sharp look, says that "some of them tales hangs together tolerable well."

Loneliness and hospitality are the two extremes of the hard existence on the coast of Maine. Elijah Tilley, one of the old fishermen, thought of as a "plodding man," has been a widower for the past eight years. "Folks all kept repeating that time would ease me, but I can't find it does. No, I just miss her the same every day." It is his habit to lapse into silence. What more is there to say? Toward the end of her life, Sarah Orne Jewett gave some words of advice to the young Willa Cather: "You must write to the human heart, the great consciousness that all humanity goes to make up." Otherwise it may remain unexpressed, as it often does in Dunnet Landing.

Joanna, Mrs. Todd's cousin, whose young man threw her over, withdrew to live alone on tiny Shell-heap Island, "a dreadful small place to make a world of." She had some poultry and a patch of potatoes. But what about company? She must have made do with the hens, her one-time neighbors think: "I expect she soon came to making folks of them." But Joanna maintained the dignity of loss. She lived, died, and was buried on Shell-heap Island. We are in a world where silence is understood.

When the time comes for the narrator to leave, Mrs. Todd, who has become a true friend, hardly speaks all day, "except in the briefest and most disapproving way." Then she resolutely goes out on an errand, without turning her head. "My room looked as empty as the day I came . . . and I knew how it would seem when Mrs. Todd came back and found her lodger gone. So we die before our own eyes; so we see some chapters of our lives come to their natural end."

Jewett is an expert in the homely and everyday who gives us every now and then a glimpse of the numinous. (That, perhaps, is why Rudyard Kipling wrote to her about *The Country of the Pointed Firs,* "I don't believe even you know how good that work is.") She does this, for instance, in a short story, "Miss Tempy's Watchers." Upstairs lies the outworn body of kindly Miss Temperance Dent, while in the kitchen, two of her old friends, keeping vigil before the next day's funeral, gradually nod off. "Perhaps Tempy herself stood near, and saw her own life and its surroundings with new understanding. Perhaps she herself was the only watcher." In one of the later Dunnet Landing stories, "The Foreigner," Mrs. Todd observes: "You know plain enough there's something beyond this world: the doors stand wide open." There are moments, too, of communication or empathy between friends that go beyond understanding. Friendship, for Sarah Orne Jewett, was the world's greatest good.

On 3 September 1902, her fifty-third birthday, she was thrown from her carriage when the horse stumbled and fell. She suffered concussion of the spine and never entirely recovered. "The strange machinery that writes," as she described it, "seems broken and confused." For long spells she was in fact forbidden by her doctors to read or write, which must have been a cruel deprivation. In 1909 she was back in South Berwick, where she had the last of a series of strokes, and died in the house where she was born.

1999

GEORGE ELIOT

The Will to Good

An introduction to *Middlemarch*

George Eliot began what is now Book Two of *Middlemarch* early in 1869. She wrote slowly, because for her it was a year of illness and trouble, and in the winter of 1870 she put this work aside and began a new story that is now Book One, "Miss Brooke." She made a note in her journal that the "subject . . . has been recorded among my possible themes ever since I began to write fiction." What is this subject?

Middlemarch is set in the years just before the Reform Bill of 1832. In Chapter 10 Mr. Brooke, the uncle and guardian of Dorothea and her sister Celia, gives a dinner party at his house, Tipton Grange. Maddening, vacillating, kind-hearted Mr. Brooke is a local magistrate and a countryman—so too, of course, is the Rector, Mr. Cadwallader, with his magnificently sharp-tongued wife. The Reverend Mr. Casaubon, scholarly, withering into dry old age, is also a man of property, as is Sir James Chettam, Brooke's guileless neighbor. But to meet these gentry Mr. Brooke has rather enterprisingly invited guests from Middlemarch itself: the upper ranks, that is, of the townspeople—Mr. Vincy, the mayor, Mr. Chicheley, the coroner, and the Evangelical banker, Mr. Bulstrode. They are talking about Dorothea and about Lydgate, the new doctor. These two have also been talking to each other, discussing model housing and the proposed fever hospital, and we get Lydgate's first impression, as he leaves the party, of Dorothea: "She is a good creature—that fine girl—but a little too earnest." She would not do, therefore, for Lydgate, who wants relaxation after his work, and smiling blue eyes. This is George Eliot's particular method of turning an incident around, so that we can look at it with her, and from different angles. In this way we have been introduced to the field of action and the beginning of what she calls "the stealthy convergence of human lots."

George Eliot's living creed—painfully arrived at—was meliorist (a word she believed she had invented). We should do all we can, during a short human lifetime, to achieve "some possible better," and the "should" is all the more binding because we cannot have a direct knowledge of God. But the individual will to good is affected by social and natural forces—by the kind of society we are born into and the kind of temperament we are born with. In *Middlemarch* Eliot is considering a money-making professional society, based on Coventry, where she lived from 1841 to 1850. Middlemarch is a manufacturing town—"the people in manufacturing towns are always disreputable," says Mrs. Cadwallader—with a corruptible local paper, electioneering for and against a reforming parliament, professional charities, and deeply distrusted advances in medicine and hygiene. Everyone knows everyone else's business. What is to be hoped for from this thriving borough, where nearly all are loudly certain of their own opinion? "I know the sort," cries Mr. Hawley, the town clerk, hearing that Casaubon's cousin, Ladislaw, is of foreign extraction; "some emissary. He'll begin with flourishing about the Rights of Man and end with murdering a wench. That's the style." At the Tankard in Slaughter Lane it is "known" to Mrs. Dollop, the landlady, that people are allowed to die in the new hospital for the sake of cutting them up, "a poor tale for a doctor, who if he was good for anything should know what was the matter with you before you died." To be "candid" in Middlemarch means that you are about to let a man know the very worst that is being said about him. "The gossip of the auction room, the billiard room, the tea table, the kitchen," as Frank Kermode puts it, "is the more or less corrupt blood of the organism." The challenges to Middlemarch come from young Dr. Lydgate and young Miss Brooke.

Lydgate has the impulse to mercy and healing and the ambition to research. But he is impatient and too self-confident and does not mind it being known that he is better born than other country surgeons. He is drawn, by fatal degrees, into the evil secret of Bulstrode's past (a favorite theme of George Eliot's and as old as fiction itself). And yet his only real error is his marriage to Rosamond Vincy. He is overwhelmed by the "terrible tenacity of this mild creature." She is, what is more, one of the world's unteachables. Whatever George Eliot's scheme of moral effort and retribution may be, Rosamond is quite exempt from it. Through all vicissitudes she quietly keeps her self-esteem. Her dream of existence is shocked, then rights itself, and she will continue, blonde and imperturbable. The world as it is seems created for Rosamonds.

Dorothea, on the other hand, never comes into direct conflict with Middlemarch. Her faults, like Lydgate's, are put to us very clearly, since George Eliot's methods are analytic. Having set herself, as she said, to imagine "how ideas lie in other minds than my own," she begins ironically, with Dorothea and sensible Celia dividing the jewelry their mother left them. Dorothea, who has renounced finery, feels an unexpected wish to keep one set of emeralds (a delicate premonition of her passion for Will Ladislaw). We are shown that she doesn't know her own nature, doesn't know life, certainly doesn't know "lower experience such as plays a great part in the world," is ruthless to Sir James and, of course, to herself, and hopelessly astray in her search for "intensity and greatness." But Dorothea is noble. On her honeymoon visit to Rome, for instance, she is so much the finest spirit there, seen in contrast not only with those around her but with the motionless statuary of the Vatican Museum. She doesn't know this. She has "little vanity." She says: "It is surely better to pardon too much than to condemn too much." We would give anything to be able to step into the novel and join Celia and Sir James in trying to stop this rare spirit from making her disastrous choice.

But why can't Dorothea aim at something greater? Why is she left, as the Finale puts it, to lead a "hidden life," and be buried in an "unvisited tomb"? Florence Nightingale, among many others, asked this question, giving as an example not herself, but Octavia Hill, the pioneer of public-housing management. It is true that Dorothea (born about 1812) was too early to have been, for instance, a student at Girton College, Cambridge (founded in 1869). But George Eliot's attitude to the position of women was, in any case, perplexing. In October 1856 she signed a petition for women to have a legal right to their own earnings, and in 1867 she told a friend that "women should be educated equally with men, and secured as far as possible with every other breathing creature from suffering the exercise of any unrighteous power." She was, however, resolutely opposed to women's suffrage. But these questions are not stressed in *Middlemarch*, and Dorothea is not shown as a great organizer, but as having "the ardent woman's need to rule beneficently by making the joy of another soul." The drawback here is that the other soul turns out, in the end, to be Will Ladislaw's; and what are we to make of Ladislaw? Critics usually consider him to be, like Stephen Guest in *The Mill on the Floss*, one of George Eliot's failures. But perhaps she intended him to be exactly what he appears—that is, at the best, "a bright creature full of uncertain promises." He becomes, of course, a Radical MP, but "in those times"— as she reminds us—"when reforms were begun with a young hopefulness of immediate good which has been much checked in our days."

George Eliot's point, however, made both in the Prelude and the Finale of her book, delivers us from having to think of Dorothea as nothing more than a noble woman who loses her head over a questionable young man. Dorothea's decisions were not ideal, George Eliot tells us, and conditions are not right for a nineteenth-century St. Theresa, but her life was not wasted: "the effect of her being on those around her was incalculably diffusive." This is part of the book's great diminuendo, not tragic but majestic, drawing back, after all its vast complications, into itself, the characters' prospects narrowing as the story closes. But we have actually seen the effect of Dorothea's being on those around her, in her generous gift to Lydgate and—in a superb chapter—her yet more generous visit to Rosamond. On these "unhistoric acts" in an undistinguished ribbon-manufacturing town in the Midlands, the growing good of the world may partly depend. We must believe this, if we can.

There was nothing in *Middlemarch*, George Eliot assured her long-suffering publisher, John Blackwood, "that will be seen to be irrelevant to my design, which is to show the gradual action of ordinary causes rather than exceptional." This, however, suggests a deliberate, even mechanical method of construction that is quite at odds with the intensely human effect of her great novel. One of the advantages of its sheer length is that there is room in it for hesitations, even moments of relenting, which give the story another dimension, like music heard at a distance. At the end of Book Four, for instance, Dorothea has not only admitted to herself the misery of her marriage to Mr. Casaubon but has glimpsed that his lifetime's work, the "Key to all Mythologies," is a meaningless accumulation of references. She has gone to her room, and waits for him in the darkness to come upstairs from his library.

> But she did hear the library door open, and slowly the light advanced up the staircase without noise from the footsteps on the carpet. When her husband stood opposite to her, she saw that his face was more haggard. He started slightly on seeing her, and she looked up at him beseechingly, without speaking.
>
> "Dorothea!" he said, with a gentle surprise in his tone. "Were you waiting for me?"

"Yes, I did not like to disturb you."

"Come, my dear, come. You are young, and need not to extend your life by watching."

When the kind quiet melancholy of that speech fell on Dorothea's ears, she felt something like the thankfulness that might well up in us if we had narrowly escaped hurting a lamed creature. She put her hand into her husband's, and they went along the broad corridor together.

The possibility is there, for long enough for us to think about it, of perhaps not happiness between them, but peace. The moment passes, as it does for Mary Garth, who has never realized that Mr. Farebrother cared anything for her, and still doesn't, fully, when he comes to see her to plead Fred Vincy's cause. But "something indefinable, something like the resolute suppression of a pain in Mr. Farebrother's manner, made her feel suddenly miserable, as she had once felt when she saw her father's hands trembling in a moment of trouble." Here Mary herself can't define her sensation. There is time in *Middlemarch*, as in life itself, for these echoes or intimations of paths not taken. Another one, which remains just under the surface but is never put into words, is: what if Dorothea had married Lydgate?

There is another complication in *Middlemarch*, which runs very deep. Meliorism looks cautiously forward, and indeed George Eliot agreed with Gladstone that there was no use in fighting against the future. But she was always true to her own past, her rural childhood when she had been a "little sister," running through green fields. All around Middlemarch stretches northeast Loamshire, "almost all meadows and pastures, with hedgerows still allowed to grow in bushy beauty, and to spread out coral fruit for the birds. . . . These are the things that make the gamut of joy in landscape to midland-bred souls." (This recalls the passage from *The Mill on the Floss*, "We could never have loved the earth so well if we had had no childhood in it. . . .") It is noticeable that although 1830 saw the height of England's agricultural distress and, in consequence, of rioting and rick burning—the Cambridgeshire fires could be seen at a distance of eight miles against the night sky—Loamshire, in this novel, is relatively tranquil. (Unrest is represented by Mr. Brooke's visit to Dagley's smallholding, where he is defied by the drunken Dagley and behaves in a way much less dignified than his own dog, the sagacious Monk.) The reason for this, surely, is that George Eliot needs to indicate an ideal experience and existence. In *Middlemarch* the country represents work, steadiness, harmony, peace. If we ask ourselves, or let ourselves feel, how human happiness is measured, we have to turn to Fred Vincy. Fred's love for Mary, in spite of his shortcomings, is the truest emotion in the book, and it is as an expert on the cultivation of green crops and the economy of cattle-feeding that he steadies down to a happy life: "On enquiry it might possibly be found that Fred and Mary still inhabit Stone Court—that the creeping plants still cast the foam of their blossoms over the fine stone wall. . . ." Their marriage is a pastoral. Then again, late on in the book, Dorothea has a moment of vision that is in the nature of an epiphany. It is after her sleepless night of extreme misery over Will Ladislaw.

> She opened her curtains, and looked out towards the bit of road that lay in view, with fields beyond, outside the entrance-gates. On the road there was a man with a bundle on his back and a woman carrying her baby; in the field she could see figures moving—perhaps the shepherd with his dog. Far off in the bending sky was the pearly light, and she felt the largeness of the world and the manifold wakings of men to labour and endurance. . . .
>
> What she would resolve to do that day did not yet seem quite clear, but something that she could achieve stirred her as with an approaching murmur which would soon gather distinctness.

Dorothea's inspiration, at this late stage, comes from the early-morning sight of the laborer and the wayfarer. This, too, is pastoral. George Eliot, of course, did not deceive herself. If her Warwickshire childhood had been an Eden, it was one that she had lost. But it remained as her surest way of judging life as it hurried forward through the unpeaceful, expanding nineteenth century.

1999

Not Herself

George Eliot, Voice of a Century:
A Biography, by Frederick R. Karl

[Burne-Jones] came across her standing monumentally alone at Waterloo Station, and, as he talked with her, they walked for a short distance along the platform. Suddenly Lewes rushed up to them, panic-pale and breathlessly exclaiming "My God! you are HERE!" George Eliot gravely admitted it. "But," stammered Lewes, "I left you THERE!"

This story (from Graham Robertson's *Time Was*) belongs to the 1870s, when George Eliot had become not only a precious charge to G. H. Lewes but also an object of general reverence as the greatest of secular teachers and (after Dickens died) the supreme English novelist. Opinion turned against her not long after her death in 1880. (A book I've got here, a *Practical Text Book for Senior Classes* published by Harrap in 1923, doesn't even include her in its chart of the Chief Victorian Novelists.) She had to wait for rescue by F. R. Leavis and above all by Professor Gordon Haight, with his nine volumes of letters and a classic biography (1968). Endlessly helpful, Haight reckoned to be able to say what she was doing at any given moment on any day of her life, even before her written diaries begin, in 1854.

Frederick Karl's new biography is seven-hundred-odd pages long and has taken him five years' hard labor. He has consulted, he thinks, all the available material, notably Eliot's brave but embarrassing letters to Herbert Spencer ("If you become attached to anyone else, then I must die"). In his acknowledgments he thanks Haight as the most dauntless of scholars, but, six hundred pages on, he calls the 1968 Life "narrow, squeezed, protective, and carefully conventional." This leads you to expect a bold treatment of some debatable points, but that would be a mistake. Of John Chapman, the publisher in whose house she lodged when she first came to London, he says "it is quite possible she and Chapman were intimate, although we will probably never have definite proof one way or another."

Why did John Cross, her second husband, twenty years younger than herself, jump from the balcony during their honeymoon into the Grand

Canal? Professor Karl examines the evidence at length, and concludes that the incident only seems amusing "if we put on hold the pain of the participants." In fact he is more protective of his subject than Haight himself, refusing to accept that she was emotionally dependent on a succession of men, beginning with her father and her elder brother Isaac.

Although she believed that "there is no creature whose inward being is so strong that it is not greatly determined by what lies outside it," George Eliot invented herself (though probably not more than most women). She let it be understood that her right hand was larger than her left because of the dairy work she did as a girl, but Isaac declared she had never made a pound of butter in her life. She gallantly defied society when she threw in her lot with the all-purpose journalist and philosopher George Henry Lewes, and yet what she longed for was acceptance and solid respectability, the right wallpaper, the right callers on her Sunday afternoons. Karl patiently admits these contradictions, but relates them to the troubled consciousness of Victorian society, with all its divisions and paradoxes. George Eliot trusted passionately in the individual, coming to believe that each of us should create his own church, but at the same time dreading the chaos and disorder to which freedom might lead. To Karl she is the "voice of the century." All her changes of name, he says—Mary Anne, Marian, Mrs. G. H. Lewes, George Eliot, Mater, Mutter, Madonna—correspond to willed transformations, the moral and spiritual versions of self-help.

Her responsibilities, as she said, weighed heavily on her, and Professor Karl can't be called light-footed either. For the most part he plods along with dignity by the side of his Mary Anne. He is strong on her years with Chapman's *Westminster Review* and on the details of her business affairs. Lewes, acting as her manager, was a sharp customer, and John Blackwood, most noble-minded of publishers, had reason to complain. But respectability had to be earned, or, as Karl puts it, "the inflow of money was an indisputable form of empowerment." In the background were Lewes's legal wife and children, whom he supported to the very end.

The book goes less well when it parts company from hard facts. In the last twenty years or so, Karl tells us, we've come to expect from the biographer "the psychological analysis of possibilities and potentialities" from patterns in the work itself. If by "we" he means the readers, then we have brought deconstructionism on ourselves. From these patterns Karl feels able to suggest that the theft of Silas Marner's life savings from the floor of his cottage "does seem linked to Eliot's uncertainty about her work," or perhaps "Eliot saw herself as part of a 'theft'. . . she had 'stolen' a particular kind of life in the face of social opprobrium," while Hetty, the kitten-like dairy-maid in *Adam Bede*, is a "subtle yet demonic double of Eliot's own desire to rise, achieve, emerge." It's as if he was allowing himself a well-earned holiday from his long search for exactness.

The search itself is on the grand scale, but never, it seems to me, quite arrives. Frank Kermode was surely right in distinguishing, in George Eliot's fiction, between the given and the calculated. Dorothea Brooke is "given." *Middlemarch*, when the novel begins to expand in Chapter 10, is "calculated." *Silas Marner* was "given" to such an extent that his image "came across my other plans by a sudden inspiration" and Eliot had to write it before she could go back to the "calculated" *Romola*. Of course, she was well aware of the difference, telling Cross that "in all she considered her best writing, there was a 'not-herself' which took possession." Certainly it would be difficult to write the story of a not-herself, but that is what is missing from this biography.

1995

MRS. OLIPHANT

The Heart and Soul of Carlingford

I. A Fighting Life

In the winter of 1860–61, Mrs. Margaret Oliphant, a penniless, undaunted little Scottish "scribbling woman," called at the office of the brothers Blackwood.

It was a very severe winter, and it was severe on me too. . . . I had not been doing very well with my writing. I had sent several articles to *Blackwood's* [Magazine] and they had been rejected. Why, this being the case, I should have gone to them . . . I can't tell. But I was in their debt, and had very little to go on with. They shook their heads, of course, and thought it would not be possible to take such a story—both very kind, and truly sorry for me, I have no doubt. I think I see their figures now against the light, standing up, John with his shoulders hunched up, the Major with his soldierly air, and myself all blackness and whiteness in my widow's dress, taking leave of them as if it didn't matter, and oh! so much afraid that they would see the tears in my eyes. I went home to my little ones, and as soon as I had got them into bed, I sat down and wrote. I sat up all night in a passion of composition, stirred to the very bottom of my mind. The story was successful, and my fortune, comparatively speaking, was made.

This is Mrs. Oliphant's own account, in what she called her "few autobiographical bits," of the origin of the Chronicles of Carlingford.* If we

---

*The first story was "The Executor," which appeared in *Blackwood's,* May 1861, but in the end was not part of the Carlingford series. These are *The Rector* and *The Doctor's Family*, published together in three volumes by Blackwoods (1863), *Salem Chapel* (1863), *The Perpetual Curate* (1864), *Miss Marjoribanks* (1866), and *Phoebe Junior: A Last Chronicle of Carlingford* (1876). During this period she published twenty-one other full-length books.

get the idea that she saw herself to some extent as the heroine of her own novel, and that she knew it perfectly well, we should be right, and right too in recognizing her as a woman with a strong visual imagination and an even stronger sense of human relationships. She sees the group in terms of dark and light, and feels the publishers' embarrassed decency and her own desperation.

For nearly fifty years she led a working, or rather a fighting life as a writer. Her industry became a legend ("I too work hard, Mrs. Oliphant," Queen Victoria said to her). She never, it seems, had more than two hours to herself, except in the middle of the night. Up to a few days before her death she was still correcting proofs. But her fortune, alas, was not made in 1861, either comparatively speaking or ever.

She was twice an Oliphant (it was her mother's name as well as her husband's) and the family was an ancient one, "though I don't think," she wrote, "that our branch was anything much to brag about." Although she was Scottish born (4 April 1828) she was brought up in Liverpool where her father worked in the customs house. It was a close-knit, plain family life, and from the outset it was a household of weak men and strong women. The father counted for very little, and her two elder brothers never came to much. All the fire and generosity of life seemed to come from the mother. Maggie herself, from a tender age, was out on the streets delivering radical pamphlets, and hot in defense of the Scottish Free Church. No formal education is mentioned. At six years old she learned to read and did so prodigiously, mostly Scots history and legends. When, in her teens, she began to write her own tales, "my style," she said, "followed no sort of law." Writing, of course, was in the intervals of housekeeping and sick-nursing. In 1849 (by which time her first novel had been published) she went up to London to look after her amiable brother Willie, who was studying for the ministry, and to keep him clear of drink and debt. "I was a little dragon, watching over him with remorseless anxiety." Lodging upstairs was her cousin Francis Oliphant, an artist; three years later, after some mysterious hesitations, she married him. This meant a hand-to-mouth studio life, in the course of which her first two babies died, and two more were born.

Although he exhibited history pieces at the Academy, Francis was by profession a glass painter, who had worked for eleven years as assistant to Pugin. (Margaret, unfortunately, had almost no feeling for art, and when he took her to the National Gallery she was "struck dumb with disappointment.") He was not the kind of man ever to succeed on his own: when he set up his own studio, in 1854, he couldn't manage either the workmen or the accounts. His failure has always been put down to the decline in demand for "mediaeval" painted glass, but in fact there was no decline until well after 1870. "His wife's success," wrote William Bell Scott, "was enough to make him an idle and aimless man." This is unkind, but certainly Margaret was the breadwinner from the first, even though she allowed seven of her first thirteen novels to appear under Willie's name in the hope of setting him up on his feet. And poor Francis was consumptive. In 1858, when he was told there was no hope, his comment is said to have been "Well, if that is so, there is no reason why we should be miserable." They went off, as invalids so ill-advisedly did in the 1850s, to the cold winter damp of Florence and the malarial heat of Rome. To spare his wife, Francis did not tell her the truth. She never forgave him this, and was honest enough to admit it. When he died she was left pregnant, with two children to look after, and about £1,000 in debts. This was mostly owed to *Blackwood's*, who had been generously sending her £20 a month, whether they printed her articles or not.

Margaret Oliphant gathered up her dependants and returned, first to Edinburgh, then to Ealing, west of London. Before long she found herself supporting not only her own children and the feckless Willie but also her brother Frank (he had failed in business) and his family of four. Like some natural force she attracted responsibilities toward her. But with this strength of hers there went a wild optimism and an endearing lack of caution. She was openhanded, like her mother. Nothing was too good for her friends. Her sons, whatever the expense, must go to Eton. Yet both of them, as they grew up, drifted into elegant idleness. Their vitality faded and she could not revive it. She had to watch them die in their barren thirties, one after the other. It is at this point that her autobiography breaks off. "And now here I am all alone. I cannot write any more."

Mrs. Oliphant's novels show little of the indulgence of Jane Austen or George Eliot toward attractive weaklings. Did she, out of her love and generosity, encourage, or even create, weakness in men? Her autobiography is deeply touching, partly because she recognizes this. "I did with much labour what I thought the best . . . but now I think that if I had taken the other way, which seemed the less noble, it might have been better for all of us." She did not think of herself as in any way exceptional. She believed she had had the "experiences of most women." They had been her life and they became the life of her books.

II. A Small Town and an Unseen World

Mrs. Oliphant's Carlingford* is described for us in much less detail than, say George Eliot's Milby in *Scenes of Clerical Life*. To draw an accurate map of it would be difficult. The railway station, with unhelpful porters, is to the south. The High Street is for shopping, George Street (with the Blue Boar Inn) is the business district. To the east of the town, Wharfside, down by the canal, is a slum, ignored by the respectable. Grange Lane and Grove Street are for the gentry, though Grove Street has "a shabby side" and backs onto narrow lanes. St. Roque's, the chapel of ease for the Parish Church, is to the north. In the last of the Chronicles, however, *Phoebe Junior*, the sun is said to set behind St. Roque's. Plainly Mrs. Oliphant is less interested in topography than in people. But in giving the atmosphere of a small community, almost resentful of arrivals and departures (although these are its main source of interest), complacent, hierarchical, inward-looking, and conscious of one direction, the canal-side, in which it dare not look—here she cannot put a foot wrong. Within these tight limits human beings must discover what a real life is, and contrive, somehow, to have it. I should like to say something here about her observation of human nature, but mustn't, because she herself thought the idea an impertinence. All she ever did, she said, was to listen attentively.

Her first approach to Carlingford (though by no means its only one) is through its churchgoing. This was a natural choice for the mid-nineteenth century. Only a few years later Dickens, close to death, fixed on a cathedral city and its clergy for his last novel. For present-day readers, Carlingford means a direct plunge into the rich diversity of Victorian Christianity. At one end of the spectrum there are "viewy" High Churchmen, inheritors of the Oxford Movement, eager to reunite England with its Catholic past and to show truth by means of ritual. Ritual, confession, vestments, candles, are all an offence to everyday wor-

---

*If Carlingford is to be identified at all, I would suggest Aylesbury, where Francis Oliphant designed some windows for St. Mary's Church. Characteristically, when no donor came forward he offered to pay for them himself.

shipers—un-English, or worse. To the Low Church, shading into the Evangelicals, plainness and simplicity are also a way of showing holiness. Church building is still in its hard Gothic heyday. (St. Roque's, where the perpetual curate is "viewy," is by Gilbert Scott.) The Dissenters have only one red brick building, Salem Chapel, in Grove Street. It is attended mainly by "grocers and buttermen." Beyond lie the poor. Here both the Ritualists and the Evangelicals see their duty. They visit, and bring blankets and coal. But what church, if any, the bargers and brick-workers attend, we are not told.

On a lower level a thriving competition is in progress between the Parish Church, St. Roque's, and Salem. How many pews are filled, how many paid-for "sittings" are taken up, will the Sunday sermon lose or gain supporters? But, unlike Trollope, Mrs. Oliphant does not treat organized religion as a variant of the political structure, occupied in maneuvers for position. The preoccupations of Carlingford are unspiritual and often ludicrous, but the church, no matter how far it falls short, is there to link them with an unseen world. In this way, although her human comedy is so much narrower than Trollope's, it has a dimension that can hardly be found in Barchester.

III. The Rector

The Rector most characteristically begins with a new arrival at Carlingford Mrs. Oliphant opens her story in a tone of shrewd irony, presenting Carlingford as its "good society" sees itself—that is, the "real town," not the tradespeople or, of course, Wharfside. This real town stays secluded in Grange Lane, behind high walls "jealous of intrusion, yet thrusting tall plumes of lilac and stray branches of apple-blossom, like friendly salutations to the world without." These households, the mainstay of the Parish Church, are half-agreeably disturbed by the thought of a new incumbent. He may be a Ritualist, like young Mr. Wentworth of St. Roque's. He may be Low Church, like the late Rector, who absurdly exceeded his duties and actually went down to preach to the "bargemen" of the canal district. To look at it from another point of view, there are unmarried young ladies in Carlingford, and it is known that the new Rector, also, is unmarried.

This, like *A Christmas Carol* and *Silas Marner*, is the novel as parable. The houses of Grange Lane, as we first see them in the May sunshine, are an earthly paradise. To open the Wodehouses' garden door—"what a slight, paltry barrier—one plank and no more"—is to be elected, to find it shut is to be cast out. As the story opens the young curate, Frank Wentworth, is already, though not securely, admitted to the garden, the falling apple blossoms making light of his "black Anglican coat." He is too poor to propose marriage to Lucy, the pretty younger daughter. When the door closes behind him he walks stiffly away along the dry and dusty road. Out goes the frustrated young man from the display of fertile greenery, in comes the shy, celibate newcomer. "A tall, embarrassed figure, following the portly one of Mr. Wodehouse, stepped suddenly from the noisy gravel to the quiet grass, and stood gravely awkward behind the father of the house" in contrast to the blazing narcissi and the fruit trees. Morley Proctor has been "living out of nature." For the last fifteen years he has been immured in the college of All Souls, preparing an edition of Sophocles. "He was neither High nor Low, enlightened nor narrow-minded. He was a Fellow of All Souls"—about which Mrs. Oliphant probably knew very little except for the irony of the name for an establishment which cared for so few of them. Proctor is honorable enough, upright and sincere, but in company he is "a reserved and inappropriate man." His heart is an "unused faculty." He is out of place, as he knows at once, in the vigorously flowering garden.

But Morley Proctor, too, has come from a Paradise to which he looks back regretfully, a haven of scholarship and "snug little dinner-parties undisturbed by the presence of women." This is in spite of the fact that his mother has come from Devonshire to look after him, a dauntless little mother who treats him with the mixture of love and impatience at which Mrs. Oliphant (in fiction as in life) excelled. Old Mrs. Proctor, young in heart, regards her son as a child, but as one who should be settled down with a wife. One of the Wodehouse daughters would do—the kindly, plain, elder one whose reserve seems an echo of Morley's own timidity, or perhaps the dazzling Lucy.

Having placed this situation, Mrs. Oliphant asks us to see it in a different light. It turns out that the new Rector has left All Souls, somewhat against his conscience, precisely in order to give his mother a good home. When he "turned his back on his beloved cloisters" he knew very well what the sacrifice was, but he was determined to make it.

I have said that Mrs. Oliphant is not writing of the religious life simply as a social mechanism, or for the sake of the psychological tension that it produces. Proctor's flight from the possibility of marriage (not without an unexpected twinge of sexuality, since Lucy is so pretty) is domestic comedy of a delicious kind, since Lucy does not want him in the least. But the crisis of the story, when it comes, is spiritual. As a sharp interruption to the dull services that he conducts and the dinner parties that he awkwardly attends, the Rector is called to the bedside of a dying woman. He is asked to prepare her soul for its last journey. His reaction to the agony is dismay, and a very English embarrassment. Without his prayer book he is at a loss for a prayer. He has to leave even that duty to young Wentworth, who providentially comes in time to the sickroom. The Rector "would have known what to say to her if her distress had been over a disputed translation." The heart of the story is his trial and condemnation, and he has to conduct the trial himself. Carlingford doesn't reject him—quite the contrary. But he perceives that Wentworth, "not half or a quarter part as learned as he," was "a world further on in the profession which they shared." Among those who are being born, suffering, and perishing he has no useful place. His training has not prepared him for such things. And yet, can they be learned by training? "The Rector's heart said No."

Mrs. Oliphant, in fact, is asking: what is a man doing, and what must he be, when he undertakes to be an intermediary between man and God? She returns to the question later, in *Salem Chapel*. The answer, in her view, has nothing to do with formal theology, or she would not have proposed it. Nor is it a matter of duty. Morley Proctor was right, in his anxiety, to consult his heart.

IV. The Doctor's Family

The Doctor's Family enlarges the view of Carlingford and takes us to a different part of it. The Doctor, however, like the Rector, has to face a painful ordeal of reality. This is all the more telling because in his hardworking medical practice he might be thought to be facing it already. But Mrs. Oliphant shows him as another, although very different example of the unused heart.

Edward Rider is a surgeon, still, at that date, professionally inferior to a doctor. He is no hero, and Mrs. Oliphant defines carefully what are "the limits of his nature, and beyond them he could not pass." He is shown as wretchedly in need of a woman, but unwilling to marry because he can't face the expense and responsibility. His surgery is in the dreaded brickworkers' district, partly because he is not a snob, but largely because he has to make a living. He would work in Grange Lane if he could, but that is the domain of old Dr. Marjoribanks, who attends the "good society." To this "poor young fellow," as Mrs. Oliphant calls him, strong-minded, short-tempered, comes a terrible visitation. His drunken failure of an elder brother, Fred, has come back in disgrace from Australia and installed himself in the upstairs room. "A large, indolent, shabby figure," he is incapable of gratitude but is always ready with a pleasant word for the neighbors, who prefer him, in consequence, to the doctor. Fred's foul billows of tobacco smoke define him and hang over the first part of the book, just as the surgery lamp shines defiantly at the beginning and the end.

Mrs. Oliphant was well acquainted with sickbeds and travel and the support of idle relations. The story seems almost to tell itself. It moves fast, as though keeping pace with the doctor's rounds in his horse and drag, the quickest-moving thing on the streets of Carlingford. One encounter follows another, each outbidding the last. Fred is followed from Australia by his feebly plaintive wife and a pack of children. All have arrived in charge of his forceful young sister-in-law, Nettie. She is a tiny, "brilliant brown creature," a mighty atom, afraid of nothing "except that someone would speak before her and the situation be taken out of her hands." Having a little money left, she undertakes to support the whole lot of them, and whisks them away to new lodgings. The title *The Doctor's Family* can now be seen in all its irony. First Rider, who has been too cautious to marry, is threatened with a whole family of wild children: Nettie comes to his rescue, but this is no relief to the doctor, who falls violently in love with her. Fred's squalid death in the canal may look like a solution, but isn't. It means, or Nettie convinces herself that it does, that she has no right to marry and desert her weak-spirited sister. All the action seems checked, until the arrival of another Australian visitor, "the Bushman," who "fills up the whole little parlour with his beard and his presence," gives it quite a new direction. From the secluded top room where Dr. Rider once hid away his brother, the whole drama has come into the open. There it has to be played out to the amazement of watching Carlingford, from the bargemen who drag in Fred's bloated body to mild, elderly Miss Wodehouse, with whose gentle observations the book comes to rest. Dr. Rider and Dr. Marjoribanks, Frank Wentworth and the Wodehouses, will return in the later Chronicles, all of them less than perfect human beings. Mrs. Oliphant is not much concerned with faultless characters. An exception, in *The Doctor's Family*, is the honest Bushman, but even he, Miss Wodehouse points out, has made a woeful mistake. And by avoiding the Victorian baroque, the luxurious contrast between the entirely good and pure and the downright wicked that even George Eliot sometimes allowed herself, Mrs. Oliphant creates a moral atmosphere of her own—warm, rueful, based on hard experience, tolerant just where we may not expect it. One might call it the Mrs. Oliphant effect. In part it is the "uncomprehended, unexplainable impulse to take the side of the opposition" that she recognized in herself and in Jane Carlyle. It is the form that her wit takes, a sympathetic relish for contradictions.

We are quite ready, for example, to accept Nettie as the saving angel of *The Doctor's Family*, but when the drunken Fred says "Nettie's a wonderful creature, to be sure, but it's a blessed relief to get rid of her for a little," it's impossible, just for the moment, not to see his point of view. Later on, when Nettie's responsibilities unexpectedly disappear, she feels, not gratitude or "delight in her new freedom," but a bitter sense of injury. She has never had to see herself as unimportant before. Again, Freddie, the youngest child, adores her and refuses to leave her. But this passion, says Mrs. Oliphant, is simply "a primitive unconcern for anyone but himself." Anybody who has looked after young children must reluctantly admit the truth of this. "When I am a man, I shan't want you," says Freddie. In *The Rector*, young Mr. Wentworth, even in his deep concern for the dying woman, cannot help feeling annoyed that the Rector was there before him. Mrs. Oliphant hardly implies that men, women, and children should not be like this, only that this is the way they are. The often not-quite-resolved endings of her novels produce the same bittersweet effect. In *Hester* (1883) the strong heroine, who has shown herself perfectly capable of an independent career, is left without hope of the work she meant to do, but with two men, neither of them up to her mark, who want to marry her. "What can a young woman desire more," writes Mrs. Oliphant dryly, "than to have such a possibility of choice?" To take a very different example in one of her short stories, "The Open Door" (1882), the ghost of a young man knocks at the door of a house in Edinburgh, ceaselessly trying to make amends to the family who lived there a century ago. A minister persuades the spirit to leave its haunting, but whether it is at peace as a result there is no way of telling.

As to the conclusion of *The Doctor's Family*, Mrs. Oliphant herself was not satisfied with it. "Sometimes," she wrote to Miss Blackwood in 1862, "one's fancies will not do what is required of them." I think she underrated herself here. Surely she was right, in any case, to leave her readers to reflect on whether the end of the story is a defeat for Nettie. This, in turn, raises the question of the balance of power between man and women, and the world's justice toward them. "If it were not wicked to say so," Nettie remarks, "one would think almost that Providence forgot sometimes, and put the wrong spirit into a body that did not belong to it." Nettie has had no education. One might call her self-invented. She speaks for her creator here. Still more so, when she has rejected Dr. Edward and let him drive off, full of love and rage, into the darkness, while she goes into the house. "As usual, it was the woman who had to face the light and observation, and to veil her trouble." This is all the more effective because of its restraint. Mrs. Oliphant is not asking even for change, only for acknowledgment.

The letter to Miss Blackwood makes it clear that her imagination was not always under the control of her will, and shows the natural spontaneous quality of all she wrote, as indeed of all she did. The mid-Victorian novel, Walter Allen once pointed out, "was an unselfconscious, even primitive form," and it suited her admirably. When she had good material—and in the Carlingford Chronicles she had—she was a most beguiling novelist. She saw her novels, she said, more as if she was reading them than if she was writing them. "I was guided by the human story in all its chapters."

V. Salem Chapel

"When I die I know what people will say of me," Mrs. Oliphant wrote. "They will give me credit for courage, which I almost think is not courage, but insensibility." In the winter of 1861 she was living in a small house in Ealing. She was deep in debt, and had three young children to support, one of them born after her husband's death. Working, as usual, in the middle of the night, she continued her chronicles of provincial life with *Salem Chapel*.

At the heart of her new book is the unwelcome clash of the idealist with the world as it is. The world, this time, is represented by Salem— the Dissenters of Carlingford, in satisfied possession of their thriving shops and of the red brick chapel which they have built themselves.

Salem, in appearance, is modest. On the shabby side of Grove Street, the chapel is surrounded by the "clean, respectable, meagre little habitations" where the congregation live. They, of course, are condescended to by the gentry; they are tradespeople. But their independent worship and their free choice of their own minister, to be replaced if he fails to suit, give them an agreeable sense of power. Salem folk, the women in particular, are never happier than when they are "hearing candidates." As a community they are inward-looking—the poor of Carlingford are the church's business, not theirs—but there is warmth and dignity in Salem, the warmth of neighborliness and the dignity of self-help. To them comes Arthur Vincent, their just-elected minister, a gentlemanly young scholar fresh from theological college, "in the bloom of hope and intellectualism," asking only for room to proclaim the truth to all men. He is met by what Mrs. Oliphant calls "a cold plunge." Salem wants him to fill the pews with acceptable sermons, and to do his duty at tea-meetings.

There is a strong hint, too, that the very best a young minister can do is to choose a wife from the flock, which in practice means the pinkly blooming Phoebe Tozer, the grocer's daughter. He is told of another young pastor who failed "all along of the women; they didn't like his wife, and he fell off dreadful." Arthur's instincts prompt him to escape. "Their approbation chafed him, and if he went beyond their level, what mercy was he to expect?" As in the two previous novels of the series, Carlingford will prove a test for the newcomer that is all the more painful because it is only half understood. *Salem Chapel* makes no claim to show the impact of Dissent on English life. There can be no kind of comparison, for instance, with George Eliot's treatment of Methodism in *Adam Bede*. Non-conformism is not even shown as a significant moral force. "As a matter of fact," Mrs. Oliphant admitted, "I knew nothing about chapels, but took the sentiment and a few details from our old church in Liverpool, which was Free Church of Scotland, and where there were a few grocers and other such good folk whose ways with the ministers were wonderful to behold." One of her earlier editors, W. Robertson Nicholl, pointed out that she got several of these details wrong. But this, even if she had realized it, would not have deterred Mrs. Oliphant.

What she did understand, from the depths of her Scottish being, was the power of the spoken word as a communication from heart to heart. Arthur Vincent's progress as a preacher, through the length of the book, is from mere eloquence to a painful success (which he no longer wants) before an assembly that "scarcely dares draw breath." In the second place, Salem, as she presents it, is a small community which, however comfortable and unassuming it is, claims a power that may be beyond the human range. Her concern is still with the urgent question that she had raised in *The Rector*: what does it mean for a man, living among men, to call himself their priest? Vincent has received his title to ordination, not from a bishop, but from the vote of the congregation itself, and when he first arrives in Carlingford he is proud of this. He agrees to deliver a course of lectures attacking the Church of England, a hierarchy paid for by the State. But the experience of ministry makes him question not only what he is doing, but who he is. If he is answerable to God for the souls of human beings, can these same human beings hold authority over him?

Almost certainly Mrs. Oliphant had in mind two great unorthodox Scottish ministers, Edward Irving and George Macdonald, both rejected for heresy by their congregations. Only a year earlier, in 1860, she had been writing her memoir of Irving, in which she let fly, with generous indignation, at the "homely old men, unqualified for deciding any question which required clear heads," who had passed judgment on the great preacher. And Arthur Vincent, like Irving, comes to dream of a universal Church, with Christ as its only head, "not yet realised, but surely real." Irving, however, was the son of a tanner, and Macdonald the son of a crofter. Both of them were giants of men, with their own primitive grandeur, quite unlike the dapper young man from Homerton. But the distant echo of their battles can be heard in *Salem Chapel*.

Arthur believes that his first duty is to save himself from "having the life crushed out of him by ruthless chapelmongers," all the more so because he constantly risks the ludicrous. His meditation on his high calling as a soldier of the Cross is interrupted by Phoebe Tozer, who blushingly comes to offer him a leftover dish of jelly. But, at all levels, the conflict is not as simple as he believes. The real fighting ground is psychological. He could, for example, have accepted the dish of jelly graciously, Mrs. Oliphant tells us, if he had not been a poor widow's son. His poverty and his Dissent give a painful edge to his ambition. English society, he finds, in Carlingford as elsewhere, is "a phalanx of orders and classes standing above him, standing close in order to prevent his entrance." He had hoped to make Salem a center of light. Now, as Salem's minister, he finds himself shaking hands "which had just

clutched a piece of bacon." And in all the pride—not to say the vanity—
of his intellect, he discovers not only how difficult it is to accept these
people, but how easy it is to manipulate them. He sees himself as a teller
of tales to children, and feels delighted, in spite of himself, with his own
cleverness. This two-edged danger returns more than once. He grows
disgusted with his own work, but "contemptuous of those who were
pleased with it."

In Mrs. Oliphant's novels, men turn for help to women. But in Carlingford the two women who mean most to Arthur act, in a sense, as his
opponents without intending it or even knowing it. Beautiful Lady Western, with whom he falls so disastrously and pitiably in love, means no
harm, either to him or to anyone else. She is quite conscious of her
power, but not of the damage it is doing. Then there is Mrs. Vincent,
Arthur's mother. The formal distance between Mrs Oliphant and her
subject is often very slight, particularly when she introduces these frail,
anxious widows who come to the rescue of their families with the unexpected strength of ten. Evidently she is drawing on her own experience
here, and indulging herself a little. There is too much about the widow's
self-sacrifice, and far too much about her spotless white caps. But Mrs.
Oliphant is still able to take a clear look at Mrs. Vincent. She loves
Arthur dearly, her simple faith puts him to shame, and in his defense she
confronts Salem, and even Lady Western, successfully, but she is a minister's widow, and to her the ministry is everything. Nothing can make
her see beyond the limits of pastoral duty. For this reason, in the end, she
can be of comfort, but not of help, to her son.

Arthur Vincent's struggle is a real one, and not only in terms of the
mid-nineteenth century. He has enough to contend with, it might be
thought, in Salem. Why did Mrs. Oliphant feel it necessary to involve
him, as she does, in such a lurid sub-plot? It starts off well enough with
the mysterious, sardonic Mrs. Hilyard, stitching away for a living at
coarse material that draws blood from her hands. She and her dark sense
of injustice are successfully presented, and it seems appropriate that she
eventually puts the crucial question of the book, when she begs Arthur,
as a priest, to curse her enemy, and he offers instead, as a priest, to bless
her. But when the eagle-faced Colonel Mildmay makes his appearance
("'She-Wolf!' cried the man, grinding his teeth"), and Arthur and his
mother begin to chase up and down the length of England to save his sister from "polluting arms," the effect is not so much mystery as bewil-

derment, turning, sooner or later, to irritation. Arthur himself is singularly inefficient—at one point he arrives at London Bridge just in time to
"glimpse" not one, but two of his suspects gliding out of the station in
separate carriages. Even Mrs. Oliphant herself became doubtful about
her contrivances. "I am afraid," she wrote to her publishers, "the
machinery I have set in motion is rather extensive for the short limits I
had intended."

Like her contemporary Mrs. Gaskell, she was not at ease with the
"machinery," and this is the only time it appears in the Carlingford
Chronicles. It is true that she was an admirer of Wilkie Collins (though
not of Dickens), and in particular of *The Woman in White*. In May 1862
she wrote a piece for *Blackwood's* under the title "Sensation Novels,"
which praised Collins for using "recognisable human agents" rather than
supernatural ones. But the goings-on of Colonel Mildmay are not much,
if at all, in the style of *The Woman in White*. They are stock melo-
drama—abduction, bloodshed, repentance—though admittedly there is
nothing supernatural about them. Mrs. Oliphant however, was determined to produce a bestseller at all costs, and she did. *Salem Chapel*
began running as a serial in *Blackwood's* for February 1862, and came out
in book form in 1863. "It went very near," she recollected, "to making me
one of the popularities of literature." It paid the family's bills, at least for
the time being, and gave her the courage to ask an unheard-of £1,500 for
her next novel.

This was a sturdy professional attitude, but I think she had another
reason for the sensational elements in *Salem Chapel*. Arthur Vincent cannot come to terms with himself, or with his gift of words, until he has
encountered what Mrs. Oliphant (who knew something about it) called
"the dark ocean of life." Poor though he is, he has been sheltered from
the sight of absolute want and misery, and at Homerton he has never
been led to think about such things. The shock of Mrs. Hilyard's mysterious poverty drives him out to visit the slums in Carlingford, even
though he has no idea how to go about it. He believes everything he is
told, gives money to everyone who asks, and returns penniless and
exhausted. This is a beginning. But the wild scenes of flight and pursuit
in which he is soon caught up distance him from Carlingford altogether.
This, I think, is the effect Mrs. Oliphant wanted. When at long last he
admits to Salem that his old certainties are gone and that now he only
faintly guesses "how God, being pitiful, has the heart to make man and

leave him on this sad earth," he is talking about things which he could only have learned outside Carlingford, and beyond it.

When John Blackwood, however, said that the novel came very near greatness, but just missed it, he was probably regretting the disappearance of Salem for so many chapters. And if some of the readers thought that the book must be by George Eliot (this caused Mrs. Oliphant an indescribable mixture of pleasure and annoyance), they, too, were thinking of Salem: Mrs. Oliphant inherited the Victorian novelist's birthright, the effortless creation of character. In Salem she is totally at her ease. She lets her readers know the people of Grove Street better than poor Arthur Vincent ever does. This is true even of those who only make two or three appearances. Mr. Tufton, for example, Arthur's predecessor, is a homely old minister who has fortunately been "visited" by paralysis—"a disease not tragical, but drivelling"—giving the congregation an excuse to retire him with a suitable present. A bland self-deceiver, he has never admitted his own failure, and the congregation (this is a convincing touch) has forgotten it. They assume that it will do the new minister all the good in the world to visit the old one and draw on his wisdom. Arthur suffers agonies of impatience in the Tuftons' stuffy front parlor, dominated by its vast potted plant. But this place of amiable self-deception is, unexpectedly, also the source of truth. The crippled daughter, Adelaide, strikes the sour note of absolute frankness and absolute unpleasantness. Her eyes have "something of the shrill shining of a rainy sky in their glistening whites." She explains that she has no share in life "and so instead of comforting myself that it's all for the best, as Papa says, I interfere with my fellow creatures. I get on as well as most people." She takes no pleasure in it; it is an "intense loveless eagerness of curiosity" that the complacent old Tuftons scarcely notice. At the end of the book Adelaide plays a curious small part in deciding Arthur's future. This kind of detail, a novelist's second sight, is characteristic of Mrs. Oliphant.

Mr. Tozer, the senior deacon of Salem, seems at first to represent the Victorian idea of the good tradesman. Never quite free of the greasiness of the best bacon and butter, he is proud of being "serviceable" to the gentry and is all that is meant or implied by "honest" and "worthy." He makes the familiar equation between morality and trade. All accounts, financial and spiritual, must be squared, and the new pastor's sermons must "keep the steam up." His household, where the apprentices eat with the family, is patriarchal, and, it is suggested, belongs to times past.

So, perhaps, does his unaffected kindness. Often, Salem knows, "he's been called up at twelve o'clock, when we was all abed, to see someone as was dying." All this is predictable, but Mrs. Oliphant refuses to simplify it. Tozer is Arthur's champion, but partly, at least, because he backed him from the first and can't endure to be put in the wrong. When Arthur touches despair, Tozer shows him Christian kindness, but doesn't conceal his pride in managing the minister's affairs. Arthur finds it hard to bear Tozer's perfect satisfaction over his own generosity. He feels, and so do we, that it would be "a balm" to cut Tozer's remarks short, and to "annihilate" him. At this point he is goodness in its most exasperating form. Yet we can't miss the weight of his reproach when the wretched young man "breaks out" (his sister is suspected of murder): "Mr. Vincent, sir, you mustn't swear. I'm as sorry for you as a man can be; but you're a minister, and you mustn't give way."

Comic characters on this scale generate their own energy, and grow beyond themselves. Tozer escapes from the confines of his "worthiness." In his own way—although Arthur feels he must be "altogether unable to comprehend the feelings of a cultivated mind"—he is a connoisseur, and even an aesthete. This appears in his description of a tea meeting, "with pleasant looks and the urns a-smoking and a bit of greenery on the wall," and, more surprisingly, in his tribute to Lady Western's beauty: "She's always spending her life in company, as I don't approve of; but to look in her face, you couldn't say a word against her." Again, Tozer's reverence for education goes deep, although he is too shrewd to expect others to share it. It would, he thinks, be unwise to charge an entrance fee to Arthur's lectures. "If we was amusin' the people, we might charge sixpence a head; but, mark my words, there aren't twenty men in Carlingford, nor in no other place, as would give sixpence to have their minds enlightened. No, sir, we're conferring of a boon, and let's do it handsomely." He, too, has his battle to fight, with his second deacon, Pigeon, who cannot believe that Salem needs a highly educated minister. And, in practical terms, Pigeon turns out to be right, but we can never doubt Tozer's claim to authority. The last sight we have of him is his red handkerchief; he has drawn it out to wipe away a tear or so, and to Arthur, preaching for the last time in Salem Chapel, "the gleam seemed to redden over the entire throng." This is Tozer heroic. Mrs. Oliphant herself, although she always refused to make any high claims of her own work, admitted that Tozer had amused her.

Salem can settle back to its own level, and find its own peace. "Unpeace"—this is Mrs. Tozer's word—is at all costs to be avoided. But there is no easy solution for Arthur Vincent, who has been called upon for something less than he can give, but has given, all the same, less than he might have done. Like *The Rector* and *The Doctor's Family*, *Salem Chapel* points forward to the future without exactly defining it. As the story ends, Arthur knows what it is to mistake one's calling, and to be misunderstood, and to suffer. He still has to learn what it is to be happy.

VI. The Perpetual Curate

Frank Wentworth, the Perpetual Curate, was one of Mrs Oliphant's favorites. "I mean to bestow the very greatest care on him," she told her publisher, William Blackwood, as she set to work, with her usual rush of energy, to expand Frank's story from the glimpses we get of him in *The Rector* and *Salem Chapel*. In this fourth Chronicle, Carlingford is as respectable, slow moving, and opinionated as ever. Frank, on the other hand, is "throbbing . . . with wild life and trouble to the very finger-points." He is a dedicated priest, he is in love, and he is still (as he was in *The Rector*) too poor to marry, certainly too poor to marry Lucy Wodehouse, the young woman he loves.

To be a perpetual curate, in the 1860s, meant exactly that.* He was in charge of a church built, in the first place, to take the pressure of work off a large parish. To a great extent he was independent. But to rise higher he had (like any other curate) either to be preferred to a family living, or to be recommended by the Rector to his Bishop. If, however, he was "viewy"—meaning if he had views that his superiors didn't accept—the result was bound to be a high-spirited clash with the Rector, with which the chance of recommendation was likely to disappear.

Frank Wentworth is "viewy." He is a Ritualist. At his little church, St. Roque's, built in hard stony Gothic, there are candles, flowers, bells, and a choir in white surplices. The worship there represents the later phase of the Tractarian movement whose effect was so disturbing that the Established Church had begun to take legal action against it. (One of the

---

*Frank's stipend isn't given, but in Trollope's *Framley Parsonage* (1861) the Reverend Josiah Crawley, Perpetual Curate of Hogglestock, earns £130 a year.

first of these cases, in fact, was brought against the perpetual Curate of St. James's, Brighton, who refused to give up hearing confessions.) Frank remains a good Anglican, and Mrs. Oliphant never makes it very clear how extreme his opinions are, only that he holds them sincerely. And his Ritualism, of course, is not a matter of outward show, but of symboliz-ing the truth to all comers. But the candles and flowers of St. Roque's are a scandal to three-quarters of Carlingford.

Frank, however—and here he is in deeper trouble—doesn't confine himself to St. Roque's. By the 1860s the Tractarian Movement had spread out from Oxford into missions to England's industrial slums. Frank's first Rector, old Mr. Bury, had asked the energetic young man to help him, for the time being, in Wharfside, Carlingford's brickworking district down by the canals. Here his daily contact with extreme hardship, and the dif-ficult lives and deaths of the poor, has brought out Frank's true vocation. In Wharfside he is respected and loved. His plain-spoken sermons fill the little tin chapel. But Wharfside is not in Frank's district. He has only come to think of it as his own. It is this that the new Rector, Mr. Morgan, finds intolerable. Unquestionably the success of his ministry has gone to Frank's head, Morgan challenges him directly. He proposes to sweep away the tin chapel and build a new church in Wharfside. This is not power politics, it is a dispute over a "cure of souls," but still a dispute. And "next to happiness," as Mrs. Oliphant puts it, "perhaps enmity is the most healthful stimulant of the human mind."

Since Frank cannot compromise on a matter of principle, he faces a future without advancement. This means the long-drawn-out waste of his love and Lucy's. Here is the central concern of the novel, and there are two minor episodes, comic and pathetic by turns, which stand as a kind of commentary on it. In the first place, the Morgans themselves have waited prudently through many years of genteel poverty. The appointment to Carlingford has been their first chance to marry. But by now Mrs. Morgan is faded, her nose reddened by indigestion, while Morgan has the short temper of middle age. With a touching determi-nation they brace themselves, after so many delays, to make the best of things. The railway for example, runs close behind the Rectory, the first house they have ever lived in together. The old gardener suggests that it won't show so much when the lime trees have "growed a bit," but poor Mrs. Morgan is "reluctant to await the slow processes of nature" the processes, that is, which have tormented her for the past ten years. Then

there is the terribly ugly, but perfectly good carpet left behind by the last
Rector. Mrs. Morgan detests this carpet. But she tells herself, with hard-
won self-control, "It would not look like Christ's work. . . if we had it all
our own way." She cannot afford to complain. Time has robbed her of
the luxury of ingratitude. And in her heart she is afraid that it has nar-
rowed her husband's mind, although this makes her more loyal to him
than ever. "If only we had been less prudent!" Mrs. Oliphant shows that,
in spite of everything, the love between the Morgans goes deep, but
Frank, passing them in Grange Lane, sees them as grotesque, and feels
his own frustration as demon thoughts.

Secondly, there is the story of the elder Miss Wodehouse, the gentle,
"dove-coloured," forty-year-old spinster who appears in *The Rector*. To
all appearances she is resigned to a life without self, devoted to her pretty
and much younger sister. But the Reverend Morley Proctor returns to
Carlingford and offers her her "chance." True, he proposes disconcertingly with the words "You see we are neither of us young." But he allows
Miss Wodehouse, for the first time, to set a value on herself, "a timid
middle-aged confidence." She even has it in her power, for a while at
least, to patronize Lucy. She will have a home of her own. When Lucy's
happiness makes this unimportant, Miss Wodehouse has "a half-ludi-
crous, half-humiliating sense of being cast into the shade." A truly good-
hearted woman, she cannot understand these new feelings. We have to
recognize them for her.

Love, money, duty, passing time, the powerful interactions of the mid-
Victorian novel, all bear down on the Perpetual Curate. But there is a
possible way out. The Wentworths are a landed family and they have a
living, with a good income, in their gift. The living is expected to fall
vacant and Frank is the natural successor, unless—and the Wentworths
have heard disturbing rumors of this—he has "gone over" to Ritualism.
To investigate this, Frank's unmarried aunts, all firm Evangelicals, arrive
in Carlingford. They are there to take stock of the flowers and candles,
to hear whether their nephew preaches "the plain gospel," and to deliver
their verdict accordingly. Although Mrs. Oliphant objected to the fairy-
tale element in Dickens, surely she is allowing herself to use it here.
Three aunts—one gracious; one sentimental, whose hair "wavered in
weak-minded ringlets"; one stern and practical—install themselves in
Grange Lane. From there they circulate through the town, at once men-
acing and ridiculous.

It is no surprise, however, in a novel by Mrs. Oliphant, to find enterprise in the hands of the women. Frank's father, the Squire, is an attractive figure, but a bewildered one, with only "that glimmering of sense
which keeps many a stupid man straight." He is shown, in fact, as acting
largely on instinct. Outside his broad acres (where he is shrewd enough)
he seems at a loss. From his three marriages there are numerous children
with conflicting interests, and he hardly seems to know what to do with
them either. And the family not only descends remorselessly on Frank
but summons him home to deal with the problem of his stepbrother
Gerald.

Gerald is the Rector of the parish of Wentworth itself. But he has
been struggling with doubts and has now been converted—"perverted,"
the aunts call it—to the Roman Catholic Church. The wound to his family and their sense of betrayal leaves them almost helpless. "Rome, it's
Antichrist," says the old Squire. "Every child in the village school could
tell you that." More monstrous still, Gerald hopes to become a Catholic
priest. And then there is a very real obstacle: he is married. His wife,
Louisa, is a fool. While Gerald struggles to be "content to be nothing, as
the saints were," Louisa complains, through ready tears, "We have
always been used to the very best society!" But she has the power of
weak, silly women, a power that fascinated Mrs. Oliphant, herself an
intelligent woman who had to struggle to survive. Gerald, obsessed with
his wife's troubles and his own ordeal, is "like a man whom sickness had
reduced to the last stage of life."

Frank's generous heart aches for his brother. The whole family relies
on him to bring Gerald to his senses, and the debate between the two of
them is extended through the central part of the novel. It begins at
Wentworth Rectory, where the solid green cedar tree on the lawn outside
the windows seems to stand for ancient certainties, and it echoes the
painful divisions in so many English families after the turning point of
Newman's conversion in 1845. Frank is aware that if Gerald resigns the
Wentworth living it will be there for himself and Lucy, but he hates himself for remembering this. Indeed, all he has time for is the distress of his
brother's sacrifice.

Mrs. Oliphant herself was no sectarian. The "warm Free Churchism"
of her early days was behind her, or rather it had expanded, in the course
of a hard life, into tolerance. Forms of worship interested her very little.
She knew only, as she told one of her friends, that she was not afraid of

the loneliness of death because of "a silent companion, God walking in the cool of the garden." Time and again she relates religion to instinct and nature. This doesn't mean that she treats Gerald and Frank's debate as unimportant, only that it follows its own lines. There is, for instance, nothing like Charlotte Brontë's romantic approach to the question in *Villette* (1853). The real point at issue is reached in Chapter 40 when Gerald explains himself in terms of authority. He needs a Church that is "not a human institution," one that gives absolute certainty on all points. Although the steps by which he has reached this decision aren't given, there is a hint here of Charles Reding, the hero of Newman's *Loss and Gain* (1848). Frank's answer is unexpected. He bases it, not upon freedom of conscience, but on the sufferings and inequalities of this life. How can the Catholic Church, which can no more explain these things than anyone else, claim that its authority is sufficient when it comes to doctrine? If trust in God is the only answer left to us for the pain of life, then, says Frank, "I am content to take my doctrines on the same terms."

Frank is to be seen here as the true priest, because he puts himself at the service of human suffering without pretending to be able to explain it. He understands, too, the relief from anxiety, which Mrs. Oliphant herself thought was "our highest sensation—higher than any positive enjoyment in this world. It used to sweep over me like a wave, sometimes when I opened a door, sometimes in a letter—in all simple ways." The complement of this is the sympathy for others which relief brings, "the compassion of happiness," and this, too, Frank feels at the last. But this is the same Frank Wentworth who has to restrain himself from whacking his aunt's horrible dog, and who lies awake maddened by the sound of the drainpipe—his landlady has "a passion for rain-water." Mrs. Oliphant is determined to keep him human. Indeed, it is only on those terms that he can truly be a priest.

After the success of *Salem Chapel*, Mrs. Oliphant had asked for, and got, £1,500 for the *The Perpetual Curate*. It was the highest payment she ever had from a publisher. John Blackwood's old clerk (she was told) turned pale at the idea of such a sum, and remonstrated with his master. The story began to run in *Blackwood's* Magazine in June 1863, and was produced under even greater difficulties than usual. Mrs. Oliphant wrote it only one or two installments in advance—this at her own request, as the monthly deadline, she said, "kept her up." In the autumn she traveled, with her usual large party of friends and children, to Rome.

There, in January 1864, her only daughter fell sick, and died within a few weeks. Maggie was ten, "the beloved companion," as Mrs. Oliphant had been as a little girl, to her own mother. "It is hard to go out in the streets," she wrote, "to look out of the window and see the other women with their daughters. God knows it is an unworthy feeling, but it makes me shrink from going out."

In spite of this, she missed only one installment for *Blackwood's*, for May 1864. Stress, perhaps, was responsible for a few mistakes (the church architect is called first Folgate, then Finial), and for the weakness of the sub-plot, involving Frank, as it does, in unlikely misunderstandings. Fourteen years earlier Mrs. Oliphant had sent her first novel, *Margaret Maitland*, to the stout old critic Francis Jeffrey; he told her it was true and touching but "sensibly injured by the indifferent matter which has been admitted to bring it up to the standard of three volumes." The difficulty remained, the standard length was still demanded in the 1860s by publishers and booksellers, and she set herself to meet it. Certainly the story, with its comings and goings from house to house, moves slowly at times. But Mrs. Oliphant, I think, is able to persuade the reader to her own pace, so that we can truly say at the close that we know what it is like to have lived in Carlingford.

Whatever we may think of the turns of the plot, she is at her shrewdest in this book, and at the same time at her most human. Her refusal to moralize is striking, even disconcerting. It is here in particular that she stands comparison with Trollope, whose titles *Can You Forgive Her?* and *He Knew He Was Right* challenge readers not so much to judge as to refer to their own conscience. In *The Perpetual Curate* the worthless do not repent. Jack Wentworth, the *bon viveur*, seems on the point of sacrificing his inheritance but the old Squire tells him sharply to do his duty. Everyone is fallible. Young Rosa, who causes so many complications, looks as though she is going to be a helpless victim of society. She turns out to be nothing of the sort. Miss Wodehouse becomes not gentler, but tougher. In Chapter 43 she is treasuring up an incident that might be useful to her in arguments with her future husband. Lucy, because she had made up her mind to sacrifice herself and marry Frank, even though it means being a poor man's wife, can't rejoice whole-heartedly at his success; it lessens her, she feels "a certain sense of pain." And when Frank speaks of poetic justice, Miss Leonora says, "I don't approve of a man ending off neatly like a novel in this sort of ridiculous way."

Frank Wentworth's story returns to the problem of *The Rector* and *Salem Chapel*—What does it mean for a man to call himself a priest? and, closely related to this—What can he do without the partnership of a woman? "Partnership" is the right word here. In *The Perpetual Curate*, the lesson Frank learns is that "even in Eden itself, though the dew had not yet dried on the leaves, it would be highly incautious for any man to conclude that he was sure of having his own way."

1986–87

The Mystery of Mrs. Oliphant

Mrs. Oliphant, "A Fiction to Herself": A Literary Life, by Elisabeth Jay

"I don't think I have ever had two hours uninterrupted (except at night, with everybody in bed) during the whole of my literary life," said Mrs. Oliphant. At night, therefore, she wrote—nearly one hundred novels, more than fifty short stories, history, biography, travel, articles "too numerous to list" in the index even of this meticulous book.

She was born in 1828 in Wallyford, near Edinburgh, and brought up in Liverpool. Her father, a clerk, seems never to have counted for much. The mother kept everything going, and this pattern—the helpless man, the strong woman—persisted through her life and in her fiction. Of her two brothers, one became a drunkard, the other a bankrupt invalid. She married her cousin, an unpractical stained-glass designer. He died (for which she found it hard to forgive him), leaving her to drift about Europe for cheapness' sake, with £1,000 in debts and three young children to feed.

Before long, her brothers, nieces, and nephews would also look to her for support. Words had to be spun into money, even when her only daughter died at the age of ten, leaving her to "the roughest edge of grief." She never expected help from her two idle, graceless sons; indeed she indulged them absurdly. Part of her rejoiced in taking charge and preferred her dependents to be weak. She knew this tendency of hers, and described it unsparingly in *The Doctor's Family*. In her new biography of Mrs. Oliphant, Elisabeth Jay calls her "completely self-aware," able to see herself in both comic and tragic lights, or as "a fat little commonplace woman, rather tongue-tied." This phrase comes from her *Autobiography*, still unpublished when she died in 1897. It reads as a spontaneous outpouring of love and grief, with sharp passages, too, when other women authors come into her mind. ("Should I have done better if I had been kept, like George Eliot, in a mental greenhouse and taken care of?") Jay, who edited the *Autobiography* in 1990, makes it her starting-point here. But she didn't want, she says, to go through the life and the work, comparing them blow by blow: a career is linear, but a woman's life is cyclical. Her part-headings speak for themselves: "Women and Men," "A Woman of Ideas," "The Professional Woman." Her only firm ground, she tells us, has been Mrs. Oliphant's attempt to "evaluate her gender role," but her book, after eight hard years of original research, is much more comprehensive than this.

Mrs. Oliphant, in any case, wasn't evaluating so much as surviving. The necessities of the long battle made her unpredictable. More than once she described her visit, in 1860, to *Blackwood's* offices—"myself all blackness and whiteness in my widow's dress," a humble supplicant who understood little about money—but when that didn't work she negotiated advances with the best. She believed that women should be given the vote, but not that she herself would ever want to use it. She could be "almost fearsomely correct and in the middle of it become audacious." Often, too, her stories don't give her readers the satisfaction of closure— a conventionally happy or even a well-defined ending. She doesn't want us to expect too much of life, certainly not consistency.

Her subjects were the staples of Victorian women's fiction—money, wills, marriages, church and chapel, disgraceful relatives, family power-struggles, quarrels, deathbeds, ghosts—though she fearlessly stepped outside this in her Little Pilgrim stories, which take place beyond the grave.

"Is she worth reading?" Elisabeth Jay has been asked time and again. The question is difficult to answer, since the books are so hard to find, and publishers who do reprint them always go back to the Chronicles of Carlingford, probably because the title suggests Trollope's Barchester series (from which Mrs. Oliphant borrowed a little when she felt like it). But although she wrote with marvelous fluency—writing, she said, felt to her much like reading—the length of the three-volume novel seems not to have suited her.

She is at her very best in novellas and short stories. Two of them, which might well be reprinted together, are "The Mystery of Mrs. Blencarrow"(1890), in which a conventional widow with a large estate falls in love with her coarse-mannered steward, and "Eleanor and Fair Rosamond" (1891). Here the wife finds out that her husband has made a bigamous marriage. She has the other woman's address, and resolutely sets out for the distant suburb, the street, the house. What follows is "tragi-farce," as Mrs. Oliphant calls it, "the most terrible of all," and she risks a conclusion that dies away into silence and echoes.

This is a valuable study, strong on Mrs. Oliphant's religious experiences and on her professional life. As to her bewildering personality, perhaps no one understood her better than the thirty-years-younger James Barrie. In 1897, when she lay dying of cancer, he called to see her and "the most exquisite part of her, which the Scotswoman's reserve had kept hidden, came to the surface." But he does not say what she told him.

1995

THE VICTORIANS

Called Against His Will

Father of the Bensons: The Life of Edward White Benson, Sometime Archbishop of Canterbury, by Geoffrey Palmer and Noel Lloyd

It's more of a difficulty than a help that so much has been written about the Bensons (Palmer and Lloyd have already done a biography of Fred Benson) and that the family should have written so much about themselves. The Archbishop kept diaries, and his wife Minnie wrote two—one a dutiful sightseer's journal, kept at her husband's suggestion on her honeymoon, another one many years later that told some, at least, of the story of her heart. (There is also a contemporary diary of Minnie's for 1862–63.) Arthur Benson wrote four and a half million words of diaries, a book of family reminiscences, a family genealogy, lives of his father, his sister Maggie and his brother Hugh, and a memoir of his sister Nellie. Fred wrote *Our Family Affairs*, *Mother*, *As We Were*, and (almost on his deathbed) *Final Edition*. He also kept a diary. The Bensons, "a rather close little corporation," as Arthur called them, had a boundless talent for self-expression, self-justification, and self-explanation. Yet they did not give themselves away.

Edward White Benson took charge of his five brothers and sisters at the age of fourteen, after the death of his father in 1842. This father had been an unsuccessful research chemist who had invested what money he had in a process for manufacturing white lead, but Edward, fearing the taint of "business," refused to let his mother carry on with it. This was probably wise, since he already had a career in the Church in mind. "To a boy of tender home affections there is perhaps no pain more acute than can be caused by the discovery that his schoolfellows think slightingly, on the score of poverty or social distinctions, of those who are dearest to him in the world." This is from the biography of one of my grandfathers, later Bishop of Lincoln: it tactfully conceals the fact that in the 1860s his father kept a shop, and got hopelessly into debt. Edward Benson was spared this, but when his mother died in 1850 he was still working for his tripos at Cambridge, and since she had been living on an annuity the family faced the future on a little over £100 a year. He was rescued by the rich and childless bursar of his college, Francis Martin, who had heard of his troubles, and offered to support him until he could earn his own living. Martin lavished affection on the handsome, hard-pressed scholar, but, the authors say, "the younger man did not fall in love with the older although he was willing to accept both the devotion and all the advantages that went with it." This seems hard. Affection can't be regulated, and by 1852 Edward had in any case determined to make eleven-year-old Minnie, daughter of his widowed cousin Mrs. Sidgwick, his future wife. Neither of his relationships, with the doting Mr. Martin or the bewildered Minnie, was considered in any way strange in the 1850s.

No one who has written about the Bensons has been able to help making Minnie the heroine of the story. They married in 1859, when she was eighteen and Edward thirty. "An utter child," she wrote, "with no stay on God. Twelve years older, much stronger, much more passionate, and whom I really didn't really love. How evidently disappointed he was—trying to be rapturous—feeling so inexpressibly lonely and young, but how hard for him."

Edward went on to be a master at Rugby, the first Master of Wellington College, Chancellor of Lincoln, the first Bishop of Truro, and in 1883, Archbishop of Canterbury. Minnie bore him six children, all of whom loved her dearly, and from her early days as a muddled extravagant housekeeper she grew into the doyenne of vast households. She liked meeting distinguished people and was certainly a great gainer from her marriage. Gladstone called her "the cleverest woman in Europe." She was not clever, but she was generously responsive, and had a genius for following her instincts even when she hardly admitted them. She was, as became clear early on, a woman who loved women, and had agonizingly keen relationships, emotional and spiritual, with a series of female friends, some of them quite dull. It says a great deal for the Bensons that they made a go of an ill-assorted marriage, a brilliant, bizarre, self-centered family, and a career that reached the very summit.

Edward's present biographers take a calm and judicious tone, but they call him a "natural bully" and say that his children all emerged "scarred," except his eldest son, Martin, who died at seventeen, and Nellie, his eldest daughter, who was not afraid of her father. But all of them, even the amiable Fred, inherited his neurasthenia and spells of black depression, and Maggie, the younger daughter, became suicidally insane, recovering only for the last few days of her life. Hugh, the treasured last-born, looks in his childhood photographs like a changeling, palely star-ing. The three sons grew up homosexual and each of them, in their distinctive way, avoided taking responsible posts. Arthur, when the point came, did not want to be headmaster of Eton. Fred became a popular novelist and a resolutely genial bachelor. Hugh, having converted to Catholicism, lived as a priest without a parish.

Their father was integrity itself, a mighty force always heading the same way, excluding other opinions with an absolute certainty of their wrongness. His system was total: music, literature, travel, social behav-ior, the careful folding of an umbrella, the management of gravy and potatoes on the plate were all judged not from the aesthetic but the moral viewpoint. We know that he was a flogging headmaster, that to Ethel Smyth (a friend of Nellie's) "the sight of his majestic form approaching the tea-table scattered my wits as an advancing elephant might scatter a flock of sheep," that conversation with him was not to be undertaken lightly, and that Hugh—for example—felt like "a small china mug being filled at a waterfall." He dearly liked his children to be near him and anxiously waited for their love. But circumstances were against him, because as schoolmaster, bishop, and archbishop his family were always on show and must be urged and interrogated into perfec-tion. Meanwhile the children themselves were longing, perhaps praying, for him to go away.

"No one," Betty Askwith wrote in *Two Victorian Families*, "who has not experienced some taste of Victorian family life (for it survived in places well into the twentieth century) can quite understand the extraor-dinary sense of living under the domination of one of those vital, strong-willed tyrants. If the tyranny be accompanied, as it frequently was, with vivid personality and wide-ranging intellectual interests, there was an excitement about it which was incommunicable."

Edward Benson was a great man, and Palmer and Lloyd give a sym-pathetic account of a formidable career. He loved to rule, although he believed the choice was not in his hands—"if calls exist," he wrote, "called I was, against my will"—and they think he was at the very height of his powers in Truro, working as a creative pioneer, with a new cathe-dral to build, and on the way to revealing his own personal conception of the episcopacy and of religion itself. As Primate "his acquaintance with the practical affairs of Church and State was slight, and he knew he would quickly have to master all the administrative problems that would surround him. Everything poetical and romantic, the very essence of his view of life, would be left behind in Cornwall." But Edward of course went courageously into new duties and controversies – temperance, patronage, disestablishment, the guidance of missionary societies, "the wretchedness of the poorest classes, their ignorance and wildness and false friends," reunion between the churches, ritual.

His Lincoln judgment of 1890 was given after months of hard work and anxiety. The Bishop of Lincoln was on trial on charges of "irregular and unlawful ritual," and in particular of adopting the eastward position with his back to the congregation during the consecration, so that the people could not see what the priest was doing. Benson finally allowed the eastern position as optional, but insisted that the consecration of the elements itself must be before the people. "What he meant by this was illustrated at my consecration in St. Paul's Cathedral," wrote my grandfather (my other one, the Bishop of Manchester). "He thus deliberately differentiated the English Holy Communion from the Roman Mass. But this provision of his has been generally disregarded." Who cares? But in February 1889, crowds besieged Lambeth Palace on the first day of the trial, long before the doors opened at eleven o'clock, and the police had to be called in to keep order.

This grandfather, by the way, although he worked himself almost to death, allowed himself not to answer letters from obvious lunatics. But Benson, apparently, told his chaplain that they must all be answered, since they might have been of importance to the men who wrote them. He never retired, but died (in October 1896) on a visit to the Gladstones, at early Communion in the church at Hawarden. "He died like a soldier," said Gladstone. And he had lived like one, too, constantly at his post. But Palmer and Lloyd might, perhaps, have said more about his interest in the supernatural. At Cambridge, in the late 1840s, he and his friends had founded a Ghost Club. He is usually said to have lost interest in such matters or even to have come to disapprove of them, but in his notebooks for 12 January 1895, Henry James writes:

Note here the ghost story told me at Addington . . . by the Archbishop of Canterbury . . . the story of the young children (indefinite number and age) left to the care of servants in an old country house. . . . The servants, wicked and depraved, corrupt and deprave the children; the children are bad, full of evil, to a sinister degree. The servants die (the story vague about the way of it) and their apparitions, figures, return to haunt the house and children, to whom they seem to beckon, whom they invite and solicit, from across dangerous places, the deep ditch of a sunk fence, etc so that the children may destroy themselves, lose themselves, by responding, by getting into their power. So long as the children are kept from them, they are not lost; but they try and try, these evil presences, to get hold of them. It is a question of the children "coming over to where they are."

Edward Benson told this story in the year before his death. There are two principles within each soul—we have to choose, we have to renew the struggle every hour. He had preached this so long and so earnestly, but here it is in the form of a powerful tale of haunting. How can it be said, then, that he left everything poetical and romantic behind him in Cornwall?

1998

The Need for Open Spaces

Octavia Hill was born in Wisbech, Cambridgeshire, England, in 1838, the youngest but two of a family of eleven children, ten of them girls. She had no formal education, for her strong-minded mother believed in letting her children do what they were best at, and in letting them be outdoors as much as possible. When Octavia was fourteen, the family moved from the country into London: she never forgot the loss of green fields and fresh air.

However, she needed to earn her living, so she became the manager of a toy-making workshop run for the benefit of girls from what was then called a ragged school. Hill went on to become a crusader for housing reform, managing small blocks of slum property and making sure the apartments were fit to live in. She grew into authority and sat on select committees and royal commissions, but without wavering an inch from her first principles.

She didn't believe in charity as such. What she asked for, for everyone, was access to education, employment at a fair wage, and, above all, space "for the sight of sky and of things growing." She felt strongly that people, and the poor in particular, needed open space, but she also set herself to see that they got it. This is the work for which she is now best remembered, as one of the founders of the National Trust. The campaign, based on the open spaces movement in the United States, began in the late 1880s with a protest against the closing of rights of way and footpaths. The first stretch of land to be presented to the trust was four and a half rocky acres on the coast of Wales. By the time Hill died, in 1912, the trust's property had expanded beyond all calculations, and some American conservationists had taken to looking to Hill for inspiration.

Evidently, to achieve so much, Hill had to be an impressive but also an infuriating woman. Tiny, stout, noticeably badly dressed, with a hat like a pen wiper (her lifetime friend John Ruskin couldn't bear her dowdiness), she was obstinate—no, more than obstinate, absolutely inflexible. She has been called one of the noblest women ever sent upon earth, but it didn't do to disagree with Octavia Hill.

1999

In the Golden Afternoon

Lewis Carroll: A Biography, by Morton N. Cohen,
and *The Red King's Dream, or Lewis Carroll in Wonderland,*
by Jo Elwyn Jones and J. Francis Gladstone

In a letter of 1874 the author of Alice described to a child friend how he had been seen off at the railway station by two affectionate friends, Lewis Carroll and Charles Dodgson. Here he is dividing himself not into two, but three. This was never a matter of conflicting selves. It was a game, though one he took seriously, as mathematicians do.

Morton N. Cohen, after thirty years of faithful research and scholarship, has undertaken a complete biography of the whole man, and finds himself driven to call him "Charles." In a certain sense, there is little to relate. Dodgson was born in 1832, the eldest child of the parsonage at Daresbury in Cheshire, where "even the passing of a cart was a matter of great interest." He was deaf in one ear and stammered. At Rugby, he suffered uncomplainingly for four years. At home, he edited nursery-table magazines, *The Rectory Umbrella* and others, for his brothers and sisters, and took responsibility for them when the parents died. In 1851, he went up to Christ Church, and spent the rest of his working life there. He was elected to a studentship in mathematics and became a rather contentious member of the very contentious governing body and Curator of the Common Room, laying down some good wine and, in 1884, instituting afternoon tea. He had rooms, first of all in the Library building, and then, when he had more money, in Tom Quad. His study was as full of devices and puzzles as a toyshop, and up and down his stairs came scores of little girl visitors and their mothers. (When speaking to children, he did not stammer.) As a Ruskinian in search of beauty and, at heart, a gadgeteer, he became a notable amateur photographer. His subjects were almost all celebrities—he stalked the Tennyson family, catching them at last in the Lake District, and children. In 1880, perhaps because the new dry-plates made the whole thing too easy, he put away his camera. In 1867, he had made an expedition to Russia with his old friend Henry Liddon; he never went abroad again, never married, and was ordained only as a deacon, never as a priest. Meanwhile he worked relentlessly, though sedately, publishing three hundred titles, of one kind or another, in thirty-five years. He also, of course, became famous, and yet perhaps the most dramatic incident of his life was the river expedition to Nuneham when his whole party, including his aunt, two of his sisters, and Alice herself, got wet through and had to be taken to a friend's house to dry off. In 1898, almost as an afterthought, Dodgson died of a cold and cough.

Morton Cohen is as heroic as a biographer, in his way, as Dodgson was with his camera. This means going painstakingly into university and college politics, and making a serious attempt to sum up Dodgson's professional career. "A modest, none too successful lecturer of mathematics," in Roger Lancelyn Green's judgment, "whose writings on the subject are hardly remembered to-day." This, naturally, is not enough for Cohen, who calls in expert opinion, mostly in favor but sometimes against, on every syllabus, textbook, and pamphlet. Then there are the puzzles and ciphers, and the almost unplayable games. (Even Cohen, perhaps, hasn't tried "Croquet Castles.") The book is arranged chronologically, but pauses from time to time to consider a subject at greater length. It is a disadvantage, certainly, that the four years from 1858 to 1862 are missing from Dodgson's diaries. These volumes would cover the beginning of his acquaintance with Liddell, the Dean of Christ Church, the strong-minded Mrs. Liddell and their young family. By 1862, Alice was nearly ten. The fourth of July was the "golden afternoon" (although Cohen anxiously points out that the meteorological records show that it was raining) when Alice and her two sisters listened to the earliest version of her adventures underground. Two years later, Dodgson had apparently fallen quite out of favor at the Deanery. He had applied in vain for leave to take the girls out on the river, "but Mrs. Liddell will not let any come in future: rather superfluous caution. . . . Help me O God, for Christ's sake, to live more to Thee. Amen!" What precisely, or even imprecisely, had gone wrong? Dodgson had disagreed with Liddell over college business, but scholars and Heads of Houses were used to arguments on a much grander scale than this, and the Dean would never have let such things interfere with personal matters. Perhaps the worst case of all for a biographer, nothing definable happened at all.

At this point, Cohen gives way to ungainly speculations. Perhaps, he thinks, in 1863, when the newly married Prince and Princess of Wales visited the Deanery, Alice might have impetuously piped up: "I'm going to marry Mr. Dodgson." And if Charles were present, perhaps taking it as a teasing remark, or not, he might have picked up the thread and replied: "Well said, and why not!" Ah, teasing. That might have much to do with the case. Young females can bat their eyes, shake their heads, toss their locks about, feign innocence, and make outrageous suggestions all with intent to shock and call attention to themselves. And the three clever Liddell sisters were probably expert in these arts.

The biographer's task, however, isn't to picture wild scenes at the Deanery, but, as Cohen tells us, "to look beyond the writings and into the artist." He has set himself to account for Dodgson's shyness, reserve, and melancholy and the springs of his magical creative power. His conclusion is that Dodgson, as a rector's eldest son, bore "scars of guilt" because he was a childless bachelor and a mathematician who would never be a priest. The father must, it seems, have been oppressive, although there is very little evidence for this and Cohen has to end the section rather lamely: "Had Charles managed to forge a union with Alice or some other object of his desire he would have been a far happier man than he was." *Alice in Wonderland*, he claims, is, in fact, about Dodgson himself, and his adolescent trials and stresses (although Alice could in no circumstances be anything but a little girl, absolutely certain of the rules she has learned and able to put down any amount of nonsense). *Through the Looking-Glass* is about Alice Liddell, but the game is more advanced. She climbs the social ladder and "becomes a woman." This doesn't account for the irresistibility of the stories, which Cohen, in orthodox style, puts down to emotional and sexual repression. He has made a checklist of the prayers entered in the diaries for purity and a new life. There are many more of these, he calculates, when Dodgson was meeting the Liddell children regularly. His diverted sexual energy "caused him unspeakable torments," but we can consider ourselves fortunate, since it was in all probability the source of his genius. Meanwhile, without ever compromising his conscience or his religious faith, he had to endure his existence as "the odd man out, an eccentric, the subject of whispers and wagging tongues."

Although Cohen accepts Mavis Batey's identification (published in 1991) of the stories with their Christ Church background, he seems never quite to realize how well Dodgson was suited to mid-Victorian Oxford. Oxford hostesses were good judges of eccentricity, and the college halls were used to nervous, stammering, opinionated, riddling, and joking guests. My grandfather, a tutor at Corpus in 1870, notes, "Heard this evening the last new joke of the author of *Alice in Wonderland*: he [Dodgson] knows a man whose feet are so large that he has to put his trousers on over his head." There is a kind of friendly resignation about this, certainly not hostility.

As to Alice herself, she was a creature of the golden age of indulged small girls, when Ruskin piled up valuable books for them to jump over, when Oscar Wilde rowed little Katie Lewis on the Thames, delighted with her selfishness, when Flaubert wrote a letter to his niece from her doll and Gladstone buttered his granddaughter's bread on both sides. And Alice becomes a queen, but her reign will be short. As the century turned, the little girls of fiction were replaced by boys (Peter Pan, le grand Meaulnes) who were either unwilling or unable to grow up, but that is not the world of Alice. "I had known dear Mr. Dodgson for years," Ellen Terry said. "He was as fond of me as he could be of anybody over the age of ten." Dodgson believed that "anyone that ever loved one true child will have known the awe that falls on one in the presence of a spirit fresh from God's hands on whom no shadow of sin has yet fallen," but between ten and fourteen the shadow did fall. On 11 May 1865, he met Alice (by now thirteen) with Miss Prickett, "the quintessence of governesses," in Tom Quad. "Alice seemed changed a good

deal, and hardly for the better probably going through the usual awkward stage of transition." Like every other child friend (though none of
them were so dear), she had withdrawn her true self into time past. In
Chapter 23 of *Sylvie and Bruno*, he expresses his nostalgia as a melancholy joke when with the help of the Professor's Reversal Watch he turns
time backward, only to find himself cruelly cheated.

It is distressing that Morton Cohen seems to care so little for *Sylvie
and Bruno*, Dodgson's parable of love and forgiveness. It is here that he
is closest to his friend George MacDonald, whose *Phantastes* was written as a "fairy-tale for adults." When (in the introduction to *Sylvie and
Bruno Concluded*) Dodgson says that he has imagined a possible psychical state in which a human being "might sometimes become conscious
of what goes on in the fairy world, by actual transference of their imma-
terial essence," he is talking about something of the greatest importance
to him. It is not enough to say, as Cohen does, that "Charles retreated
inward when he should have traveled outward."

Cohen, however, may well think that after thirty years' patient study
of the material he has earned the right to his own interpretations. Certainly he has avoided "the eccentric readings [that], while they may
amuse, do not really bring us any closer to understanding the work,"
although, judging from his true grit as a biographer, he has probably
read them all. *The Red King's Dream* is yet another one. Here the
authors, Jo Elwyn Jones and J. Francis Gladstone, set out with the
apparent advantage of living at Hawarden Castle, a few hundred yards
from the Gladstone Library at St. Deiniol's. Their quest seems to have
started there, with a strange conviction that, in Tenniel's *Wonderland*
illustration, the Lion is Disraeli and the Unicorn (in spite of his unmis-
takable goatee beard) is Gladstone. Tenniel was a political cartoonist,
therefore the whole book must be a contemporary satire. (Dodgson, in
fact, chose Tenniel not because of his work for *Punch*, but because the
animals were so good in his *Aesop's Fables*.) The White Knight must be
Tennyson, and Tennyson's two sons (not twins) must be Tweedledum
and Tweedledee. In default of other evidence, an anagram will do. For
instance, it is decided that the Mad Hatter is Charles Kingsley, so that
the Hare must be his brother Henry: the Hare's reply, "It was the best
butter," is an anagram (though unfortunately it isn't quite) of "The
Water Babies." But "we still did not know who the Dormouse could
be . . . we could not fit him into the Kingsley coterie." It is anybody's

guess, but fit in he must, and he turns out to be F. D. Maurice, while Dean Stanley is the Cheshire cat, and Millais, because of his commercial success, is the Lobster who is baked too brown. And so on, faster and faster.

The only compensation is that the authors seem to be enjoying themselves so much. In this way at least their research is part of what Dodgson called "those stores of healthy and innocent amusement that are laid up in books for the children that I love so well."

1995

Old Foss and Friend

Edward Lear: A Biography, by Peter Levi

Edward Lear (1812–1888) made his reputation as a watercolorist after almost no training, and invented himself as an Old Man with a Beard. He is a very attractive example of Victorian self-help. It was not an easy life, of course. English humorists are all depressives, and Lear suffered to the very end from "fits of the morbids."

Vivien Noakes's *Edward Lear: The Life of a Wanderer* (1968), her book on his painting, and her catalogue for the 1985 Exhibition are classics. Peter Levi acknowledges her work without reserve. It has left him free to write an eccentric, affectionate biography, and to indulge himself as well as his subject. Lear was born in Holloway in 1812, the youngest of twenty-one children. When he was four, his father, a stockbroker, was declared bankrupt. Edward had perhaps five years at school and scarcely knew some of his family. He was lucky that his much older sister Anne looked after him tenderly, and he never had to go out to work as a clerk. He was unlucky in having poor sight until he was given spectacles, everything he saw was "formed into a horror" in being epileptic and asthmatic, and in having (at the age of ten) been put through an experience by a brother and a cousin that he remembered as "the greatest evil done to me in life excepting that done by C." Who was "C"? Lear kept diaries, but later destroyed all of them up to the year 1858.

By the time he was sixteen, he was "drawing for bread and cheese," then made a serious start as a bird painter, and was summoned to Knowsley by the old twelfth Earl of Derby to draw the menagerie. Another benefactor, Lord Egremont, asked him: "But where is all this going to lead to, Mr. Lear?" It led to the life of a wanderer, or rather of a voluntary exile. In 1837, Lord Derby (and others) paid his passage to Rome. Lear got himself an attic in the via del Babuino, and began to learn Italian. What was to be drawn was beyond anything he could have imagined, not the antiquities, but the views. At that time, as Levi points out, you could still see the tip of Mount Soracte from the middle of Rome, glittering white in winter, and then there was the Campagna.

Levi believes that Lear "became happy from the time he decided to become a landscape painter." After nine years in Rome, and the publication of two volumes of *Excursions in Italy*, there was an unexpected interlude when the Queen, pleased with the *Excursions*, sent for him to improve her drawing. This was a new opening, perhaps, but it came to nothing. From Rome he went on, traveling in discomfort inconceivable, to Calabria, Sicily, Corfu, Greece, Turkey, Albania, Egypt, Palestine, Athens, Crete. It was his ambition to paint the whole Mediterranean coast, with one last expedition to India. In the 1870s he eventually settled down in a villa at San Remo. As a young man, he had walked almost the whole distance from Milan to Florence. As an old one, he had to be lifted in and out of railway carriages "like a bundle of hay." But he continued to work. In recording the lands of summer, he made something like ten thousand watercolors.

Levi writes finely about images he loves of countries which he himself knows well. Temperamentally, I think he is drawn to sketches more than to finished pictures, to "dew-freshness and variety," "the heavenly-fresh sketch of the bridge at Scutari," yet, on consideration, he believes that the chromolithographs of the Ionian islands are Lear's masterpiece, and out of these he selects for his one permitted color illustration the view of Zante, which had worried Lear because he didn't see how it could be made picturesque.

> In fact it was that failure which lay at the root of his success. . . . He drew
> a picture of perfect provincial peace and quiet, enlivened, if at all, only by
> a few normal-looking goats, but in doing so he expresses the true genius
> of place. . . . The image has stood still in his eye.

Lear was deeply interested in technical processes that might create a larger market for him, photography in particular; he didn't seem to see how threatening it might become to a painter of views. Meanwhile, he continued to make a living in the only way he knew, and as his hero, Turner, had done he either got commissions, or showed his finished works to people who might be likely to buy them. Apart from these, there were his travel albums and the Nonsense books, both of which sold moderately.

Apparently he thought seriously of marriage and proposed twice to the same girl, but since she was forty-six years younger, he must have been certain of a "No." Friends, the visits of friends, their unaccountable behavior, their many-paged and always-answered letters, were the defense against "cruel loneliness" and the support of his life, partly because he lived a good deal through theirs. Frank Lushington, the dearest of all, he followed to Corfu. When he heard that another close friend, Chichester Fortescue, had been made Secretary for Ireland, he threw a fried whiting, in his joy, across the hotel dining room. There were tears, also, and "angries." Not a hint of homosexuality here, Levi insists, but this ignores the many lights and shades of that golden age of male friendship. Undoubtedly, however, the real married couple of the household were Lear and his grumbling old Suliot servant, Giorgis, an unsatisfactory cook ("Fried oranges again!") but faithful to the death. Giorgis did not think a poor man should want to live more than sixty years, and in fact died before Old Foss, Lear's favorite cat, the other presiding genius of the villa at San Remo.

Lear had escaped the fate of a mid-Victorian jester to the gentry, established his own life and planted his own garden. Now, accepting his stoutness, his beard, his strange nose, he mythologized himself, delightfully, though more wistfully, perhaps, than the circumstances warranted, as the desolate Yonghy-Bonghy-Bò and finally as Uncle Arly, who wandered the world in shoes too tight for him. There was a mythical version, too, of Old Foss.

Levi wanders amiably and sometimes confusingly in and out of the diaries and letters, and up and down the years. But the book arose, he tells us, "from an attempt to put together a lecture on Lear as a poet," and it seems a pity that in the end he has left himself so little room for this. Lear was a skilled metrist, partial to dactyls ("Calico," "Pelican," "runcible"), and a magic songwriter, with something like a reverence for the absurd. Levi says something about this, and, as a poet, he defends the limericks from anyone who may have found them disappointing because of the repeated last rhymes. But he goes over the edge, surely (as he does several times in this book), when he says that in the 1880s Lear was writing poetry which "no one but Tennyson (until Hardy) could rival for its lively and startling originality." What's become of Browning?

1995

The Sound of Tennyson

I think of Tennyson as one of the greatest of the English-rectory-bred wild creatures. In matters of theology, love, doubt, grief, and loss he is usually felt to have said what most people wanted to hear, but when he was in the grip of his daemon, as he surely was in "Break, Break, Break," or "Tears, Idle Tears," with its strange series of comparisons, or "In the Valley of Cauterez," or the last five verses of "To the Marquis of Dufferin and Ava," he is not definable and not resistible. He was a superb metrist, who scarcely needed to care for the opinions of Indolent Reviewers, but did care, and he was someone who could hear the authentic voice of the English language. By this I don't mean onomatopoeia (in any case many of his subjects for this—immemorial elms, church bells, steam trains — have unfortunately almost disappeared), but the sound of the language talking to itself. Take his round "o"s, which can be heard as he pronounced them himself in his recorded reading of "The Ballad of Oriana": "When the long dun wolds are ribbed with snow. . . ." When my grand-father, as Bishop of Lincoln, preached the centenary sermon at Somersby, he quoted "Who loves not knowledge?" and was told afterward "You should have said *know-ledge.* Lord Tennyson always pronounced it so." Every round "o" had its weight and its considered position. "Row us out from Desenzano, to your Sirmione row!"—"Naay, noä mander o' use to be callin' him Roä, Roä, Roä [Rover] / For the dog's stoän deaf, and 'e's blind, 'e can neither stan' nor goä." That is the Spilsby variation, of course. At times Tennyson seems to me to be listening, rather as Pavarotti does, in apparent amazement simply to the beauty of the sounds that he is inexplicably able, as a great professional, to produce.

1992

The June-blue Heaven

Emily Tennyson: The Poet's Wife, by Ann Thwaite

In 1984, Ann Thwaite wrote, most successfully, the biography of Edmund Gosse, the Man of Letters. Now she has made a close study of another almost extinct profession, the Great Man's Wife. It was a role that could end tragically, as it did for the second Mrs. Watts, who had to live on in the painter's house and studio for more than thirty years after his death, while his reputation faded to almost nothing. Emily Tennyson only survived her husband by four years, giving her time to work, with her son Hallam, on the two volumes of Memoirs.

They first met each other as Lincolnshire children. She was the daughter of Henry Sellwood, a Horncastle solicitor; he came from the disastrous Rectory family at Somerton. She did not marry her Ally until she was thirty-six years old. By this time the worst of his financial troubles were over (although he had formed a chronic habit of grumbling about money), and a few months later he was appointed Poet Laureate. But for the past seven years the two of them had been eating their hearts out, while her well-meaning father forbade them to correspond. Sellwood was thinking of the drinking and smoking, the restlessness, the black moods and indeed the "black blood" of the Tennyson family, the father an epileptic drunkard, one brother in an asylum, another one violent, a third addicted to opium from Lincolnshire's homegrown poppies. Beyond this, Emily was a steadfast believer, while Tennyson was tormented and unresolved, particularly over God's reason for creating sin and suffering. Another gulf to cross was the "deeper anguish" of Arthur Hallam's death, which had left Tennyson, as he said, "widowed," so that he "desired to die rather than to live." But this, at least, was not a drawback to Emily. As a strengthening influence, she thought of herself as Hallam's appointed successor. It seems a difficult concept, but it illustrates the depth, the purity, and the strange nature of Victorian emotional relationships.

Even Ann Thwaite, the most thoroughgoing of researchers, can't tell exactly how it was that the crisis was resolved. They were married on 13 June 1850, at Shiplake-on-Thames. Tennyson said, in apparent surprise, that it was the nicest wedding he had ever been at.

Now Emily embarked on her profession, which was primarily a defensive campaign on many fronts. Tennyson had to be protected against distress of body and mind—against noise and disturbance, against the servant situation (which Georgie Burne-Jones, herself an expert campaigner, described as "a bloody feud or a hellish compact"), against visitors, sightseers, vexatious relatives, against a monstrous daily post (every amateur poet in the country sent their verses for his opinion), against contemptible hostile criticism and a writer's own self doubt and self-reproach. He seems to have managed up till then without her, largely by moving about. Indeed, even after his marriage, the Tennysons moved often, and for years Emily had two houses to run, Farringford, at Freshwater on the Isle of Wight, and Aldworth, near Haslemere, where they went in summer to avoid the holiday makers. Ann Thwaite's book is long, but her painstaking method is the only way to give an idea of Emily's immensely troublesome, immensely rewarding daily life. Almost everything that could go wrong with the two houses did, including that traditional enemy, the drains. In 1856, for example, Emily was weeding potatoes, binding Alfred's manuscripts, and planning a new dairy. She paid the bills and subscriptions, kept the accounts, found tenants, organized and supervised builders. She became deeply involved with the Farringford farm when they took it over in 1861. Emily would often consult Alfred—about the rent they should ask for the chalkpit, for instance—but he would say, "I must leave it in thy hands to manage."

In 1865, Queen Emma of the Sandwich Islands arrives with her Hawaiian entourage. The children's rooms are needed for the royal party, and they are crammed into the lodge, while Emily's cousin and aunt, who are staying "indefinitely," are stowed away elsewhere. Later, Dr. James Acworth arrives; his wife is a spiritualist medium and "in A's study," Emily's diary records, "a table heaves like the sea." In 1871, there is a full house at Aldworth, but Mrs. Gladstone is told to come and bring as many of the family as possible. "We have room, both in house and heart." Some guests have to be encouraged, some consoled. Tennyson, although a generous host, is unpredictable. In 1859, Edward Lear, a favorite guest, is so rudely treated that he goes upstairs to pack; Emily soothes him and buys one of his drawings. Meantime, her two sons, Hallam and Lionel, are brought up from golden-haired darlings, encouraged to walk on the dinner table, to become unrebellious, affectionate, quite dull young men.

Thwaite gives them almost as much importance in her biography as they must have had in their own family. She is following, she says, Christopher Ricks's advice to her—"Parents are formed by their children as well as children formed by their parents." But did Emily ever change? Some personal difficulties she solved simply by letting them be—the poet's dirty shirts, for example, his dark muttering or bellows of complaint after dinner, his skirmishes with pretty women visitors and his compulsion to wander. "I trust Saturday will indeed bring thee back, but do not come if there is anything for which thou wouldst wish to stay," she writes in 1859.

These indulgences irritated friends of long standing who saw Emily as a kind of saint, certainly much better than Alfred deserved. "Do not throw away your life," Jowett wrote to her. He thought "there was hardly enough of self in her to keep herself alive." Lear (half envious of the closeness of marriage, half repelled by it) wrote in his diary that "no other woman in all this world could live with [A.T.] for more than a month." They were mistaken, however, if they thought Tennyson was ungrateful. He knew very well that he was blessed, and would, he said, have worked as a stonebreaker to be allowed to marry her earlier. "If she were not one of the sweetest, justest natures in the world, I should be almost at my wits' end." And the two of them faced together the death of two children—their first son, who was stillborn, and Lionel, who died at sea in 1885 on the passage home from India.

The usual image of Emily Tennyson is that of one more sickly Victorian woman, ruling from her sofa. (That, certainly, was how Virginia Woolf represented her in her play *Freshwater*.) From early childhood she had been considered a weak creature and as a married woman she was often in too much pain to walk, and yet, as Thwaite points out, when her sons were little she writes of climbing ladders, scrambling over rocks, and getting down the Alum Bay cliffs with her feet in eel-baskets. It was not until Hallam and Lionel were students that she had some kind of serious collapse. But nineteenth-century ailments defeat twentieth-century biographers. Reducing sufferers to a wreck, pain was accepted as a lifetime companion. Patience was prayed for, a cure was hardly expected. It's a relief to know that Emily was a great believer in champagne, and brandy in her bedtime arrowroot.

After five years of research, Thwaite asks herself and the reader: was Emily Sellwood's life (as Jowett put it) "effaced"? After she left school to become an angel in the house, she educated herself, like so many spirited

Victorian daughters, by reading. (My own step-grandmother entered in her diary on her wedding day: "Finished *Antigone*; Married Bishop.")

Emily read Dante, Goethe, Schiller, science, and theology, as Thwaite says, "as though in preparation for eternity." When she was introduced to Queen Victoria, they talked "of Huxley, of the stars, of the millennium, of Jowett." Did she squander her intelligence, or worse still, did she wear herself out for nothing? Mrs. Gilchrist (the widow of Blake's first biographer) told William Rossetti that she believed that Emily did positive harm, when, "watching him with anxious, affectionate solicitude, she surrounds him ever closer and closer with the sultry, perfumed atmosphere of luxury and homage in which his great soul—as indeed any soul would—droops and sickens." Edward Fitzgerald, the sardonic friend, considered, in the 1870s, that Alfred would have done better with "an old Housekeeper like Molière's," or perhaps "a jolly woman who would have laughed and cried without any reason why"; Tennyson's best things, he thought, had gone to press in 1842. What, then, is the value of a woman, and what is poetry worth, even one poem, say "Maud," or "To the Rev. F. D. Maurice"? Thwaite, although she gently reproves Fitzgerald, doesn't discuss these things. She has set her own limits, and she is not writing a book about Tennyson, but about Emily.

In fact, Tennyson understood, or at least comprehended, his wife very well. He knew that she was motivated by love in its highest form of compassion, not only for himself but for every other human being. Motherless herself, she was conscious every hour of the day of "the forlorn ones." It wasn't only that she dreamed on a large scale of old-age pensions for the poor, justice in Schleswig-Holstein, furnished rooms for single working women. Her instinct to rescue and console extended to the future and the past. Admiring Turner's paintings, she added, "How one wishes one might have done something to make his life happy." Simply to be unfortunate was a good enough claim on Emily.

Her faith, Tennyson wrote in the dedication to his last poems, was "clear as the heights of the June-blue heaven." Easy enough to treat this ironically or even satirically, but Ann Thwaite has done neither—she has gone right in among these people like a good, if inquisitive, neighbor who becomes a lifelong friend. She persuades us, or almost persuades us, that Emily mustn't be thought of as a victim, since she believed her work was as important as it was possible to be. This doesn't mean that she was satisfied with it. "I could have done more," she said on her deathbed.

1996

Twice-Born

Christina Rossetti: A Divided Life, by Georgina Battiscombe

Christina Rossetti (1830–1894) wrote "If I had words" and "I took my heart in my hand" and "If he would come today, today" and "What would I give for a heart of flesh to warm me through" and:

> *I bent by my own burden must*
> *Enter my heart of dust.*

Her poetry she described as "a genuine 'lyric cry,' and such I will back against all skilled labour." Biographers, though not Christina herself, feel themselves obliged to explain where the passion came from, how it was restrained, and what ought to have been done with it. Then they have to face her preoccupation not only with death but with the grave, and the sensation of lying, remembered or forgotten, under the turf. There was, too, a sardonic Christina, whose comment on art and life was this:

> *The mangled frog abides incog,*
> *The uninteresting actual frog:*
> *The hypothetic frog alone*
> *Is the one frog we dwell upon.*

But she was also, and this was central to her whole existence, twice-born. At the age of about thirteen she became, in company with her mother and sister, a fervent High Anglican. The keynote, which Pusey and Keble had set, was self-sacrifice. To find enough to sacrifice and to suffer for, "not to keep back or count or leave"—the same impulse as Eliot's "Teach us to care and not to care"—became her prayer, in extremity. She saw herself as a stranger and a pilgrim in this world, waiting for release.

She was born the youngest of a family of happily settled Anglo-Italian exiles: a pedantic, sentimental, slightly cracked father, an imperturbable mother, Italian visitors and refugees in and out at all hours. The children had their grandfather's fruit garden near Amersham for a paradise, poverty to keep them from contact with the outside world, admiring relatives to pet them, and their mother to educate them. Dante Gabriel and Christina were the "storms" of the family, and, when in a rage, Christina could be a ripper and a smasher. The elder sister, Maria, and loyal William Michael were the "calms." On "My heart is like a singing bird" William's editorial comment was: "I have more than once been asked whether I could account for the outburst of exuberant joy evidenced in this celebrated lyric; I am unable to do so." Christina needed both the saintly narrow minded sister and the "brothers brotherly," and there they were: "wherever one was, the other was, and that was almost always at home."

Like Emily Brontë, Charlotte Mew, and Eleanor Farjeon, she knew the greatest happiness of her hushed life-drama very early on. No wonder that the most radiant of her lyrics are the children's verses of "Sing-Song," or others that children readily understand ("In the Bleak Midwinter," "Does the Road Wind Uphill?") or half-understand and can't get out of their minds, like "Goblin Market." It is easy to remember this luscious and suggestive temptation poem not quite as it is—or perhaps one remembers it wrong on purpose. "The central point," as William insisted, is that "Laura having tasted the fruits once, and being at death's door through inability to get a second taste, her sister Lizzie determines to save her at all hazards; so she goes to the goblins, refuses to eat their fruits, and beguiles them into forcing their fruits upon her with so much insistency that her face is all smeared and steeped with the juices; she gets Laura to kiss and suck these juices off her face, and Laura, having thus obtained the otherwise impossible second taste, rapidly recovers." It is a story of salvation, which Christina, for what reason we can't tell, dedicated to her sister Maria.

As it turned out, she never left the family's shelter. She became a fountain sealed, a Victorian daughter aging in the company of her aunts and her beloved mother. Dante Gabriel described her "legitimate exercise of anguish under an almost stereotyped smile." She broke off two engagements to be married on religious grounds—not, surely, as Maurice Bowra thought, because she was afraid of "the claims of the flesh," but because she had twice found a sacrifice that was worth the offering.

Of the dozen or so biographies of Christina, the latest, by Georgina Battiscombe, is the most readable and certainly the most judicious. As an Anglican who has written lives of both Keble and Charlotte M. Yonge, Mrs. Battiscombe understands the wellspring of Christina's religious experience, and she explains it admirably. She is very good, too, on the dutiful day-to-dayishness of the outer life. With calmness and accuracy she counters earlier interpretations that seem to her out of proportion— by Lona Mosk Packer (obsessed with the idea that William Bell Scott was Christina's lover), Maureen Duffy (engrossed in the phallic symbolism of "Goblin Market"), Maurice Bowra, Virginia Woolf. She has, of course, her own explanation. She sees Christina as a warm-blooded Italian conforming through strength of will to a strict Anglicanism—an awkward fit.

> The poetry's tension arises when her thwarted experience of eros spilled over into her expression of agape; but to explain her intense love of God simply in terms of repressed sex is too cheap and easy an answer. Love is none the less genuine because it is "sublimated."

The subtitle of the book is "A Divided Life." On the technique of the poetry, as apart from its subject matter, she has less to say, and she doesn't do much about relating it to the Tractarian mode, as Professor G. B. Trevelyan has done in his recent Victorian Devotional Poetry. But the story itself could not be more clearly told.

1982

WILLIAM MORRIS

His Daily Bread

William Morris: An Approach to the Poetry,
by J. M. S. Tompkins

As a schoolboy, Rudyard Kipling used to stay in North End Road, Fulham, with his aunt and uncle, the Burne-Joneses. One evening William Morris came into the nursery and, finding the children under the table and nobody else about, climbed onto the rocking-horse and

> slowly surging back and forth while the poor beast creaked, he told us a tale full of fascinating horrors, about a man who was condemned to dream bad dreams. One of them took the shape of a cow's tail waving from a heap of dried fish. He went away as abruptly as he had come. Long afterwards, when I was old enough to know a maker's pains, it dawned upon me that we must have heard the Saga of Burnt Njal. . . . Pressed by the need to pass the story between his teeth and clarify it, he had used us.

Morris's open-heartedness, his shyness, his reckless treatment of the furniture, his concentration on whatever he had in hand as though the universe contained no other possible goal, all these can be felt clearly enough. Kipling, however, was really listening not to Burnt Njal but to the Eyrbyggia Saga. This was first pointed out by a sympathetic but strong-minded scholar, Dr. J. M. S. Tompkins.

For twenty years, both before and after publishing her *Art of Rudyard Kipling*, Joyce Tompkins worked on her study of Morris's poetry. In December 1986 she died, at the age of eighty-nine. Now her book is out at last, not quite in finished form. She grew old and ill, never had the chance to consult the original manuscripts, and could not make her final revisions.

Morris did, though, and protested forcibly against so many things that the critic has to protect himself. He may know a lot about the first generation of European Communists but less about papermaking or indigo or Victorian business management, Morris being one of the pioneers of a "house style." In spite of this, all the emphasis today is on his wholeness. In the annotated bibliography that they bring out in two-yearly installments, David and Sheila Latham "resist categorising under such subjects as poetry and politics because we believe that each of Morris's interests is best understood in the context of his whole life's work." Joyce Tompkins, also, wants to see Morris whole. "The wide and varied territory," she says, "has an integrity which adds to the complexity of study." But commentators have to advance in separate fields, keeping in touch as best they can. Although she doesn't make the claim herself, her book can be seen as a complement to E. P. Thompson's *William Morris: Romantic to Revolutionary* (1961). "We have to make up our minds about William Morris," Thompson said. "Either he was an eccentric, isolated figure, personally admirable, but whose major thought was wrong or irrelevant and long left behind by events. On the other hand, it may be that [he] was our greatest diagnostician of alienation." Joyce Tompkins is making the case for the Morris who has lost his readers, the narrative poet.

The telling of tales, as Kipling had realized, was essential to Morris, both before and after he declared for socialism. "They grew compulsively," Joyce Tompkins writes, "from his private imaginative life. It is this imaginative life which is my subject." But stories, Morris believed, were also necessary as daily bread to human beings, who should listen willingly. If, a hundred years later, they seem to be unwilling, what can be done?

Her book is divided into six parts, each one aimed at "the chief omissions in contemporary understanding and evaluation." She begins with *The Defence of Guenevere*. This was Morris's first book of poems, appearing in 1858, the year before Tennyson's *Idylls of the King*. Ballads inspired by (or possibly the inspiration of) Rossetti's watercolors stand side by side "with hard-edged Froissartian themes: 'The Haystack in the Floods,' 'The Judgment of God.'" Here Joyce Tompkins believes that modern readers are adrift through ignorance. They are no longer familiar with the field of Arthurian reference. She has noticed, however, that although they have lost the sense of magic, they respond to the tougher element in the poems, the sound "between a beast's howl and a woman's scream."

Godmar turned grinning to his men,
Who ran, some five or six, and beat
His head to pieces at their feet.

Ten years later, in *The Earthly Paradise*, Morris's voice has changed. This was to be "the Big Book," his dearest project in the late 1860s, in which he hoped to unlock the world's tale-hoard from the North, the Mediterranean, and the Middle East. But in spite of their wide range, it was the serene and even soporific quality of the stories that gave them great success. (Florence Boos, in a study of the Victorian response to *The Earthly Paradise*, quotes Alfred Austin's review: "Under the blossoming thorn, with lazy summer sea-waves breaking at one's feet—such were the fitting hour and mood in which—criticism all forgot—to drink in the honeyed rhythm of this melodious storier.") Knowing that "it is not easy now to feel good will towards Morris's linear narrative," Joyce Tompkins tells us to read the stories with attention to their rich detail. We ask, she thinks, not too much of them, but too little. There are two kinds of movement in *The Earthly Paradise*, one defined by Walter Pater as "the desire of beauty quickened by the desire of death," the other a gradual progress through the melancholy and distress of the second and third parts to the "tolerance and resolution" of the fourth, where in "Bellerophon in Lycia" the hero learns first to forgive himself, then to forgive others.

To *Sigurd the Volsung*, the great epic of the North drawn from all the versions of the Volsung and Nibelung story that Morris could lay hands on, her approach is somewhat different. Jessie Kocmanova, in *The Maturing of William Morris*, interpreted *Sigurd* as corresponding to three stages of society—the barbarian, the early Nordic, and the feudal—which brought dissent and ruin. Joyce Tompkins sees Sigurd as a redeemer, and the whole poem not as Christian, but presented at least "in words and images that recall the Christian legacy."

This is one of the underlying ideas or perhaps hopes of her book. She takes, for example, the cold and empty glance of the King of the Undying in *The Story of the Glittering Plain* as representing Morris's loss of faith as a young man. About this, however, he never showed the slightest regret, anchoring himself in human happiness and human work, and to "the earth and all things that deal with it, and all that grows out of it." He refused, in any case, to discuss religion, and "in the circumstances"—as she says—"there is perhaps nothing to do but to imitate his silence."

The last section of the book is left for the late romances, on which so much work has been done in the past few years. As always, Joyce Tompkins is thorough, discussing in detail the neglected *Child Christopher* and *Fair Goldilind* and the unfinished *Desiderius* and *Killian of the Closes*. One of her main concerns is to rescue Morris's land-wights, sending-boats, and magic islands from a rigid political interpretation. Both the young Morris and the harassed middle-aged socialist looking back on his former self can, she thinks, be recognized here. The stories "testify to the constant habits of his imagination."

1988

Something Sweet to Come

An introduction to *The Novel on Blue Paper*, by William Morris, edited by Penelope Fitzgerald

The novel that William Morris began to write early in 1872 is unfinished and unpublished and also untitled. I have called it *The Novel on Blue Paper* because it was written on blue lined foolscap, and Morris preferred to call things what they were.

The only firsthand information we have about it is a letter that Morris wrote to Louie Baldwin, Georgie Burne-Jones's sister, on 12 June 1872.

Dear Louie,

Herewith I send by book-post my abortive novel: it is just a specimen of how not to do it, and there is no more to be said thereof: 'tis nothing but landscape and sentiment: which thing won't do. Since you wish to read it, I am sorry 'tis such a rough copy, which roughness sufficiently indicates my impatience at having to deal with prose. The separate parcel, paged 1 to 6, was a desperate dash at the middle of the story to try to give it life when I felt it failing: it begins with the letter of the elder brother to the younger on getting *his* letter telling how he was going to bid for the girl in marriage. I found it in the envelope in which I had sent it to Georgie to see if she could give me any hope: she gave me none, and I have never looked at it since. So there's an end of my novel-writing, I fancy, unless the world turns topsides under some day. Health and merry days to you, and believe me to be

Your affectionate friend,
William Morris

The tone of gruff modesty, and in particular the catch phrase from Dickens (the Circumlocution Office's "How Not to Do It"), is habitual to Morris and can be taken for what it is worth. In spite of the disapproval of Georgiana Burne-Jones, whose opinion he valued at the time above all others, he did not destroy his MS, but kept it, and after what was presumably further discouragement from Louie, he kept it still. He must have been aware, too, why he had been given no hope. J. W. Mackail tells us, in his Life of Morris (1899), that Morris "had all the instinct of a born man of letters for laying himself open in his books, and having no concealment from the widest circle of all," and (of the Prologues to *The Earthly Paradise*) that there is "an autobiography so delicate and so outspoken that it must needs be left to speak for itself." That, we have to conclude, was the trouble with the novel on blue paper; it did speak for itself, but much too plainly.

The background of the novel—the "landscape"—is the Upper Thames valley, the water meadows, streams, and villages round about Kelmscott on the borders of Oxfordshire and Gloucestershire. Morris had gone down to inspect Kelmscott Manor House in May 1871, and in June he entered into a joint tenancy of the old house with Rossetti at £60 a year. The gray gables, flagged path, enclosed garden cram-full of flowers, lime and elm trees "populous with rooks," white-paneled parlor, are all recognizably described in this novel, although Morris when he wrote it had never spent a summer there. It was the house he loved "with a reasonable love, I think." Rossetti, not a countryman, had hoped that the place would be good for his nerves. But in the seclusion of the marshes his obsession with the beauty of Jane Morris, and his compulsion to paint her again and again, reached the point of melancholy mania. Morris had a business to run and was obliged to be in London a good deal. The seemingly intolerable tension arose between the three of them that has been so often and so painfully traced by biographers. To Morris it was "this failure of mine." Mackail, cautiously describing the subject of the novel as "the love of two brothers for the same woman," evidently saw no farther into it than the failure. Once, however, when I was trying to explain the situation, and its projection as myth, to a number of overseas students, one of them asked a question that I have never seen in any biography: "Why then did Morris not strike Rossetti?"

I hope to show that this question is very relevant to the novel on blue paper. Certainly Morris was not "above," or indifferent to, his loss. It is a mistake to refer his much later opinions, as reported by Shaw ("Morris was a complete fatalist in his attitude towards the conduct of all human beings where sex was concerned") or Luke Ionides ("Women did not seem to count with him") or Wilfrid Scawen Blunt ("He was the only man I ever came in contact with who seemed absolutely independent of sex considerations"). It is a mistake, too, to refer to opinions expressed in *News from Nowhere* to his "restless heart" of 1868–73. Which of us would like to be judged, at thirty-nine, by our frame of mind at the age of fifty-seven? Morris himself knew this well enough. "At the age of more than thirty years," he wrote in *Killian of the Closes* (1895), "men are more apt to desire what they have not than they that be younger or older."

And Morris might have been pressed into a violent demonstration at this time by yet another cruel test, the profoundly unsettling behavior of his greatest friend, Edward Burne-Jones. Burne-Jones had been married since 1860 to Georgie, the charming, tiny, and indomitable daughter of a Methodist minister. The Neds had started out in lodgings with £30 between them, and their happy and stable marriage, together with Burne-Jones's designs for the Firm, were part of the very earth out of which Morris's life and work took growth. But in 1867 the quiet Ned suddenly claimed, much more openly than Rossetti, the freedom to love unchecked. He had been totally captivated by a most tempestuous member of the Greek community in London, Mary Zambaco. Of this radiantly sad and unpredictable young woman he drew the loveliest by far of his pencil portraits: "I believed it to be all my future life," he told Rossetti. The affair came and went and came again, to the fury of Ionides and the sympathetic interest of the Greek women.* It lingered on, indeed, until 1873. Morris, stalwart, stood by his friend, but the effect of this new confounding of love and loyalty, on top of his own "failure,"

---

*The head of the Greek community in Victorian London was Constantine Ionides, "the Thunderer," a wealthy stockbroker and a generous patron of the arts. Mary Zambaco was a granddaughter of the House of Ionides, a wealthy beauty with "glorious red hair and almost phosphorescent white skin" who had left her commonplace husband in Paris in 1866 and come to London. She was also a talented sculptress, with a temperament that Burne-Jones described as "like hurricanes and tempests and billows . . . only it didn't do in English suburban surroundings." In 1868 he made his first attempt to break with her; she threatened to throw herself into the Regent's Canal. In 1869 he painted her as Phyllis pleading with Demophoön, with the epigraph *Dic mihi quod feci? nisi non sapienter amavi* (Tell me what I have done, except to love unwisely). Rossetti was in their confidence, writing in 1869 to Jane Morris that Mary had become more beautiful "with all her love and trouble . . . but rainy walks and constant journeys are I fear beginning to break up her health."

must have been hard to master; the effect of Mary herself can be guessed at, perhaps, from the strange intrusion of one of the characters, Eleanor, into the novel on blue paper.

Meanwhile, Georgie was left to manage her life and her two children as best she could. In his loneliness and bewilderment Morris felt deeply for hers, and at this time he was unquestionably in love with her.

Some of his drafts and manuscript poems of 1865–70 show this without disguise, though always with a chivalrous anxiety. He must not intrude; he thanks her because she "does not deem my service sin." A pencil note reads on one draft "we two are in the same box and need conceal nothing—scold me but pardon me." He is "late made wise" to his own feelings, and can only trust that time will transform them into the friendship that will bring him peace. Meanwhile the dignity and sincerity with which she is bearing "the burden of thy grief and wrong" is enough, in itself, to check him.

> . . . nor joy nor grief nor fear
> Silence my love; but those grey eyes and clear
> Truer than truth pierce through my weal and woe. . .

Georgie, in fact, was steadfast to her marriage, and strong enough to wait. "I know one thing," she wrote to her friend Rosalind Howard, "and that is that there is love enough between Edward and me to last out a long life if it is given us."

In the meantime, what was Morris's outward response to the assault on his emotions? Work, as always, was his "faithful daily companion." After returning from Iceland in September 1871 he illuminated the *Rubaiyat* of Omar Khayyam, designed the Larkspur wallpaper, began his novel, and fiddled about in "a maze of re-writing and despondency" with his elaborate masque, *Love Is Enough*. But the moral of *Love Is Enough* (as Shaw complained) is not that love is enough. Pharamond, coming back from his quest for an ideal woman to find that his kingdom has been usurped by a stronger man, accepts that frustration and loss are worthy—"though the world be a-waning"—to be called a victory in the name of love. But Morris knew, as Shaw knew, that this is nonsense. The victory, melancholy as it is, is for self-control. Renunciation is achieved through the will and strengthens the will, not the emotions. And this, with a far more positive hero than poor Pharamond, is, I believe, the real subject of the novel on blue paper.

Morris had been delicate as a child, but as soon as he grew into his full strength he was subject to fits of violent rage, possibly epileptic in origin. To what extent these were hereditary it is impossible to say. His father was said to be neurotic, and may well have clashed with his eldest son; when Morris was eleven he was sent as a boarder to his school at Woodford, although it was only a few hundred yards away from his home. What seems strange in his later life is the attitude of his close friends, who appear to have watched as a kind of entertainment his frenzied outbursts, followed by the struggle to control himself and a rapid childlike repentance. At times he would beat himself about the head in self-punishment. "He has been known to drive his head against a wall," Mackail wrote, "so as to make a deep dent in the plaster, and bite almost through the woodwork of a windowframe." Yet with the exception of the day when he hurled a fifteenth-century folio at one of his workmen, missing him but breaking a door panel, there is no record of his making a physical attack on anyone. To return to the student's question, Morris did not strike anybody, least of all the ailing Rossetti, because he waged almost to the end of his life a battle for self-control.

The recognition of restraint as an absolute duty may he referred back to the tutor who prepared Morris, when he was seventeen years old, for his entrance to Oxford. This tutor, the Reverend F. B. Guy, was one of the faithful remnants of the Oxford Movement who had survived Newman's conversion, or desertion, to Rome. Morris believed at this time that he was going to enter the Church, and could not fail to learn from Guy the Movement's insistence on sacrifice and self-correction, even in the smallest things. The Tractarians saw the religious impulse not as a vague emotion, but as a silent discipline growing from the exercise of the will. All that we ought to ask, Keble had said, is room to deny ourselves. And Morris, willingly enlisted in a struggle that he was never to win, persisted in it long after he had parted from orthodox Christianity. At the age of twenty-three he concluded that he must not expect enjoyment from life—"I have no right to it at all events—love and work, these two things only." In 1872, when love had betrayed or rejected him, he wrote: "O how I long to keep the world from narrowing on me, and to look at things bigly and kindly."

The most telling expression of Keble's doctrines in fiction was Charlotte M. Yonge's *Heir of Redclyffe* (1853). It was said to be the novel most in demand by the officers wounded in the Crimean War, and it was the first book greatly to influence Morris. Here he read the family story of a tragic inheritance. Guy, the Heir, has the ferocious temper of his Morville ancestors, and has to struggle as best he can with "the curse of sin and death." All his "animal spirits," all his great capacity for happiness is overshadowed by the temptation to anger, and he is driven to strange extremes, cutting up pencils, biting his lips till the blood runs down, and refusing, in obedience to a vow, even to watch a single game of billiards. "Resistance should be from within." He sees his whole life as "failing and resolving and failing again." Philip, on the other hand, the high minded young officer, provokes the Heir and leads him, from the best possible motives, into temptation. Here the novel sets out to show the evil that good can do, and when Guy dies to save him from fever, Philip is left to suffer forever "the penitence of the saints."

The Heir of Redclyffe, as an exemplary text, asks for a kind of inner or even secret knowledge from its readers. From page to page we are reminded of Kenelm Digby's Broadstone of Honour (1822–27), which held up the example of mediaeval chivalry to Young England. That is why Guy's nearest railway station is called Broadstone. Again, Guy and his sweetheart Amy are, in a sense, acting out the story of Sintram (the book which Newman would only read when he was quite alone).*

Sintram, tempted by the world, the flesh, and the devil, and burdened by his father's crime, has to toil upward through the snows to reach Verena, his saintly mother. That is why the widowed Amy calls her child Verena. And Sintram itself makes mysterious reference to its frontispiece, a woodcut version of Dürer's engraving The Knight, Death, and the Devil, over which Morris and Burne-Jones, as students, had "pored for hours."

These potent images remained with Morris, even though in The Earthly Paradise he had unlocked half the world's tale-hoard. In the second of his late romances, for example, The Well at the World's End (1892–93), Sintram's evil dwarf reappears. In 1872, the time of his greatest emotional test and stress, he set to work on this novel that is a temptation story, although the hero must proceed simply on his own resolution,

---

*H. de la Motte Fouqué, The Seasons: Four Romances from the German (English trans: 1843). Sintram and His Companions is the winter romance.

without prayer, without divine grace, without the saving hand of the loved woman. And, most unexpectedly, Morris returned from his dream-world, the "nameless cities in a distant sea," to place the story in a solid English parsonage, or, to be more accurate, in Elm House, Walthamstow, the first home that he could remember.

Morris opens his tale with the sins of the father. One of those impulses which "sometimes touch dull, or dulled, natures"—a distinction which Morris was always careful to make—arouses the train of memory in Parson Risley. Eleanor's letters follow. The parson's sin is not that he was Eleanor's lover. This is shown clearly enough later in Mrs. Mason's reproach: "Mr. Risley, if my husband likes to make love to every girl in the village, he has a full right to it, if I let him"—a remark that blends well with the "sweet-smelling abundant garden" and the fertile melon beds. Risley's guilt then, is not a matter of sexuality but a denial of it, firstly through cold cowardice in rejecting a woman "like the women in poetry, such people as I had never expected to meet," and secondly through his vile temper. These two aspects of his nature are his legacy to his sons.

The Parsonage, as has been said, recalls the house in Walthamstow where Morris was born, and in the two boys, John and Arthur, he represents the opposing sides, as he understood them, of his own character. In some ways the brothers are alike or even identical. Both are romantically imaginative and given to dreaming their lives into "tales going on," both are fond of fishing (not a trivial matter to Morris), both, of course, love Clara, both dislike their father yet resemble him. "As to the looks of the lads, by the way, it would rather have puzzled anyone who had seen them to say why the little doctor should have said that either was not like his father. Some strange undercurrent of thought must have drawn it out of him, for they were obviously both very much like him." John, however, is manly, open, friendly, bird-and-weather-noticing; Arthur is a bookworm, and sickly. ("Love of ease, dreaminess, sloth, sloppy good-nature," Morris said, "are what I chiefly accuse myself of.") Arthur is "versed in archaeological lore," while John is in touch with earth and water—"with a great sigh of enjoyment he seemed to gather the bliss of memory of many and many a summer afternoon into this one"—and yet, perversely, Arthur is to be the farmer and John the businessman.

From the guilty father John inherits anger, Arthur cowardice. John's loss of temper alarms Arthur; "Are you in a rage with me? Why, do you know, your voice got something like Father's in a rage." But just as Parson Risley fails to answer Eleanor's letter, so Arthur conceals John's.

John's struggle for self-control is marked by very small incidents. Resistance, as the Heir of Redclyffe recognizes, must be from within. At the beginning of the day's outing, when Clara greets Arthur tenderly, "they did not notice that John turned away to the horse's head." At Ruddywell Court, when Arthur begins to do the talking and Clara is entranced, John "got rather silent." On the return to the farm, when Clara kisses Arthur, John is left "whistling in sturdy resolution to keep his heart up, and rating himself for a feeling of discomfort and wrong." When she is poised for a few moments between the two of them in the rocking boat, but at length sits down by Arthur, so that both of them are facing the golden sunset to which John's back is now turned, he pulls at the oars "sturdily," exerting his strength for them in silence. These small everyday victories of the will lead up to a disastrous failure, the furious and destructive letter, and the despairing attempt to redeem it by a post-script—"tell Clara I wrote kindly to you."

Arthur, on the other hand, the "saint" of the novel, is shown indulging himself in the sweetness of his dreams and the horror of his nightmares, and even when he becomes the center of consciousness this self-indulgence is obvious. Clara's love for him is founded, in the Chaucerian mode, on pity. When he reads John's letter, he is afraid. He lies to Clara, who against her better judgment accepts the lie. Arthur is, in fact, almost without will power, while John, in his blundering way, understands keenly the importance of the will. "Nobody does anything," he tells Mrs. Mason, "except because he likes it. I mean to say, even people who have given up most to please other people—but then, they're all the better people, to be pleased by what's good rather than by what is bad." And he has "a feeling, not very pleasant, of not being listened to."

In 1872 Samuel Butler published *Erewhon*, Hardy, *Under the Greenwood Tree*, and George Eliot, *Middlemarch*. All of these seem very far removed from the unfinished tale-telling on blue paper. But when Morris told Louie Baldwin that he was impatient at having to deal with prose, he underrated the poetry of his story. This lies in the interrelationship of the three journeys—the passage of a summer's day, the first walk upstream to the paradise of the farm, and the crucial turning point of John's adolescence. The June prologue of *The Earthly Paradise* opens (also in the meadows of the Upper Thames)—

> *O June, O June, that we desired so,*
> *Wilt thou not make us happy on this day?*
> *Across the river thy soft breezes blow*
> *Sweet with the scent of beanfields far away,*
> *Above our heads rustle the aspens grey,*
> *Calm is the sky with harmless clouds beset,*
> *No thought of storm the morning vexes yet.*

This is the exact poise of the novel, between past darkness, present happiness (John when he first goes to Leaser is "happier than he was last year"), and the coming unknown discontent. And so John, at seventeen, stands on the confines of his own home, with "the expectant longing for something sweet to come, heightened rather than chastened by the mingled fear of something as vague as the hope, that fills our hearts so full in us at whiles, killing all commonplace there, making us feel as though we were on the threshold of a new world, one step over which (if we could only make it) would put life within our grasp. What is it? Some reflex of love and death going on throughout the world, suddenly touching those who are ignorant as yet of the one, and have not learned to believe in the other?" Mackail quotes this passage in part, but dismisses the novel as "certainly the most singular of his writings." Jane Morris's comment on the Life, however, is interesting: "You see, Mackail is not an artist in feeling, and therefore cannot be sympathetic while writing the life of such a man."

1982

"Whatever Is Unhappy Is Immoral"

A protector by nature, Morris felt for women tenderness with hardly a hint of patronage. When he was at work on *The Earthly Paradise* he disliked writing about the thrashing of Psyche, and "was really glad to get it over." His care for his wife extended to her tedious sister, and his affection for his handicapped daughter, who got so dreadfully on Janey's nerves, was described by Mackail as "the most touching element in his nature." Called upon for advice to a deserted lover, he suggested: "Think, old fellow, how much better it is that she should have left you, than that you should have tired of her, and left her."

Tenderness and responsibility, of course, are not the same as understanding, still less a recognition of equality. It can be fairly said, however, that as soon as his own personality defined itself, Morris began to treat women as people. Quite certain, from his own experience, that pleasurable work was necessary to happiness, he tried to find out what they could do. Embroidery became, under his persuasion, their natural activity. It was a queen's work, and also a peasant's, and guarded against the threat of idle or empty hands. Mary Nicholson, who kept house for Morris and Burne-Jones in the 1850s, was perhaps the first to learn. Morris stitched, she copied his stitches. "I seemed so necessary to him at all times," she said—this, if unconsciously, being part of the persuasion. During the early years of his marriage—"a time to swear by," wrote Georgiana Burne-Jones, "if human happiness were doubted"—Morris and Janey worked together on English embroideries, unpicking old pieces to see how they were done. In the Seventies he admired and promoted the work of Catherine Holliday, who remembered that "when he got an unusually fine piece of colour he would send it off for me or keep it for me, and when he ceased to dye with his own hands I soon felt the difference."

Yet Mrs. Holliday and her skilled colleagues were for the most part executants rather than designers, and no better off in this respect than the "paintresses" of the Potteries. This was a limitation of Morris's own mind. Writing in 1877 to Thomas Wardle about a figure designer for high-warp tapestries, he says he has "no idea where to find such a man, and therefore I feel that whatever I do I must do chiefly with my own hands . . . a cleverish woman could do the greeneries, no doubt." On the administrative side, May took over the management of the embroidery section from 1885 onwards, but there was apparently never any suggestion that she should become a partner in the Firm.

There is not much evidence, in fact, of what Morris thought about women in the professions, or in public life. He worked, of course, side by side with them in the Movement, and made a strong protest at the arrest of Annie Cobden-Sanderson, but Mrs. Besant tried him sorely—not only, I think on account of her Fabianism, but because she was Mrs. Besant. By the time Georgie Burne-Jones entered local politics, "going like a flame" through the village of Rottingdean, Morris had ceased to have much interest in "gas-and-water socialism," or in anything short of total change. In that same year (1884) he watched the haymakers, men and women both, distorted and ugly through overwork, and dreamed of the outright battle that would be needed to restore the fields to the laborers. But might he not, in any case, have agreed with Yeats that a woman in politics is a windy bellows? In an unpublished letter to Bruce Glasier he allowed himself some tart remarks about the Woman Question:

> But you must not forget that childbearing makes women inferior to men, since a certain time of their lives they must be dependent on them. Of course we must claim absolute equality of condition between women and men, as between other groups, but it would be poor economy setting women to do men's work (as unluckily they often do now) or vice versa.

Old Hammond, in *News from Nowhere*, undertakes to discuss it, but becomes evasive. There are no women members of Parliament in Nowhere, he says, because there is no Parliament.

Ruskin, in his strange treatise on woman's education, *Of Queen's Gardens* (1865), gives her the distinctive powers of "sweet ordering, arrangement, and decision," to which Morris would have added perspicacity and strength. That strength he greatly respected—he told his sister Isabella, who worked in the slums of South London, that she practiced what he could only preach—and he depended perhaps more than he knew on his wife, and more than he could ever express on Georgie Burne-Jones. There is a confusion of viewpoints in the later poems and romances, where, as E. P. Thompson puts it, "the mournful Pre-Raphaelite ladies of earlier days have given way to maidens who can shoot with the bow, swim, ride, and generally do most things, including making love, a good deal more capably than their young men." In *The Pilgrims of Hope* the speaker, his wife, and his friend set out to join the Communards in besieged Paris, "we three together, and there to die like men." *News from Nowhere* depicts a land of effortless female superiority, and Ellen is the spirit of the earth itself and all that grows from it. On the other hand, in *A Dream of John Ball*, Will

Green's daughter is sent away from the skirmish and told to "set the pot on the fire, for that we shall need when we come home," and, to return to *Nowhere*, Mistress Philippa is an Obstinate Refuser, who works obsessively at her wood-carving although the men could manage without her ("Could you, though?" grumbled the last named from the face of the wall). It has to be admitted, also, that at the Guest House the comely women (however much Old Hammond tries to explain it away) are waitressing.

But Morris had dedicated himself, in the face of all discouragements and even of his own inconsistencies, to the transformation of human existence throughout the whole social order. Nothing less than this would do, "nor do I consider a man a socialist at all who is not prepared to admit the equality of women as far as condition goes." This last phrase sounds like a qualification, but Morris is as clear as spring-water in his condemnation of the marriage and property laws, which made women the slaves of slaves: "Whatever is unhappy is immoral. We desire that all should be free to earn their livelihood . . . with that freedom will come an end of these monstrosities, and a true love between man and woman throughout society."

To his old friend Charlie Faulkner, who was exercised on the subject and wished to "blow off," Morris expanded his views a little. "Copulation is worse than beastly unless it takes place as the result of natural desire and kindliness on both sides." The divorce laws he saw as particularly hard on the poor, who were cooped together for good like fowls going to a market. In a true partnership husband, wife, and children would all be free, the children having their inalienable right of livelihood. A woman would not be considered "ruined" if she followed a natural instinct, and separation would always be by consent, though Morris adds "I should hope that in most cases friendship would go along with desire, and would outlive it, and the couple would remain together, but always be free people."

The most striking thing about this letter, written ten years before Morris's death, is that he had married Jane Burden in 1859 with much the same convictions. There is no other way to explain the patience of this impatient man during the "specially dismal time" from 1869 to 1873, when his marriage was at breaking point. Whatever the pain of it, Morris regarded Janey as a free agent, because he believed she was truly in love with another man, and love has a right to freedom, and, on the other side, a right to grant it. He left his wife to make her choice because anything else would have been "shabby," and twenty years later had not changed his mind. "A determination to do nothing shabby . . . appears to me to be the socialist religion, and if it is not morality I do not know what is."

1984

ARTS AND CRAFTS

Lasting Impressions

The Kelmscott Press: A History of William Morris's Typographical Adventure, by William S. Peterson

William Morris did not think the human race was ever likely to solve the question of its own existence, but he wanted society to change in such a way that the question would not be "Why were we born to be so miserable?" but "Why were we born to be so happy?" By 1890 he knew he probably would not see these changes in his lifetime. He felt old, he knew he had diabetes, and he realized that his outstanding natural energy was deserting him. Work was his natural recreation. It was at this point that he turned to the last of his handcrafts, making books.

It was to be "a little typographical adventure," to see whether he could produce books through traditional craftsmanship "which it would be a pleasure to look upon as pieces of printing." At first there was no thought of selling, although later on Morris found he had to do so to meet some of the costs. Characteristically, he spent a year of inquiry and research into how things should be done. With an expert friend, the printer and process engraver Emery Walker, he looked into presses, inks, and handmade papers. (The artist Robin Tanner, lecturing in 1986 at the age of eighty-two, held up a sheet of the paper Morris chose: "Listen to it! How it rings! What music!") New types, of course, had to be designed. For his Golden type Morris turned for a model to fifteenth-century Venice, and for the black-letter Troy to fifteenth-century Germany. What mattered to him most was the total effect of the integrated pages, verso and recto together. Disagreeing fiercely with many other designers, both then and now, he believed that the page should be a solid, brilliant black and white.

Between 1891 and 1898 the Kelmscott Press (named for Morris's house by the river in Oxfordshire) issued fifty-two wonderful books. Some were illustrated, some had lavish borders and initials designed by Morris himself, some were small, delicate 16mo volumes. The only way to judge them is to hold them and turn the pages. The culmination of the whole series, the great Kelmscott *Chaucer*, was finished only just in time. In June 1896, after more than three years in production, the sumptuous first copy was put into Morris's hands. Three months later he was dead. "But I cannot believe," he had said, "that I shall be annihilated."

This year, 1991, is the centenary of the Kelmscott Press, and its history has now been written by William Peterson, a professor of English at the University of Maryland, who also, in 1984, produced the bibliography of the press. He says that he suspects more has been written about William Morris than any other printer but Gutenberg. But a great deal of new evidence has become available since the last full-length study, in 1924, by Henry Halliday Sparling, Morris's unsatisfactory son-in-law. All of it is here, in the clearest, most readable, most scholarly form that anyone could ask for.

First Mr. Peterson gives the background of Victorian book production, correcting the notion that the Kelmscott Press arose, without precedents, out of nowhere. He considers the life-giving force of Victorian medievalism and Morris's part in it, and, on the other hand, Morris's awkward position as a socialist employer and as a producer of fine books that only the rich could afford. Mr. Peterson follows the story of the press itself step by step, with all its improvisations and successes. In a particularly helpful chapter he pauses to give the production history of three individual Kelmscott books—Morris's own *Poems by the Way* (1891), *The Golden Legend* (1892), and Wilfrid Scawen Blunt's *Love-Lyrics & Songs of Proteus* (1892). All these illustrate Morris's progress as a typographer, and *Songs of Proteus*, as Mr. Peterson says, "gives off echoes of very odd psychological resonances" since Blunt, only a few years earlier, had been the lover of Morris's wife, Jane.

The history of the press, in fact, is also a history of human emotions and human friendships. Fortunately, Mr. Peterson is as interested in these as in the art of the book. He doesn't let us lose sight of the helpful, patient, skilled craftsman, Emery Walker, who nursed Morris in his last illness; the invaluable but deeply self-satisfied secretary, Sydney Cockerell; and the oldest friend of all, the artist Edward Burne-Jones. If he is capable of unfairness Mr. Peterson is perhaps a little unfair to Burne-Jones. True, his delicate, silvery pencil drawings for the *Chaucer* meant endless hard work for other people before they could appear as wood engravings, but Morris wanted Burne-Jones illustrations and no others. At every turn, however, Mr. Peterson's attitude is courteous and sympathetic, above all to Morris himself. Indeed, Morris and Mr. Peterson seem to be in a kind of partnership, interpreting together Morris's genius and his shortcomings.

The influence of the "typographical experiment" was powerful in northern Europe and the United States until the turn of the century, but is difficult to assess today. Reluctantly Mr. Peterson concludes that the gap between the private printer and "the automated realm of offset presses and computerized typesetting" has come to define two separate worlds. But he still believes that "the profound questions that Morris posed about the triumph of the machine" are relevant to everyone in a technological society. Can we recover not only simpler and slower methods and infinitely higher quality, but a joy and freedom in work which, perhaps, once existed? Can we rebuild the foundations?

Meanwhile it's difficult to know how to design a book about a great book designer. *The Kelmscott Press* is set in Bembo, which is a 1930 revival of a type cut in 1495; the rubrics are in Golden, spaced much more widely than Morris would have approved, and the initial letters are also Morris's designs. There is a splendid range of illustrations, but the reproduction varies in quality. Quite certainly, however, Mr. Peterson's book is a superb account not only of the press itself but also of Morris's final conclusions on "how we live, and how we might live."

1991

Designs and Devices

Rare Spirit: A Life of William de Morgan, 1839–1911, by Mark Hamilton

William de Morgan had the pertinacity of mild-mannered people. He didn't move with the times, never shaved off his beard, remained true to his early friends, worked side by side with William Morris, but took no interest whatever in politics. From 1872 to 1907, he single-mindedly decorated clay tiles and pots, buying them in, to start with, ready-made, later employing his own throwers.

He was a great, and sometimes rash, inventor of devices and dodges. He began his career by building a kiln into the fireplace of his room and burning off the roof of the house, and went on to revive the metallic lusters of fifteenth-century majolica and to undertake majestic schemes such as the Arab room at Leighton House, where he had to match exactly the peacock-blue Iznik tiles. These processes were not secret, he said, and he was ready to share them with anyone who was interested. May Morris divided his work into three periods, corresponding, more or less, to his three potteries—"the early Chelsea time, the bold-minded period (Merton Abbey) with big strong masses enriched with small ornaments, and then the later work (at Sands End), elaborate and full of curious invention." To describe their color and deep luminosity, she says, is "to tell how the jewel-like birds fly across a blue-black sky, the pallid fish shine through green water, how the turquoise and purple flowers star the wooded lawns." There is, too, a kind of graceful grotesqueness in his bird and animal designs. They could only have been produced in the same century as Tenniel's Dodo, or Lear's Owl.

As an employer, de Morgan was very successful—his kiln-master, Frank Iles, stayed with him for thirty-five years—but he was not a businessman, and there was a chronic shortage of money. He seemed, in fact, born to attract disaster. But he had a survivor's instinct—not shrewdness, but a hidden sense which told him, in the gentlest possible manner, when the burden of his difficulties must be shifted onto somebody else. In 1885, he needed to build a larger pottery, but couldn't afford to. By 1887, he was married, for the first time, at the age of forty-eight, and his wife had invested £4,000 in the business. He was one of those people who are in a sort of amiable conspiracy with chance and circumstance. Everyone loved de Morgan.

The same thing could not quite be said of his wife. Burne-Jones (although Mark Hamilton doesn't mention this in his new biography) was downright frightened of Mrs. de Morgan, "a plain lady, whom I never look at when I talk to her." But her determination and confidence were exactly what was needed.

Hamilton, rather unexpectedly for a biographer, says "it is pointless to speculate on the intimate details of a marriage which took place over a hundred years ago." Evelyn de Morgan, at any rate, was a Pickering from Yorkshire, who trained, in the face of family disapproval, as a painter, and worked all day long and almost every day at her meticulously colored allegories and myths. Anyone lucky enough to have listened to her younger sister Wilhelmina Stirling will have some idea of what Evelyn was like. Until her death in her hundredth year in 1965, Mrs. Stirling—latterly from a wheelchair—showed her guests round her home, Old Battersea House. The walls and recesses glowed with color. She had made a notable collection of William's ceramics and Evelyn's paintings, both, at that time, out of fashion, but what did she care about that? As she moved stoutly ahead of her visitors, there was something valiant about her, even heroic.

Evelyn was prepared to support the pottery to her last penny, and looked after William (who referred to her as "the Missus") untiringly. They lived in The Vale, Chelsea, of which Hamilton prints a delightful photograph. But by 1891 one of his brothers and three of his sisters had died of TB, and he was advised to winter in Italy. Florence, of course. This meant that for six months of every year the pottery had to be run by post between de Morgan and his partner in London, the architect Halsey Ricardo. They managed, but only just. The firm closed in 1907. But by that time William de Morgan, after more than thirty years of ceramics, had taken on a second, unannounced, career. He had become a novelist. They were in Florence; William was in bed, suffering from depression; Evelyn handed him a pencil. He began—"just to see what I could do"—to write *Joseph Vance*, and, as Bernard Shaw put it, "suddenly became a pseudo-Dickens and filled his scanted pockets by writing prodigiously long novels in the style of *Nicholas Nickleby*." There were nine in all, and they sold well.

Mark Hamilton, like everyone else who writes about de Morgan's life, has to rely largely on Mrs. Stirling's memoirs. On his art and craft much more has been written, and Hamilton records it, as a dutiful amateur. But what is truly distinctive in his book is his approach to the novels. He was encouraged, he tells us, by his father to read *Joseph Vance* as being "one of the funniest books in the English language." It wasn't until he had finished the next one, *Alice-for-Short*, that he discovered "the extraordinary plates, pots, and tiles." He has never lost his enthusiasm for the nine de Morgan novels with their nostalgic picture of the Victorian London suburbs and seaside, their gallant young heroines and yarn-like plots—lost memories, buried skeletons, the evils of drink. In six chapters he summarizes what might seem the unsummarizable, and in doing so he restores a lost balance. The pots and tiles are now collected in a class by themselves. None of the novels is in print, but Hamilton, a literary agent by trade, thinks it quite possible that some enterprising firm might republish them. That would be, as de Morgan himself would have said, the rummest go.

1997

The Gospel of Joyous Work

The Simple Life: C. R. Ashbee in the Cotswolds, by Fiona MacCarthy

Charles Ashbee—C.R.A., as he asked to be called—must be counted as a successful man. He was an architect whose houses stood up, a designer whose work has always been appreciated, a homosexual who in his fifties became—almost absent-mindedly, it seems—the father of four daughters, and a dreamer who, by founding the Guild of Handicrafts, put his ideals into practice and then kept them going for twenty years. He has not many competitors there.

For a complete view of this much-loved, offensively beautiful, tactless, irritating, unknowable man—unknowable in spite of his frank gaze—we have to wait for the family biography and for the definitive study by Alan Crawford. Meanwhile Fiona MacCarthy has written *The Simple Life*, an excellent introduction to C.R.A. and his most ambitious experiment. This was the Great Move of 1902, when he led his band of 150 craftsmen from the East End of London to an unknown land, Chipping Campden in the Cotswolds. In the picturesque and then half-decaying little town he envisaged workshops and kitchen gardens for his cabinet-makers, jewelers, blacksmiths, weavers, and printers. He had already written an inspirational book for his apprentices, *From Whitechapel to Camelot.* Even more courageously, he took the foremen down to look at Campden in November, though he does appear to have given them plenty to drink. Then, as a socialist, he took a poll—one man, one vote. One of the apprentices walked eight miles through the snow to bring Ashbee the result. It is interesting to learn that the cabinet-makers, the most unionized of all the workshops, were decisively in favor of the Move.

C.R.A. was born in 1863, the son of Henry Spencer Ashbee, a wealthy businessman and bibliophile and, as his granddaughter has pointed out to me, a serious pornographer. The mother was from a good Hamburg Jewish family, of the kind that in every generation produces a sensitive aesthete to plague them. C.R.A. refused to enter the business, and is said to have been cut off with £1,000. At Cambridge, where his closest friends were Roger Fry and Lowes Dickinson, he was passionately open to influences, as to the winds that blow. In 1886, Edward Carpenter came on a visit, and

> after supper we had a delightful walk through the green cornfields in the afterglow. He unfolded to me a wonderful idea of his of a new freemasonry, a comradeship in the life of men which might be based on our little Cambridge of friendships. Are we to be the nucleus out of which the new Society is to be organised?

Deeply impressive were the sage's words about the simple life, and, apparently as part of it, the "homogenic force" that transformed homosexual love into an energy that would redeem society. Carpenter was Ashbee's man, though the Guild, of course, was inspired by William Morris. This was in spite of the fact that Morris had thrown "a deal of cold water" on the idea: for him, by that time, nothing would do short of revolution. But undoubtedly Ashbee had shown the Lamp of Sacrifice. He could perfectly well have salved his conscience in his high-minded practice as an architect. Instead of this, he set out with his men for the Promised Land.

His mission was not so much to revive traditional crafts—that had been done already. It was to restore the workers' birthright of fresh air—as Fiona MacCarthy points out, his role was "close to the Garden City prophets"—and to spread the gospel of joyous work. The like-minded Romney Green once said that if you leave any man alone with a block of wood and a chisel, he will start rounding off the corners. Ashbee's trust, in defiance or perhaps in place of experience, had this quality. And what was more, leave him alone with any group of craftsmen and he would have them singing glees or producing an Elizabethan play, or giving readings from Carpenter and Ruskin.

The Simple Life in the Cotswolds had three golden summers, with all the workshops commanding good prices, then a decline, and by 1908 it had foundered. Mismanagement perhaps, and unfair competition from Liberty's and other commercial semi-mechanized craft enterprises. But C.R.A. blamed society, which had not seen fit to support his great experiment. Bitterest of all to him was the dismantling of the print shops, which he had taken over, together with Morris's honorable grumbling old socialist foreman, from the Kelmscott Press. But his optimism survived: so, too, did his cantankerousness. In 1918 he was appointed Civic Adviser to the British Military Governor in Jerusalem, with responsibility for planning both the old and the new cities. But he did not last long in the job. He disliked being told what to do, and his sympathies were inconveniently with the Arabs.

In preparing her book, Fiona MacCarthy has found plenty of original material. The main sources are the diaries of Ashbee and his wife—for, against all expectations, C.R.A. married a young girl, Janet Forbes, who took swimmingly to the Simple Life and the awkward position of "comrade wife" among the many "comrade friends." We are told that she called her husband "Dear Lad." Ashbee's journals were meant to be edited, and he did edit them, all forty-four volumes; Janet's entries are in a different key, full of spirit and bounce.

Both their points of view are reconstructed here with skill and delicacy. Then there is the view of Chipping Campden itself. A long drama began when the local gentry, the vicar, the Parish Council, and the cottagers heard that 150 crazed socialists were expected from London. Even more unsettling were the visitors, for C.R.A. was determined to show his experiment to the world. Teachers, lecturers, and American well-wishers poured in, tourists came with the swallows and buttercups. Laurence Housman and Masefield came and wrote folk-ballads; the Webbs came, and C.R.A. sang "Widdecombe Fair" to them "in a singularly sweet tenor voice," beginning: "Mrs. Webb, will you lend me thy grey mare?" Yet in four years' time the Guild and even its new experiments in rural education were acceptable to and accepted by Campden. Perhaps only someone as highhanded as C.R.A. could have seen it through. That might stand as his greatest achievement.

It should be added that Ashbee, unlike most of his fellow dreamers of dreams, ran his Guild as a genuine profit-sharing co-operative. But his temperament never allowed him to face, as Morris did, the great tormenting paradoxes of his position. How can nostalgia for an imagined past be reconciled with an unimaginable future, a future whose news is from nowhere? Morris himself, across the supper table, had told him "the thing is this, if we had our Revolution tomorrow, what should we socialists do the day after?... We should all be hanged because we are promising the people more than we can give them!" Ashbee does not seem to have understood. Again, how can the Romantic solution, which must be total, and therefore boundless and free, be realized through constant restrictions—so much machinery and no more, so much comfort and no more, the Simple Life? Even more obtrusive was the absurdity of selling simplicity only to wealthy patrons. This difficulty C.R.A. avoided, at first by thinking as little as he could about them, while involving them in considerable expense by allowing his craftsmen "to do the job well and take their time." Later he showed a certain indulgence toward the beauty loving people of the world and in particular towards the "British aristocratic."

The Simple Life can't, in its eight chapters, discuss these questions at length, nor does it make clear how far Ashbee supervised or even dictated the designs that the Guild workshops produced. But the book maintains an expert balance between C.R.A.'s career, the movement he represented, and his private life. It is easy to accuse him of the bad habits of faith and hope. To treat him ironically is even easier, and seems consoling. But Fiona MacCarthy, although she has a keen sense of humor, is always just. For example, in describing his eccentric choice of Guildsmen—one of them was "called" from a cat's-meat barrow—she writes: "His ideal method of selection (and who has found one better?) was to grasp the man's hand to see what mettle he was made of, simultaneously gazing searchingly into his eyes. . . . The making of the object and the making of the man went together, as he frequently explained to anyone who cared to listen to him." All the ridiculous and the sublime of C.R.A. are there.

1981

RHYME AND METER

Obstacles

Edward Thomas: Selected Letters, edited by R. George Thomas

It would be quite possible to read about Edward Thomas (1878–1917) and wonder how it was that so many people made such allowances for him. A man who had a house built and then refused to live in it, he tormented his wife and children with his restlessness—he calculated that he was never happy for more than a quarter of an hour in the day. Two women, his wife Helen and the good-hearted but overwhelming Eleanor Farjeon, spoiled him as much as they dared. He couldn't get on with his son and was sometimes ruthless with his friends—"people soon bore him," said Walter de la Mare sadly—although most of them were called on to help him in his struggle with depression. But Edward Thomas was, and is, greatly loved. His scholarly biographer, George Thomas, irritated as he is by what he calls the "dithering" of Edward Thomas's early life, treats him not only with respect but with love.

Thomas saw himself with bitter clarity. "I suppose one does get help to some extent by being helpless, but when one doesn't—it's as if one had no pride at all." In October 1907 he wrote: "I went out and thought what effects my suicide would have. I don't think I mind them. . . . W. H. Davies would suffer a little, Helen and the children less in reality than they do now, from my accursed temper and moodiness." Even so, it might be true of him, as Ian Hamilton once wrote of Robert Frost, that "he knew his own failings, knew what the world would think of him if it found him out, and yet believed the world was wrong."

In this short selection of Edward Thomas's letters, George Thomas has aimed, he says, at reflecting the entire writing life while using, as much as possible, unpublished material. To do this he has examined, or re-examined, nearly three thousand autograph letters—including the new acquisitions of the National Library of Wales, in Aberystwyth—of which 126 are included in this collection. The book is meant, I think, not so much to illustrate his 1985 biography but rather as a possible first introduction to Edward Thomas. For this reason George Thomas includes a note (although a late one) written to Dad Uzzell, the Wiltshire gamekeeper, poacher, and Salvation Army convert who taught the very young Edward Thomas about "twig, leaf, flint, thorn, straw, feather," how to read the weather, skin moles, and so forth. After this he has to show, and does show, the teenager eagerly approaching a distinguished man of letters, James Ashcroft Noble ("my note-book would show you that I am not wasting my time out doors the least"); his dissipations at Oxford; the complexity, beauty, and bloody-mindedness of his love for Helen Noble; the disheartening untidiness of life in a cottage with three children; the wearisome search for work and commissions for "open-air" books, for which his enthusiasms often faded some way before the last chapter. This was an excellent time for open-air and open-road literature of all kinds: in the summer of 1907 Elizabeth von Arnim took a large party, including E. M. Forster, through Sussex by caravan, while the Neo-Pagans were camping out in the New Forest. Even so, with the rent of his cottage "a quarterly worry," Edward Thomas had to make ends meet with the reviewing he hated. It became an effort for him, by 1911, not to look on a new book as an enemy.

Sympathetic understanding kept him in more or less perilous balance, and nearly three-quarters of the letters here are to friends. George Thomas says that "each was chosen for particular needs." Harry Hooton, who was something in the City and married to an old school friend of Helen's, was consulted about the difficulties of the marriage. Walter de la Mare, Edward Garnett, and the dramatist Gordon Bottomley were ready to give literary advice and criticism and to send "suggestions, warnings etc as they came to mind." "Perhaps I am not quite just to myself," Thomas wrote to Bottomley in December of 1909,

> in finding myself very much on an ordinary everyday level except when in a mood of exaltation usually connected with nature and solitude. By comparison with others that I know—like de la Mare—I seem essentially like other men in the train and I should like not to be.

No way seemed open, however, and Thomas was on the verge of having to write a tourist's guidebook to Hampshire and Wiltshire. Meanwhile he gave generously, as well as took. It's a pity it wasn't possible to include any letters to W. H. Davies; there is nothing, therefore, to show his generosity in encouraging Davies to write and in getting him a grant for a decent wooden leg. Thomas believed, and told Helen more than once, that his own nature was incompatible with love, and that he was never quite at ease in the company of two or more people. But his salvation, he said as early as 1906, would depend on the one right person.

In 1913 Robert Frost arrived with his family from New Hampshire, unsuccessful as a farmer and not well known as a poet. George Thomas includes some of the first notes between them ("My dear Frost—I wish you were nearer so that we could see one another easily with our children"), and after that, Frost said, "1914 was our year. I never had, I never shall have again, such a year of friendship." Thomas took his family to stay near Ledington, on the Gloucester–Herefordshire border, two fields away from the Frosts. The meadows were full of windfalls from the old cider-apple trees, and at every gate and stile they paused and talked "of flowers, childhood, Shakespeare, women, England, the war, or looked at a far horizon, which some gap or dip occasionally disclosed." Possibly they also talked about alienation, loneliness, self-disgust, and self-forgiveness, since both of them were something other, or more, than the bird-and-weather writers their readers knew.

In May 1914 Thomas tells Frost that he ought to get started on a book about speech and literature, "or you will find me mistaking your ideas for mine and doing it myself." He has been reading Frost's *North of Boston*, abstemiously, only one poem an evening, and now, halfway through the letter, he asks: "I wonder whether you can imagine me taking to verse. If you can I might get over the feeling that it is impossible— which at once obliges your good nature to say 'I can.'"

He began to write poetry in December 1914, and all his poems were written by December 1916. Credit for this is usually given to Frost, certainly by Thomas himself, although Frost declared that "all he ever got was an admiration for the poet in him before he had written a line." Certainly they were agreed at once on the relationship between traditional meter and the tones and half tones of the spoken voice, a kind of counterpoint. But Frost's practical advice to his friend in 1914 was to look at certain passages in his latest book, *The Pursuit of Spring*, and to write them again in verse form, but with exactly the same cadence. It seems unusual advice, not quite using words "as poets do," and Thomas sometimes tried it the other way round, turning poems back into prose, though he did describe this as "unprofitable." The mystery of his transformation remains, although George Thomas himself doesn't hold with the idea of a significant division in Edward Thomas's inner life. Despite his "immense prose output and the later flowering of his verse," he says, "the name and nature of poetry was his dominant lifelong concern."

His poetry is a question of fine apprehensions, "intuition on the edge of consciousness," Leavis wrote, "which would disappear if looked at directly." He is listening, "lying in wait for what I should, yet never can remember", he cannot bite the day to the core. Now that the war has begun "to turn young men to dung," he sees himself as a "half-ruined house":

> I am something like that,
> Not one pane to reflect the sun,
> For the schoolboys to throw at—
> They have broken every one.

In 1915 he had been considering whether he should follow the Frosts to America. He was thirty-seven. In July he resolved his own perplexities and enlisted in the Artists' Rifles (later he transferred to the Artillery because they allowed a better pension to widows). He expected his friends to forget him, knowing that his appearance was completely changed by his first army "shortcut," when he lost his longish hair, described as dull gold. "Nobody recognises me now," he wrote to Frost in May 1916, "Sturge Moore, E. Marsh and R. C. Trevelyan stood a yard off and I didn't trouble to awake them to stupid recognition." But Helen divined that what she called (in her memoir As It Was) "his old periods of dark agony" had gone forever. Among the memoirs included at the end of this book is one written by an old friend, R. A. Scott-James, who was at training camp with Thomas and found him "scarcely recognisable for the same man." As a sergeant instructor, it turned out that he was not only a good soldier but a good teacher of soldiers, and surely no siege battery can ever have had an observation officer better suited to his job. Thomas himself put this another way, writing to his parents: "I have done all the things so far asked of me, without making any mess."

His last letters are to Helen. "Still not a thrush—but many black-birds," he wrote to her, a few days before the battle of Arras.

My dear, you must not ask me to say much more. I know that you must say much more because you feel much. But I, you see, must not feel any-thing. I am just as it were tunnelling underground and something in my subconsciousness directs me not to think of the sun. At the end of the tun-nel there is the sun.

The first publisher of Edward Thomas's poetry was James Guthrie of the Pear Tree Press, who in 1916 published six poems under Thomas's pen name, Edward Eastaway. Otherwise Thomas was not fortunate. An introduction to Edward Marsh was a failure, and Marsh did not include him in any of the five volumes of *Georgian Poetry*. Harold Monro of the Poetry Bookshop, a friend, also rejected Edward Eastaway. "Many thanks for saying it," Thomas wrote to him. "I am sorry because I feel utterly sure they are me. I expect obstacles and I get them." Professor Thomas might perhaps have explained that the enemy was not Monro himself so much as his highly-strung partner, Alida Klementaski. She associated Thomas with Frost, whom she detested. "I could have pulled that Frost man down the stairs by his coat when he said he was going up to see you," she told Monro. In this way Monro, a deeply harassed man who missed many opportunities, missed one of the greatest of all.

1996

The Poetry Bookshop

The Poetry Bookshop, both as a shop and as a publishing venture, existed from December 1912 to 1935—I should like to say "flourished," but it hardly did that. It was never quite out of financial difficulties, and more than once close to bankruptcy. Yet it was considered a success by everyone who knew it, and remembered with affection. It had one object and one only, to bring readers and poetry together. It has to be judged, therefore, I suppose, by how close they seem together now.

The Bookshop was the idea of one man, Harold Monro, who was born in 1879. His family were Scottish in origin, and before his father there were three generations of doctors. The Monros owned a private lunatic asylum, and there would have been money enough for Harold to live his life in modest comfort without making much effort. He had begun, in fact, as a drifter, expelled from school, tormented by his ambitions as a poet, and, after seven miserable years of marriage, separated from his wife. "She for whom I had built such cloud-capped summits of ideals," he noted, "cares for nothing better than to play tennis and reads novels the whole week." Here was the source of anguish, for Monro was deeply affected—though his wife evidently was not—by the mind-climate of the new century with its expectation of joy and freedom, expressed through Fabianism and Utopianism, through Tolstoyan settlements, garden cities and vegetarianism tea-rooms, through Shelley's Spirit of Delight and the Spirit of Ecstasy and the new Rolls-Royce. In 1908 he had tried to fit himself to join the Samurai, a movement that aimed, through clean living and spiritual training, to evolve a higher human type. There is a feeling here of sincerity pushing itself too hard, and at an early stage Monro began to drink, to struggle against drink, and to be haunted by his dreams. These were often nightmares of locked doors, or of grotesque chases and falls, or, once, of Christ begging him not to drink, but "because Christ meekly implored, I drank it down." But Monro had good friends, and it was his English friends in Florence, where he often stayed, who told him he ought to go back to London and concentrate his scattered efforts on "doing something about poetry."

Why should this be necessary? Certainly, at the beginning of the twentieth century, English people still read poetry. They read Kipling, Masefield, and Yeats, they took anthologies on walking tours through Scotland and Switzerland, and in particular they read *The Golden Treasury*. My own aunt and uncle, when they were engaged to he married in 1911, corresponded by postcard, giving a reference to *The Golden Treasury*. But rebellious elements were at work—the Imagists, the Vorticists, the Futurists, the new Georgians. Ezra Pound had arrived in London to call everyone to order. Edward Thomas believed that the trouble was too much poetry. Anyone with £5 to spare, he said, could get a book of verse printed, and "reviewers and booksellers have not been able to keep their heads above the stream." To Monro, poetry was a constant and necessary element in the life of man, particularly industrial man. It had to be restored to its right place.

Monro came back to London in the autumn of 1911. His happiest relationship was always teacher to pupil, and he brought with him a young man, half Italian, half English, Arundel del Re. "His weakness and paleness did not impress us," Virginia Woolf wrote of him in 1919, "but then, perhaps weakness and paleness are the necessary qualities." Del Re, on this first visit, was "thrilled by everything," even "the long terraces of tall, grimy-looking, flat-faced houses peering down on the street." In one of these flat-faced houses, 35 Devonshire Street, Monro established his office.

Devonshire Street (now Boswell Street) was in Bloomsbury, "which at that time," del Re remembered, "had not yet become the favourite haunt of the younger highbrows." It was an unsavory place, full of cats and dustbins, and the ground-floor workshops made it noisy. At No. 35 there was only one cold-water tap for the whole building. But it was near the British Museum and the Central School of Arts and Crafts, and it was cheap. Monro had the habit, as he noted himself, of taking on responsibility for other young lives, and if you do that you must be careful with your money.

Needing advice, although he did not always take it, Monro turned to his friends, and in particular to two of them, Arthur Romney Green (1872–1945) and Frank Flint (1885–1960). Romney Green has been described as a "craftsman, woodworker, boat builder, sailor, mathematician, social reformer, friend and lover," but referred to himself as a small workingmaster. Carpenters and poets, in his opinion, faced the same problems, and he held that any man left with a chisel and a straight piece of wood will want to round it off—what was more, when he ran workshops, during bad times, for the unemployed, he proved that he was right. Extravagant and cranky though he was, Monro knew him for his good angel. Frank Flint was Monro's invaluable expert on French literature. His childhood was spent in London's old East End, one of a family that flitted from one home to another when the rent was due, and even before he left school at the age of thirteen he was working as a soapboy in a barber's shop. In 1909, having made his landlady's daughter pregnant, Flint married her, but he managed, during intervals of his work as a clerk in the Civil Service, to learn nine—some say ten—languages. After bringing out his three small volumes of poetry—two of them published by Monro—he became cautious of expressing his emotions. But he was one of the few who attended Monro's funeral, and with the coffin, he said, disappeared "the largest and best part of my life."

Monro's first move, as soon as he felt his friends around him, was to recommend himself to what might be called the establishment, the august Poetry Society. They agreed to lend their support to a new journal, the *Poetry Review,* and to enclose in it their dismal list of fixtures, the *Poetical Gazette.* Although Monro was to do the work and meet some of the expenses, his attraction for the Society was probably partly his appearance. His moustache and upright bearing made him look like a Guards Officer ("a dejected Guards officer," said John Drinkwater) and "safer" than most young poets. Late in 1912, however, he parted company with the *Review* and started up his own quarterly, *Poetry and Drama,* on the principle, said del Re, "that poetry was to be judged as poetry and not according to standards that, more often than not, have nothing whatsoever to do with poetry." Meanwhile, in September 1912, he was approached by Eddie Marsh, who asked him to publish an anthology of the new Georgian poets.

Marsh was Winston Churchill's Private Secretary, a patron of the arts and, in a guileless and generous way, of artistic young men. It was Rupert Brooke who had suggested the anthology (and, indeed, had offered to write the whole thing himself) and Marsh, though his taste was conservative, was taken by the idea of new young voices, rejecting the Victorian past, outshining *The Golden Treasury.* The selections, of course, he wanted to make personally, but it says a good deal for Monro, who had no experience of publishing beyond the Samurai Press, that Marsh should have chosen him to bring the book out, even though once again he took some of the financial risk. *Georgian Poetry 1911–1912* sold more than fifteen thousand copies, and it was ready on the center table for the customers who came to the opening of Monro's new venture, the Poetry Bookshop. Thirty-five Devonshire Street was to become a shop that would stock every book published in English by a living poet. The offices were moved up to the second floor, and downstairs, as the sculptor Gaudier-Brzìska put it, they would "sell poetry by the pound."

Shopkeeping was new to Monro, and he never quite took to it. "Conscientious but incompetent" was his own description, although the shop in itself realized his dearest ambitions. Coming down from his office with stiff bows and hesitant smiles he would give heartfelt advice to the customers, often advising them to choose something more worthwhile but less expensive. The office boy was "slow and dreamy" and del Re, who never managed to master the Bar-Lock typewriter, drifted away, becoming a protégé of Logan Pearsall Smith. But Monro had the luck that courage deserves when he met a beautiful young woman, Alida Klemantaski, who asked for nothing except the chance to serve humanity. She came from a Polish refugee family, and was "free," living largely on tea and cigarettes in a single room. A few days later she wrote to him: "The only way to make life worth living is to try and make other people love beauty as much as we do, isn't it? That is what I try to do." Teaching herself everything that was necessary as she went along—stock keeping, accounting, copyediting, hand printing, hand lettering—she became his shop assistant at twenty-five shillings a week.

She had thrown in her lot with him, and was eager to live with him and to bear his child, "a record of our love." Monro, after all, had a son by his first marriage, who sometimes came to see him—so too did his first wife, who was living cheerfully in London with her lover, and sending her friends gifts of port wine. "She is just a woman I married," he explained. He loved Alida. To him she was "Dearest Child," his safe refuge. "We are most nearly born of one same kind"—but they were not, and he could never find the right words to tell her that he had been homosexual ever since his schooldays. Possibly he thought that since Alida had joined "the ranks of the emancipated" she would understand him without difficulty, but she could not and did not, either then or ever.

Monro dreamed, night after night, that he was being buried alive. Both Romney Green and Frank Flint believed that Alida was a cool and balanced young woman who converted Monro from a romantic to a cynic. But in fact her temperament was one of heights and depths, and her love (though she had a generous heart) had its reverse side in wild jealousy, even of the visiting poets. Monro never lived with her, and was frequently away. Having become something like the official spokesman for English poetry, he worked devotedly at one of the most tiring of all occupations—traveling and giving talks. One of his lists reads "Workers' Educational College, National Home Reading Union, Village Clubs Association, Carnegie Trusts, Shakespearean Reading Circle." Sometimes the wheels of the train, as they rattled along, seemed to him to he repeating "Windy bore, windy bore." He could rely on Alida to send him every detail of the shop's fortunes. While the tragicomedy between them played itself out, she never failed the confidence he had put in her.

During its first years the Poetry Bookshop was crowded, and known as a welcoming place, warmed in winter by a coal fire with Monro's cat Pinknose and Alida's dogs stretched out in front of it, and with seats where you could sit and read without being asked to buy. The seats, and indeed all the furniture, had been made by Romney Green out of massive oak. What became of these pieces in the end is a mystery, but it is hard to believe that they could ever have been destroyed. The shop was also a meeting place, and poets arriving in London, or even in England, made their way there as though by instinct. It was assumed that they would he needy, and the small rooms at the top of the house were available for them at the low rent of 3s 6d a week. The D. H. Lawrences, the Epsteins, the Frosts, all lodged there, and Wilfred Owen, who came there to get good advice, found that the place was full and had to take refuge in the local coffeehouse. Flint, however, noticed that none of them stayed there long. Devonshire Street was too much for them, he thought.

Monro, of course, was also still a publisher, on the lookout for good poetry. He never arrived at a definition of it, although he believed it had something to do with rhythm and sense becoming identical. He might have added, however, after a few years' experience, that poetry was what demanded, at all costs, to he published. In *Poetry and Drama* for June 1914 he had rashly said that he would "be glad at all times to receive letters from authors who consider themselves unfairly treated." In the *Chapbook* No. 23, May 1921, he specifies that manuscripts brought to the shop by hand will not be received, and even when sent by post "they cannot he examined within any specified period," but before that he had become used to abuse and reproaches of all kinds. Rejected authors called him "Your Lordship" and complained that he was reducing them to starvation, and even those who were accepted often protested bitterly.

> *You bloody Deaconess in rhyme*
> *You told me not to waste your time—*
> *And that from you to me!*

> *Now let Eternity be told*
> *Your slut has left my books unsold—*
> *And you have filched my fee.*

This was from that "magnificent gypsy of a woman," as Louis Untermeyer called her, "gnarled in her own nervous protests," Anna Wickham. No greater contrast with Anna could he imagined than the pale, withdrawn, enigmatic Charlotte Mew, Alida's "Auntie Mew," who also wrote sharply to Monro about his arrangements for her first book, *The*

Farmer's Bride. To both these poets, and to all the others, he sent out careful and regular accounts.

In 1913 the Bookshop's work was extended in two directions. It began to publish and sell its own illustrated rhyme sheets as cheaply as possible (they started off at a penny plain, twopence colored) and it announced twice-weekly poetry readings. These in themselves were nothing new—Monro had met Alida at a Poet's Club evening at the Café Monico, where she had read and he had been the guest of honor. But at the Bookshop's Tuesday and Thursday evenings, where comfort was not thought of, there was a spirit of quiet intensity. The room was up a flight of ladder-like stairs. The desk was candle-lit, later lamp-lit, with a shade of dusky green. Audiences, except for Yeats, were not large, and the takings (out of which the reader was paid) were small. Alida often read herself, or, if not, "managed" the highly-strung poets, although W. H. Davies—for example—whined from nerves like a baby. Monro had always thought of a poem as a printed score, brought to life by the human voice. His own (although he was a good amateur singer) he thought was too gloomy, and if any of his work was to he read, he left it to Alida. After the reading came "selling time," which often turned out to be talking time, late into the night. Yet these sparse occasions turned into immortal hours, and their reputation mysteriously spread. When Richard Aldington joined up in 1916, he (one might think rashly) told the Quartermaster Sergeant that he was a poet. "Oh, are you? Have you ever heard of the Poetry Bookshop?"

The war meant that Monro, like other publishers, lost his cashier and his traveler, ran out of paper, and found it difficult to sell any poetry except "trench verse." London, and particularly Bloomsbury with its wide squares, became like an armed camp. In August 1916, Monro got his own calling-up papers, and was sent first to an anti-aircraft battery, where he felt wretchedly out of place, and then to the War Office. "Dear child, what shall I do?" Alida, distracted with worry for him, had no doubt about what she ought to do. The shop had to be kept open, even though she had to do the packing herself and made deliveries with a handbarrow. In the evenings, if there were no Zeppelin raids, she colored the first series of rhyme sheets and some of the chapbook covers in watercolor, sometimes with the help of Charlotte Mew. Sidgwick & Jackson offered to travel the books for her, but they asked for 10 percent commission and that would have left her with less than nothing.

In the early Twenties, when, in Rose Macaulay's words, "there was a kind of poetry-intoxication going about" and John Masefield sold eighty thousand copies of his *Collected Poems,* the shop, to all appearances, should have done well. But though Monro had been untiring in his efforts to sell both his authors and the rhyme sheets in America, he had no capital to expand. Worse still, the shop's early success had given rise to competition. Arundel del Re himself opened a Chelsea Bookshop in 1919, and began to issue the Chelsea Broadsides. But he also sold modern pictures, while other establishments offered smocks and pottery and even tea and scones alongside the books of verse. This was quite foreign to Monro's original conception. But his account books told him one thing, his ideals another.

In 1920, apparently at the insistence of McKnight Kauffer, he married Alida at Clerkenwell Registry Office. Up to the last moment he had tried to explain his difficulties without success, and she had been left "terror-stricken" by hints that she did not understand. Her heart, she said, was raw. As soon as the ceremony was over he disappeared, leaving her to go down to the country alone. Yet they still made their appearance in the shop together, although the customers talked and read rather than bought, and in 1923 bankruptcy seemed to threaten. "Will they sell my dogs?" Alida asked.

Drink, in one of Monro's earlier poems, he had called his "strange companion," not pretending that he could ever do without it.

> *We never smiled with each other.*
> *We were like brother and brother,*
> *Dimly accustomed.*

Out of a residual sense of duty and his love for Alida he undertook during the 1920s a series of cures in France and Germany—"not the best places," she thought, "to fight such a battle," as wine was so cheap there. Meanwhile, the Devonshire Street lease would be up in 1926, and they arranged to rent new premises in 38 Great Russell Street, opposite the British Museum. With not much hope, surely, of success, Monro put out a proposal for the conversion of the Bookshop into a limited liability company. In this scheme the stock is valued at £3,500 and Romney Green's oak furniture at £500; the approximate turnover is given, but there is no mention of current profits. A few friends put themselves down for shares, but the idea came to nothing.

The second Bookshop, however, opened gallantly, with McKnight Kauffer's new sign and an interior decorated in orange, pink, and purple, the colors of the all-conquering Ballets Russes. But this room had to be partitioned and shared with the publishers Kegan Paul, and the readings were moved to a nearby hall, which meant that there was no "selling time" at all. Worn out with the move, Alida arranged things as best she could. The big book table and the wide seat still stood in the light from the windows, but there was no fire, only a gas stove, and she felt the old magic was lost. The rhyme sheets were still pinned up and could be read by passersby, but Monro had been obliged, in spite of everything, to stock general books on literature and art. It was no longer in the truest sense a poetry bookshop.

Monro by now had not much hope of recovery. In Great Russell Street he had taken to drinking at the local public house, the Plough, with the rough trade. "Red Mudie," "Albert," and "Italian Lou" figure in his scattered diary. Once the police had to be called in, and Alida's letters to him are in the truest sense pathetic. It is only the Strange Companion, she tells him, who stands between "the two helpless creatures that we are." And yet something in Monro, something that lay deep at the bottom of his mind, seemed to tell him that he was close at last to what he had always wanted to write about. He made a note to himself: "Can't I eat up some of these pornographic experiences and digest them hot and spit them out again as beauty?"

Monro died on 16 March 1932. In his will he had asked for his ashes to be scattered at the root of a young oak tree, though only if the idea proved practicable. The Poetry Bookshop was to be wound up. Alida did not take the decision to do this until June 1935, trying to persuade herself, she wrote to her friends, "that the moment had not come." But she told them that she would continue to live upstairs at 38 Great Russell Street and would be delighted to see any of them, "as if the Bookshop were still in existence."

Georgian Poetry 1911–1912, the Bookshop's first publication, was also its greatest success. The sales of the series dropped with the fifth volume, although *Georgian Poetry 1920–1922* still sold eight thousand copies. Finally Eddie Marsh was left looking back on his past success as an editor "very much as I should towards having been Captain of Cricket at Westminster." This remark in itself shows why Monro was anxious not to identify himself with the Georgians as a group, and why he appeared sourly gratified by their decline in reputation. Meanwhile in 1914 he brought out Ezra Pound's *Des imagistes,* and in 1915 Richard Aldington's *Images (1910–1915)* and Flint's imagist *Cadences.* With Futurism he would probably have gone much farther than he did if Alida had not expressed an absolute horror of Marinetti. All this was in line with the original idea of the shop as a "depot" where poets of different views could meet and talk far into the night, while their volumes confronted each other from the shelves. Through war, through money troubles, through alcoholism he continued doggedly to look for new poetry. His only competitor in the field was Grant Richards, who wrote to him in December 1920 that "we might between us clear up the poets of the country." Monro remains as the publisher of Charlotte Mew, Anna Wickham, and Frances Corn ford, and of Robert Graves's first book.

The Bookshop's list falls short of what it might have been. When the Big War (as he preferred to call it) became inevitable, Monro forcibly refused to print "patriotic rubbish," but from the young serving officers he managed to get only Robert Graves's early *Over the Brazier* and *Magpies in Picardy** by his young friend T. P. Cameron Wilson, who was killed in 1918.

Apart from this, Monro was reproached, and reproached himself, for his rejection of T. S. Eliot and Edward Thomas. Thomas had been an early friend both of *Poetry and Drama* and of the shop, and it seems inexcusable that the "Edward Eastaway" poems, which he sent round in May 1915 in a sad brown-paper parcel, should be returned to him. But Alida decisively objected to Thomas, probably as a friend of the dreaded Robert Frost. She also complained (March 1917) that Ezra Pound had been in "hawking" T. S. Eliot's poems. "We don't want them but he wouldn't take 'No' and said he'd send them to be seen." In both cases Monro came to recognize his mistake and did what he could to atone for it. After Thomas's death in action, he wrote to his widow, Helen, offering to publish, and must have felt that he deserved the reproachful snub he got in reply. Eliot's early poetry he frankly found hard to understand (so, too, did Leonard and Virginia Woolf, who took it for the Hogarth Press). But by 1915 he was able to "hear" Prufrock—"I consider that

---

*Monro could not resist "improving" the title poem by leaving out the last two verses. But Field Marshall Lord Wavell, when he included "Magpies in Picardy" in his anthology *Other Men's Flowers* (1944), was able to remember the verses from the *Westminster Gazette,* where they had first been printed.

Harold is dawning," Pound wrote to Harriet Monroe—and in 1921 the
Bookshop distributed the remaining copies of *Ara Vos Prec.* Monro
wrote well, though cautiously, about *The Waste Land* (*Chapbook* No. 34,
February 1923), and Eliot, who remained a loyal friend, wrote the Critical Note for Monro's *Collected Poems* (Cobden-Sanderson, 1933).
Monro, he said, was not a technical innovator, but a poet needs a new
technique "only as far as it is dictated, not by the idea—for there is no
idea—but by the nature of the dark embryo within him which gradually
takes on the form and speech of a poem."

As an editor Monro was at his happiest, or, to be more accurate, at his
least unhappy. His gloomy enthusiasm was persuasive. Although *Poetry
and Drama* was kept going by the royalties from *Georgian Poetry
1911–1912,* he was unable to pay his contributors, and yet the hard-up
Edward Thomas and the penniless Flint worked their best for him. Aiming high, he tackled Robert Bridges, the Poet Laureate, and Henry Newbolt, both of whom responded. These were names from the past, but his
drama critic, Gilbert Cannan, boldly supported Gordon Craig and the
experimental theatre. Flint's "French Chronicle" in particular is written
with information and feeling. The September 1914 number leaves him
watching the North Sea roll in on a flat English beach, having heard that
Charles Péguy is dead, wondering whether Guillaume Apollinaire will
survive. But the war put an end to *Poetry and Drama,* and Monro
showed good sense in not trying to revive it. Its place was to be taken by
The London Mercury (1919), edited by John Squire, and Eliot's *Criterion*
(1922), although *The Criterion*'s circulation was never more than nine
hundred. "There are too many periodicals," Monro noted in his diary,
"yet who is going to stop? There is not enough stuff to go round." Meanwhile he had devised the monthly *Chapbook,* a delightful miscellany,
sometimes unexpectedly lighthearted. For this he spirited up his old
illustrators and some new ones to decorate the front covers and often—
although it would have paid better to use the space for advertising—the
back ones. Anyone who is lucky enough to possess a run must be glad to
have No. 29, designed by Terence Prentis, the last of Monro's admiring
disciples, or Ethelbert White's covers in plum red, white, and yellow for
No. 33, or Paul Nash's No. 35. The paper, of course, did not pay, although
Monro tried a number of editor's devices, including the unusual one of
lowering the price (Nos. 25 to 38). It was erratic during 1921, the year after
their marriage—Harold and Alida went abroad independently of each

other and publication lapsed for six months—but this was part of the *Chapbook*'s ragged, Petrouchkalike charm. With almost every issue the subscribers could expect something different. Nos. 6 and 18 offered songs with music, No. 20 a crazy but deeply interesting piece by Gordon Craig on the political aspect of puppet shows, No. 29 a roaring satire by Osbert Sitwell on the Georgians under the guidance of their goddess Mediocrity, No. 32 Harold Monro's "morality," *One Day Awake,* where the wretched protagonist, threatened by the voices of Business, Food, and Furniture, pours himself out a glass of wine as the scene closes. These were in addition to the issues on contemporary American, French, and English poetry.

The idea of the rhyme sheets may have come to Monro from the Dun Emer Press broadsides and the Flying Fame rhyme sheets, which the Bookshop took over in 1914, but they became distinctively his own. In the *Chapbook* No. 35, March 1923, he wrote that "certain distinctive qualities are essential to a successful Broadside, and it will be found, if these are studied, that only a few poems possess them." What are they? He never made this quite clear, perhaps, even to himself, but an important point was their impact. The poems vary a good deal in length, but they are usually short, sometimes cut down, even when (as with Blake's "Schoolboy," The New Broadside No. 6) this means changing the meaning entirely. In commissioning his illustrators Monro showed none of his hesitation with authors. They were the best he could get—Lovat Fraser, Charles Winzer (who designed two signboards for Sylvia Beach's Shakespeare & Co.; both were stolen), John and Paul Nash, Albert Rutherston, later David Jones, McKnight Kauffer, Edy Legrand, Edward Bawden. The illustrations, particularly Lovat Fraser's, were often decorations, almost independent of the text. But Monro, in the spirit of William Blake, wanted the verse and the picture to make their impression together. The sheets were meant to be pinned up and replaced at will, but the memory would retain the song and the last word would belong, not to time, but to joy, a memory which would last when the sheets were thrown away with the rubbish or blown with the wind. Robert Frost, waiting for a train on Beaconsfield station during his first visit to England, had seen a bit of paper blowing about at his feet, and picking it up he had read for the first time Ralph Hodgson's "Eve," printed as a "filler." This kind of chance, this kind of contact, was what Monro hoped for with the rhyme sheets. As to poetry, he once said, "the less of it printed the better; and the more of it carried in the memory and conveyed by the voice, much, much the better." This, surely, is one of the strangest remarks ever made by a hard-working publisher. But the rhyme sheets' verses were carried in the memory. The writer William Plomer, looking back through thirty years, remembered how as a boy at Rugby he had hung the rhyme sheets on the walls of his room, "best of all, de la Mare's 'Arabia,' with gaudy decorations by (I expect) Lovat Fraser." Sylvia Townsend Warner wrote in August 1952 to Leonard Bacon,

> Your mention of Ralph Hodgson and his broadsides swept me back to the public at fisticuffs. Broadsides were what one bought at Munro's [sic] Poetry Book-shop, only I think we called them rhyme-sheets. Like a galley proof, as you say, with rough coloured woodcuts heading and tailing them, often drawn by Lovat Fraser. And we tacked them on our walls, above our beds and our baths. I remember one I was particularly attached to, that began

> *Oh, what shall the man full of sin do,*
> *Whose heart is as cold as a stone,*
> *When the black owl looks in through the window,*
> *And he on his deathbed alone?*

(This particular poem was the first to be issued, and surely only the conscience-ridden Monro would have chosen it.) Sylvia Townsend Warner couldn't remember the author, and Plomer couldn't remember the artist (in fact Charles Winzer), which is not surprising, since these names were usually printed as small as possible. In a sense, they didn't matter; this was poetry, as Monro described it to Amy Lowell, to be "sold anywhere and everywhere, carried in the pocket, read in the train." This makes it hard work, of course, for today's collector and bibliographer.

Finally, in both the first and the second Bookshops, children were not forgotten. Although Harold and Alida were, in their different ways, rather intimidating for a young child, and cats, kittens, and dogs were needed as intermediaries; everything they published for children was successful. There were special rhyme sheets for them in both the two series and in the New Broadsides, which opened with de la Mare's "The Huntsmen." (It was disappointing, perhaps, that Ethelbert White had drawn the horsemen riding up the stairs to bed at the top, but not, in the tailpiece, going downstairs again.) Eleanor Farjeon gave readings of her verses from the Nursery Sheets, while Lovat Fraser's "Rhymes for Children" in the November 1919 *Chapbook* was so popular that they were reprinted on their own. Other poems, not in the first place intended for children, were dearly loved—Charlotte Mew's "The Changeling" (from *The Farmer's Bride*), Frances Cornford's "To a Fat Lady Seen from a Train" (from *Spring Morning*), and Harold Monro's "Overheard on a Saltmarsh" (from *Children of Love,* and reprinted as a rhyme sheet), which has been called "as complete and inexplicable as a thing seen suddenly and clearly between sleeping and waking" and was inspired by the green glass beads of an actress, Vera Tschaikovska. Osbert Sitwell declared that the children of a racecourse tough who lived next door to the Bookshop were offered some of the rhyme sheets but tore them up and stamped on them. This Monro would have to mark as another defeat. But it is fair to say that the Poetry Bookshop made a lasting impression on two generations.

1988

Miss Lotti's Story

Charlotte Mew: Collected Poems and Prose,
edited by Val Warner

During her lifetime Charlotte Mew was either greatly liked or greatly disliked, and now, more than fifty years after her death, those who are interested in her are very much interested. There are at least two collections of her papers which nobody is given permission to see—not quite with the feeling that she ought to be left to rest in peace, but, rather, that she shouldn't be shared indiscriminately with outsiders. She was a writer who was completely successful perhaps only two or three times (though that is enough for a lyric poet) and whose sad life, in spite of many explanations, refuses quite to be explained.

Val Warner, who has worked for so long and against so many difficulties to produce this edition, is to be congratulated. The prose pieces and seven of the poems have been collected for the first time, there are five new poems, and the fifty-four lines which were cut from "In Nunhead Cemetery" in Duckworth's collected edition of 1953 have been put back. There is a level-headed introduction and a bibliographical note (to which Sir Sydney Cockerell's diaries should be added). Val Warner, herself a poet, is not primarily interested in biography. I am therefore hoping to expand and correct one or two points.

Charlotte Mew, who lived from 1869 to 1928, changed very little for about thirty years of her life. She was tiny, trim, curly-haired, and pale, wearing size-two boots—doll's boots. Her eyebrows were fixed in a half-moon of surprise, apparently at a joke. What joke? Possibly one that she liked to tell: a hearse-driver runs over a man and kills him, and a passer-by shouts: "Greedy!" She was the sort of person whose luggage is carried by helpful young men, and yet she regarded the world with defiance, answering inquiries with a toss of the head, and carrying her umbrella like a weapon. This umbrella, with which she repelled tiresome children on the beach, was part of her Victorian character as "Miss Mew" or "Miss Lotti." Among what she called "good five o'clock people," she guarded this personality carefully. Only when she felt sure of her company would she sometimes let herself go, and, like most melancholics, prove wildly entertaining. But at the same time Charlotte Mew was writing, and indeed living, *à rebours,* under the threat of insanity and in the dark thrill of self-inflicted frustration. The split could not be concealed indefinitely, and by the 1920s her appearance had altered, and shocked. "Her wind-blown gray hair, her startled gray eyes, her thin white face, belonged to a reluctant visitor from another world, frightened at what she had undergone in this one." The biographer has not so much to reconstruct her life as to account for what life did to her.

Charlotte Mew was the third child (out of eight) of Fred Mew, a farmer's son from the Isle of Wight, who had come to London to be trained as an architect by H. E. Kendall. In 1863 he married Kendall's daughter, a tiny, silly woman who was "above" him, and always made him feel so: he was made to describe his own father, on the marriage certificate, as "Esquire." Charlotte remembered her childhood as happy. Looking back, she was quite sure, as English poets are, that there had been a happier time. That had been in the two top rooms of 10 Doughty Street, with the round table and the rocking horse, and a doll's house designed by Fred. Here Lotti, radiant, passionate, and excitable, ruled the nursery, hopped up beside the driver whenever a cab was called, and was half-mad with excitement at Christmas. She told Florence Hardy that she "never outgrew the snowflakes." And yet when she was only seven, two of her brothers died—one a baby, one, her great playmate, a six-year-old. Lotti, as was then considered right, was taken in to see him in his coffin. The steadying influence was their Yorkshire nurse, Elizabeth Goodman, tenderly described in Charlotte's article "An Old Servant": "as fixed a part of the Universe as the bath (cruelly cold in winter) into which she plunged us every morning, and the stars to which she pointed through the high window, naming some of them, in the evening sky." But it was also this faithful servant who imprinted on Lotti's mind the Evangelical sense of guilt and retribution. Every sin—and every happiness—has been calculated in advance, though not by us, and must be paid for.

> *Sweetheart, for such a day*
> *One mustn't count the score;*
> *Here, then, it's all to pay,*
> *It's good-night at the door.*

This was the poem, "Fin de Fête," that in 1916 attracted the attention of Thomas Hardy and convinced him of Charlotte Mew's talent. Hardy, of course, didn't need to be persuaded that the Spirit of the Universe was exacting, and Charlotte had the kind of temperament that accepted this without question, even in the nursery.

In 1882 Charlotte was sent to the Gower Street School, which had connections with Bedford College. Here, at the age of fourteen, she fell violently in love with her headmistress, Lucy Harrison. Miss Harrison was one of the great educationalists of the turn of the century. "There was something royal in her nature," Octavia Hill wrote. There was also a strongly masculine element. She was one of the conspicuous successes of the liberal and unsectarian Bedford College: a brilliant scholar (as well as an expert carpenter) and a supporter of liberal movements—she kept as a souvenir a cigar given her by Mazzini. Her aim was to open windows for her pupils, both for the body and the mind. During this first important post the strain on her temperament proved too great, and in 1883 she was forced by what was called "a breakdown in health" to resign. One of the old Gower Street pupils, Mrs. Alice Lee, said that when the news was given out Charlotte, who had been playing the piano, "jumped up and in a wild state of grief started to bang her head against the wall."

Alice, who was younger, wondered if she ought to bang her head too. Miss Harrison retired for the time being to Hampstead, where she continued to coach her favorite girls. Lotti was one of them: Fred Mew innocently believed that it would "stabilize" her to keep in sight of the beloved teacher. Her friends remembered that at this time she was in such high spirits, and so amusing, that the walk from Bloomsbury to Haverstock Hill seemed short. After two years, however, Lucy Harrison fell deeply and permanently in love with Amy Greener, who had taken over the Gower Street School. "Dearest, I do not feel at home anywhere without you now," she wrote. "With the person you love comes a halo and a glow over everything, however miserable and poor, and without that presence the light seems to leave the sun itself. This is a trite remark, I am afraid." Miss Greener later wrote on this delicate subject delicately, saying that she had often been asked whether her friend's life had "lacked the perfect rounding love can bring." She assured her readers that it had not, and the two of them lived for many years of unclouded happiness together in Yorkshire.

Besides this first experience of desertion, Lucy Harrison left with Charlotte her ideals of restraint and self-discipline, even in small things ("if a pudding is begun with a fork, the help of a spoon must not be called in half-way through"), and a passion for English literature. The books she read with the inner group allowed for a certain release of emotion—in fact, for Miss Harrison's soppy side: the Brownings, the Brontës, Alice Meynell, Francis Thompson, Tagore's "King of the Dark Chamber" and "The Post Office." When Charlotte Mew found her individual voice, all these influences persisted, just as her school friends remained her first and last refuge throughout her life. With them there was less need for concealment, because they had grown up with Charlotte and knew the unpleasant secrets of the Mews' new home at 9 Gordon Street. By 1888 the eldest son, Henry, and the youngest, Freda, were both incurably insane. Both had to be confined, Henry with his own nurse, in Peckham Hospital, Freda in the Carisbrooke Mental Home on the Isle of Wight, the town which Charlotte described, twenty years later, in "Ken":

> *So when they took*
> *Ken to that place, I did not look*
> *After he called, and turned on me*
> *His eyes. These I shall see—*

Ken, however, is represented as an amiable idiot, whereas both Henry and Freda were victims of what was then called dementia praecox—that is, schizophrenia. "In Nunhead Cemetery" sets out to represent the process of the split mind—"a sudden lapse from sanity and control," as she explained it—by the dreadful heap of earth and flowers in the grave-yard. Meanwhile the guilty identification with the two unfortunates, and the heavy expense of having them looked after, darkened the Mews' respectable daily life. Charlotte wrote of 9 Gordon Street as "The Quiet House." She had a wretched fantasy that one evening when the front-door bell rang, she would answer it and face herself, waiting outside in the street.

In September 1898 Fred Mew died of cancer. During his long illness Charlotte had made her first appearance in print with a short story, "Passed," which was published in the *Yellow Book* for July 1894. I think she probably began to write in order to make some money. Mrs. Mew was left, or made out that she was left, badly off, and lamented that she would have to let off half of the house. Anne had trained at the Queen's Square Female School of Art as a screen and furniture painter. Charlotte had been trained for nothing, so she wrote. She wrote slowly, and, like the heroine of *New Grub Street*, did her time in the British Museum Reading Room, grinding articles ("The Governess in Fiction," "Mary Stuart in Fiction") out of other people's books. Original to the point of willfulness when the impulse to poetry came, she seems, with these prose contributions, to have studied the market. In "In the Curé's Garden" she is imitating *Villette*, in "Mark Stafford's Wife" she is imitating Henry James, in "The Wheat" she is imitating May Sinclair, and in "The Fatal Fidelity" she seems to be having a shot at W. W. Jacobs.

Her first story, "Passed," is the most impulsive and interesting of the lot. The subject is guilt. A respectable young woman hardens her heart when a prostitute appeals to her for help. Later she wanders into a Catholic church as the candles are lit for Benediction, and sees a girl patiently helping her imbecile sister. She knows then how far she has failed in human love. "Passed" is appealing because the painful emotion is felt as true, but it is a period piece: apart from the scene at the altar and the prostitute, we get the prostitute's dying sister, the cynical club-man who seduces them both, and the haunting scent of violets in a cheap china cup. No wonder it was accepted immediately by Henry Harland, the *Yellow Book*'s editor. To her old friends—rather left behind at this point—Lotti seemed one of the New Women. She went about London unescorted, smoking hand-rolled cigarettes, her hair cut short as Miss Harrison's had been, and wearing a smaller version of Miss Harrison's black velvet jacket, collar, and tie. She was now in the orbit of Harland's contributors and John Lane's Keynotes—"George Etherton," Evelyn Sharp, Netta Syrett, and the languid but sharp-witted Ella D'Arcy. These young women were not Bohemians: they were dandies. They objected when Frederick Rolfe left lice on the furniture; Beardsley was "a dear boy" to them. At the Victorian Club for Professional Women, or in the new flats and studios, they talked with passion and spirit. As Evelyn Sharp puts it in her reminiscences, "We were on the crest of the wave, and felt that everything must go." Meanwhile they lived on very small incomes. It was a gallant fellowship, but precarious. When her brother died in 1901, Charlotte made a run to Paris and the companionship of Ella D'Arcy. When she describes how she walked through the rain and the dazzling lights to help Ella arrange her bed-sitting room in the Rue Chat we get a last glimpse of the decade that had suited her best.

She was soon recalled to London. Mrs. Mew rarely let her daughters stay away for long. But the tyrannous old mother was, it turned out, indispensable. In the end, Charlotte's attachment to her home and family was stronger than her desire to be free: they promised normality, which implies peace. During these apparently quiet years, when, as "Miss Lotti," she was ordering the dinner or doing social work in the Girls' Clubs, she became a poet. Hers is a poetry of tensions, which Val Warner defines as "passion unfulfilled by the loss of youth, by death, by the working of a malign fate, by the dictates of conventional morality, by renunciation and even by the glorification of renunciation of all love into itself a kind of passion," to which I would add the overwhelming conviction of guilt. This is only too clear in "Fame," where Charlotte Mew sees herself with disgust "smirking and speaking rather loud" at London parties, "where no one fits the singer to his song," or "On the Asylum Road," where she is one of the crowd passing the darkened windows which cut off the inmates, or "Saturday Market," where a wretched woman tries to hide her disgrace under her shawl and sets the market "grinning from end to end." The images leave the writer, as she put it, "burned and stabbed half through." They are not experimental, but they are not quite under control either. In the main, the shorter her lyrics are the better, partly because her ear for meter was uncertain over a long stretch (she calculated by syllable, not by stress), and partly because they are *cris de coeur*. Explaining this in a letter, she gives examples of genuine *cris de coeur*: Margaret Gautier's "je veux vivre" and Mrs. Gamp's "Drink fair, Betsy, wotever you do." Cries have to be extorted: that is their test of truth. The quality of emotion is the first requirement of poetry, she said. Given that, she liked to speak in different voices, and for both sexes. She is a "cheap, stale chap" in "Nunhead Cemetery" and an adolescent French schoolboy, set on edge with frustration, in "Fête." In "The Farmer's Bride" the young wife has "turned afraid" and sleeps alone, while the farmer sweats it out only a flight of stairs away.

> *"Oh, my God! the down,*
> *The soft young down of her, the brown*
> *The brown of her—her eyes, her hair, her hair!"*

"Sexual sincerity is the essential of good emotional work," complained Wilfred Scawen Blunt, who, predictably, didn't like the personae and was "often left in a puzzle by the situations." But the uncertainty, of course, was in itself sincere, and made a strong, half uncomfortable appeal to readers as different as Hardy and Virginia Woolf.

One of these early admirers was the novelist May Sinclair. Charlotte had written to her in 1913 congratulating her on *The Combined Maze*, a novel in which the image for the human condition is a men and women's evening gym class at the Polytechnic. The outcome for the hero is sacrifice and repression of "the murmur of life in the blood," a theme well understood by Charlotte. May replied, ready to embark on another of her many literary friendships, but within a few months Charlotte had begun to fret. May Sinclair was a small, pretty, cat-loving woman and an entirely professional writer. She had many interests, including philosophy and what was then called medico-psychology, and kept an escape route for suffragettes across her back garden. She could deal competently with most situations, and her letters show that when the friendship grew warmer and Charlotte became importunate, she knew how to put her quietly in her place. "When I say, 'I want to walk with you to Baker Street Station,' I mean I want to *walk,* and want to walk with you, and I want to walk to Baker Street Station. . . . Better to take things simply and never go back on them, or analyse them, is not it?" At the same time May was generous in her appreciation of the poems, which Charlotte read

aloud to her in her hoarse little male impersonator's voice. She recommended them to Ezra Pound (who printed "Fête" in *The Egoist*) and,
indeed, to every critic she could think of. She perhaps encouraged Charlotte unduly when she wrote to her: "I know one poet whose breast beats
like a dynamo under an iron-gray tailor-made suit (I *think* one of her
suits is iron-gray) and when she publishes her poems she will give me
something to say that I cannot and do not say of my Imagists." It was
surely a loss on both sides when the friendship abruptly ended, in
1916–17. After the breach, there was not much poetry left in Charlotte
Mew. In 1969 an American scholar, Theophilus Boll, who was most
painstakingly writing the Life of May Sinclair, began to turn this episode
over in his mind. "If I should find something awful enough," he frankly
admitted, "I might produce a bestseller, instead of an academic 'doubt-
sell.'" In this he was disappointed, but Dame Rebecca West allowed him
to see a letter from G. B. Stern, recalling how May Sinclair had told
them, in her "neat precise little voice," that Charlotte Mew had chased
her upstairs into her bedroom, "and I assure you, Peter, and I assure
you, Rebecca, I had to leap the bed five times." Dr. Boll says he pon-
dered this, working out with true academic caution how far May Sinclair,
who was then over fifty, would really have been able to leap.

It is not surprising, then, that when she first called at the Poetry Bookshop and was asked, "Are you Charlotte Mew?" her reply was: "I am sorry
to say I am." The Bookshop, during those years the natural meeting-place
of poets, was a small room off Theobald's Road in what was then a slum
area of Bloomsbury, and it was largely run and managed by an intense,
energetic Hampstead-Polish girl, Alida Klementaski. Alida had read
"The Farmer's Bride" in *The Nation,* and was "electrified." "This poem
I immediately committed to memory, and a year or two later repeated it
to Harold Monro, who had recently opened the Poetry Bookshop with
the avowed intention of publishing the work of young poets and presenting them to a large audience." Charlotte was no longer young, but in
1916 the Bookshop brought out "The Farmer's Bride" and sixteen other
poems in an edition of five hundred copies, with a cover design by Lovat
Fraser. After Charlotte's death Alida, with a good deal of difficulty, composed a memoir that, up to now, has been the standard source of information. There are some unforgettable passages—the chloroforming, for
example, of the Mews' savage old parrot (a job which Alida reluctantly
undertook), and the tragic account of the sisters' last days. But Alida,

though a staunch friend, was not qualified to understand the nature of Charlotte's emotional life. Homosexuality dismayed her. In 1916 she wrote in distress to Harold Monro that she had missed the last 19 bus and been stranded in the rooms of a fellow suffragette: during the night she had been terrified and "nearly went off my head when the young woman came into my room—I said 'go and get a dressing-gown'. . . but she said in a curious voice, 'No, it's too much fag.'" In consideration for this new friend, Charlotte produced an edited version of her life-story. She did not tell Alida the truth about May Sinclair, and she accounted for her distrust of men (except for the old and tamed) by saying that a lawyer had once cheated her out of a sum of money. So Alida, the first and closest biographer, was also the first to be mystified.

To her, the fiftyish Charlotte was "Auntie Mew," and as an eccentric auntie Charlotte became a habituée of the Bookshop. Now that she was modestly well known she was more farouche than ever and more suspicious of patronage, refusing to visit the Sitwells, dodging Lady Ottoline Morrell, intimidating Virginia Woolf, but in the fire-lit bookshop, with Alida's dogs and Harold Monro's cat, there was no need for defensiveness. During the Twenties she acquired, also, an elderly beau. Sydney Cockerell, the director of the Fitzwilliam Museum, had been struck by "The Farmer's Bride," though he was timid at first about "the brown of her": "I suppose her sunburnt arms and neck?" he suggested. In time, Charlotte became one of the middle-aged artistic ladies with whom he conducted decorous flirtations. She was, he noted in his diary, "both witty and profound." He invited her to Cambridge to see the Fitzwilliam's Brontë manuscripts, and "after tea we sat on the grass, looking at the waterlilies." In London they had little suppers in restaurants and saw Charlie Chaplin in *Shoulder Arms* and Noël Coward in *Hay Fever.* To Cockerell it seemed that she was subsisting on tea and cigarettes, since Charlotte, like most women living on a fixed income, had the illusion of being much poorer than she really was. In 1924 he arranged a Civil List pension for her of £75 a year, calling on the "Big Three" (Thomas Hardy, John Masefield, and Walter de la Mare) to give their recommendations. It didn't matter, he explained when she objected that she was writing nothing—the pension wasn't dependent on that. For all this kindness she was thankful, but when she needed, as she put it, to listen to her own heart she turned to his wife, Kate, or to Thomas Hardy's second wife, Florence.

In 1922 the Mews moved to 86 Delancey Street. It was a smaller house, but they could look down and see the children and the Punch and Judy in the street below. This had always been a resource to Charlotte. "The Shade Catchers," which Alida thought the best of her poems, simply describes two barefoot children shadow-hopping down a sunny London pavement. The move upset Mrs. Mew. She fell, contracted pneumonia, and in May she died. Four years earlier Edith Sitwell had described Charlotte as a gray and tragic woman "sucked dry of blood (though not of spirit) by an arachnoid mother," but the death did not come as a release. On the contrary, Charlotte felt adrift, "like a weed rooted up and thrown over the wall." "Was not able to be of any use," Cockerell noted in his diary. The two sisters retreated to Anne's studio off the Tottenham Court Road. It was the bachelor establishment that, in the Nineties, they had never had, but without the spirit of those lost days. They looked on it, indeed, as a comedown, and all Charlotte's warring emotions were concentrated on the protection of her sister. Anne, who had not been able to work for some time, was ill. The illness was cancer of the liver, and Anne began gradually to die in public, for callers were still received. "They ought to be allowed to put her to sleep," wrote Alida.

> As I talked to her and she shut her eyes I felt they were sealed on her face and would never open, but they did. Auntie Mew says the Dr says any moment she may go down to earthy mould. Poor little Mew it is more tragic than I can tell you—Her rough little harsh voice and willful ways hiding enormous depths of feeling—now she will be entirely alone and her relation with Anne has been one of complete love, and I imagine the love of sisters (or brothers) more marvellous than any other as there can be no fleshly implications or sexual complexities.

When Anne died in June 1927, Charlotte felt a survivor's guilt. It was not the search for recognition, or even the search for love, that was to extinguish her, but the determination to be punished. She convinced herself first that Anne might, as the result of her negligence, have been buried alive, and next that she herself was contaminated and that the black specks in the studio were the germs of cancer. A doctor examined the specks: they were soot. Charlotte was persuaded to go into a private nursing home where the matron was not the kind of woman to understand her, and the view from the window was blocked by a stone wall.

After living there alone for about a month, Charlotte Mew went out, bought a bottle of Lysol, and drank half of it. A doctor was called, but she only came round sufficiently to say: "Don't keep me, let me go."

"24 February 1928," Cockerell wrote in his diary. "A tragic ending to the tragic life of a very rare being. After dinner wrote a little memoir of her for the *Times*." In the following year the Bookshop brought out *The Rambling Sailor*, with thirty-two more poems—all that could be found by Charlotte's executors. By the 1930s the grave where Charlotte and Anne lay buried together was neglected, but collectors had begun to buy Charlotte's letters. In 1940 the research staff of the H. W. Wilson Company were at work on their *Twentieth-Century Authors,* and evidently quite at a loss over her entry. They settled for: "She was educated privately, she lived for some time in Paris, she loved someone deeply and hopelessly, she endured poverty and illness and despair." She was given a pension, they added, "so that she should not starve." So the half-myth perpetuated itself. None of this would matter if it did not concern a poet "who will be read," as Hardy insisted, "when others are forgotten."

1982

A Questioning Child

Imagination of the Heart: The Life of
Walter de la Mare, by Theresa Whistler

Walter de la Mare believed that children—if they could be got to listen at all—were the best listeners. I remember as a small girl hearing him at afternoon readings upstairs at the Monros' Poetry Bookshop in Devonshire Street. I did not consider that he read satisfactorily, though he was better when he took turn and turn about, as he often did, with the valiant Eleanor Farjeon. And he did not *look* like a poet. I knew how poets ought to look, because at that time they walked about the streets of Hampstead. De la Mare was at the same time too stout and too trim for someone who had met at eve the Prince of Sleep, as I did not doubt that he had. But he was the man who had written *Peacock Pie*. That was enough.

But poetry, he said, "depends for its life on being remembered," and no one knew better than de la Mare that iron rusts, Time returns mock-

ing answers, and poets become what publishers call "due for reap-
praisal." Waterstone's catalogue lists him as "not always fashionable, but
always popular." Even this seems uncertain. Theresa Whistler, in a
strong-minded and sympathetic prologue to *Imagination of the Heart*,
tells us that she was determined *not* to write "yet another comprehensive
biography of someone formerly esteemed, now neglected, who knew
everybody worth knowing." Rather than that, she has based her book on
a conversation she had with de la Mare at the end of his life, in 1950, at
South End House in Twickenham. He suggested then that imagination
took distinct forms, and she could tell from his voice that the one he valued most was "the imagination of the heart." On this element she
decided to concentrate, tracing it like a river whose outfall turned out to
be very close to its source.

Theresa Whistler's qualifications to write this book couldn't be bet-
tered. She is the granddaughter of Sir Henry Newbolt, de la Mare's great
benefactor, she knew de la Mare himself very well, she has made her way
through countless drawersful of papers (he kept everything) and spent
several years in research. All the same, I found it difficult to accept the
pattern of the heart's imagination. For half a century, while his mind
took journeys into space and eternity, he presented the outside world as
it had first come to his notice in the 1870s. Tailors sit cross-legged, children sent to bed blow out their candles, crickets sing behind the wain-
scot, sweeps and bakers push their carts through the morning streets.
The atmosphere, however, is hostile. The fish in the frying pan says
"Alas!" but no help comes, and children are drowned with their silver
penny or shut up in a bag and stolen. Everywhere there are the cold and
solitary, watching from behind closed windows. And why do the rats run
over John Mouldy in his cellar, and what does Miss Emily want with that
long, shallow box? Sometimes a bargain can be made with the mysterious persecutors by settling—like the poor old Widow in her Weeds—for
very little, or simply by running away, as in the stupendous "Tom's
Angel." Every now and then, there is an epiphany of a moment's total
happiness or innocence—in "Chicken," in "Full Moon" ("One night
when Dick lay fast asleep"), and in the miraculous three verses of "The
Funeral." But James Reeves, in his Penguin anthology *Georgian Poetry*
(1962), includes "Drugged," "Dry August Burned," "The Feckless Dinner Party" (they are trapped in the cellars), "The Marionettes" ("Let the
foul scene proceed"), "Echo" (which repeats "Who cares?"), "The

Dove" (its voice "dark with disquietude"), "Treachery," and "Tit for Tat," where the trapper Tom Noddy ends up hanging still from a hook "on a stone-cold pantry shelf." In some of these poems there is regret and dismay, but the imagination they show is not of the heart but of second sight, or rather second senses, icily alert. "Their atmosphere is like that of overpowering memory," Edward Thomas thought. "Never was child so tyrannous a father to the man."

Her account of de la Mare's early life turned out, Whistler explains, "rather like a row of late-nineteenth-century engravings." It begins in a small, overcrowded house in Charlton, now part of Woolwich, where Walter (always called Jack) was born in 1873, the sixth of seven children. When his father died, the family moved to Forest Hill. His biographer thinks that that these outer suburbs, on the shadowy borderline of London and country, were an image to him of persistent straying between dreaming and waking. In any case, he seems never to have lost the child's special faculties—daydreaming, make-believe, questioning. In middle age, he would still deliberately ask himself: what is it like to be a river? a house? a blind man? To him, as to Blake, the child was an exile who must make the best of his way home.

De la Mare was educated at St. Paul's Choir School, where, although not an angel chorister, he did well enough. "Music," he thought, "even if not closely attended to, is on this earth what the soul can unwittingly breathe, to its infinite benefit." At the age of sixteen, he started as a copy clerk with the Anglo-American Oil Company. In the evenings he sat down to study grammar and poetry. "When he opened his books his real day's work began." Although the office was not congenial, the Nineties were, and it seems that he was drawn to stories of the exquisite and the violent, and grew his hair to an aesthetic length. It was at this point that he changed the spelling of his name from Delamare, to emphasize his Huguenot ancestry. But his nights of self-education began with words. "Sound and meaning are inseparable," he wrote in "How I Became an Author," "and the words themselves become the means of make-believe—one of the richest of human consolations." He was turning himself into a wordmaster—a craftsman in sound "beyond Music's faintest Hark!" Meanwhile, he had a growing collection of editors' rejection slips.

De la Mare met his wife, Elfrida Ingpen, at an amateur dramatic society. She was more than ten years older than him, and they did not marry until 1899, by which time Elfie, perhaps in desperation, had become pregnant. (Whistler believes that de la Mare was passionately interested in birth and death, but not in sex.) He did, in any case, the decent thing, struggling to support four children on £3 a week. Worry about money, he said, "thrust its foul nose into [my] thoughts," although Elfie was an excellent manager, "working tirelessly to preserve whatever small graces of living she could, since they meant so much to Jack."

De la Mare was less cautious than Eliot in escaping from his city desk. The order of release came through Henry Newbolt, then literary editor of the *Monthly Review*, who began to accept de la Mare's verses and stories. In 1908, Newbolt (a great fixer) succeeded in getting him a grant of £200 from the Civil List. On the strength of that, he gave in his notice to the Oil and scarcely thought of it again. By now he was in the generous care of the Settee, which consisted of Newbolt, living in mysterious harmony with his wife, Margaret, nicknamed "Lad," and his mistress, Ella Coltman, Margaret's cousin. The writer Mary Coleridge made up a gracious fourth. De la Mare, who had been used since he was a little boy to a protective female household, responded and expanded, while Elfie, usually not invited by the Settee, aged rapidly in the cramped house in SE20.

He still worked very hard, reviewing, reading for Heinemann—both tasks that ground away the soul—and writing, at the rate of about fifteen hundred words a day, novels which were ventures into "the other real." The novels made their way slowly. When, however, *The Listeners and Other Poems* and *Peacock Pie* both came out in 1911, de la Mare became one of the best-loved poets in England. The following Christmas, when Eddie Marsh collected his first volume of *Georgian Poetry*, he included five poems from *The Listeners*, and for de la Mare "invitations multiplied—to join the English Association and the Omar Khayyam Club, to improve André Gide's conversational English, to lunch with Asquith at 10 Downing Street. . . . De la Mare accepted and accepted."

The years of success are a biographer's nightmare. Friends and patrons begin to crowd the page, but all are firmly dealt with by Whistler, who concentrates on those who "seemed to give fresh bearings on my theme." This means that some loyal supporters (Percy Withers, for example, and Sydney Cockerell) hardly get a mention, but there is a close and sympathetic account of the dearest friend of all, Edward Thomas, who actually got de la Mare to take a five-mile walk. The two of them loved England's earth and sky perhaps about equally, although de la Mare valued the past not for its weight of history but simply for its pastness. This partly accounts for his disconcerting goblin diction, "the dusk of words"—*pelf, hark, nay, shoon, e'en, saith*, and so on. Thomas couldn't be doing with this, and said so, but their friendship held.

Equally careful is the chapter on the handsome journalist Naomi Royde Smith. Said by Storm Jameson to be like the younger Queen Victoria, she might be considered a tiresome woman, but Mrs. Whistler makes us see how de la Mare came to love her for nearly five years. She herself was certain that it was good for her to be with him—it was not good, of course, for Elfie—and he waited until 1930 to describe what he had felt in *Memoirs of a Midget*. "The core of the book is the Midget's passion for the full-sized Fanny, beautiful and false," Whistler says. "The condition itself is unmistakeably what he had known for Naomi."

Imagination of the Heart shows de la Mare, by and large, as he describes himself in *A Portrait*—a child gone gray, "haunted by questions never answered yet"—and his day-to-day life is given in absorbing detail. The one thing missing is the different climate of artistic and intellectual correctness that was developing around him almost without his noticing it. In 1912, for instance, the Post-Impressionist Exhibition had been open a year, the Ballets Russes had made their first visit, and Conrad Aiken had arrived in London with *Prufrock* for sale, while Yeats had given warning that in future his poetry would be walking naked. Meanwhile, Barrie was causing the Peter Pan statue to "appear" in Kensington Gardens, and Constable was bringing out *Peacock Pie*. Walter de la Mare's strangeness and greatness might have detached themselves more clearly against a middle distance.

In "The Old Man," written when he was about fifty, he had thought of the old as caged and riddle-rid, lost to Earth's "Listen!" and "See!", but nothing of the kind happened to him, and Theresa Whistler has a long, tranquil, attentive old age to record. It wasn't that he had nothing to suffer. Elfie declined slowly and painfully, and his younger daughter, Jinnie, became an alcoholic. But Florence, his eldest, was at hand, as his sister Flo had been, and a private nurse, Nathalie Saxton (to whom the book is dedicated), devoted herself to him entirely. In fact, Walter de la Mare was spoiled for eighty-three years, as poets probably should be. He knew this and was grateful for it, as he would be grateful for this fine biography.

1993

The Consolations of Housman

"I can no more define poetry," A. E. Housman wrote in 1928, "than a ter-
rier can define a rat when he comes across one; and I recognise poetry
by definite physical sensations, either down the spine, or at the back of
the throat, or in the pit of the stomach"—a warning, surely, that poetry
can't be usefully argued about. Housman also said that he didn't begin
to write it until the "really emotional part of my life [that is, his unre-
turned love for Moses Jackson] was over." I accept what Housman
says—no biographer has made it much clearer, nor does Tom Stoppard's
play *The Invention of Love.*

Last Poems came out in 1922, when I was nearly six years old, and in
fact my copy is a first edition, published by Grant Richards, with discreet "printer's flowers" at the end of each poem. Most of them had been
written much earlier and recall *A Shropshire Lad*'s themes of guilt, longing, distance, absence, the dead friend, and the soldier who trades in his
life for thirteen pence a day ("everything comes un-stuck," as George
Orwell complained, while admitting grudgingly that Housman was
likely to be immortal). But in *Last Poems* there is more relaxation of
Housman's glacial severity:

> *I, a stranger and afraid,*
> *In a world I never made.*

He has been born, however, as we all are, within the confine of the
laws of God and the laws of man. The daily effort has to be made. "Oh
often have I washed and dressed," Housman says:

> *Ten thousand times I've done my best*
> *And all's to do again.*

England, meanwhile, is beautiful (and was much more so in 1922), and
at the end of *Last Poems* is the unforgettable "Tell me not here," a
description of his own border country, so quiet that a single pine cone
falling to the ground and the cuckoo that "shouts all day at nothing" are
the loudest sounds in it. But he reminds us that although we may be

beguiled, as he was, for a lifetime, it will be at our own risk. "Heartless, witless nature" makes no response to us whatsoever.

These are the verses of a reserved, unbending man who was first a clerk at the Patent Office, then a meticulous Professor of Latin. I cannot explain why I find them such a great consolation.

1998

M. R. JAMES

Monty and His Ghosts

An introduction to
The Haunted Dolls' House and Other Stories

There is something dismaying in a life with nothing to regret and nothing to hide. In the case of Montague Rhodes James, however, this has to be accepted. "No loveless childhood to be thrust out of mind," wrote his biographer, Michael Cox, "no parental iniquities to be kept secret." Monty (as he preferred to be called) did not like talking about himself. How much, in fact, did he have to say?

He was the fourth and youngest child of the rector of Livermere, near Bury St. Edmunds. Born in 1862, he spent almost his entire life between Eton and King's College, Cambridge, the two foundations of Henry VI. After entering Eton (on his second attempt) as a King's Scholar in autumn 1876, he spent there, as he always acknowledged, the happiest years he could remember. He was twenty years old before he left Eton. Passing on to King's he took a double first in classics and was appointed Junior Dean, Dean, Provost, and, in 1913, Vice-Chancellor of the University. During this time he had made himself one of the leading authorities on the Apocryphal Books of the Bible and on western medieval manuscripts. In 1918, just before the armistice, he was called back to Eton as Provost. In 1930 he received the Order of Merit. He died in his Lodge in June 1936, while in Chapel they were singing the *Nunc dimittis*.

Monty's sedate memoirs are called *Eton and King's* (1926). "It's odd," Lytton Strachey wrote after reading them, "that the Provost of Eton should still be aged sixteen. A life without a jolt."

Monty never married, although he remained on affectionate terms with his brothers and sister, and acquired, in the course of time, a surrogate family. They were the widow and daughter of a pupil who became a friend, James McBryde. McBryde died early, and Monty became guardian to little Jane, taking his responsibilities very seriously. But he was still a bachelor, and a late-Victorian bachelor at that. It has been pointed out that in every photograph of Monty, from his childhood to his seventies, he has the same benevolent but almost expressionless look, latterly behind round, wire-rimmed spectacles. Probably he felt the greatest pressure on him in 1905, when he was appointed Provost of King's. "You will have to get a Provostess, that's that," a distinguished friend told him. And Monty, well used to deflecting this argument, would hint at his admiration for a certain actress who was appearing in *Peter Pan*, but nothing came of it. Much more important to him, although what he said about it is not on record, was the question of ordination. Like Lewis Carroll, he became a deacon but never a priest.

Monty is remembered today for his ghost stories. They are entirely his own, written in an irresistibly appealing manner, in accordance with rules which he had invented for himself. Writing at the end of the 1920s about contemporary "tales of the supernatural," he said, "They drag in sex . . . which is a fatal mistake; sex is tiresome enough in the novels; in a ghost story, or as the backbone of a ghost story, I have no patience with it." Certainly sex doesn't trouble his protagonists. It is their unclouded innocence, combined with their serious scholarship, which is precisely Monty's strong card. By way of contrast there are deferential inn-keepers, agents, and chambermaids, who may know a little more than their employers, may wink or smile, but are a thousand miles from guessing the shocking truth.

It would be a mistake to think of these stories as something separate from his life. His predilection began early. His biographer quotes from a contribution to the *Eton Rambler* in 1880 (when he was seventeen):

Everyone can remember a time when he has carefully searched his curtains—and poked in the dark corners of his room before retiring to rest— with a sort of pleasurable uncertainty as to whether there might not be a saucer-eyed skeleton or a skinny-chested ghost in hiding somewhere. I invariably go through this ceremony myself.

To the skeleton and the ghost we may add spiders, owls, the sound of voices talking just out of earshot, a creature covered with long hair, a figure cloaked or cowled or with its head in a sack. The Apocrypha, too, which had fascinated him very early and continued to do so all his life, has been described by Richard Holmes as "a somewhat twilight field, neither orthodox Biblical studies nor entirely medieval folklore, and it contains many strange presences, such as Solomon and the Demons." At the same time, Monty's recreations remained guileless—long bicycle rides with two or three friends, church music, animal grab sometimes in the evenings, then (like Anderson in "Number 13") "his supper, his game of patience, and his bed."

Having written "Canon Alberic's Scrap-Book" some time after April 1892 (when he visited St. Bertrand-de-Comminges in the Pyrenees) but before 1893 (when he read it aloud to the Chitchat Club in Cambridge), and "Lost Hearts" at about the same time, Monty produced his ghost stories at regular intervals, and read them to a Christmas audience of friends in his rooms at King's, blowing out every candle but one. They were published at regular intervals: 1904, *Ghost Stories of an Antiquary*; 1911, *More Ghost Stories of an Antiquary*; 1919, *A Thin Ghost*; 1925, *A Warning to the Curious*; and 1931, *The Collected Ghost Stories*, for which he wrote five additional pieces, "There Was a Man Dwelt by a Church-yard," "Rats," "After Dark in the Playing Fields," "Wailing Well," and "Stories I Have Tried to Write." He also wrote a preface, in which he cautiously answered the question, did he believe in ghosts: "I am pre-pared to consider evidence and accept it if it satisfies me." That is to say, he used the same criteria as he did in his life as a scholar, teacher, and administrator.

"Places have been prolific in suggestion," he wrote. The stories are not only set in, but arise from real localities, and Monty himself was a deeply engaged traveler, with his map spread out on his knee—like Mr. Davidson, for example, in "The Uncommon Prayer-Book," who spends the first morning of his holiday taking a train a couple of stations west-ward and walking back to his hotel along the river valley. Denmark, Swe-den, Felixstowe, Belchamp St. Paul in Essex—not exotic places, but that is why he selects them—respectable hotel rooms, libraries, cathedral cities, modest country houses, seaside towns out of season, dark passages leading to candlelit bedrooms where there is something wrong with the window. The reader, of course, is always one or more steps ahead of the victim, and would like to tell him not to pick up objects from archaeo-logical sites, or to put his hand on carved figures on a choir-stall, or, if he dreams, that it is only a dream.

But that would not be quite accurate, because in *Ghost Stories of an Antiquary* Monty introduces dreams that wonderfully suggest the feeling of suffocation and powerlessness that comes with "dreaming true." There is Stephen Elliot's dream of a figure of a "dusty leaden colour" lying (and smiling) in an old disused bath, W.R.'s dream of a sickeningly bloodstained Punch and Judy show, Professor Parkins's dream (or vision) of a man desperately climbing over the groynes on Felixstowe beach, Mr. Dillet's dream (or nightmare) in "The Haunted Dolls' House." They are equally likely to be projected from the past (like Frank's in "The Rose Garden") or from the immediate and unescapable future. In either case, they anticipate the climax of the story, but don't diminish it. Whether Monty himself was troubled by dreams I don't know. In January 1907 he told Arthur Benson (who noted it in his diary) that he was only happy in bed or looking at manuscripts. This hardly sounds like a dreamer, but I am not sure that Monty told Arthur Benson the whole truth.

He was, from first to last, a man of books. "The library was the obvious place for the after-dinner hours. Candle in hand and pipe in mouth, he moved round the room for some time, taking stock of the titles." This is from "Mr. Humphreys and His Inheritance," but might just as well be about its author. With old-fashioned courtesy he welcomes his readers to his world, just as, when Provost of King's, he welcomed students and friends with tobacco and whisky decanters already laid out in the hall, while the lock had been replaced by a plain handle. A natural mimic in real life, he could imitate the style of any period that interested him—it seemed less a deliberate imitation than a natural process, like protective coloring. There was Medieval Latin, of course, the "fragments of ostensible erudition," as he called them, which persuade us into accepting as real the manuscripts, the inscriptions, the "rather rare and exceedingly difficult book, the *Sertum Steinfeldens Norbertinum*." This last is in the possession of a Mr. Somerton, an antiquary, but his story, "The Treasure of Abbot Thomas," takes place in 1859, and Monty is careful to adjust himself to that date, three years before he himself was born. "Martin's Close" begins "some four years ago" but consists largely of the verbatim report of the trial in 1684 (it is said to be in seventeenth-century shorthand, so there has been some delay in translating it) of George Martin for the murder of a half-witted girl, Ann Clark. Lord Chief Justice Jeffreys is the judge, and Monty, using, as he says, the State Trials, has reproduced Jeffreys' style so exactly that it seems ventriloquism. Almost as good, and almost as chilling, is the diary of Archdeacon Haynes from August 1816 onwards in "The Stalls of Barchester Cathedral." Monty approaches slowly. First he tells us that he read an obituary of Haynes "quite by chance" in an old copy of *The Gentleman's Magazine*, then, "quite lately," he is cataloguing the manuscripts of the college to which he belongs. The first hint of something unusual comes when the librarian says he is "pretty sure" that a certain box is one that the old Master of the college said they should never have accepted. It contains the diary. Now Monty has shut the trap on us. He can rely on the guilt and fascination that all of us feel when we open a private diary. The placing of the entry "There *is* no kitchen cat" is a masterstroke.

Ghosts, he declared (in his introduction to *More Ghost Stories*), should be "malevolent or odious," never amiable or helpful. The haunted should be "introduced in a placid way, undisturbed by forebodings, pleased with their surroundings, and in this calm environment let the ominous thing put out its head." This may be the result, by accident or design, of long-buried secrets, setting retribution to work. Something of the kind seems almost a professional hazard for his visiting scholars and librarians. They have to face, also (in one of Monty's own phrases), "the malice of inanimate objects," such objects as the wallpaper in "The Diary of Mr. Poynter" (who lives quietly with his aunt) and the sand-filled whistle in " 'Oh, Whistle, and I'll Come to You, My Lad.'" He speaks, too, of the rules of folklore, and says he has tried to make his ghosts act in ways "not inconsistent with them." One of the rules of folk stories is that the bad shall come to bad ends, and to this Monty was faithful. But the good (whose only failing may be that they have lived undisturbed so far) are rewarded rather unequally. Take, for example, what to my mind is the best story he ever wrote, "The Story of a Disappearance and an Appearance." W.R.'s uncle has not been a wrongdoer, has no hideous secret like Mr. Abney in "Lost Hearts," hasn't disturbed any long-dead or made any rash experiments, or (most unwise of all) bought or borrowed any questionable old books. In W.R.'s dream of Punch and Judy there is "a sturdy figure clad in black and, as I thought, wearing bands: his head was covered with a whitish bag." This must be a projection of Uncle Henry, but Monty does not explain why he should be there, and seems to have come in this story as close as he ever did to compulsive writing, or being carried away. There is true inspiration in the names of the Punch and Judy men—Foresta & Calpigi, which changes to Kidman & Gallop.

How seriously did he take these stories? "I am told that they have given pleasure of a certain sort to my readers," he wrote. "If so, my whole object in writing them has been attained." It was his lifelong habit not to make too much of things. However, they were more than a diversion, they were a declaration of his position. From his schooldays onward he not only disliked but detested maths and science. In *Eton and King's* he reduces both these subjects and their teachers to a stream of mildly satirical stories. "As a warning to scientists I must record how a question of mine, to which I really desired an answer, was met by [Mr. Carpenter]. 'Sir, what is the difference between a frog and a toad?' 'Well, that's perfectly simple; one's Rana, and the other's Bufo.' I am convinced that there must be a better solution than that." T. H. Huxley he referred to as "a coarse nineteenth-century stinks man." Mathematics he equated with suffering. He extended his disapproval, which was more like an intense physical reaction, to philosophy. When he was Dean of King's he overheard two undergraduates disputing a problematic point, and, according to his colleague Nathaniel Wedd, he rapped on the table sharply with his pipe and called out: "No thinking, gentlemen, please!" "Thought," Wedd notes in his unpublished memoirs, "really did disturb Monty throughout his life." What truly distressed him, however, was the division of King's into the Pious and the Godless (Wedd himself, although an admirer of Monty's, was an agnostic), while in the Cavendish Laboratory young physicists were at work—with cardboard and string, it was said—constructing new models of a world without God. It was, of course, not scientific accuracy Monty objected to—that was necessary to all scholarship—but a sense that mankind was occupying the wrong territory. In 1928, toward the end of his life, he spoke at Gresham's School in defense of an education in the humanities as against "modern invention or the most intimate knowledge of things that have no soul."

"'Oh, Whistle, and I'll Come to You, My Lad'" is the story which in literal fact is about a "sheeted ghost"—it has "a horrible, an intensely horrible face of *crumpled linen*." Its victim is Professor Parkins, said to be the Professor of Ontography, which I suppose makes him an expert on things as they are. He is certainly a scientist, "young, neat, and precise of speech," and emphatically a disbeliever, above all in ghosts. Disarmingly, Monty gives Parkins credit where it is due. He is "something of an old woman—rather hen-like, perhaps," but "dauntless and severe in his convictions, and a man deserving of the greatest respect." He is also the man who, after he has summoned his gruesome visitor, would either have fallen out of the window or lost his wits if help had not come. "There is nothing more to tell, but, as you may imagine, the Professor's views on certain points are less clear-cut than they used to be. His nerves, too, have suffered." So, faced by the obstinate disbeliever, Monty takes his not-so-mild revenge.

2000

THE WORLD OF *PUNCH*

Thin, Fat, and Crazy

When *Punch*, a year ago, gave an elaborate-sounding party for its 150th anniversary, I didn't go, feeling that the celebrations were unfortunately out of place. This year, 1992, the tough little paper has quietly given up publication. I rang up the offices to ask what was going to become of the Table round which the editorial staff had sat, for a century and a half, to decide on the week's political cartoons— the Mahogany Tree, as Thackeray called it, although it's really made of deal, and on which generations of staffers have carved their names. What would become of it? They didn't know. It was as though they had been stunned by an expected, rather than an unexpected, blow. And in fact the death of a humorous paper is a serious thing.

My father, E. V. Knox, was the editor of *Punch* from 1932 to 1949. His connection with the paper started long before that. His first contribution (not accepted) was sent in four years after the death of Queen Victoria. At that time he was a poet, indeed he always remained one, but he was too diffident ever to say much about it. He admired A. E. Housman, and in particular a seemingly effortless couplet like

> *I, a stranger and afraid,*
> *In a world I never made.*

He admired G. K. Chesterton and R. L. Stevenson, and he very much admired Mark Twain. Meanwhile, he went up to London from Birmingham, in the industrial Midlands, as a young man determined to earn a living, at a time when one of a writer's highest ambitions was to get something into *Punch*. A joke was said either to be, or not to be, "good enough for *Punch*." Once in, it was repeated and admired as the paper circulated out to the limits of the British colonies. Arriving by sea several weeks later it was ready to be appreciated again. Durability was essential to a joke in those days. Of course it might well have been produced, as my father's certainly were, by an almost desperate young man in lodgings who polished his boots every morning in order to be smart enough to call on London's editors.

I would like to take a look at two of my father's remarks—or rather asides, for everything that was of real importance to him he said as an aside:

1. "What is the difference between journalism and literature? None, except that journalism is paid, and literature is not." Here, like a true professional, he is speaking up for his trade, but he is also defending, I think, the concept of lightness—"light verse" in particular. This kind of verse, which was a specialty of *Punch*, and at which he himself excelled, is often the last resort for subjects that have got beyond rational comment. It struck my father, as it struck a good many others, that the world was increasingly ruled by misguided people, in that they no longer seemed able to create a system that benefited even themselves. They could only be appropriately described in light verse.

2. He once said that humorists, if it was necessary to understand them at all, could be divided into fat men and thin men, although they could on occasion take each other's parts. Thin men are, of course, dangerous, and they are resentful, indignant, clear-sighted, possibly savage. They either have less (or more to suffer) than others, or remember what it is to have less, or can identify with those who have less. Ovid, Villon's *Testaments*, *Gulliver's Travels*, *Mansfield Park*, *A Connecticut Yankee in King Arthur's Court*, *The Catcher in the Rye* are thin persons' books. Fat men are genial, expansive, company-loving, seem to make the sun shine simply by coming into a room, and so forth. Horace, irrespective of his personal appearance and his personal situation, was a fat man. *Barchester Towers*, *Diary of a Nobody*, *Carry On, Jeeves*, *Lake Wobegon Days* are fat men's books, providing, as thin men's books don't, consolation.

During the eighteenth century, a third kind of comic genius arrived, the fantasist. "She went into the garden to cut a cabbage-leaf, to make an apple-pie; and at the same time a great she-bear, coming up the street, pops its head into the shop. 'What, no soap?' So he died, and she very imprudently married the barber." This was part of a monologue by Samuel Foote (1720–1777), who liked to give one-man performances because they cost him almost nothing. He defied anyone else to memorize "She went into the garden." But it was not nonsense, it was free association, and so, on a grand scale, was *Tristram Shandy*. Beyond this, Sterne claimed to have a philosophical backing for his novel, that is, Locke's claim that the mind's association of ideas is based on something other than reason. As Freud put it, "it is easier to mix up things than to distinguish them, and it is particularly easy to travel over modes of reasoning unsanctified by logic." Possibly easier, and certainly more amusing.

There you have it, then. Humorists are either thin, fat, or crazy. And yet Thackeray, one of the earliest of *Punch*'s contributors, wrote that "the humorous writer professes to awaken and direct your love, your pity, your kindness; your scorn of untruth, pretension, imposture; your tenderness for the weak, the poor, the oppressed, the unhappy. To the best of his means and ability he comments on all the ordinary actions and passions of life almost." And this, also, is true.

Punch started out in 1841 in rather confused circumstances—there were several other journals with the same name—but most emphatically as a "thin" paper. It was violently radical, campaigned against capital punishment, prostitution, slums, and the brutishness of Members of Parliament, attacked the Prince Consort, named names, and joked recklessly about Jack Ketch, the hangman, and the suicides from Waterloo Bridge. The cover design was settled only after a few hits and misses. It was by Richard Doyle (who later left the paper because as a Catholic he could not stomach the violent attacks on the Pope) and showed the figure of Mr. Punch leering disreputably and somewhat the worse for drink. Toby sits beside him, sunk in the true Toby-dog's melancholy. Punch's followers are from the procession in Titian's *Bacchus and Ariadne* in London's National Gallery; they are supposed to have fled to his protection from the Gallery's incompetent picture-restorers. This cover appeared, with only minor modifications, every week until the 1950s, and when, largely at the insistence of bookstall managers, it was abandoned, *Punch's* fortunes departed with it. The paper's finances were precarious—Mark Lemon, one of the original editors, had to write and sell farces to meet the weekly printing bills and the early statement of aims was pitched pretty low—much lower, for instance, than Ross's in the first number of *The New Yorker*, which offered to "present the truth and the whole truth without fear or favor." *Punch*'s writers were all anonymous, the editor's name was never listed, and the tone was wonderfully convivial and uncompromisingly "low"—what was then called a "chophouse" or "pot-house atmosphere." But from the start *Punch* was ferociously political, and at the height of its influence could be seen, in celebrated cartoons, reproving Gladstone and Disraeli (shown as two tiresome schoolboys) for throwing mud at each other, or riding onto the battlefield to reproach Napoleon III. In a casual and very characteristic way, the paper, which had been expected to last only a few years, acquired power without ever meaning to.

The subjects of the cartoons were settled—and continued to be settled, as far as I know, to the very end—at a weekly dinner, which later became lunch, round the *Punch* table. In May 1859, after Disraeli had presented his Reform Bill to the House of Commons, "we begin discussing politics even before the venison. . . . Thackeray thinks of workmen coming among gentlemen of Parliament and asking 'What have you done for me?'"

Of course, the riotous staff of the early days had never given up their right to turn serious at the appropriate moment. That was always understood, even though Mark Lemon had announced the first issue as "an asylum for the thousands of orphan jokes now wandering about without so much as a shelf to rest upon." No editor ever made a decision comparable with Ross's when he allocated a whole number to John Hersey's report on Hiroshima, but in 1843 (in the Christmas number) Lemon printed Thomas Hood's *Song of the Shirt*. Hood sent it in rather diffidently, saying it could be thrown away if not wanted. But *Punch* did want it, and the ballad of the South London seamstress who got five farthings a shirt, out of which she had to find her own needles, was translated into every language in Europe. The circulation of *Punch* tripled. Hood was gratified, but was obliged to point out that he was dying. Death's door, he said, had opened so wide that he could distinctly hear its hinges creak.

Punch, at this point, had the chance of turning into the English *Simplissimus* or *Krokodil*, a risk-taking satirical weekly in the European mode. But by the 1860s it had grown less political, and, under Thackeray's influence, much less radical. On the other hand, it acquired a succession of fine black-and-white artists—John Leech, Charles Keene, George du Maurier, Linley Sambourne, Phil May—who turned the mid- and late-Victorian *Punch* into a superb journal of record. As a small girl I used to sit on rainy afternoons in the corner of the dining room, where the old bound volumes of *Punch* were kept, turning the pages and entering, without needing to understand, the quite different worlds of Keene and du Maurier. Keene, the greatest genius of them all, drew London, Paris, and Scotland exactly as he saw them. As Forrest Reid puts it in his *Illustrators of the 1860s*, "he left nothing to chance. . . . If he wanted to draw a typewriter or an old boot he procured his original; if he wanted a turnip field for a background, out he tramped into the country till he found one. Frequently he made use of himself as a model, keeping a large mirror in his studio for the purpose—a habit not without its drawbacks, as the trousers of some of his 'swells' bear witness." It's true that you hardly ever find a pair of unwrinkled trousers in Keene. His is a world of drunks and railway porters and cabdrivers (also often drunk, and almost always abusive), of umbrellas glistening in wet streets, snug firesides, and stout wives. With du Maurier, on the other hand, you are with the Duchesses, in drawing rooms and concert halls, surrounded by the absurd musicians and artists they patronize and the yet more absurd nouveaux riches who are gently but decisively put in their place. "I have generally stuck to the 'classes' because Keene seems to have monopolised the 'masses,'" du Maurier said, but in any case he conducted a lifelong romance with a half-imaginary English aristocracy, improbably tall and elegant, with drooping moustaches and casual male strength corresponding to womanly beauty, dark or blonde, inherited from numerous generations. To Henry James it seemed that Keene expressed himself in terms of ugliness, and du Maurier in terms of beauty. I don't quite know what he meant by this. The lights and shades of Keene's umbrellas and bony cab horses are surely beautiful, if the quality of the drawing is to count for anything at all.

But are the jokes funny? *Punch*, after all, can't be judged entirely by its contribution to social and political history. The usual answer, I think, would be that the jokes themselves have become a joke. There are too many words, too much explanation, and too many comments by the artist ("collapse of stout party" was one of Keene's). Here is one of du Maurier's, for 31 March 1883. The scene is a musical soirée, where the young ladies will shortly be asked to sing at the piano.

DANGERS OF INDISCRIMINATE PRAISE

(A CAUTION TO MOTHERS)

MRS TOMLINSON (*to extremely eligible young lady*): 'I'M SURE YOU'LL LIKE MY SON RICHARD, MY DEAR MISS GOLDMORE; NOT THAT HE'S EXACTLY BRILLIANT, YOU KNOW, BUT HE'S SO STEADY AND GOOD. SPENDS ALL HIS EVENINGS AT HOME, AND ALWAYS IN BED BY ELEVEN! HE'S NEVER GIVEN ME AN HOUR'S UNEASINESS IN HIS LIFE!'

'GOOD GRACIOUS!' EXCLAIMS MISS GOLDMORE, AND INSTANTLY CON-
CEIVES FOR RICHARD A FRANTIC AVERSION. (*Which is not lessened when
she discovers that he's that modest youth in the background, pulling on
his gloves.*)

This directs us to the background of the picture, where we can see the
modest youth, who probably shouldn't be pulling on his gloves, since the
other men don't seem to be wearing them, and we can see too that he is
short and stout, crimes in the eyes of du Maurier. Du Maurier called his
text, with its stage directions at the end, his "scrawl."

Some of the scrawls, of course, take much longer to get to the point.
"Indiscriminate Praise" is a fair average. But the fact is that these are not
jokes at all, but what the nineteenth century thought of as "good things,"
that is scenes or moments which, like James Joyce's epiphanies, express,
when they're successful, an entire relationship or even an entire lifetime.
One of the last of them, and perhaps the best loved of all, appeared in
October 1906. It was by Gunning King, an artist who modeled himself
on Charles Keene—a drawing of an old woman sitting by the fire.
"Sometimes I sits and thinks; and then again, sometimes I just sits." All
the resignation of old age and natural exhaustion are in the words and
the picture.

The last great Victorian editor of *Punch* was Francis Burnand, who
accepted "Sometimes I sits and thinks" and (as a serial) *The Diary of a
Nobody*. Burnand lived at Ramsgate, on the coast, and when he came up
to the *Punch* offices at 10 Bouverie Street, the staff knew he had arrived
from the loud thud as he took off his boots and threw them into the passage. As the new century advanced Burnand (who had been Sullivan's
librettist before Gilbert appeared) perhaps recognized himself as out of
place. In 1906 his efficient deputy editor, Owen Seaman, took over. Seaman was a good organizer, a skilled writer of verse, and a dignified man
of the world who knew everyone and went everywhere. His one weakness was the (in his own view) guilty secret that his family had been "in
trade"—his father had been a ladies' haberdasher. The fact that this
should have weighed so heavily with Seaman (later Sir Owen) is an ominous sign of the stifling respectability that gradually overtook the paper.
Punch after the First World War became not only conservative but a conservative institution. What it offered its still-faithful readers was not so
much humor (for Seaman believed humor should be taken seriously) as

whimsicality and the killing sayings of young children. This meant, however, that he welcomed the Christopher Robin poems, although he could never get on personally with A. A. Milne, considering him a dangerous radical.

Seaman was persuaded to resign with the greatest difficulty in 1932. My father then had to see the paper through the end of the slump and the rise of the dictators, which *Punch* most consistently opposed. The management talked him into staying on through the Second World War (he had been seriously wounded in the first one), during which the circulation reached two hundred thousand copies, the highest in its history. He had also, from a professional point of view, to face something that Seaman had regarded with horror, the challenge of the crazy man in the form of American (or, as it was usually called, *New Yorker*) humor. The idea of this, fortunately, didn't at all distress my father, who, quietly correct though he seemed, had always been attracted by the point where poetry and humor meet and forget, for the moment, their responsibilities. 21 July 1937 was the significant date when *Punch* printed the "hippopotamus" joke. Two hippopotamuses are basking side by side in the river; one of them says, "I keep thinking it's Tuesday." Impossible now to convey how deeply the readership was divided as to whether this was funny or could ever have been meant to be funny. And if it was funny, still it was surely not British.

In 1953 the management brought in Malcolm Muggeridge as editor. He was expected to overhaul everything completely, to find new writers and new social and political material, and (for the first time in more than a hundred years) to introduce jokes that hinted, at least, at sex. All these things he did, but after only four years he lost, not his nerve, but his interest in reforming the paper and in what, to him, was the agonizing business of making the British public laugh. I don't think that anything would be gained by following the courageous struggles of the editors that came after him. Historians are never agreed about the point of no return.

To me, *Punch* means the old Fleet Street, which has itself disappeared, with the paper lorries maneuvering down narrow lanes to the printing presses, and the Law Courts and the Houses of Parliament within shouting distance. When the newspapers migrated and the art of printing was transformed I still believed that *Punch* would survive. But I was quite wrong, *Punch* is dead. At the end of the marionette play, which you can still see on the beach or at the fairground, Punch, having got the better of his wife, his baby, his dog, his doctor, and the crocodile, succumbs to the hangman and the undertaker, but—if the text is followed out to the sardonic end—comes back to life in time to collect the audience's money. But for the once loved and feared old weekly there is no hope of resurrection. Although for several years there hadn't been much in it worth reading, I still feel very much poorer for the loss.

1992

Evoe's Choice

Foreword to *In My Old Days*,
a selection of poems by the author's father, E. V. Knox
("Evoe"), privately printed by his widow in 1972

This selection of poems was made by Evoe himself in 1969. It covers nearly fifty years of his life—from 1909 to 1956—and he gave it the characteristically wry title of *In My Old Days*.

The majority of the poems appeared week by week in *Punch*, finished as it seemed miraculously just in time for the deadline—often while he was shaving—on whatever subject was interesting at the moment. In this way they form a kind of rueful commentary on English history through two world wars, though he himself would never have called them this. They were designed to amuse and touch the readers, and they did both. But every art is based on a craft. Evoe was a professional poet. If he had not known *how* to write verse he would not have written it. In his ear were the rhythms of Latin poetry. His children took it for granted that when their pets died and had to be buried in the back garden he would produce for them—even for a badger—a Latin epigraph composed on the spur of the moment. In this selection, "Embattled London" is written in Virgillian hexameters simply because they were appropriate. But the rhythms of English are even more difficult, because they are less law-abiding, than Latin. Evoe had great respect for the nineteenth-century masters, Calverley and Hood, but he set a standard which was distinctively his own. All his poems need to be read aloud. Only then do you notice—to take a single example—how skillfully he introduces the strange wildflower names into "A Meadow Wreath," until the poem, winding on to its sad conclusion, is like a wreath itself.

Light verse is a product of civilization, for it is a sign of being civilized to be able to treat serious things gracefully. The concern can be felt, however, beneath the surface. These poems range from the daily sufferings of the commuter and the humane man in a world apparently run by maniacs, to the deep faith Evoe felt in his own country ("Fiat Justitia"). Of the parodies (although Robert H. Ross in his *Georgian Revolt* (1967) has called him "the most persistent and masterful parodist of the Georgians") Evoe did not want to reprint much. He has kept "String, in Lieu of" (A. E. Housman), "Crooked Paths" (John Masefield), and "My Own Old Garden" (Walter de la Mare), all of them affectionate tributes rather than satires.

Just as his light verse is based on strong-mindedness, so his kindness was based on courage, and what always goes with true courage, reticence. To be thanked was for Evoe a dreadful experience. He was often unwilling even to be acknowledged. But something of what he was like can be guessed, even by those who never knew him, from the poems of *In My Old Days*.

1972

Kipper's Line

There must have been hundreds of people who called Ernest Shepard Kipper, or Kip. I used to think that the name was a variant of Skipper and had something to do with his boat, *Grey Owl*, which (though he had sold her by that time) went over with the little ships to Dunkirk. But he explained that he had been given it much earlier, in student days, when his friends considered him "a giddy kipper." It sounds late Victorian, and Kipper, although he had the gift of making the best of every day as it came, was, to the end, a late Victorian, most certainly in his professional life.

He was very highly trained, entering Heatherley's (which figures in Thackeray's *The Newcomers*) at the age of sixteen and winning a scholarship to the Academy Schools a year later, in 1897. He was preparing, if luck went his way, to be a full-dress, gold-framed, twice-yearly Academy exhibitor (his *Followers*, painted in 1904, was sold to the Durban Art Gallery), but when it became clear that he was a draftsman rather than a painter he was quite happy to settle, as Tenniel and Charles Keene had done before him, for illustrations and cartoons.

He worked hard and methodically, kept pretty well everything in case it might be useful later, and did all his preliminary sketches from life. There are innumerable notes of people, clothes, animals, and weather, sometimes no more than a passing shadow, or the effect of the wind on a hat brim.

Shepard collectors have nearly eighty years' work to consider. There are working notebooks, roughs and finished drawings for the weeklies, illustrations for a hundred or so books, ranging from a romantic novel called *Smouldering Fires* to Pepys and Boswell's *Life of Johnson* (the gray wig Kipper used for Dr. Johnson is still in the family dressing-up box), jokes and Second World War cartoons for *Punch*, travel sketches, English landscapes in oil and watercolor. It was part of his calm professionalism that he knew what he could and couldn't do. He never found it easy to get a likeness, even (or perhaps particularly) in 1945 when he became senior cartoonist of *Punch*. Nor could he manage the sheer indignation that gives political satire its weight, or the ruthless lines that he admired in Charles Keene and Phil May. What was more, there were some books which he felt couldn't be illustrated; he refused to try *Peter Pan*, for instance, just as Charlie Chaplin refused to act in it.

Kipper's specialty is the clear line based on his knowledge of how things, including the human body, work or how light falls, and above all of movement and relaxation. Once he had found his own distinctive style he was able to let his figures blow across the page, and in or out of it, with a kind of graceful and airy determination. When he was over eighty he still had the instinct for stir and movement. You can recognize it in one of his last original drawings, a study of his brother Cyril as a young man cutting long grass with a fag-hook. The braces are only just sketched in, but you can see how they take the strain.

Kipper himself was amiable, cheerful, hospitable, surprised at his own eventual fame, thought of, I suppose, as an "easy" man but not at all easy to fathom. His mild light blue eyes gave away very little. He had had to suffer at least some of life's hardest trials. His mother died when he was ten. Between 1915 and 1918 he served as a gunner officer and was awarded the MC, but his much-loved brother was killed during the first offensive on the Somme. After the war, when his children were born and he was beginning to be successful, his wife went into hospital for a minor operation and died of it. During the Second World War his only son, Graham, went down with his ship. Kipper, I think, never said much about these things, and indeed when he called on me after a loss of my own—a miscarriage—he handed me a bunch of flowers without a word.

My brother, Rawle Knox, who wrote the definitive biography, *The Work of E. H. Shepard*, thought that Kipper never changed, "until, perhaps, he grew too old to care very much; and if he ceased to care at the end, that was only because he was unable to work, and work—art—had meant more than anything else in life."

Kipper would cheerfully have admitted that all his work rose in value because of Christopher Robin and because of Pooh. His relationship with A. A. Milne was an unemotional, pipe-smoking, astoundingly successful collaboration, which began in 1924 between two men who never really got to know each other. But which of the two was really responsible for the immortality of Piglet, Pooh, and all the rest of them? Malcolm Muggeridge thought that Milne was not a childlike man in any way but liked children, and wrote about them from the outside as an approving adult, which was why adults were so fond of the books. Children only pretended to like Pooh in order to ingratiate themselves with the grownups. Here he was getting close to Winnie-the-Complex. Kipper, on the other hand, was certainly not either childish or childlike, but he had a certain transparency or luminosity of the memory which made him able to distinguish faultlessly between the inner life of children, animals, and toys.

When Milne was asked to dramatize *The Wind in the Willows* as *Toad of Toad Hall*, he complained about Kenneth Grahame's lack of logic. The river animals have to be thought of, he said, as sometimes human, sometimes not, sometimes walking on four legs, sometimes on two. But this no more worried Kipper than it had Beatrix Potter. He was able, too, as she had been, to indicate space and freedom, open air and fresh water, in a very small space, so that although his illustrations to *The Wind in the Willows* were in competition with Arthur Rackham's (which have a much better sense of the element of ancient fear in the book), they were a much greater success from the first with the readers. Grahame himself approved of them, and they have lately undergone another translation into Alan Bennett's current production for the National Theatre.

Ultimately, of course, like every artist of every century who gets it right, Kipper relied on certain moments of inspiration. He drew Winnie-the-Pooh, for example, from his son Graham's Growler, but the great improvement was in the placing of the eye, much lower down and further back than in any teddy bear before him, and certainly much lower than Growler's. The new position suggests little intelligence, but boundless loyalty and sweet temper. In this way the hard-working draftsman becomes a mythmaker.

1991

YEATS AND HIS CIRCLE

A Bird Tied to a String

John Butler Yeats: Letters to His Son W. B. Yeats and Others, 1869–1922, edited by Joseph Hone and abridged, with an Introduction, by John McGahern

In 1916, John Butler Yeats wrote to his younger son: "Hereafter, when I have become a silent member of the company existing only in memory, it will be pleasant to think that you have written to me many times. So do write." What could be more persuasive than this man and his letters?

J.B.Y. was descended from Church of Ireland rectors and was intended first for the Church, then for the Bar, but not long after his marriage to Susan Pollexfen, of Sligo, he threw up everything for an artist's career. Their family grew to two boys, William and Jack, and two girls, known as Lily and Lolly, and they moved in 1868 from Dublin to London, but J.B.Y. did not then or ever acquire any kind of business sense. He had inherited property, and there was no reason why he should not have lived on his income, but all was mortgaged and lost. Commissions for portraits he had, but took an obsessively long time to carry them out, and could not bring himself to charge enough for them. Willie maintained himself as a man of letters and Jack as a painter, but for their sisters there was no education and no prospect of marriage, and it was much to their credit that they made some sort of a living from embroidery and fine printing. In 1907, when his last mortgage was paid out, J.B.Y.'s tolerant friends raised a subscription to take him to Italy. But he preferred New York, and died there in February 1922, without ever returning to Ireland.

Two selections of his letters were published in his lifetime, then another, more comprehensive, in 1944, edited by Joseph Hone, the biographer of W. B. Yeats. From Hone's book, John McGahern, the novelist, has made this further selection. J.B.Y., he tells us in his compassionate introduction, "was a well-remembered presence in Dublin when I was young, sometimes referred to affectionately as 'the old man who ran away from home and made good.'" In fact, he scarcely did that, but as he himself insisted, "affection springs out of memory," even memory gone astray. These letters have been selected to show not only what W. B. Yeats's father was really like, but also the kindly myth that was created around him.

They are written to Lily, his favorite daughter, with a few to Lolly, to Oliver Elton, an old friend who became Professor of English at Liverpool University, to Ruth Hart, the dear daughter of another old friend, only one to Lady Gregory, several to John Quinn, his great American patron, but nearly half of them to W.B.Y. himself. After twenty-seven letters, J.B.Y. is permanently in New York, more often than not as a lodger of the Petitpas, three Breton sisters who ran (illegally, as it later turned out) a lodging house in West Twentieth Street. Here he continued drinking late and talking and writing, on the grand scale, on the things that mattered to him most—poetry and art. Sometimes he is inconsistent: the world, he says, must learn to reason less and feel more; art and poetry deal with what cannot be expressed in action or in thought, "being as inarticulate as the cry of a woman in childbirth." On the other hand, the world will not be right till poetry is pronounced to be life itself, our own lives being but shadows and poor imitations. And life means change, death being only one change the more.

McGahern says that "many of the son's central ideas came from the father," but there is no real meeting point here with W.B.Y.'s vision of cycles of recurrence. J.B.Y., in any case, did not believe—or said he didn't—in argument, rather that friends and enemies should give voice to their most deeply held opinions, side by side. W.B.Y. himself tells us, in his *Reveries Over Childhood and Youth*, that "it was only when I began to study psychical research and mystical philosophy that I broke away from my father's influence." But J.B.Y. has a largeness of utterance that warms the heart.

Sometimes he listens to the voice of conscience, but rather as if it was something imposed on him from the outside world. "A man shackled by impecuniosity is like a bird tied to a string. The bird thinks the string very long, as it sometimes is, and forgets it is there at all, and so flies up to tumble back distractedly." With the loan of a few dollars, which meant that he could treat his friends, the distraction passed.

I have been an unconscionable burden to you and George [W.B.Y.'s wife] on your comparatively slender resources and I do assure you that I have sleepless nights thinking of it. . . . When you see my magnum opus, I think you will forgive me. I mean it to be ahead of any portraits Quinn may have and to know this will soothe my last moments. 'Ripeness is all.'

This self-portrait was still not finished when he died, in the upstairs room of the Petitpas lodging house. "He lived in hope and I think the past hardly existed for him," W.B.Y. wrote to Lolly. He and his father had disputed bitterly. But there had once been a barber in Sligo who observed that "the Yeatses were always respectable," and both father and son drew comfort of a kind from that.

The illustrations are all pencil sketches (with one pen drawing) by J.B.Y. himself. Lady Gregory was surely right in saying that these were what he did best, because he had not the chance to get at them and alter them from the first impression.

1999

Too Long a Sacrifice

"Always Your Friend": The Gonne–Yeats Letters, 1893–1938,
edited by Anna MacBride White and A. Norman Jeffares

"An overpowering tumult" entered W. B. Yeats's life in 1889 when Maud Gonne, aged twenty-two, first arrived in a cab at his home in Bedford Park. This was in January, even though in *The Trembling of the Veil* Yeats speaks vaguely of a great heap of apple blossom, which her complexion rivaled. "She vexed my father by praise of war," and Willie Yeats, bowled over, felt compelled to support her arguments, which vexed his father even more. Later, it was revealed to him that such women come to dislike their own beauty because it is created from the antithetical self and will not allow them to develop their souls in peace.

Maud came with an introduction from the sister of the old Fenian John O'Leary. What is not clear is why she came at all. She had had a free and loving but unsettled childhood in Europe and Ireland, where her father had been posted with his regiment after the risings of 1868.

After his death she had lived in France and taken a middle-aged lover, a French politician, Lucien Millevoye. Both of them were agents of the Boulangists, called in this book "a strange mixture of republicans, royalists, and socialists" but sometimes described as proto-fascists. Later, she and Millevoye took a vow to join the world's violent protesters, he for Alsace-Lorraine, she for Ireland. In her high eagerness, Maud can surely never have hoped for much from John Butler Yeats, who was a moderate Home Ruler, and his student son, Willie.

Maud, led by "inspirations which come to me and always guide me right," gloried in public demonstrations and secret activities, stormy meetings and wild journeys. Yeats's place in Ireland's history was with the Revival and with literary politics. At times, he saw the contrast between himself and Maud ironically, as Maud could not. "I was sedentary and thoughtful; but Maud Gonne was not sedentary, and before some great events she did not think but became exceedingly superstitious. . . . Once upon the eve of some demonstration, I found her with many caged larks and finches which she was about to set free." Irony, however, never restricted the passion which Maud accepted, he wrote, "with scarce a pitying look." Being deeply engaged with Ireland's ancient presences, Oisin, Cuchulain, and Maeve, he began to create his own mythology for the twentieth century, where she could be assured of immortality:

> *Maud Gonne at Howth station waiting a train,*
> *Pallas Athene in that straight back and arrogant head.*

Were they ever lovers? George Moore, according to his own account, was the only person to put this question to Yeats directly, and he received a riddling reply. "There was about Yeats," wrote Michael Mac Liammoir, "as about so many respectably bred Irishmen, something endearingly old-maidish." Maud, on the other hand, disliked sex, except for the procreation of children. She refused Yeats's many proposals of marriage, but asked him for a spiritual union compared to which "material union is but a pale shadow." In this collection of letters there is a brief period, at the end of 1908, when she addressed him as "Dearest" instead of "Dear Willie" or "Dear Friend," but she also says that she has prayed for all earthly desire to be taken out of both her love and his, and, in December, that she believes that, if necessary, she could "let him marry another."

These letters are published here for the first time, and no one could ask for better editors than the two that Maud Gonne has been granted—Professor A. Norman Jeffares and her own granddaughter, Anna MacBride White. They have provided a detailed commentary, two introductions, a chronology, notes, and explanations of almost everything. These are not only closely researched but have about them the voice of prolonged friendly discussion—the voice of Dublin itself: "Let me see now, May Gonne, what was she to Maud?" There are, unfortunately, only twenty-nine letters from Yeats: "[MG] told me," says Professor Jeffares, "when Free State soldier raided her house in St. Stephen's Green, the great loss was that most of her papers were burned in the street and among them her letters from him." There is very little before 1923, although a draft is included of his plea to her not to marry John MacBride, on the curious grounds that if she took "one of the people" as a husband they would cease to trust her. Papers later than 1923 were stored elsewhere, and there are twelve further letters from Yeats. Here at last we have the two of them confronting each other, but by then their friendship had sunk to low ebb. "We will never change each other's politics," Yeats wrote. "They are too deeply rooted in our characters." Even their common interest in the unseen and in supernatural communication had begun to drift a little. "Now that you do so little occult work," she told him, "I never know at a distance as I used to what you are thinking. You did not even know when I was almost dying, & for three days almost unconscious & when I wrote to you the words didn't convey anything to you. I think you were astonished yourself they did not."

The correspondence covers forty-five years, during which time Maud had born another child to Millevoye and left him, founded the Young Ireland Society in Paris and the Daughters of Erin, opposed the Boer War, devised a plan to hide bombs in the coal-bunker of British troop-ships, appeared in Yeats's play *Cathleen ni Houlihan* as the personification of Ireland, was received into the Catholic Church, married the revolutionary John MacBride and divorced him for adultery and indecent behavior, started the Women Prisoners Defense League, nursed the war wounded, and fed, consoled, and took up the cause of many. Yeats, she soon felt, was not to be trusted with "the outer side of politics." When the two of them were trapped in a Dublin tea shop by demonstrators protesting at Queen Victoria's Diamond Jubilee, he refused to let her go out and face a charge by the police. "Do you know," she asked him (June 1897), "that to be a coward for those we love, is only a degree less bad than to be a coward for oneself. The latter I know well you are not, the former you know well you are." He had higher work to do, she told him, whereas she was born to be in the midst of a crowd. "For the honour of our country, the world must recognise you as one of the Great Poets of the century." He had been chosen to write poetry for the glory of Ireland. She would have rejected with indignant words Joyce's "Art has no purpose, but it has a cause." For her, the purpose and the cause were the same. She didn't like *Portrait of the Artist*, didn't like Yeats's "Easter 1916" (which he sent her after MacBride's execution). Both of them were unworthy of Ireland.

Yeats was also there to carry out errands. You cannot be Maud Gonne and devote yourself, soul and body, to a cause without making good use of those who happen to be helplessly in love with you. "My dear Willie, are you going to Sligo and when? If you are, will you try and do something for me not at all in your line. . . . There is a poor old man called Durkan who Lord Arran evicted under very hard circumstances"; "Could you get Mr. O'Leary to write a letter which could be published saying he is satisfied as to my Irish descent?" "I thank you for all the trouble you have taken for me—perhaps you will have to take a little more & get us all permission to return to Ireland." Anna MacBride White tells us that "Willie was the long-time friend remembered with affection, toleration and amusement," and there is a good deal of that in these letters, where Willie's help is treated as a kind of natural resource. When Maud's daughter Yseult made an unsatisfactory marriage, Yeats undertook to disentangle it. When her son Sean MacBride, who was opposed to the treaty of 1921, was arrested by the Free State Government forces, Yeats made himself responsible for the boy. When Maud herself was taken to Mountjoy Gaol in 1923, he wrote to Olivia Shakespear that the day before her arrest she had told him "that if I did not renounce the Government she renounced my society for ever. I am afraid my help in the matter of blankets, instead of her release (where I could do nothing), will not make her less resentful."

Meanwhile Yeats had married, and, however necessary he thought it to choose between perfection of the life and of the work, had become a harassed public man. He was disturbed by the increasing bitterness of Irish nationalism, and in particular by the way Maud was hurling the little streets against the great and, in the process, transforming herself into an old bellows full of angry wind. It seemed to him that her actions were based on hatred. "In 1910 or 1911," he wrote to her in 1927, "when you were working on the feeding of school children I met you in Paris & you told me that you were convinced that all the misfortunes of your life had come upon you because you had taken up movements which had hate for their motive power."

Maud's beauty had once made young and old stop and stare at her in the street (this, by the way, seems to have been a much commoner habit in Edwardian days). It faded early, although her dignity remained, as photographs show. In describing her to those who had never seen her, Yeats was defending her against Time, although he could hardly claim, as he did with Eva and Constance Gore-Booth, that Time was her only enemy. He had also cast his own heart into his verse, but Yeats, although painfully candid in poetry, was much less so in his memoirs. (Compare, for instance, Maud's letter of September 1903 about the opening of *Cathleen ni Houlihan* with the account in *Dramatis Personae*.) One of the objects of this book, Maud's granddaughter tells us, is to set the record straight and at the same time to save her from marginalization as no more than an "adjunct of Yeats." We are being asked to read the letters, not for old sake's sake, but for her own.

They show the ferociously busy life of a romantic revolutionary— Maud's day-to-day troubles, consoling spirit visions, very occasional times off when she went conger-eel fishing by moonlight in Clew Bay or painting in Seine-et-Marne ("but I am not made for a peaceful life"). Unfortunately, although she often recorded her dreams, "it never comes naturally to me to write of thoughts or impressions." Yeats noted in one of his journals, quoted by Jeffares, that her dread of the sexual relation probably affected her whole life, "checking natural and instinctive selection and leaving fantastic duties free to take its place." In terms of his vision, however, she was a Helen born out of her time and mismatched to her phase of the moon, to whom Ireland could not offer an adequate catastrophe. These explanations may have satisfied Yeats. Maud herself comes close to one when she writes (July 1900),

> I have chosen a life which to some might be hard, but which to me is the only one possible. I am not unhappy only supremely indifferent to all that is not my work or my friends. One cannot go through what I went through & have any personal human life left, what is quite natural & right for me is not natural or right for one who still has his natural life to live.

Sixteen years later, however, when Yeats wrote that too long a sacrifice can make a stone of the heart, Maud objected bitterly (November 1916): "Though it reflects your present state of mind perhaps, it isn't quite sincere enough for you who have studied philosophy & know something of history." Her reminiscences, which were published in 1938, are not of much help here. She began a second volume, but never finished it, finding it too painful to go on.

Partly on account of her own temperament, partly because as a woman she could not be admitted to the political organizations, Maud worked as a freelance. Although in these letters she appears surrounded by children, lawyers, friends, prisoners, dogs, birds, and old servants, Yeats more than once in his poems calls her "that lonely thing." She was driven in upon herself, it seems, but without feeling the need to explain what she found there. Her granddaughter remembers that in old age "she wished to be gone and said she hated the lingering process." But about this there was nothing disheartening. Maud Gonne believed that beyond the grave our energies are renewed as when we were young. We can then begin the struggle again.

1992

Lily and Lolly

The Yeats Sisters: A Biography of Susan and Elizabeth Yeats, by Joan Hardwick

W. B. Yeats says very little in his *Autobiographies* about his two younger sisters, Lily (christened Susan) and Lolly (Elizabeth), except that they sometimes "dreamed true," which interested him. However, in 1994, Gifford Lewis published *The Yeats Sisters and the Cuala Press*, and in 1995 came William M. Murphy's *Family Secrets: William Butler Yeats and His Relations*. Both of these books make good use of Lolly's diary and Lily's scrapbooks. We have had a chance, then, lately, to know them much better.

Joan Hardwick is still indignant on their behalf, and although they never took the risks of the Rossetti girls (who printed an anarchist newspaper in the basement), or put up, as Somerville and Ross did, with being treated as the joke of the family, still, they can be seen as under-rated and hard done by. For the Yeats family, it wasn't only a question of keeping a home together but of maintaining any kind of an entity with a feckless (call it easygoing) artist father and a melancholic mother whose actions, William said, were "unreasonable and habitual, like the sea-sons." They moved from Ireland to England and back again so often that it might seem like flitting, and very nearly was. They went from Sandy-mount to various seedy addresses in London, then to respectably bohemian Bedford Park, back to Howth, Bedford Park again, and in 1901 a return to Ireland, this time to Dundrum. Their one real security was the mother's family, the Pollexfens, who took them in for long holi-days, so that for the rest of their lives they were homesick for the bare mountaintops and the voices of Sligo people.

Wherever they went, the pattern remained the same. Lily was the father's favorite. Lolly, he thought (although she undertook the house-keeping), "should have been a man." William also preferred Lily to the restless, talkative Lolly. Jack, the youngest, the future artist, was suffi-cient to himself. Meantime, it was said that on one occasion in Bedford Park, there was only twopence in the house. Neither of the girls had had much in the way of education or training, but with admirable courage they set about earning a living. Lily ventured out first, as an embroiderer in May Morris's workshop, later as a designer in her own right. Lolly trained as a compositor at the Women's Printing Society. Her friend (unfortunately later her enemy) Evelyn Gleeson, a power in the Arts and Crafts movement, had raised enough capital to open a workshop near Dundrum, and this was the first home of what became the Cuala Press. William's *In the Seven Woods* was the first title to appear, in the familiar gray cover with the glazed spine.

Hardwick goes to the attack, however, as well as to the defense. Although she acknowledges the usefulness of the material in Murphy's *Family Secrets*, she interprets it quite differently. She has no patience with John Butler Yeats, who finally abandoned (if that's not too positive a word) his family, to live the rest of his life in New York. Distrustful, on the whole, of charm, she sees him as nothing more than a scrounger. She defends the passionate, awkward Lolly against her seemingly gentler elder sister. William, she thinks, should have done more for both of them, though it is hard to see how they could not have got on without his introductions. Surprisingly little is made of his Nobel Prize award. The Bounty of Sweden, as he called it, helped with the expenses of Lily's illness (she was tubercular) and of the Cuala, never without its difficulties. Lily sank back in gratitude, but Lolly felt thrust aside and resisted the appointment of new directors (both men). "My sister and I quarrelled at the edge of the cradle and are keeping it up on the grave's edge," William wrote in 1937. He had mythologized his ancestors, his friends, and himself, but his sisters never.

The Yeats Sisters is clearly but somewhat flatly written, without much feeling for what Gifford Lewis calls "the unstable broth" of Anglo-Irishness—still less for the wasteful virtues that, Yeats felt, gave it grace. But Lolly, for so many years the odd one out, would be grateful to Joan Hardwick for this generous account of her.

1996

Monsieur Moore of Mayo

A Peculiar Man: A Life of George Moore, by Tony Gray

Tony Gray is a Dubliner who writes on Irish subjects, but seems to have hit on this one by chance. Two years ago, in what he calls a "spoof Booker contest"—it was actually a discreet promotion by Everyman— George Moore's *Esther Waters* was named as the best novel of 1894. According to Gray, "the general reaction was 'George Who?'" In reply, he has put together this biography, as he frankly tells us, from good ready-to-hand materials, in particular the Life (1936) by Moore's crony, Joseph Hone.

George Moore was born in 1852, the eldest son of a Mayo landowner. At the age of eighteen he inherited 12,500 acres and (when they could be collected) rents of over £5,000 per annum. Poverty was never a threat. During his wretched years at Oscott, he had learned almost nothing, but became convinced that he would make an artist. "He had gone to Paris straight from his father's racing stables," Yeats wrote, "from a house where there was no culture . . . acquired copious inaccurate French, sat among art students, young writers about to become famous, in some café; a man carved out of a turnip, looking out of astonished eyes." His appearance seemed the one important thing about him. Sickert saw him as "an intoxicated mummy," Henry Tonks as "a spoilt child of four," Gertrude Atherton as "a codfish crossed by a satyr." Manet, who did three portraits of him, thought "he had the look of a broken egg-yolk." In Paris, Moore discovered that he couldn't paint, but must write. Neither Zola, with whom he had scraped acquaintance, nor any of the painters he sat with in the Nouvelle Athènes, expected him to come to anything.

Having read nothing, Moore now set himself to read everything, and, as might be expected, began by writing French Naturalist novels in English. As such, they caused scandal, helpful to a beginner. The value of publicity was something he understood well, and he ably supported his publisher, the risk-taking Henry Vizetelly, and visited him during his spell in prison. At the same time, Moore began to be known in London as an art critic and, by some mysterious but gradual process, as "G. M.," the great Irish wit and armchair conversationalist. He had created himself, though never quite without caution: "to be ridiculous has always been *mon petit luxe*." But he knew that a man who had written *Esther Waters* could never, in fact, be considered entirely ridiculous.

"It is all about servants," he explained to Clara Lanza, one of his many women correspondents, "servants devoured by betting. It begins in a house where there are racehorses." A Zolaesque theme, then, of corruption and obsession, while the story of a patient young woman "in service" in a great house, made pregnant and disgraced, is told in a faultlessly unsensational voice. But the distinctive beauty of the novel, which Moore was never able to reach again, comes from the return of Esther's story to its beginnings. She comes back at last to the mistress who once turned her out, and the two of them settle down together, two aging women in a silent, decaying house. This surely is the "rhythmical sequence of events described with rhythmical sequence of phrase" that Moore said that he was aiming at. And although he thought his family home in Mayo was ugly, and was quite content with the £7,000 compensation he got when it was burned down by the Insurgents, the years he had spent there had to be written out of him, so that *Esther Waters* is also about the mortality of great houses. In *Memoirs of My Dead Life* (1906), he wrote movingly of his return to Moore Hall at the time of his mother's death. "The lake which I hadn't seen since childhood I did not need to look at, so well did I know the place of every island." There is an echo here of the novel Moore loved best, Pater's *Marius the Epicurean*, where Marius in the end goes home and looks as Moore had done himself into the dark family vaults.

Yeats, greatly admiring *Esther Waters*, invited Moore back to Ireland to collaborate on a play, *Diarmuid and Grania*. Moore saw this as a sacred mission; indeed, walking down Royal Hospital Road, Chelsea, he heard a voice—"no whispering thought it was," he says in *Hail and Farewell*, "but a resolute voice, saying 'Go Back to Ireland.'" There he thought to become the champion of the Gaelic League—perhaps of the whole Irish Literary Renaissance—but was received without much enthusiasm by the president, Douglas Hyde. The mission changed direction; Moore saw now that he was fated to become Ireland's Voltaire and to produce what Gray rightly calls "an autobiographical fantasy," showing up everybody, and the Renaissance and the Catholic Church in particular. "I knew the book to be the turning-point in Ireland's destiny."

As a novelist, he no longer followed the French masters. Zola had died in the autumn of 1902, asphyxiated by a charcoal stove. "Innumerable paragraphs and leading articles made Moore jealous and angry; he hated his own past in Zola. He talked much to his friends on Saturday nights. 'Anybody can get himself asphyxiated.'" This is from Yeats's *Dramatis Personae*, in which *Hail and Farewell* is quietly annihilated.

Tony Gray gives the later novels, *The Brook Kerith* (1916) and *Heloise and Abelard* (1921), a fair hearing, but he also wants to explain his subtitle, "A Peculiar Man." This was one of Moore's descriptions of himself, implying satisfaction with his distinctive work. Gray, however, applies it to his private life. What would Moore have seen if (in James Joyce's phrase) he had "put down a bucket into his own soul's well, sexual department"? Moore, Gray concludes, though he tried to give the impression of a reckless Irish bachelor, was no more than a voyeur from first to last. As a student, he was obsessed with naked models, and when he was in his seventies, he persuaded Nancy Cunard, who knew him as a friend of her mother, to take off her clothes for him. On the other hand, everything which he said took place—for example, in *The Lovers of Orelay*, "in the middle of a great Empire bed, under the curtained tester"—existed, most likely, only in his mind. Peculiar, too, Gray thinks, is Moore's love of unfamiliar words. He quotes "fluctuant tides," "tedded grass," "wis," which, he says, is "in the dictionary, it means 'know'. . . it is still a very odd word to use." And then, Moore was a liar, not only about sex. He worked usually from some basis of reality, but had some all-purpose tall stories; was it Emerald Cunard or Mrs. Pearl Craigie whom he once kicked in Green Park, "nearly in the centre of the backside, a little to the right"? Here Gray seems more bewildered than necessary. Both these tendencies—to collect unusual words as if they were jewels, and to tell lies on the scale of Wilde and Whistler—were Aesthetic, and Moore, even as a Naturalist, remained at heart an aesthete.

By the end of the 1920s he had separated himself from nearly all his old friends, "Æ," Yeats, St. John Gogarty, his own brother Maurice. At his home in Ebury Street, a new circle attended to him devotedly, but "by fifty," he said, "we should have learned that life is a lonely thing and cannot be shared." To some of his readers—"Dear ones! Dear ones!" as he calls us this is saddening. But his genial, energetic biographer doesn't dwell on this. He says he's come to think of Ireland as a fatal disease, from which both Moore and himself "were lucky enough to escape for the greater part of our lives."

1996

NEW WOMEN AND NEWER

Dear Sphinx

The Little Ottleys, by Ada Leverson,
with an introduction by Sally Beauman

Ada Leverson (1862–1933) said she had learned about human nature in the nursery. A little brother got her to help him make a carriage out of two chairs, but when he was taken out in a real carriage he was not in the least interested. Certainly she never underestimated the human capacity for imagination or for disappointment.

The nursery was in lavish 21 Hyde Park Square, and her father was a successful property investor. Her mother, descended from a distinguished Jewish family, was beautiful, talented, and leisurely, with moments of intuition, called "Mamma's flashlights." They did not warn her that Ada was going to escape, as she did at the age of eighteen, into a luckless marriage. Ernest Leverson, a diamond merchant's son, was unfaithful, a gambler, and couldn't manage the money, although it is true that Ada was extravagant, and notably more so after she met Oscar Wilde. She became Wilde's fast friend, and for a few golden years was surrounded by London's artists, actors, and first-nighters. (Max Beerbohm, of course, was a second-nighter; he advised on the decoration of her new house.) Ada Leverson was not worried by Wilde's *train de vie*. To another friend, who said he was on a strict regimen "in the hope of keeping my youth," she replied: "I didn't know you were keeping a youth"—this, like other unpredictable things, in a low voice, almost thrown away. To use her circle's favorite word, she was *impayable*. She had the gift, too, of amiability (Henry James felt that in her at last he had found the Gentle Reader) and of pure high spirits: all the family had them—one of her brothers was the original of Charley's Aunt. After Wilde's disgrace and death she may have lost heart a little. But just as she had stood by her ruined friend, so she put a brave face on her marriage until Ernest, on the verge of bankruptcy, was sent away to Canada in the company of his illegitimate daughter, at the diamond merchant's expense. Then Ada retreated to Bayswater with her children.

Wilde had told her that she had all the equipment of a writer except pen, ink, and paper, and in fact she had already contributed, on and off, to *Punch* and the *Yellow Book*. Now Grant Richards, who says in his *Memories of a Misspent Youth* that "an introduction to Mrs. Ernest Leverson was one of the most important things that could happen to a young man," persuaded her to turn novelist. Her grandson, Francis Wyndham, has told us that she hated writing, though it seems almost perverse of her not to enjoy something she did so well. Six novels came out between 1907 and 1917. After that, Grant Richards—although she was in love with him—could only persuade her to write the introduction to a fortune-telling book, *Whom You Should Marry*, which amused her. Three of the novels, *Love's Shadow*, *Tenterhooks*, and *Love at Second Sight*, make up a trilogy, and these have now been reissued by Virago.

It was indeed confusing of Oscar Wilde to call Ada Leverson "Sphinx." ("Seraph" would have been better—that is, if seraphs laugh.) Still, Sally Beauman worries unduly about this. There were many Sphinxes about in the Nineties. One of them appeared to Richard Le Gallienne as he sat in a restaurant eating whitebait, others to Gustave Moreau and to Khnopff. Nor would I agree with Sally Beauman that the tone of the Sphinx's novels is "unmistakably descended from Jane Austen." It seems to me much more nearly related to her own contemporaries, Paul Bourget and "Gyp." The passing remarks of Bourget's characters ("*tout est pour le mieux dans le meilleur des demi-mondes*," "*avec les femmes tout est possible, même le, bien*") are in the Leversonian mode, so is the worldly entanglement of *Mensonges* (which Edith, in *Tenterhooks*, is reading for the first time). But Ada Leverson never indulged in the clinical analysis of the psychology of love, for which Bourget pauses between almost every speech. She has her own lucid shorthand for the emotions. "Gyp," on the other hand, wrote almost entirely in dialogue, whereas we couldn't do without the Sphinx's droll commentary.

I don't mean that Ada Leverson was an imitator: rather, that she was enchanted by the times she lived in. The three novels that make up *The Little Ottleys* change subtly with the passing years, not only in reference but in atmosphere. In *Love's Shadow* (1908) there are aging poets surviving from the Nineties, *nouveau art*, amateur theatricals. In *Tenterhooks*

(1912) you can choose whether to take a hansom or a taxicab, Debussy and Wagner are "out," and at dinner parties "one ran an equal risk of being taken to dinner by Charlie Chaplin or Winston Churchill." The Turkey Trot is discussed along with Nijinsky and Post-Impressionism: "Please don't take an intelligent interest in the subjects of the day," the hero begs. In *Love at Second Sight* (1916) he is in khaki, and wounded. At the same time the viewpoint grows, not less intelligent, but more sympathetic to the absurdity of human beings in a trap of their own making.

Unashamedly her friends are pictured in her novels, and her own unhappiness, and, for that matter, the courage with which she faced it. Perhaps because of this, they show a great advance on her *Yellow Book* stories, "Suggestion" and "The Quest for Sorrow." *Love's Shadow* is a set of variations on the theme of jealousy. Ada herself felt that jealousy was allowable, but envy, never. Hyacinth Verney's guardian is in love with her, Hyacinth is in pursuit of the fashionable Cyril, Cyril has a hopeless *tendresse* for Mrs. Raymond, who is neither young nor beautiful but seems merely "very unaffected, and rather ill." For counterpoint, there is Edith Ottley, who is beginning to be tired of her own patience with her husband, Bruce, but who is not yet the victim of human emotion. Critics, and even the Sphinx's own family, found the book frivolous, but I don't know that any book that proclaims so clearly the painful value of honesty can be frivolous. Its real heroine is the uncompromisingly plain Anne Yeo, hideously dressed in a mackintosh and golf-cap, and "well aware that there were not many people in London at three o'clock on a sunny afternoon who would care to be found dead with her." Sharp-tongued Anne is in love with Hyacinth, the only genuine passion in the novel. When she has done all she can to help Hyacinth to capture Cyril in marriage, she is seen for the last time on her way to Cook's. She has decided to emigrate.

Whether Ada Leverson originally intended it or not, the Ottleys become central to the next two novels. Grandly careless in small details, she changes Edith's age and the color of her hair, and makes her far more witty and admired. Bruce is, if possible, more monstrously selfish and witless. (When Ernest Leverson came back on one of his infrequent visits from Canada, it was said that "he talked just like Bruce.") Possibly the Sphinx is too hard, at times, on her creation. Faultless is Edith's clarity, ruthless are the sharp-eyed inhabitants of the nursery. But, after all, Bruce is well able to protect himself. "With the curious blindness common to all married people, and indeed to any people who live together," Edith has not noticed that Bruce is making sly advances to the governess. Meanwhile, she herself has fallen in love with the impulsive Aylmer Ross, but "how can life be like a play?" she asks sadly, and to Bruce's relief (for he can now feel injured) she simply gets rid of the governess. In contrast to her self-restraint, there is the interlocking story of her devoted friend Vincy. A dandyish observer of life, Vincy has a mistress, Mavis, an impoverished young art student whose red hair is "generally untidy at the back." Her poverty, which brings her close to starvation, is disquieting, but Vincy discards her without pity: "Shall you marry her?" "I'm afraid not," he said. "I don't think I quite can." For all their humor and good humor, these novels can sometimes seem unrelenting. At length, the easily persuaded Bruce runs off with Mavis. Edith, however, for the sake of her children, rescues him once again.

But Ada Leverson is writing in terms of comedy, and Edith Ottley must be left happier than she was herself. To bring this about, she introduces, in *Love at Second Sight*, a grotesque creation, powerful enough to dominate the situation. Eglantine Frabelle, perfectly well-off and perfectly self-satisfied, is a guest in the Ottleys' small London house and shows no signs of ever going away. She is, wrote Siegfried Sassoon, like "a really great impressionist picture by Whistler or Manet," who, "to tell you the truth, rather dumps the others, dear Sphinx." Sassoon was right. Edith and Aylmer are less interesting than this stately, tedious widow of a French wine-merchant, whose name has undertones of *frappant* and *poubelle*. Always knowledgeable, and invariably wrong, she is detestable, and admired by everybody: even Edith is devoted to her. When Bruce (it is 1916) finds that listening to the war news is affecting his health, and he must leave for America, he elopes—and we know he will never escape again—with Madame Frabelle. Once she has left the book, even though Aylmer and the delightful Edith are free to marry, the interest fades. We seem to be waiting for her to come back.

How can Bruce manage to think that he must "throw in his lot" with her? Through willful misunderstanding. Their day out on the river is tedious. The only boat left for hire is *The Belle of the River*, as battered as an old tea-chest, and they find that they have very little to say to each other. But both of them have the impression that it has been a great success. With such non-events, or anti-events, Ada Leverson is marvelously skillful. Oscar Wilde had wanted *The Importance of Being Earnest* to be not paradoxical, but nonsensical—pure nonsense, he said. The first act ends not with an epigram, but a wail: "But I haven't quite finished my tea!" This is the art of inconsequence, possible only in a society where consequences can still be grave. The Sphinx, also, had a most distinctive ear for nonsense. "With a tall, thin figure and no expression," she writes, "Anne might have been any age, but she was not."

1983

Out of the Stream

Olive Schreiner: Letters, Volume 1: 1871–1899, edited by Richard Rive

Rebecca West said that Olive Schreiner was a "geographical fact." Others were reminded of a natural force, admired and dreaded, unchecked by illness, war, or poverty, something new coming out of Africa. To fit her into the history of South Africa, of literature, or of women's movements is an exhausting business. "The day will never come when I am in the stream," she said. "Something in my nature prevents it I suppose."

Olive Emile Albertina Schreiner (named for three brothers who died before her) was one of nine children born to a German missionary and his wife, Rebecca, a member of Moorfields Tabernacle. The family was reared in the strictest possible Bible Christianity. Gottlob Schreiner was an unfortunate man, difficult to place in the Lord's vineyard, arriving finally at a mission station in Wittebergen on the edge of Basutoland. Here he was forced to leave the ministry, having broken the strict regulations against trading. As a trader he was even less successful, but Olive never ceased to love the ruined father. Left homeless, she was taken in by her eldest brother, Theo, who first ran a school, then went to try his luck in the diamond fields.

When Olive was five she sat among the tall weeds behind the house and understood, without having the words for it, that they were alive and that she was part of them. At six, she was whipped for speaking Cape Dutch, and felt "a bitter wild fierce agony against God and man." At nine her little sister died and Olive, who had slept with the body until it was buried, lost her Christian faith. At sixteen she was possibly engaged to, possibly seduced by, an insurance salesman who let her down: "the waking in the morning is hell," she wrote in her diary. At about the same time she was lent a copy of *First Principles*, by Herbert Spencer. She had three days to read it, and Spencer's vision of human evolution toward the Absolute remained with her for a lifetime. At eighteen she had a long conversation, which was profoundly important to her, with an African woman. This woman said to her: God cannot be good, otherwise why did he make women? At nineteen she was close to suicide, but found strength to go on from reading Emerson and John Stuart Mill. These are her own landmarks, "disconnected but indelibly printed in the mind." At twenty, she began to write *The Story of an African Farm*.

If she had been the child of an English Evangelical parsonage, she would have been conforming, in her struggle from faith to freethinking, to a recognizable pattern. But Olive was self-created. It's true that *African Farm* is, in some ways, much what might be expected from a young woman in the 1870s, jilted, working as a governess, writing in a leaky farmstead by candlelight. The heroine, Lyndall, is very small, with beautiful eyes (Olive is small, with beautiful eyes), a penniless orphan, "different." Her lover rides a hundred miles to see her, and her dull cousin's fiancé, Gregory Rose, leaves everything to follow her. "What makes you all love me so?" she asks. But Olive, by her own account, had read, at this stage, no other fiction at all. And the *African Farm*, as it goes on, is a very strange book. Lyndall, in the end, is nursed on her deathbed by Gregory Rose, disguised as a woman in long skirts. He has shaved off his beard and watched the ants carry off the hair to their nests—an example of the book's perilous balance between fantasy and observation. More than anything else it is a book of dreams, and specifically the dreams of children. Lyndall has a vision of independence and free choice for women. She refuses to marry the man who has made her pregnant, because she doesn't love him enough. Waldo, the son of the farm overseer, represents another side of Olive. He dreams, in his "seasons of the soul," of studying the earth and rocks around him as a scientist. A stranger who rides in from the Karoo tells him a story—"The Search for the Bird of Truth." But Waldo, though he understands the allegory, dies without getting his opportunity. "In after years," Olive wrote, "we cry to Fate, 'Now, deal us your hardest blow, give us what you will, but let us never again suffer as we suffered when we were children.'"

She sent the manuscript to a friend in England, who recognized as she opened the parcel "the strange, pungent smell of the smoke of wood-fires, familiar to those who know a Karoo farm." It was published in 1883, partly on the recommendation of George Meredith, and with its great success Olive Schreiner entered on her passionate dialogue with the world at large. Of all Lyndall's confused perceptions, the clearest is: "When I'm strong, I'll hate everything that has power, and help every-thing that is weak." Olive was not a leader, or even an organizer, but she was a great advocate, and the evangelist her father had failed to be. The only necessary claim on her attention was weakness. She needed, as she freely admitted, to be needed. For women's right to financial and sexual independence, for the Boers against the British, the small farmer against the capitalist, the blacks (always "Kaffirs" or "niggers" to Olive) against the whites, she spent herself recklessly. All this was in the face of a chronic illness, apparently asthma, which is often said to be psychoso-matic (though never by any one who has had asthma), and an inability to settle for long in one place. Her restlessness meant, as her biographers Ruth First and Ann Scott point out, that she "lacked a constituency." In spite of her record of friendships, she felt the pain of isolation, both per-sonal and political. "Indeed the two were joined, for her sense of politics included the necessity for the individual to define her independence and make it an inviolable part of herself."

First and Scott's *Olive Schreiner* was written in the context of the women's movements of the Seventies. The earliest biography, by her hus-band Cron Cronwright, has been under fire ever since it appeared in 1924, and indeed even before that, since several of Olive's women friends refused to lend him their letters. Cronwright, as a practical man, a farmer and lawyer, probably felt he had done a fairly good job and put the best face on things, but he allowed himself omissions and even alterations. Now the Clarendon Press has published the first of two authoritative selections of the Olive Schreiner letters.

The book is divided into three parts, beginning in 1871, when Olive was sixteen. One of the troubles about collecting letters is that before the writer becomes famous no one is likely to keep them: there is only a handful of family letters here, but they are touching in their awk-wardness and affection. Hard work, scarcity, the death of nieces and nephews, all in a careful copybook style. In 1880, with the help of her brothers, she scraped together £60 and sailed to England, meaning to study medicine. She never completed her training, either as doctor or nurse, and this was one of the personal failures—as opposed to her great public successes—which made her call herself, at the end of her life, "broken and untried." At last, however, except for persecuting landladies, she was free, and, after a day spent "worrying an idea to its hiding-place," she had people to talk to, and was understood. A celebrity after the publication of *African Farm*, she launched herself into socialist circles of the Eighties, and joined the Fellowship of the New Life. "It's dreary work eating one's own fire"—but now she no longer had to, and her relief can be felt like a kind of intoxication. The most important letters are to three new friends, Havelock Ellis, Edward Carpenter, whose *Towards Democracy* came out in 1881, and the mathematician Karl Pearson. With Carpenter she was always on easy terms, he was "my dear old Ed'ard." She does not discuss in her letters, and perhaps never recognized, his homosexuality, nor does she criticize his version of the Simple Life, although she tells him that he has been overfed with education whereas she is "dying of hunger." Havelock Ellis, still when she first knew him a medical student, offered her a long and tender friendship that was perhaps intellectual only, although in *My Life* he recalls her dashing naked out of the bathroom to explain an idea that had suddenly come to her. Rive himself, in his introduction to the 1975 edition of *African Farm*, mentions Olive's "inability to exercise restraint over the number of themes which interested her." In the *Letters*, Havelock Ellis is asked, as her "other self," to respond to them all. Karl Pearson, on the other hand, set definite limits on their friendship that Olive seems not to have been able to keep. He was the moving spirit of the Men and Women's Club, which met for free discussion of all matters concerned with relations between the sexes. And Olive does discuss them freely, leaving herself without defenses. "I would like to think you could make any use of me as a scientific specimen, it would be some compensation to me." The break with Pearson was a dark night of her existence. She wrote, but could get nothing finished, and dosed herself with dangerous medicines. Her influence over most people she met was as strong as ever—"I sometimes am filled almost with terror at the sense of the power I have over them," she tells Havelock Ellis—but she had begun to long for South Africa. Her last letter in this selection is to Edward Carpenter (October 1889). "Goodbye, dear old Brother. You will have to come out after me some day, when you hear about the stars and the black people and all the nice things. I'm going to be quite well."

By this time her younger brother Will was legal adviser to the Governor of Cape Colony, and she made a forceful entry into Cape politics. "There is one man I've heard of," she tells Havelock Ellis (April 1890): "Cecil Rhodes, the head of the Chartered Company, whom I think I should like if I could meet him; he's very fond of *An African Farm*." She did meet him, four months after he became prime minister of the Cape, and began what Rive calls "a complex relationship," although it might perhaps be seen as grandly simple. At first she felt a "curious and almost painful interest" in Rhodes as "the only big man we have here." She had the highest hopes of him politically and perhaps in other ways, walking away from him at Government House where "it had been said that I wished to make him marry me." But after he voted in favor of the Strop Bill (making it legal to flog farm servants for certain offences) she never forgave him. He came to stand, in her eyes, for the greatest of all political evils, capitalism. "It's his damnable and damning gold which has first ruined himself and is now, through him, ruining South Africa." As to the Jameson Raid, she saw his complicity at once, although her old friend, the journalist W. T. Stead, did not. A point was reached when Olive and Rhodes were passengers on the same ship and, as she told Will Schreiner in 1897, "he was so afraid of me that he dared not come and wash his hands in his own cabin, because he had to pass my cabin and might meet me." But when there were rumors that the "almighty might-have-been" had suffered a breakdown, she felt "intense personal pity."

Olive believed, or thought she believed, that women must take responsibility for their own future—this is the subject of one of her allegorical *Dreams*—but she had to combine this with her evolutionism, with the eugenics learned from Karl Pearson, and with Lyndall's declaration in *African Farm*: "I will do nothing good for myself, nothing for the world, till someone wakes me." In 1894 she married Cron Cronwright, seeing him as he at first saw himself, as "something like Waldo, but fiercer and stronger." Cron, eight years younger than Olive, deeply respected her genius and sacrificed a good deal for her: he changed his name to Cronwright-Schreiner and gave up farming, which he loved, for the sake of her health. Olive calls her marriage "ideally happy," and indeed continued to do so in the years to come when they found it impossible to live under the same roof or even in the same country. Only five of her letters to Cron are given here, showing their early years together as "tenderness itself," though deeply shadowed by the death of their child, who lived for only sixteen hours. "Morally and spiritually"—which for Olive was the same thing as politically—they were, at first, completely in tune. They campaigned together against Rhodes and the Chartered Company. The "Native Question" was not Olive's main concern as yet, although she saw, as perhaps no one else in South Africa did, that it was another aspect of the world's confrontation of capital and labor. In the Nineties her pressing duty was to champion Boers, the small upcountry farmers, the patriarchs of her childhood. Olive's vision of Africa was pastoral and republican. On the other side were principalities and powers, the "wild dogs of gold." "All my friends (liberals) from home write saying there cannot be war," she tells her brother in July 1899. "But for us there is a worse possibility than war, that of slowly falling into the hands of speculators." On 9 October 1899, the Transvaal presented its ultimatum. Two days later, war began.

Olive, too ill to go to the Front as a war correspondent, as she had been asked to do, braced herself to do all she could in "my poor little handful of life," confident that her time of work would come when the war was over. Her letters show her courage, her integrity, and her intuition, and, with them, the alarming neurotic force of the Victorian "wonderful woman." It was this, probably, that made the liberal politician J. X. Merriman call her "one of those persons one admires more at a distance."

1988

Keeping Warm

Sylvia Townsend Warner: Letters, edited by William Maxwell, and *Sylvia Townsend Warner: Collected Poems*, edited by Claire Harman

Sylvia Townsend Warner expected her correspondence to be published; indeed, she sensibly provided for it. "I love reading Letters myself," she told William Maxwell, her *New Yorker* editor and literary executor, "and I can imagine enjoying my own." She was born in 1893, an only child. Her father was a Harrow master, who, in a way not very complimentary to his profession (but quite right for S.T.W.), never sent her to school. She was allowed to study what she liked, and was devoted to him, emerging from the "benignly eccentric household" as a musician: she was about to go to Vienna, to study under Schönberg, when the First World War broke out. When her father died, leaving her, as she put it, "mutilated," she saw that it would be better to earn her own living than stay in the country and quarrel with her mother. She came to London, and worked as an editor on the monumental *Tudor Church Music*. Plain, frail, shortsighted, not quite young any more, and, for the first time in her life, rather poor, she set out to enjoy herself. "I am sure that to be fearless is the first requisite for a woman: everything else that is good will grow naturally out of that."

In her first novel, *Lolly Willowes* (1926), she puts the situation in terms of fable. The decorous Lolly sees that she must escape her family. This intimation comes to her in the greengrocer's, when she looks at the plum jam and feels herself in a darkening orchard, where the birds are silent. To find where the jam comes from, she gets an ordnance survey map— as S.T.W. did when she set off in search of T. F. Powys, the writer she most admired. When a well-meaning relative pursues Lolly even to her country cottage, she asserts her will by transforming herself into a witch. Admittedly, she has now been captured by Satan, "the loving huntsman," but she has proved that she "prefers her own thoughts above all others," and, in any case, she feels that she knows more than Satan— more about death, for example, "because, being immortal, it was unlikely he would know as much." This is reassuring, and typical of the writer. What S.T.W. herself wanted to do, and did, was to write (though sometimes she thought she was better at sawing and digging), to hear music, and to live in the country with the human being she loved best, Valentine Ackland. The two women settled in one cottage after another, and finally at Frome Vauchurch, in Dorset.

What happened to them? That was left in their letters, journals, and poems for the world to understand. In 1935 they became 1935-ish members of the Communist Party. In 1936 they went to Spain together for three weeks to help in the British Red Cross bureau. By 1950 Valentine had joined the Catholic Church, and S.T.W., while remaining fiercely anti-clerical and ready to fight to the death against privilege or bullying, allowed a little irony to modify her left-wing views. "It takes reckless resolution now," she wrote, "to admit that one has known a more civilised age than the present. It is painful to admit it to oneself, and apparently shameful to mention it to others. Everyone is busy pretending that even if they once or twice went out to tea they always drank the tea from a mug." In 1949 Valentine (described as a "sea-nymph who can split logs with an axe and manage a most capricious petrol-pump") fell in love with another woman, a young American, and S.T.W. courageously faced solitude, preferring "the sting of going to the muffle of remaining." The crisis passed, because, S.T.W. thought, "I was better at loving and being loved," and they returned to a life that she could only call blessed. She meant travel, many friendships, gardening, jam-making, perilous motoring, cats, books, and music. Guests might find the cottage exceedingly cold (Maxwell says that the temperature was the same indoors and outdoors and the front door stood wide open), but the welcome could hardly have been warmer. These years brought S.T.W., not prosperity, but recognition, both here and in America, as a deeply imaginative writer whose novels and poems were most distinctively hers. More than this she didn't expect: when, in 1967, she was invited to become a Fellow of the Royal Society of Literature she mildly pointed out that it was her first public acknowledgment since she was expelled from kindergarten for upsetting the class.

In 1968 Valentine died of lung cancer. "I have always prayed that I might not die first," S.T.W. wrote, "though my age made it probable that I should." As she went through her dead friend's possessions, she found in the coat-pockets notes from herself, "on the lines of Keep Warm, Come Back Soon." They had agreed that S.T.W. should live on at Frome Vauchurch, and this, until May 1978, she did. "With a heart as normal as a stone" but quite undaunted, she was still writing and reading voraciously—and giving dinner parties and denouncing Mrs. Thatcher—to the very end. Misfortune and egoism, she thought, turned women into vampires—very different from witches—and this she was determined to avoid.

Her letters, from which I have been quoting, are formal, in the sense that S.T.W. hardly knew how to write carelessly. It isn't that she is considering the effect: she produces one, from a long habit of elegance. She knew that herself. "I can't say it yet," she wrote to Leonard Woolf after *Beginning Again* came out. "Already I am writing like a printed book, and falsifying my heart." Often, however, her formality couldn't be improved upon—for example, to David Garnett: "I was grateful to you for your letter after Valentine's death, for you were the sole person who said that for pain and loneliness there is no cure." It enabled her to deal with publishers, and, most difficult of all, to give away money gracefully: "I can well afford it; I have always made it a rule in life to afford pleasures." Every now and then a short story that she never had time to write rises quietly to the surface:

> Now I will sit down to tell you about two very old and distant cousins of mine, brother & sister, who live together. She is in her nineties, he is a trifle younger. They were sitting together, he reading, she knitting. Presently she wanted something, and crossed the room to get it. She tripped & fell on her back. So she presently said: Charlie, I've fallen & I can't get up. He put down his book, turned his head, looked at her, and fell asleep.

Just as careful, and just as brilliant, are the descriptions of day-by-day life in the cottage and the village, often to correspondents who had never seen either. All records of passing time were precious to S.T.W., from Proust to Gilbert White's notes on his tortoise. "Continuity," she said, "it is that which we cannot write down, it is that which we cannot compass, record or control. . . . An old teapot, used daily, can tell me more of my past than anything I recorded of it." Few people can ever have described a teapot as well as S.T.W.

Editing this volume was clearly a labor of love, and not an easy one, for William Maxwell. Unfortunately, he has cut and edited the letters on a system peculiar to himself ("I have used three dots, unbracketed, to indicate an omission at the beginning of a letter. . . . I have not used three dots to indicate that there is more than the last sentence"), and, disappointingly, there is only a sketchy index. Addicts of collected letters will tell him that this is a serious mistake. S.T.W.'s index would have read, in part:

> celibacy, S.T.W. recommends
> clearing up, S.T.W.'s passion for
> coalshed, T.H. White's diaries lost in
> cold baths, S.T.W. advises, if piano kept in bathroom
> *Contre Sainte-Beuve*, S.T.W. translates

As to the selection, the correspondence with Valentine Ackland is being published separately, while some other series have disappeared or been withdrawn: still, there is plenty here. It is only a pity (though no fault of William Maxwell's) that he has found nothing from America for 1927, when S.T.W. was guest critic of the *New York Tribune*, and that there is so little reference to her poetry.

It is sad that she should have died such a short time before the publication of her *Collected Poems*. Claire Harman begins with the unpublished and uncollected work, arranged as far as possible in chronological order. S.T.W. is shown as an endless reviser, hard to satisfy. *The Espalier* (1925) and *Time Importuned* (1928), with their demurely ironic titles, are the only two collections she brought out in her lifetime. *Opus 7*, a satirical narrative in the style of Crabbe, based on the story of a "drinking old lady . . . a neighbour for many years, and I had the greatest esteem for her because she knew what she wanted," came out in 1931. The late poems were privately printed, except for *Boxwood*, which S.T.W. thought of simply as verses for Reynolds Stone's wood engravings (although it includes the haunting "People I never knew"). The rambling joint collection with Valentine Ackland, *Whether a Dove or a Seagull*, has not been reprinted here, for the tactfully put reason that "it exists on its own terms."

S.T.W. was a Georgian poet, and my only complaint against Claire Harman's excellent introduction is that it takes the word "Georgian" as an insult, and I had hoped that it no longer was. She was Georgian in her subject matter and also in her professional skill, composing, as she said, "with piteous human care." Here she can bear comparison with Walter de la Mare, the master of the two-stress line:

> *Winter is fallen early*
> *On the house of Stare. . .*

S.T.W. almost always succeeds with this precarious meter, which sounds nostalgic in "The Repose," mysterious in "Nelly Trim," and in "Blue Eyes" exactly suggests Betsy's disappointment:

> *Down the green lane*
> *She watched him come,*
> *But all he did*
> *Was to pinch her bum.*

With half-rhymes and unstressed rhyme she made a number of delicate experiments, letting the meaning control them, so that in "Anne

Donne Undone" the rhyme gradually disintegrates as Anne struggles with weakness and fever, while in the triplets of "Journey by Night" it almost disappears. In one of her *New Yorker* pieces, "Interval for Metaphysics," S.T.W. remembers what it was like, as a small child, to relate the world of words to the world of things, and stand looking at a wooden paling "which had suddenly developed its attaching gravity, and had gathered to itself the pale primrose that forsaken dies, and a certain expression that the sky puts on at dusk, and that I had rarely seen, since l was supposed to be in bed by then." Yet she was surprised, twenty years later, to find she was a poet. "I haven't yet got over my surprise that I should be doing it at all."

Her sharp-wittedness had always made her more, rather than less, sympathetic to other lives, past or present, birds and animals as well. In a tiny lyric, Winter is an old beggar standing motionless in the fields:

> All day he will linger
> Watching with mild blue eyes
> The birds die of hunger.

Loneliness, I think, she considered, after mature reflection, the worst suffering of all. It is at the heart of her finest poem, "Ballad Story," and her novel set in a medieval convent, and dedicated to Valentine Ackland, has the epigraph: "For neither might the corner that held them keep them from fear." But, in the end, what is most striking about this civilized poet is her affinity with whatever it is that defies control. By this I don't mean either sin or magic, for she regarded both of these as perfectly amenable, but what she liked to call "the undesigned." Against Nature we oppose human order—the lawn must be mowed and appointments must be kept, even though "the clock with its rat's tooth gnaws away delight." But, conversely, we can accept the threat of disorder, even if it is never let loose, as the most precious thing we have. "I have tamed two birds," she wrote in "The Decoy," "called Metre and Rhyme"

> At whose sweet calling
> All thoughts may be beguiled
> To my prepared place;
> And yet by blood they are wild.

1982

The Real Johnny Hall

Our Three Selves: A Life of Radclyffe Hall, by Michael Baker

When *The Well of Loneliness* came out, in July 1928, the reviewers were not astonished. Both Leonard Woolf and L. P. Hartley thought the book sincere, but overemphatic. *The Times Literary Supplement* also called it sincere, and Vera Brittain said it was "admirably restrained." It sold quite well, going into a second impression, and Radclyffe Hall, with her lover Una Troubridge, thought of taking a cottage in Rye. She may have felt some disappointment, having planned her novel in a crusader's spirit. She claimed to have written the first full-length treatment in English of women who loved women. In Rosamond Lehmann's *Dusty Answer*, she said, "the subject was only introduced as an episode." (She seems not to have known Dickens's Tattycoram and Miss Wade.) She wanted to "smash the conspiracy of silence," but found herself instead mildly successful at W. H. Smith and the Times Bookshop.

The case was altered only by James Douglas, the editor (also in a crusader's spirit) of the *Sunday Express*. Douglas decided, a month later, to feature the book and its photogenic author, in her "severe" smoking jacket, as evidence of "the plague stalking shamelessly through public life and corrupting the healthy youth of the nation." The rest of the popular press divided up for or against the *Express*'s stunt, *The Well* sold out, the Home Secretary gave his opinion against the novel, and Cape was summoned to Bow Street to show cause why it should not be destroyed in the public interest. John Hall (to give her the name she preferred) was not called upon to give evidence, and was silenced, when she tried to interrupt, by the magistrate. In this way the Beaverbrook press started *The Well* on its career as the best-known lesbian novel in the English language.

At heart, *The Well* is a nice long solid Great War–period romantic novel. The ethos is that of *If Winter Comes*, or *The Forsyte Saga*. Stephen, the hero/heroine, driven out of her grand ancestral home, joins an ambulance unit, is wounded and gets the Croix de Guerre, and won't declare her compromising love until she is sure it's returned. When Mary succumbs she supports her by writing, but has to work such long hours that Mary, left on her own, takes to drink. To save her from degradation and childlessness, Stephen, in a great act of self-sacrifice, drives her into the arms of a man, who marries her. Those were the days of Boots Circulating Libraries, and *The Well* only needs one adjustment, though an important one, to make it a first-class Boots book. This, in fact, has always been the objection of its most serious readers. Stephen's final plea, "Acknowledge us, oh God, before the whole world," doesn't mean "I am different, let us be different in peace" but "I am the same, why can't you admit it?" Stephen is a transsexual, but the suggestion is that she wants to conform to society and can't, just as Peter Pan, as Barrie finally admitted to himself, wanted to grow up but couldn't. Women are treated in *The Well* without much sympathy, and almost always as empty-headed. The whole book supports the view that men are naturally superior, which is why Stephen would prefer to be one. Another drawback to its defense of lesbians ("my people," as John called them) is the frightful gloom and ill-fortune attending on the minor characters, who grow consumptive or deranged, or commit suicide in garrets. Stephen's circle of friends, it seems, is doomed. Whatever else the novel does, it doesn't show the lesbian life as recommendable.

Michael Baker has taken on the task of relating *The Well* to John's own life. "It is arguable," he writes, "that had John drawn more on her own personal knowledge, a better novel would have resulted." But she would have had, of course, to romanticize herself less. Her other novels, in particular *Adam's Breed* and the touching *Unlit Lamp*, speak for the victimized and repressed. The life of Radclyffe Hall herself was not tragic, not sacrificial, not self-denying. Writers are not obliged to be like their books. But there is something disconcerting, which Baker evidently feels, about the discrepancy here.

John was born as Marguerite Antonia Radclyffe-Hall, in a house in Bournemouth called Sunny Lawn. She was not a masculine-looking child; Sir Arthur Sullivan called her "Toddles." But Toddles suffered deeply from the division between her rarely seen father and her violent, hysterical mother. (The bewilderment of children growing up without love was what she was to do best in fiction.) In 1901, with not much in the way of education, she came of age and inherited her grandfather's fortune. This meant freedom to travel, and in 1907, at Homburg, she met Mabel Batten, a dashing, well-connected older woman who was there to take the waters and play roulette. Mabel had a warm mezzo-soprano voice; she was the kind of woman Sargent painted, and he did paint her. She was thought to have been one of Edward VII's mistresses.

By 1907 Mabel was fifty, had spread emotionally and physically, and was known as "Ladye." Ladye's hot-water bottles were called Jones and Charlie, and she petted and spoiled them. As John's first lover, she did duty, too, for the unsatisfactory mother. Together they began to cruise to "dear abroad," leaving Ladye's complaisant husband to spend his time at his clubs. There was no scandal, Ladye having a truly Edwardian adroitness in managing the pleasures of the flesh. She was a Catholic convert, and John, too, was received by the Jesuits at Farm Street. Both of them were convinced that they must have met in some previous existence. But in a few years' time Ladye's forces had begun to wane. John became first impatient, then unfaithful. In 1915 she met Una Troubridge, who wrote in her Day Book that "our friendship, which was to last through life and after it, dated from that meeting."

Baker's title (unlike, for instance, I. A. R. Wylie's *My Life with George*) doesn't refer to the homosexual's divided nature. "Our Three Selves" were Ladye, John, and Una. During the war there was a tormenting *ménage à trois* at the Vernon Court Hotel, which made Ladye (she too kept a diary) "sick at heart. Atmosphere sad beyond words." In 1916 she died of a heart attack. She had been at a tea party, singing one of her own patriotic compositions, and came back, tired out, to find that John was not there. The resultant guilt and self-reproach, John found, could only be absolved by communication with the spirit world. With the help of Mrs. Leonard, who was undoubtedly a powerful medium but sometimes, perhaps, resorted to likely guesses, Ladye was heard to forgive. "She says . . . 'I understand you and know you never hurt me intentionally.' . . . I say most emphatically nothing could or shall prevent our meeting or my coming to you as long as God permits." Subsequently Ladye gave John permission to cut her hair short. The son/daughter was recognized as Una's husband. Admiral Troubridge returned from action to find himself unwanted and his little daughter neglected. He was obliged, under protest, to apply for a legal separation. "A great peace and relief upon me," Una noted. "Deo Gratias."

The Twenties were John and Una's heyday, a period of what Baker calls "hectic socializing." The two of them were instantly recognizable figures at first nights and private views, and were, of course, well-heeled travelers. "We stopped where we felt inclined," Una wrote, "and allowed the ex-chefs of royalty to feed us." Life was kept at fever pitch by quarrels and reconciliations, illnesses real or imaginary, and the false exhilaration of moving house. If all else failed, they could call in doctors and solicitors, or buy more and more pet dogs, or sack the servants. In politics they supported "our class" and Mussolini's Italy. Through all this Una remained John's faithful wife, providing the reassurance that writers need. "After a day and a night spent like Jacob, wrestling with the angel of her own uninspired obstinacy, [John] would hand me the resulting manuscript . . . and command me to read aloud . . . having been asked if I was tired and told I was reading abominably and sometimes informed that I was ruining the beauty of what I read, the manuscript would be snatched from my hands and torn to shreds." But no price was too high to pay. If the marriage was necessarily sterile, at least the books had been born. All Una's emotional capital was invested in John's genius.

Michael Baker doesn't claim to be a critic and therefore makes no attempt to decide whether her faith was justified. In any case, to Una, as to Ladye, John was unfaithful. During the hot summer of 1934, when they were in France, they had to call in a nurse from the American hospital in Paris. She was a White Russian, Mongolian or "Chinky-looking," and, Una thought, "quite unmistakably of our own class." John, at fifty-four, fell insanely in love with Evguenia Souline. She was restrained, but only for a short time, by the thought of the example of infidelity that she would give to "my people" (Havelock Ellis had claimed that lesbian relationships were by their nature unstable). But Souline, who treated John as a source of easy money, was unpredictable and hard to get, and John, perhaps because of this, couldn't exist without her. In her many hundreds of letters to her "sweet torment" she began to refer to Una as a "terrible obligation" and a load that might be beyond bearing. Only the Second World War separated these later Three Selves.

At intervals throughout the long story a curious heartlessness appears. Ladye stands deserted in the darkening hotel room. Admiral Troubridge is left astounded and embittered when Una hints to her friends that he has infected her with syphilis. Una's small daughter is found wandering in the street with no one to care for her. As an adolescent, she is asked to call John "Uncle." Una, after twenty years of loyalty, is left hanging about, recovering from a hysterectomy, while out at Passy John is in bed with Souline. In the words of *The Well of Loneliness*, "God alone knows who shall judge of such matters."

Michael Baker has written this biography with a calm, flat-footed perseverance that contrasts effectively with the agonies of his subject. He has turned up a considerable amount of new material. In addition to Una's Day Book, which was also used by Richard Ormrod in his *Una Troubridge* (1984), he has had access to Mabel Batten's diaries and to the letters to Souline. But while Ormrod declared "a measure of personal empathy" with Una, Baker doesn't precisely explain what led him to write such a long book about Radclyffe Hall. Perhaps what attracted him, in the end, was her courage. Courage is not the same thing for the well-off as for the poor. John thought of herself as a martyr, but it was a martyrdom de luxe. I'm not thinking, however, of her defiance of the law or even of her fortitude in her last illness, but of her experience, through so many years, of being treated as somewhat ridiculous. Rupert Hart-Davis's remark "It was always said that at a dinner-party, when the women left the table, Johnny Hall found it hard to make up her mind whether to go with the women or remain with the men" says it all. But Radclyffe Hall was never deflected, either by friends or by enemies. She never wavered in her immense seriousness. She continued to hold her head high, even in the face of English jokiness.

1985

An All Right Girl

An afterword to *Thank Heaven Fasting*, by E. M. Delafield

"Thank Heaven, fasting, for a good man's love" is Rosalind's sharp rejoinder, in *As You Like It*, to the proud shepherdess. As advice it is ambiguous, because Rosalind can only give it while she is passing herself off as a man. And E. M. Delafield's book, delightful (like everything she wrote) to read, is not as straightforward as it looks at first.

Most recollections of E. M. Delafield are of the handsome country-woman and J.P., organizing and well organized, the competent mother, the successful public speaker, a director of *Time and Tide*. "A witty, extremely *soignée* person" an American interviewer found her in 1942. One might not have guessed that her sympathies were with the Labour Party, and there are other unexpected glimpses of her, for example on her visits to Russia where she had arranged to meet the young journalist

Peter Stucley. "With a hat," he wrote, "from Marshall & Snelgrove on her head, and in her hand a bag which always contained, at moments of exhaustion, a supply of ginger biscuits," they toured Moscow together, although their last outing, to a reformatory for prostitutes, was cancelled. In her own account she describes how she washed his handkerchiefs and saw him off "in deepest dejection," feeling like *l'orpheline de Moscou*. The total impression—and this, I believe, accounts for the comic and pathetic tension of her books—is of a woman who would like to free herself and understands how it is to be done but can never quite bring herself to the point of doing it. "Realize, not for the first time," writes the Provincial Lady, "that intelligent women can perhaps best perform their duty towards their own sex by devastating process of telling them the truth about themselves. At the same time, cannot feel that I shall really enjoy hearing it." What held her back—and she knew this, of course, better than anyone—was partly inborn, partly imposed. At convent school, she said, she had been taught for life that "a good reason for doing something was that I knew I should hate it." An even stronger influence was her mother.

This mother was also a novelist. Mrs. Henry de la Pasture had a great popular following, and when Elizabeth began to publish she called herself "Delafield" (a translation of sorts), apparently to keep clear of her mother's success. Why not, however, a different name altogether? Mrs. de la Pasture's books went into many editions, including Newnes' Sixpenny Novels and Hodder & Stoughton's Sevenpenny Library. Among her titles are *The Grey Knight: An Autumn Love Story* (1908) and *The Lonely Lady of Grosvenor Square* (1907). Her advice to her daughter was to write about something of which she had personal experience, but in her own novels this experience is certainly heightened. You get dash and spirit from Mrs. de la Pasture, and generous wish-fulfillment. Her heroines are the middle-aged enchantresses dear to middle-aged women authors. Take Lady Mary in *Peter's Mother* (1905). She is a widow, pale, sad, but still beautiful, and free at last to marry her first love. But her son comes back wounded from the Boer War and expects her to make a home for him. When she asks, in a sudden outburst, whether she doesn't deserve a life of her own, she meets total incomprehension. What is disconcerting is to find that in E. M. Delafield's last novel, *Late and Soon* (1943), the same situation appears, though in more painful terms. The Provincial Lady notes "*Mem:* a mother's influence, if any, almost always entirely disastrous." The struggle to escape from it, however, greatly strengthens the critical faculty.

Thank Heaven Fasting was published in 1932, when E. M. Delafield had been writing for twelve years. The period of the story is not precisely given (the First World War is never mentioned), but in Eaton Square the power of money, parental authority, and social status is still absolute. Power needs force to support it, and it is the overwhelming force of received opinion that divides the All Right from the Not Quite and makes the unmarried woman something worse than odd—a failure, a disgrace to herself and to what in racing would be called her "connections." The term is the right one, because the young women are bred and trained entirely with the object of getting them successfully married within three years, after which they are regarded, and regard themselves, as leftovers. Grotesquely artificial as the system is, it is biologically predictable. The All Right—even if some of them are Only Just—must reproduce themselves with the All Right to maintain the species. In itself this is a bizarre spectacle, one of nature's processes gone hopelessly astray, which must lead eventually to extinction.

The story opens on a note of keen irony. "Much was said in the days of Monica's early youth about being good." (Monica was one of E. M. Delafield's own names and one may guess that she would rather not have been given it.) Goodness, in this context, means what is convenient to those in authority. Certainly, it has nothing to do with truth. Monica has been carefully trained to behave to men—beginning with her own father—exactly as they expect, and to say to them only what they want to hear.

> "Have you been to play whist at the Club, father?"
> The question dated from Monica's nursery days. She asked it several times weekly, and never realized that it was a matter of complete indifference to her.

At her first dance she catches sight of herself in one of the great ballroom mirrors and "saw that she was wearing too serious an expression. Both her mother and the dancing-mistress had warned her about this, and she immediately assumed an air of fresh, sparkling enjoyment." At home, after dinner, she sometimes plays the piano.

> "That will do now, darling," said Mrs. Ingram. "I can hear father coming, and he may want to talk. Ring for coffee."
> Monica obeyed.

She was not really particularly interested in either the *Adieux* or *Sobre les Olas*, although she vaguely liked the idea of herself, in a simple white frock, dreamily playing under the lamplight and it always rather annoyed her that her conception of her own appearance had to be spoilt by the fact that, having no faculty for playing by ear, she was obliged always to keep her eyes fixed upon her music.

Monica, then, is not a protester. She is conscious of the duties of her station as a young girl and accepts them without question. All time is wasted—so too is all friendship and all music—unless it can be shown to "lead to something," that is, a proposal of marriage, although it is assumed that the man is likely to try and get out of it if he can. If the offer is not made within the first three seasons, the daughter will have to share with her mother the cruel burden of guilt. Fathers can distance themselves; mothers, if they have failed, must live with failure.

A possible exception to this rule is the handsome, formidable Lady Marlowe (her first husband had been a German Jew, but her second had been English, "so that was all right"). If her two daughters, Frederica and Cicely, prove unattractive to men, Lady Marlowe intends, so she frankly says, to banish them to a separate house and disown them. But such strength, and indeed such cruelty, can hardly be expected of all mothers, nor is it surprising that Frederica and Cicely droop, with dark shadows under their eyes and "pale, inefficient hands."

Monica does not have to suffer from this kind of brutal contempt. The novel would be very much weakened if she did, since another irony of the opening chapters is that her prospects seem so hopeful. She starts out with the goodwill of the entire household, although she knows very little about some of them—"she had a dim idea that the kitchenmaid did actually sleep in the boxroom." She is crimped and squeezed into the desirable shape and launched into the drawing-room world. Once there, her first conversation on her own is a success. She has been able, for several minutes, to think of something to say to a man. It looks, then, as if she will be able to justify her existence and the fact that she was not born a boy. Her parents, who remind her so frequently of all they are doing for her, will not have to be disappointed.

Every now and then E. M. Delafield indicates briefly (she is a very economical writer) how much human material is being wasted or suppressed. Left to herself, Monica has a good heart and a healthy capacity for normal happiness. She loves dancing for its own sake, and, disastrously, she loves Captain Christopher Lane. At his appearance on the scene, her eighteen years of training—social, emotional, and religious—collapse at a touch. "God must understand her, and must not allow her mother to guess anything at all." Captain Lane, to be sure, is not altogether real to her—"he was masterful, exactly like people in books"—but he is also a powerful physical presence which has nothing to do with books. At the funfair—a strong metaphor for sexual excitement—she finds that she has forgotten her mother and her friends and, as the evening goes on, even time itself. She will never be allowed the chance to do such a thing again. Almost at once time reasserts its power, and becomes a threat. Although the flashy Captain only finds the opportunity for a few kisses before he is posted back to India, Monica's reputation for niceness has gone. She has lost her marketable freshness. She and her mother will be left to count the anxious years as they pass. They are not quite hopeless, but their hopes will be pitched sadly lower and lower.

"The Anxious Years" is the title of the second, and by far the longest, part of the novel. Monica, Mrs. Ingram, and Parsons, the faithful lady's maid, are left in a kind of unholy alliance to keep up appearances in Eaton Square. Monica, once a devourer of fiction, now creates it, inventing, with her mother, new variations of the true story. "They displayed for one another's benefit a detached brightness that ignored everything below the surface," conscious, day in, day out, of "an undercurrent of sick envy and mortification." E. M. Delafield calls their pretense "gallant" as they go through the daily formalities of dressing, shopping, driving out and back home again, which are all they know and which it would never occur to them to give up. Without these things their life would not be endurable.

The men who are supposed to give meaning to their lives are a poor lot, almost all of them self-satisfied and self-deceiving. But the thin characterization of the men, in this particular novel, works very well. They are to be seen as a necessary condition of life rather than as human beings. Poor Monica is patronized by her father, sexually awakened and then ditched by the Captain, disillusioned by Carol Anderson, without understanding any of them. It could be said, indeed, that the true marriage, as the story works itself out, is between Monica and her mother. They have "the intuition peculiar to those who live together." From Monica's first childish dependence she grows into the desperate conspiracy of the middle chapters, until almost imperceptibly she becomes the stronger of the two. "Darling, there's no such thing as friendship between a man and a woman," is Mrs. Ingram's comment when Carol Anderson appears, but for the first time her voice is timid. Her last resort is the pretense that she can't bring herself to let her daughter marry and leave her by herself. "Not that I'd ever grudge you your happiness, my precious one, but just for a few years more—I don't suppose it'll be for very long." And Monica, listening, feels "sick with pity."

Earlier in the book she has been jealous of the affection between her parents, and when Vernon Ingram is killed in an accident she envies her mother's hysteria, her right, so to speak, to violent grief. Jealousy, in the peculiarly English form of accepted defeat (everyone else is more fortunate and more worthy of being fortunate), was of particular interest to E. M. Delafield. Unlike lechery and greed, it can never provide satisfaction in itself, only in the thought of someone else's failure. In creating character, she held that

> to show one side only is to falsify it and therefore deprive it of all value . . . there are no wholly "nice" people, or wholly "nasty" people in real life, and they therefore have no place in the particular form of *roman psychologique* in which I happen to be interested.

The jealousy that bedevils the gentle and pliant Monica is a product of "the whole tradition of her world, daily and hourly soaking into her very being, so that it became an ineradicable part of herself." There is, for example, the beginning of a real friendship between Monica and Cicely Marlowe. But the news of Cicely's engagement (even though the man is not All Right), while Monica herself is still doggedly waiting and hoping, is almost too painful to be borne. "It added to her misery that she was ashamed of it, and despised and reproached herself for her unworthy jealousy." Still more disgraceful is her relief when the whole thing, after all, comes to nothing.

Thank Heaven Fasting would be a somber book if it were less witty, and less deceptively mild. Proceeding, as it does, in the kind of short paragraphs that were then thought suitable for the Woman's Page, it concentrates from beginning to end, and with admirable clearness, on the main story. In this sense, it must be counted a classic. Characters and places are carefully limited. The tone is detached, or seems so. E. M. Delafield had, she said, "consciously striven, throughout the whole of my writing life, for ability to observe impartially, unbiased either by sentiment or by cynicism, and courage to record faithfully and without dramatic emphasis." She isn't impartial, of course. What is the use of an impartial novelist? But she is accurate, calm, and lucid. She possessed what she called a phonographic memory, and could repeat, word for word, conversations that she had heard or overheard many years earlier. Dialogue, even in short snatches, is one of her great strengths as a writer. In *Thank Heaven Fasting* the conversations are often—as they are in real life—duels, open or disguised. Mrs. Ingram has an easy victory over Monica.

> "Sit down, my pet."
> "I'd rather stand."
> "Mother said, Sit down, Monica."
> Monica sat.

The neurotic Frederica also challenges her mother, together with the whole system to which she has been condemned.

> "I don't want to get married. I hate men. I wouldn't marry anyone—whoever it was."
> Lady Marlowe gazed at her in astonishment for a moment, and then laughed again.
> "So you've got to that stage, have you?" was all she said.

And Frederica, left alone, sinks her teeth into the flesh of her thin wrist to control herself. At the other end of the scale is Mr. Pelham, amiably chatting on one of his punctual calls.

> "The other day," remarked Mr. Pelham, "I heard of a fellow who was sitting out a dance with a girl. They'd talked about all the usual things and didn't seem to have anything more to say, and whatever he asked her she only seemed to answer Yes or No—so what do you think he suddenly did?"
> "What?"
> "He suddenly asked her: 'Do you like string?' Without any preliminary, you know."

Monica smiles, though only because she sees that she is expected to. But she understands as well as he does that between people who are obliged to talk but have nothing to say, anecdotes, even about string, are precious currency. There is something touching, however, about Mr. Pelham's admiration of the resourceful fellow, whom he doesn't even know, but has "heard of." Mr. Pelham is tedious—he is the sort of man who always calls a walk "a ramble"—but in his voice one can distinguish human kindness.

If E. M. Delafield had a good ear, she also had an exceptionally sharp eye for (to quote one of her own titles) The Way Things Are. The house in Eaton Square dominates *Thank Heaven Fasting*. In Monica's bedroom

> the furniture itself was all painted white, so was the narrow little mantelpiece on which stood the collection of china animals dating from nursery days. The pictures were framed in gilt—mostly "copies from the flat" of Swiss scenery, and Italian peasantry, but there were also reproductions of one or two "really *good*" pictures. These had been given to Monica from time to time, usually on birthdays, and she always felt that she ought to have liked them much better than she really did.

In a rebellious moment she had wanted to take down the Sistine Madonna, but had not been able to summon the courage. Her upbringing has taught her that nothing must be taken more seriously than appearances. When she goes to her mother's room after a party "to tell her all about it," she sees the nighttime Mrs. Ingram, with whom she is quite familiar—her hair in a double row of steel wavers, her face glistening with cold cream, recruiting her forces for the next day's grand pretense. Heavy meals come up from the basement kitchen, clothes are worn which can't be taken off without the help of a servant, fires blaze, bells are rung, hairdressers arrive by appointment—every morning and evening bring the spoils of a comfortable unearned income. It is the only home Monica has ever known, and we have to see it turn first into a refuge for the unwanted, and then into a prison.

In *Thank Heaven Fasting* E. M. Delafield returned to a theme she had treated much earlier, in *Consequences* (1919). In this novel, which was one of her own favorites, the heroine, Alex, is as naïve as Monica, but much less able to do what is expected of her. She has suffered—unlike Monica, but like E. M. Delafield herself—from years of spiritual regimentation in a strict Belgian convent. Emerging, bewildered, at the age of eighteen, she finds that her parents expect her—what else has she been growing up for?—to get married. She accepts a proposal from a man she doesn't love, and who removes his pince-nez, with deliberation, before he kisses her. (This is also true of Mr. Pelham and of Cecil Vyse in *A Room with a View*; it seems to be an Edwardian novelist's warning signal.) With very real courage, Alex breaks off the engagement. In consequence, her mother's world rejects her. She is undirected, untrained, thought to be odd and difficult. Her brother and sister do not want her, and as a last solution she drowns herself. Monica's story, then, could be seen as a revised version of Alex's; we must accept that comedy is crueler than tragedy. It is interesting to see how E. M. Delafield has quietly removed what might be called the extenuating circumstances. Alex dies because her sincerity is unforgivable. Monica retreats to the pretenses of Eaton Square. Nanda, in Henry James's *The Awkward Age* (who becomes unmarriageable because she is thought to have read a daring book), is shown as finer than all the men and women around her. Monica is not. Gissing's Odd Women lose their means of support. Monica remains comfortably off. In a conforming society, she is a conformist. Her claim to sympathy is only that.

And the reader does sympathize with Monica, all the more because she is unheroic, and finds it almost unbearable when, at the very end of the book, she wakes sweating and sobbing, afraid that after all there may be some hitch to prevent her marriage. One feels almost ashamed to be seeing her desperation at such close range. Was she capable of acting otherwise than as she did? So tightly does her world close around her that it seems, at first, that there are no choices open to her. She has heard faintly of alternatives—the New Woman, the suffrage movement—but she has been taught to regard them with horror, and is duly horrified. Lady Marlowe considers that women who demand votes are simply hysterical old maids, or wives who can't get on with their husbands (she herself has worn out two). No New Women make an appearance (there is a hint of one in Mary Collier, who wears her hair straight and her clothes plain, but it is not developed) and there are no female salary earners—not even writers—among Monica's acquaintance. At one point in the novel, however, when Cicely falls ill, the Marlowes call in young Dr. Corderey (clever, but not All Right). Corderey has studied the unhappiness of idle women, and considers it an illness. They need treatment, he thinks, as much as any other patients. To Monica he says,

"I suppose you were never sent to school either, and you live at home, and have nothing to do . . . and if you were forced to earn your living to-morrow, you'd have to starve."

Monica, for an instant, felt offended, because she knew that her mother would think she ought to be offended. But he had spoken with so much sincerity that she could not pretend to disagree.

"It's quite true."

Monica is listening here to the voice of truth. She has heard it before, more than once. She heard it when she wanted to take down the print of the Sistine Madonna. She expresses it, if only for a moment, when she cries out "Why can't one have a career, or even work, like a man?" She knows that her mother's grief has turned into self-indulgence. She has the capacity even to know herself, but what she sees dismays her. Better to look away. Here E. M. Delafield is relentless. We are not allowed to question the happiness of the happy ending. Quite against the tradition of comedy, the older generation has been proved, apparently, right. And all Monica has to wish for is that if ever she has a child, it will be a boy.

1989

Passion, Scholarship, and Influence

Dorothy L. Sayers: Her Life and Soul, by Barbara Reynolds

When she dined at Somerville High Table, as she quite often did in the late 1930s, we used to look up at Dorothy Sayers as she sat there in black crêpe de Chine, austere, remote, almost cubical. She told the dean that the students dressed badly and had no sense of occasion. We resented this because we felt that, although most of us had not much money, we had done the best we could. These, as it happens, are the very words of her illegitimate son, whom she supported but never acknowledged in her lifetime: "She did the very best she could."

We, of course, could never have envisaged such a situation. We couldn't have guessed at the weight of feeling behind her story "The Haunted Policeman" (in which Lord Peter Wimsey's son is born) or at the images which appear on the cover of this new Life—a frilly child, a slender young woman with a Leonardo smile, a jolly undergraduate dressed as a man and impersonating the conductor Sir Hugh Allen.

Biographies of Dorothy Sayers—four at least, including Janet Hitchman's *Such a Strange Lady*—have been published already, but this is the most authoritative by far. Dr. Barbara Reynolds, who is editing Sayers's letters, has read more of them than anyone else, and she met and corresponded with her for eleven years and collaborated with her on her Dante translations. (About this she has written already in *The Passionate Intellect*.)

As her subtitle suggests, she is particularly concerned with Sayers as a committed and dogmatic Christian and as a scholar—a scholar even of detective fiction, as she showed in her introduction to the well-loved Gollancz collection *Great Short Stories of Detection, Mystery & Horror* (1928). "I do feel rather passionately about this business of the integrity of the mind," she wrote to Victor Gollancz. There she felt unassailable. Emotionally and physically, however, she had a rough ride, with some compromises to make. Like many children of the manse (her father was Rector of Bluntisham-cum-Earith in Huntingdon) she had to make the best of oddly conflicting impulses. After a wretched entanglement with an elusive poet, John Cournos, she "chummed up" with a car salesman and motorbike fitter who amused her, told her dirty stories, and left her pregnant. (Fortunately she had a cousin, Ivy Shrimpton, who made a living by fostering and teaching children.)

Then, in the 1920s, when she was reviving her interest in Old French literature and preparing to translate *Tristran*, she married Mac, a motoring journalist, who enjoyed a few drinks and a visit to the Holborn Empire, and so did she. With him she took to good food and wine and majestically increased in weight. She was able to give up her slogan-writing job at Bensons, where she had worked successfully on the campaigns for Guinness and Colman's mustard, and become a writer only.

But, distressingly enough, in the shadow of her success Mac diminished. From then on she managed her own life admirably, supported by loyal friends and taking on publishers, the press, the BBC, even the hierarchy when there was trouble over the broadcasting of her brilliant life of Christ, *The Man Born to Be King*.

She was one of the intellectuals entrusted by the Ministry of Information to encourage the nation at war, and she fearlessly accepted controversy. As a matter of fact, although she was argumentative, argument was not her strong point. (In *The Mind of the Maker*, for example, she claims that the process of artistic creation is threefold and so an analogy of the Trinity, without any evidence at all except that that was how she felt herself when writing.) What she had, as Frank Swinnerton puts it in *The Georgian World*, was "that inconvenient readiness of comment which flows from a mind lively and in good order."

Speaking what she believed to be the truth she regarded as a duty. "She was influential," says Barbara Reynolds, "and other influential people took notice of what she said." This, of course, is true, but there were many strong-minded women, in sensible hats, on call at that time, and it is heartening to remember that Dorothy Sayers's influence was due to an imaginary amateur detective who had "walked in complete with spats" in 1920, and who was not at first meant to be taken seriously.

Barbara Reynolds is a cautious writer, devoted to her subject and, as the founder of the Dorothy Sayers Society, scrupulous over detail. Take the question of the almost too amiable chaplain of Balliol, Roy Ridley. He did, it's true, wear spats and a monocle and did claim, to Sayers's vexation, to be the original of Peter Wimsey. But she was quite wrong in saying she had never met him until after she had written her books, and Reynolds shows that she was wrong.

It is always a biographer's job to look for the relationship between the life and the work, even though Sayers, like most authors, said that there wasn't one. "None of the characters that I have placed upon this public stage has any counterpart in real life." Reynolds can only say that this is "disingenuous." After all, it is Lord Peter himself, in *The Nine Tailors* (by which time he's become pretty serious), who says that the writer's creative imagination "works outwards, till finally you will be able to stand outside your own experience and see it as something you have made, existing independently of yourself." Writers, he adds, are lucky.

1993

BLOOMSBURY

A Way into Life

Virginia Woolf, by Hermione Lee

More literary biographies are published than any other kind, presumably because writers like writing about writers. And they find readers who like reading them, although those readers are not seen at their best in the introduction to Hermione Lee's new biography of Virginia Woolf. "I have noticed," says Lee, "that in the course of conversation about the book I would, without fail, be asked one or more of the same four questions: Is it true that she was sexually abused as a child? What was her madness and why did she kill herself? Was Leonard a good or a wicked husband? Wasn't she the most terrible snob?" Lee seems not to have been asked about Virginia Woolf's parents or her sister Vanessa Bell, and certainly not about her novels. She does not complain about this, noting it down simply as part of the process of mythmaking. As a biographer she is calm, patient, strong, deeply interested and interesting. Although she does not believe that complete objectivity is possible, she will answer all the questions in their proper place.

She could not start her book, she says, as Quentin Bell started his twenty-four years ago: "Virginia Woolf was a Miss Stephen." She begins instead with Virginia Woolf's own obsession with "life writing" and with the relation between the inmost personality—"the wedge-shaped core of darkness"—and the daily hard-working self. The biographer is bound by facts, but must go ahead, like the miner's canary, to test the air for falseness and out-of-date conventions. Hermione Lee herself is certainly on the lookout for falsifications, but her real concern is to restore order, dignity, and sympathy. Her book, marvelously informative as it is about food, money, houses, clothes, pets, doctors' prescriptions, and the complexities of love and sexual jealousy, is still a heroic life of Virginia Woolf, and perhaps even more so of Leonard.

"Virginia Woolf and her contemporaries are poised on the edge of the revolution which has turned biography into the iconoclastic gossipy art form it is now, when the only taboo is censorship," Lee writes. Failure to make money is of course also a taboo, and literary figures wait like bundles of washing for regular collection ("reassessment") every ten years or so. Lee's publishers absent-mindedly, or perhaps recklessly, say that this is the first major Life for twenty years, ignoring James King's (rather dull) *Virginia Woolf* in 1994, Phyllis Rose's *Woman of Letters* (1978), John Mepham's *Virginia Woolf: A Literary Life* (1991), and Lyndall Gordon's in 1984, not to speak of Louise Desalvo's *Virginia Woolf: The Impact of Childhood Sexual Abuse in Her Life and Work* and Jane Dunn's *A Very Close Conspiracy: Vanessa Bell and Virginia Woolf* (1990)—but here we are out with the auxiliaries, with the dizzying circles of intimate and less intimate friends and relations and their emotional baggage trains. Meantime, six volumes of letters and five volumes of diaries have been published, and last year Woolf herself emerged from copyright.

Why do people want to read so much about her? Not, it seems, to identify with her, rather to feel how much she was "other." As a child, a journalist's daughter, I felt most clearly the distinction between the undemanding Georgian world I lived in and the world of Bloomsbury. My world was Hampstead, muffin men, autumn leaves, *Peter Pan* at Christmas, the Poetry Bookshop where Walter de la Mare, W. H. Davies, and Eleanor Farjeon read aloud our favorite verses (for this was the last era when poets and the general public were on easy terms with each other). Bloomsbury was brilliant, poetryless, Cambridge-hardened. In comparison, we knew we were homely.

But Bloomsbury has been the survivor. Noël Annan, asked in 1990 for an assessment, described its position on the stock exchange of culture.

> Stracheys reached a high between the two wars, but suffered a catastrophic decline in the 1950s and 1960s and have never totally recovered their one-time value. . . . On the other hand, Forsters have proved to be remarkably firm right up to the 1980s, although they have eased somewhat since then. Woolfs were bought by discerning investors in the 1920s, but it was not until the company diversified with the publication of the [Quentin Bell] biography . . . that the stock went through the roof.

He gives Michael Holroyd the credit for introducing these people (in his *Lytton Strachey*, 1967) as living, disturbing, suffering human beings. The Georgians, however, also suffered—they rotted away in the trenches, loved, hated, and sometimes could not pay the rent—but although Edward Thomases have stayed in favor, Walter de la Mares (in spite of Theresa Whistler's fine biography) and John Masefields have sunk, it seems, almost too low for recovery.

But Hermione Lee has not written this book because Woolfs have gone through the roof. She mentions an attack of "archive faintness" at the thought of the vast reserves of material that would make it possible to recover what Virginia Woolf said, felt, and did pretty well every day of her life. Like some other researchers, she has felt almost ashamed to interview the still living friends and acquaintances who have obliged so often already with their reminiscences of this one famous woman, "as though the rest of their lives counted for nothing." But Lee's book is not only very good but very necessary.

One of her objects, although not at all the only one, is to place the half-Victorian Virginia in her right context of twentieth-century feminism. Virginia's own explanation, early arrived at, was that her father-dominated upbringing at 22 Hyde Park Gate was an image for her of the noisiness and infantilism of a male-organized society and the tyranny of the state. She said this charmingly in *A Room of One's Own* and more forcefully and raggedly in *Three Guineas* (which was originally called "On Being Despised") Leslie Stephen, her father, although he held, or said he held, that women should be as well educated as men, found the money for his sons' education but not for his daughters'. (Lifelong resentment led Virginia to refuse every academic honor offered to her and even an invitation to deliver the Clark lectures.) After his second wife's death his demands for sympathy were monstrous, he was insatiable, and she knew and said that if he had lived much longer she would have been obliterated. None of this is in doubt, but Lee describes, better than anyone else has been able to do, what a complex business it truly was. Virginia loved her father, and she had inherited from him a Victorian nonconformist conscience painfully detached from its God. She tried to exorcise him, but he escaped her, just as Mr. Ramsay, at the end of *To the Lighthouse*, steps ashore, ignoring his son and daughter, with his brown-paper parcel in his hand. At the age of fifty she still shook with anger at the thought of his emotional blackmail and his obtuseness to music and painting. "Virginia wrote and rewrote her father all her life," says Lee, but she also read and reread him. She was drawn back, against the grain, to the honesty of his books and their courage.

Lee accepts that Leslie Stephen, first editor of the *Dictionary of National Biography*, "chanting and groaning on his way up to his study," was at the root of Virginia's erratic radical politics. But she also makes a convincing connection between her feminism and her concept of biography. Perhaps (as Stephen Spender suggested) because she felt her own experience was too limited, she was unashamedly interested in other people's lives, women's in particular; hidden, obscure lives. What was the way into them? Among her correspondence, after *Three Guineas* came out in June 1938, was a woman called Agnes Smith, a factory worker who lived near Huddersfield. She was out of a job, managing on fifteen shilling a week. She asked what was the use of telling women to become "outsiders" and refuse to manufacture arms, when so many of them would be glad to be paid to manufacture anything? Virginia answered this and Agnes Smith's subsequent letters, always admitting that she belonged to a privileged social class and wrote from among them and addressed herself to them. But the "unnarrated lives" that she wanted to bring into brilliant clarity were not documentary, they were imaginary. She envisaged a point where fiction and history met, or could be believed to meet. One of the best-loved passages she ever wrote is the story, in *A Room of One's Own*, of Shakespeare's young sister—who never existed—and her pitiable expedition to London—which never took place.

What we cannot tell is how this idea might have worked out in the autobiography that, in one way or another, she had been writing ever since she left the nursery. She did not feel able to live long enough to finish it. We cannot tell either what she would have said about this wonderfully fluid, imaginative, but strictly researched book, where every chapter has its own pattern, as though the biographer was following Virginia Woolf's own advice to herself "to get down into the depths, and make the shapes square up."

1996

Breathing Together

A Very Close Conspiracy: Vanessa Bell and Virginia Woolf,
by Jane Dunn

I associate these close conspiracies of sisters with "long" families in many-storied and -railinged London houses. It was a primitive form of association, with all the morbidity and natural strength of true Victorianism.

> Come and kiss me.
> Never mind my bruises,
> Hug me, kiss me, suck my juices—

This is what Lizzie cries out to Laura in Christina Rossetti's "Goblin Market." "Eat me, drink me, love me"—and Laura is brought back from the edge of death, "for there is no friend like a sister." D. G. Rossetti's drawing *Golden Head by Golden Head* illustrates the closeness, this time with a suggestion of magic.

The sisterly alliances were defensive and protective against family pressure and, if necessary, against the outside world. The groupings, of course, varied. In the Benson family the two sisters, with only a year between them, were in a strong position, bridging the gap between the older boys and Fred, with the strange little Hugh in the nursery. The five Strachey sisters remained close enough until at last Pippa (the Angel Standby, as her mother called her) found herself, somewhat resentfully, left as "the daughter at home." Octavia Hill, the ninth of eleven children, kept her elder sister Miranda (or "Andy") close to her to the very end. From family to family the same handicaps had to be faced—the fascinating, demanding father (perhaps wounded himself, as Edward White Benson was by the loss of his eldest son), the hard-pressed but miraculous mother, an inheritance of black melancholia, financial ups and downs, inquisitive relations, cruel and totally unexpected early deaths. All these things lay in wait for the Stephen sisters, and, in addition, while their brothers were given an expensive education, they were not. This was in spite of Leslie Stephen's declared principle "I chiefly hold that women ought to be as well educated as men." As well as this setback, which they might well have expected to escape, Vanessa and Virginia had the fortune or misfortune to be deeply in love with each other. "I've been in love with her since I was a green-eyed brat under the nursery table, and so I shall remain in my extreme senility," wrote Virginia in 1937 when she counted on living long, for there was a great deal still left to write.

Marriage, of course, was the chief threat, a new conspiracy that might fatally weaken the old one. It was surely not until Vanessa married Clive Bell that Virginia discovered some of her own painful disadvantages of temperament. The pact made in childhood that she would be a writer, her sister a painter, seemed almost to insure them against competition, but Virginia was plagued by self-reproaching jealousy, and with it an acute and delicate version, in fact the agnostic version, of the Evangelical conscience. In the December of 1927, for example, she enters "a severe reprimand" in her diary for "the habit of flashy talk":

> Nessa's children (I always measure myself against her and find her much the largest, most humane of the two of us) think of her now with an admiration that has no envy in it; with some trace of the old childish feeling that we were in league together against the world; and how proud I am of her triumphant winning of all our battles; as she takes her way so nonchalantly, modestly, almost anonymously, past the goal, with her children round her; and only a little added tenderness (a moving thing in her) which shows me that she too feels wonder, surprise, at having passed so many terrors and sorrows safe. . .

This, from one point of view, is Jane Dunn's subject matter. She is writing the history of a relationship, and it must have been a very difficult thing to do. In the first place the sources have been gone over so often, though she is not disheartened by this. The families, she says, have helped her "as if I had been the first rather than the five-hundred-and-first researcher to stumble through their pasts." Secondly, the incidents and even the time sequence are not important to her in themselves. This means that events may be repeated to show them in a different light, or even left out altogether. After the first four chapters, Jane Dunn tells us she has "pursued themes in their lives, as for instance the tension between the demands of life and their art, and so weave back and forth through time and place."

In spite of the careful division of spheres—Vanessa maternal, painterly, inarticulate, triumphant in the bed, the nursery, and the kitchen; Virginia sexless, imaginative, language-loving, elegant, wild, famous—Jane Dunn looks at the two of them as a unity. There was "an essential reciprocity." They were conspirators in the true sense of breathing together. But the oneness was composed of sympathies and antipathies that she traces very far back. Vanessa, challenged by a naked six-year-old Virginia in the bathroom, admitted that she loved her mother best, and Virginia "went on to explain that she on the whole preferred her father." This is one of the central arguments of the book—that Vanessa became more and more like her mother, and scarcely knew what to think when Virginia restored or re-created Julia Stephen in *To the Lighthouse*. Virginia, on the other hand, with the motherly sister before her eyes, had to write her parents out of herself or perish. "I used to think of father and mother daily; but writing *Lighthouse* laid them in my mind."

One of Jane Dunn's achievements is to show the change in the relationship when Julian Bell was killed in Spain and Vanessa, up till then always the protector, healer and rescuer, was herself in need of healing. Virginia gave up every other concern to be with her, and Vanessa recalled "lying in an unreal state hearing Virginia's voice going on and keeping life going as it seemed when otherwise it would have stopped & later every day she came to see me here." Jane Dunn suggests that it was now at last that Vanessa forgave her sister for her ill-timed flirtation with Clive Bell. But the two of them must, even so, have felt profoundly uneasy. "It was discomforting to have the pattern of a lifetime reversed." But still the conspiracy held.

This is a very good book, possibly a bit too reverential, but deeply felt and deeply researched. Perhaps, as a common reader, I might be allowed to take issue on two points. The first is the influence, if any, of painting as an art on Virginia Woolf as a writer, and, in particular, the relationship between Lily Briscoe's picture and *To the Lighthouse* itself. To be sure, Lily's canvas (unlike Mrs. Ramsay's knitting) is finished at the same time as the novel, but it is subject to all the limitations of painting that made Virginia Woolf impatient. It seems uncertain (and Jane Dunn isn't certain either) whether it is Impressionist or Post-Impressionist, but it is carried out in a limited color range of greens and blues, with a triangle of violet and finally a dark line down the center. My feeling has always been that, until perhaps the last page, Lily's picture is a mess, and who can say this, at any stage, of *To the Lighthouse*? Certainly the picture's subject is fixed forever at the window. It can't convey, as the novel so beautifully does, changing place and passing time. "It was a miserable machine," Lily thinks, "an inefficient machine, the human apparatus for painting or feeling; it always broke down at the critical moment." Virginia Woolf sometimes spoke enviously of artists' lives (by which she meant life at Charleston) because they could work "alongside," whereas the writer is in a lonely agony, "blown like an old flag." When speaking or writing to painters she often used metaphors from painting, in the hope of being understood. But they were people who fussed about a change of light, fussed about a viewpoint. It is the novelist who has fifty pairs of eyes, plus "some secret sense as fine as air," which can move both inside and outside Mrs. Ramsay. But in any case, if we're comparing the arts, isn't *To the Lighthouse* in sonata form? E. M. Forster had been told this, and he accepted it.

My second point is, I suppose, a small one. Jane Dunn deals most sympathetically with the crucial decision (apparently made over Virginia's head) that the Woolfs must remain childless. How much human unhappiness this caused is not to be guessed at, but I should like to defend Leonard Woolf from the suggestion that he was too orderly or perhaps too repressed to welcome the idea of young children. That can be corrected, I think, by one quotation from Richard Kennedy's *A Boy at the Hogarth Press*:

> When I got back LW was up smoking his pipe and seemed pleased to see me. He told me that we were going over to see the Bells at Charleston for the day. So after breakfast I went with him in his Singer to Lewes to do some shopping. Children pounded along the village pavement. "The first day of school," remarked LW, his features softening.

1991

Living Doll and Lilac Fairy

Carrington: A Life of Dora Carrington, 1893–1932,
by Gretchen Gerzina, and *Lydia and Maynard: Letters Between
Lydia Lopokova and John Maynard Keynes, 1918–1925,*
edited by Polly Hill and Richard Keynes

These two books, a full-length biography of Dora Carrington and the edited correspondence of Maynard Keynes and Lydia Lopokova from 1918 to their marriage in 1925 (more volumes to follow), suggest that there is still a good deal of reading to be done about Bloomsbury. Both show the fate of newcomers, arrivals in Bloomsbury from the outside.

"Most people were at that time ordinary," said Frank Swinnerton, looking back with nostalgia to the beginning of the century, and Dora Carrington might have had the good luck to stay ordinary. In 1970 David Garnett, introducing his selection from her letters and diaries, felt that the reader might ask: "Who was this woman Carrington?" She derived her importance from the fact that she lived with Lytton Strachey. Hostesses, he went on, like the Asquiths and Lady Colefax, who welcomed Strachey, "would no more have invited Carrington than the cook." Knowing her very well, he thought she was a complex and original character in a strange situation, but did not say what effect on her the strange situation had.

Dora Carrington was born in 1893, the daughter of an engineer in the East Indian railways. She lived at a house called Ivy Lodge, went to Bedford High School, was good at drawing, bad at spelling, and loved her father more than her mother. She studied at the Slade under the all-powerful trinity of Frederick Brown, Wilson Steer, and Tonks. It was 1910, and the students were advised not to attend Roger Fry's Post-Impressionist exhibition. By 1914 Carrington, a mild bohemian, had cut her hair short. Mark Gertler and C. W. Nevinson were in love with her, and the world outside the Slade lay open.

Reading a good biography means thinking of unfulfilled conditionals. If chance or affection had given Carrington a push in another direction, she might have painted, cooked, traveled, and made love in something like contentment. She was at the Slade with Paul Nash (who gave her his suspenders, taking them off on top of a bus), and through him or through Nevinson she might have become an illustrator, as they were, for the

Poetry Bookshop. She could have learned etching from Sickert, always generous to beginners, or have worked with James Guthrie at the Pear Tree Press. She might have lived in Hampstead and gone to Robert Bevan's Sundays, or tramped with Eleanor Farjeon to Edward Thomas's cottage. As it was, she found herself in Bloomsbury. Even if they were, as Quentin Bell called them, "as amorphous as friends can be," they were nearly all highly literate, and judged accordingly. They treated her as a kind of peg-top doll, a sailor doll with blue eyes, "a thought unnaturally wide open," or, at best, as a child. Neither Duncan Grant nor Vanessa Bell was seriously interested in her pictures. When, after Lytton's death, she shot herself, Gerald Brenan said that her suicide was not a great tragic act "but had something childish and thoughtless and pitiful about it." Perhaps, if pathos is the tragedy of the bewildered, Carrington might be called tragic. After her death, no one could remember whether she had been cremated or not, or, if so, where the ashes had been put.

Her letters are beguiling but quite often apologetic and self-accusing. Her strange spelling (perhaps dyslexia) grew no better. On the honey labels that she designed for David Garnett at Charleston, even "Charleston" is spelled wrong. This was in spite of her great capacity for enjoyment and her strong physical appeal, which made her, to a number of men and women, irresistible. Here, too, Carrington was anxious to please, but not to tell the truth, and for a long time (she would have preferred to have been born a boy) she was not anxious for sex. Affectionate words were easier, and gave so much pleasure. Gerzina's chapter headings—"The First Triangle," "The Second Triangle," "Separations and Unions," "Picking Up the Pieces," "Compromise"—suggest how much pain and havoc were caused. One of Mark Gertler's letters to her in 1917 stands out in its naked misery:

> . . . for years I wanted you—you only tortured me, then suddenly you gave yourself to such a creature, and you yourself said if he wanted your body you would without hesitation have given it to [that] emaciated withered being. I, young and full of life, you refused it, tell me Carrington what am I to think of life now . . . he will deaden you in time & that is what hurts me so. You are absolutely at his feet. You follow him about like a puppy . . .

This book is beautiful to look at, decorated with Carrington's little pen-and-ink drawings, which are often more light-hearted than the text.

Gerzina starts from the suicide, and the rest of her book calmly and scrupulously explains it. She is not a historian. Her concern is with Carrington's thirty-nine years of life. Her best work was probably done in the early years at Tidmarsh, but Gerzina is careful to point out that Lytton was encouraging and (except when his own comfort was at risk) generous. "His homosexuality allowed them full rein in all other aspects of their relationship, and both were productive in their life together." The hardest question, then and now, is How could she care so much? Gerzina, quite rightly, does not attempt to answer this. "Love is love and hard enough to find."

For Carrington Bloomsbury felt at least some pity. Lydia Lopokova aroused terror. When, in 1922, Maynard Keynes began his serious courtship of Lopokova, one of Diaghilev's most popular stars, they could hardly believe, at first, that he was caught. "She has him by the snout," wrote Virginia Woolf, "a sublime but heartrending spectacle." "Don't marry her," Vanessa Bell advised. "However charming she is, she'd be a very expensive wife and would give up dancing and is altogether to be preferred as a mistress." Lopokova was delightful in a way in which they didn't want to be delighted. Her pranks put them all on edge. The Lilac Fairy was impossible, they felt, at close quarters, and Maynard would be lost to them. "How we all used to underrate her," said Morgan Forster.

Their early correspondence has been edited by a niece and a nephew, Polly Hill and Richard Keynes, who rightly believe that it will be "of value and interest and will not offend their ghosts." In an excellent introduction, they admit that Lydia, in the early stages, must have worn herself out in flattering Maynard. She had abandoned her husband and Diaghilev, and although she was still dancing with Massine, and was only thirty, her great days were over. In spite of innumerable friends, she was adrift. Maynard was working very hard, traveling between London and Geneva: he had installed her at 50 Gordon Square, where Vanessa Bell was also living, terribly disturbed by Lydia's *entrechats* upstairs. For Lydia the necessary thing was to hold on to Maynard, who was prepared to take responsibility for her financial affairs. "Maynard," she writes, "you are so brilliant I think sometimes I say things not as bright as you expect. Anyhow I try to develop my mind." She doggedly reads everything he recommends, and takes more interest in his ailments even than his mother. Maynard writes as a busy man, affectionate and expecting to be amused. But Lydia never loses her sense of her own value as a woman and a professional artist. Before long they are writing each other true lovers' letters.

When they are apart they write almost every day. Maynard is at conferences, Treasury meetings, college feasts, and, at one point, rather absurdly, a stag hunt. Lydia can tell him what Picasso said or what Nijinsky did, but she also has, as the editors put it, "a creative taste for ordinary day-to-day living," so that even a bus ride or a stomachache becomes an absorbing *skandal*. At the end of the letters there are endearments invented for her Maynarochka: "I have no chemise. I touch your bosom without a shirt," "Your pale chaffinch," "If it is cold where you are, as it is here, I warm you with my foxy licks," "Recurrent dismals of sympathy," "The jolts from my heart for you." Lydia's cunning misuse of the English language enchants Maynard, and sometimes, out of tenderness, he tries to imitate it, but cannot. It is an artistic version of English, just as her Highland divertissement was an artistic version of a fling. In May 1925 she writes to him

> I took your key, read 1/4 of *Mrs. Dalloway*, it is very rapid, interesting, and yet I feel in that book all human beings only puppets. Virginia's brain is so quick that sometimes her pen cannot catch it, or it is I who is slow. However I shall pursue the book to the end in a short time, and be established in the critisism. . . .
>
> I thank you for the papers [banknotes]. I shall buy "Eau d'Atkinson" and sprinkle myself everywhere except the hairy spots.
>
> Be comfortable and I am so very fond of you.
>
> L.
>
> P.S. I have been on the bicycle since but my skins make my pantelettes flick before the passers-by. I could not do for long.

These letters have been judiciously edited and cut, on principles that the editors explain, and carefully annotated (though I think "Rupert Dome" on page 191 must be Rupert Doone, and they don't give the meaning of the Russian word *pupsik*, which the lovers use so frequently). The notes and indexes don't take away from the immediacy of the letters. They have the kind of warmth that, in *To the Lighthouse*, frightens Lily, the detached artist. "They turned on her cheek the heat of love. . . . It scorched her and she flinched."

1989

MODERNS AND ANTI-MODERNS

The Great Encourager

Ford Madox Ford, by Alan Judd

Most people first come to be interested in Ford Madox Ford through reading his novel *The Good Soldier*. This must be one of the most carefully organized fictions ever written. Ford himself, however, was almost as disorganized as a human being can be. Ezra Pound told him that even if he were placed naked and alone in a room without furniture he would reduce it, in an hour's time, to total confusion.

Ford was the grandson of a fine old Pre-Raphaelite painter, Ford Madox Brown, so there was that to be lived up to, or got away from. He was tall, blond, and vacuous-looking in his youth, and as the years passed and he drank more he became very stout. He was compared to a white whale, a behemoth, an English squire, Falstaff, Lord Plushbottom.

His father was a German musicologist. Ford was educated partly in France and Germany, and he always thought out his novels in French. All his family lived for music, painting, and language. Whatever the disappointments, nothing else could be truly worth the doing. During his whole life Ford worked unremittingly to support himself and others by writing, but he was not a person who could ever make money. In a sense, he scarcely needed it. It was there to be lent, or borrowed, as fate decided. Ford needed luxury (good wine, food, and conversation) but not comfort. In the shabbiest lodgings he could maintain his grand manner.

Ford married in 1894, when he was only twenty years old, and it was in those early penniless days that he met Joseph Conrad, whose ideas stayed with him for the rest of his life. In 1908 he was editor of the influential *English Review*. In 1909 he left his wife, Elsie, and their two daughters. He was ordered to pay them a weekly maintenance, refused on principle, and spent eight days in Brixton jail. From 1911 onward he lived with the sharp-tongued literary hostess Violet Hunt. She desired to marry him, and he extricated himself with difficulty. When World War I broke out he joined the army (he was over forty), and came back from the battle of the Somme shellshocked. In 1918 he was lucky enough to meet an Australian painter, Stella Bowen, who was prepared to live with him in a remote, rat-infested cottage in Sussex and to bear him a third daughter. In the 1920s they decamped to Paris, where Ford edited *The Transatlantic Review*, getting contributions from Conrad, Pound, Gertrude Stein, Hemingway, Joyce, Paul Valéry, and William Carlos Williams.

Ford was less lucky in meeting the waiflike Jean Rhys, whose talent he encouraged (he was a great encourager). She described their affair, without forgiveness, in her novel *Quartet*. As Alan Judd shows in *Ford Madox Ford*, at all times he was surrounded by friends, who sometimes became enemies, and always he found ways to be hospitable. At fifty-six he found, or was found by, his last lover, the American Janice Biala. He had always been more appreciated in America than elsewhere and lived for years in the United States. But eventually he took his new wife back to Europe. He had been driven, he said, by an overwhelming nostalgia for French cooking. But time had run out. His health declined rapidly on the voyage to France, and he died on 26 June 1939, in a clinic in Deauville, at the age of sixty-five.

Ford conducted his life unwisely. To explain him is exceptionally difficult because he was a shape-shifter, giving a series of contradictory versions of himself to anyone who would listen. For mere facts, he said, he had a profound contempt. "What he is really," said H. G. Wells, "or if he is really, nobody knows. . . and he least of all." At heart he saw himself as the gallantly uncomplaining English gentleman of his finest novels, the victim of ruinous women or of some guileless-seeming manipulator, like the narrator of *The Good Soldier*. Yet Ford was overcome by little worries; he was prone to nervous collapse; he wept on the shoulders of others. Often he was not taken seriously. His devotion to literature was absolute, but he was, perhaps, a holy fool on a large scale.

The standard biography up till now—though not the only one—has been *The Saddest Story*, by Arthur Mizener (1971). Mr. Judd acknowledges Mizener's work and follows his chronology, but doesn't agree with what he calls Mizener's negative interpretation of Ford. In fact, Mr. Judd's fiercely energetic, absorbing book is in part a defense of Ford against Mizener. It starts unexpectedly with the words "There are also the rich in spirit." Although he can hardly claim that Ford was a happy man, he refuses to consider him a failure: "The point, surely, is that he was a writer. It doesn't matter what else he was or pretended to be—pig farmer, country gentleman, cook, man-about-town, editor, man of letters, soldier, cricket enthusiast. . . . If anyone was ever sent into the world to be something, Ford was; and he achieved it."

Ford started by collaborating with Conrad, then turned to light novels and historical fiction. *The Good Soldier* came out in 1915. After the war came the brilliant *Parade's End* tetralogy, then reminiscences, essays, criticism, *A History of Our Own Times*. Mr. Judd covers as much of this as he can, and quotes rather too much of Ford's tepid poetry.

He seems, in fact, prepared to defend almost everything Ford wrote but settles, as he is bound to, for the novels. Between 1906 and 1908 Ford brought out a trilogy, *The Fifth Queen*, based on the marriage of Catherine Howard and the aging King Henry VIII. To Mr. Judd this is one of the best historical novels in the language. But *The Fifth Queen* could not hope to compete with bestsellers by people like Rider Haggard or Robert Louis Stevenson, who had said that historical romance should appeal to our "nameless longings" and provide the adult version of child's play.

That was not at all the sort of thing Ford could do. Conrad and he had agreed that the general effect of fiction must be "the effect life has on mankind." This Ford believed could be achieved not by either romance or realism but by re-creating states of mind. These, of course, can be deceptive, as they are in *The Good Soldier*, a story of two married couples and a young girl—well-off, respectable, and supposed to be good friends. Only gradually does it show itself to be what Ford first wanted to call it, "The Saddest Story," a frightening pattern of love and death. Those who have "heart" are perhaps better human beings, but they are liable to grotesque disasters. A good deal is asked of the reader, who is led through dazzling shifts of time and viewpoint, without hope of finding a final solution, since Ford believed that "there is in life nothing final."

When Mr. Judd tells us that "it is better to read and re-read *Parade's End* rather than read about it," it is clear that he himself is something much more genial than a literary critic. He is, in fact, a novelist himself and, on the evidence of this book, a tolerant man, sympathetic to human passions and dilemmas and to commonplace human embarrassments. Accordingly, he is particularly good on the subject of "Ford's women" (they were known as that). Ford was successful with women, Mr. Judd thinks (in a way that astonished James Joyce), because he liked them, and needed to talk to them. They didn't expect him to provide, but knew he would give. Did he enjoy sex? "It may be that what he most sought was the emotional intensity, intimacy and dependence engendered by sexual relationships rather than sex itself." The keynote of Ford's character, as Mr. Judd sees him, is generosity. For this all his shortcomings, even his disregard for truth, must be forgiven.

Mr. Judd provides his book with few notes and no references, telling us that Ford cared nothing for such things. This, I think, was a mistake, but in every other way he is the reader's good friend, persuading, lecturing a little, and bringing his subject unforgettably to life. "Not," he says, "that complete understanding is possible; the point is to get as near to it as we can, to know all that can be known in order to stand, if only for a moment, at the edge of what cannot."

1991

A Student of Obliteration

An introduction to *The World My Wilderness*, by Rose Macaulay

Rose Macaulay was born in 1881, and died in 1958. As a young woman she went bathing by moonlight with Rupert Brooke, and she lived long enough to protest, as a well-known author and critic, against the invasion of Korea. *The World My Wilderness* was published in 1950, when she was thought to have given up fiction, not having written a novel for nearly ten years.

The book disturbed her readers, because it was not what they expected. The most successful of her early novels had been social satires. They were delightful to read, and still are, brilliantly clear-sighted without being malicious (or at least more malicious than necessary), but they took a detached view; humanity was so misguided that one must either laugh or cry, and Rose had felt it best to laugh. *The World My Wilderness* showed that the power of ridicule, after all, was not the most important gift she had.

Rose Macaulay herself was most characteristically English, tall, angular, and given to wearing flat tweed caps, or hats like tea cosies—English, too, in her gaiety and wit, which, at heart, was melancholic. But almost any conclusion you came to about her would be wrong. From the ages of six to thirteen she had grown up with her brothers and sisters in a small fishing town on the Genoese coast, and this interlude of scrambling about the Mediterranean hills and foreshore was as important to her as all her English education. Again, Rose was often thought to be sexless, or, as Rosamond Lehmann put it, "sexless though not unfeminine." But in fact she had, at the age of thirty-six, fallen irretrievably in love with a married man, Gerald O'Donovan, and in spite of much heart-searching she never broke with her lover till the day of his death. Both these episodes have a good deal to do with the writing of *The World My Wilderness*.

The book's seventeen-year-old heroine Rose herself described as "rather lost and strayed and derelict." Barbary Deniston has grown up in wartime Occupied France, only half attended to by her worldly, sensual charmer of an English mother. This mother, Helen, has been divorced from Deniston, and her second husband, "an amiable, thriving French collaborator," is dead. Meanwhile Barbary and her stepbrother have lived in and out of the house as children of the Maquis, trained by the Resistance in sabotage and petty thieving. Like Auden's boy with a stone, Barbary has never heard of any world where promises were kept. When she is sent from her fishing village to the respectable Deniston relatives in London, she is doubly lost. Like seeking like, she escapes from pallid WC2 to join the drifters and scroungers in the bombed area round St. Paul's, where "shrubs and green creeping things ran about a broken city." "Here, its cliffs and chasms seemed to say, is your home; here you belong; you cannot get away, you do not wish to get away, for this is the *maquis* that lies about the margins of the wrecked world." Ironically enough she begins housekeeping at once, tidying and cleaning the gaping ruins of a church. She is not a wanderer by nature, it is only that she needs a home that she can trust.

In Rose Macaulay's earlier novels, notably *Crewe Train* (1926) and *They Were Defeated* (1932), there are young girls of Barbary's sort, precociously adult and yet clinging for reassurance to childhood. Many have names that could be either masculine or feminine (Denham, Julian, Eve-lyn), as though rejecting all society's definitions. All of them are unwilling exiles from some lost paradise. They remember sunshine and freedom, as Rose remembered her Italy. But in this story of the 1940s, the world that Barbary longs for and looks back to is a black-marketing France. The paradise itself is corrupt. And the civilization to which she is packed off is an equally shabby affair. Deniston, the honorable man, is an odd man out in post-war London. His son Richie describes himself as a "gentle, civilised, swindling crook" who by bending the law a little— as all his friends do—hopes to make himself a comfortable life. Barbary is no doubt right, on the beach at Collioure, to examine the word *civilization* "and to reject it, as if it were mentioned too late." In any society, she will remain a barbarian. The novel's painful question is: what have we done to our children?

The war years had brought deep personal trouble to Rose. In 1939 she was responsible for a serious car crash in which her lover was injured. In 1941 her flat was bombed and she lost nearly everything she possessed. In 1942 Gerald O'Donovan died, and Rose entered her own wasteland of remorse. How much could be forgotten, and how much could she forgive herself? In spite of this, or more probably because of it, she is more compassionate in this novel than in any other. To be self-satisfied, to be stupid, to be cruel (Rose had always said) is undesirable, if we are to consider ourselves civilized, but at the same time she was not at all easily shocked. Asked on one occasion by a question-master whether she would prefer death or dishonor, she replied: "Dishonour, every time." And *The World My Wilderness* is remarkable for the pleas in mitigation she makes for all her characters. Helen has no conscience, it seems to have been left out of her, but she creates pleasure for others. Deniston is stiff, bland, and resentful, but his integrity must count for something. Richie is a young aesthete who prefers to withdraw rather than to be too much involved, but then he has been fighting through three years of "messy, noisy and barbaric war." Mrs. Cox, the house-keeper, can't distinguish—which of us can?—between interference and what, to her, are good intentions. Even Pamela, Deniston's second wife, wholesome tweedy Pamela ("all Pamela's clothes were good, of the kind known as cheaper in the end"), Pamela the young committeewoman, not at all Rose's favorite kind of person, redeems herself by suffering with dignity. If there is a responsibility to judge these people the author is asking us to share it.

In the same way, every turn of the story brings a different confrontation, genial against skeptical, honorable against amoral, will against emotion, rough against smooth, wild against tamed. And these encounters, too, are left unresolved. In the closing chapters, for instance, Helen comes back to London. At the Denistons' house she takes command, a supremely inconvenient guest. Her motives, as we have to admit, are generous. But poor Pamela has to hold her own against the sumptuous intruder. The contest of possessiveness, jealousy, and genuine love is so finely balanced that most readers would be hard put to it to say exactly where their sympathies lie. Rose has written the novel in terms of comedy, but all the satirist's air of knowing what's best for everybody has gone. Indeed there is, perhaps, no "best" for any of them.

Rose Macaulay liked to insist that ideas for novels came to her as places—"backgrounds" would hardly be a strong enough word for them. In *The World My Wilderness* (if we take the "respectable, smoke-dark houses" of London as a kind of negation of place) we have three of them—Collioure in the South of France, Arshaig in the Western Highlands, and the wilderness itself. Each corresponds to its own moral climate. Collioure is described in the most seductive terms. "The cool evening wind rustled in the cork forest, crept about the thymey *maquis*; the sea, drained of light, was a wash of blue shadow, sparked by the lights of fishing boats putting out for the night's catch." By day, the Villa Fraises offers serene warmth and relaxation for all comers, but always with a hint of excess. The garden is "crowded," Helen "lounged her days away," the most striking of her pictures is "a large nude who was a French mayor, reclining on a green sofa with a blue plate of strawberries in his hand; the flesh tones were superb." Arshaig is equally beautiful, but austere, with misty dawns and steel-pale water, and at the shooting lodge are a whole family of Barbary's relations, "formidably efficient at catching and killing Highland animals." But in saying this Rose reminds us that there has also been killing and hunting—of men as well as animals—in the forests of Collioure, "savageries without number," from the days of the Saracens to the Gestapo and the Resistance. And on the beach there Barbary and Raoul had stood watching the fish in the nets as they struggled, leaped, and died.

Barbary herself becomes a creature of the wilderness, the ruins of the city of London. In 1950 the rubble was still lying where it had fallen, carpeted with weeds and inhabited by rats and nesting birds. The whole area fascinated Rose—how much, can be felt in the lyrical opening to Chapter Eighteen. To her they were the new catacombs. "I spent much of today in the ruins round St. Paul's, which I like . . . part of my new novel is laid in this wrecked scene," she wrote to Gilbert Murray. Many people must still remember, as I do, the alarming experience of scrambling after her that summer (she made no distinction of age on her expeditions) and keeping her spare form just in view as she shinned undaunted down a crater, or leaned, waving, through the smashed glass of some perilous window. Foxgloves, golden charlock, and loosestrife were flourishing everywhere they could take root in the stones, but Rose did not sentimentalize over the wild flowers. It was not man's business, in her view, to abandon what he has won from nature. She was studying obliteration.

Descended from historians, trained as a historian herself, she makes the ruins into something more than a metaphor for Barbary's desolate state; they give the novel a dimension in time. They are still alive with the indignation of all the generations who have lived and done business in the city, or worshiped in its fallen churches. "The ghosts of churches burnt in an earlier fire, St. Olave's and St. John Zachary's, the ghosts of taverns where merchants and clerks had drunk" all haunt their old precincts, even under the midday sun, so do the long-dead clerics and shopkeepers themselves. When Barbary is on the run, the phantoms of five centuries of London crowd together to watch, from their vanished buildings, the pitiful end of the chase. They are not sympathetic, they want her caught. History, as might be expected, is on the side of authority.

At the end of the book Richie is seen alone on the brink of the "wrecked scene," and the squalor in front of him makes him feel sick. He reflects that "we are in rat's alley, where the dead men lost their bones," quoting *The Waste Land*, from which Rose took one of the novel's epigraphs (she wrote the first one herself).* But *The Waste Land* is also a fitful quest for spiritual healing, and Richie, in the end, takes the track from Moorgate Station "across the wilderness towards St Paul's."

---

*"The world my wilderness, its caves my home, / Its weedy wastes the garden where I roam, / In chasm'd cliffs my castle and my tomb. . . ."—Anon.

This is one of several hints in the book of a religious solution, or, at least, of curiosity about one, even though Barbary and Raoul perceive that "if there is anything, there must be hell. But one supposes there is nothing."

The World My Wilderness is, in fact, not a pessimist's book—heartfelt, yes, but pessimistic, no. However faulty the main characters may be, there is one striking fact about them; their mistakes are not the result of caring nothing about each other, but of caring too much. It is because he still loves Helen that Deniston fails to forgive her, and Helen herself learns in the end not only how much she loves her daughter, but a way to help her. "She must have sunshine, geniality, laughter, love; and if she goes to the devil she shall at least go happily, my little savage." This is probably the best that Helen can do. And if the inhabitants of this earth, in spite of the mess, the slaughter, and the desolation they cause, can give up so much for each other, they must be redeemable. In the last resort, Rose Macaulay thought so. And she was, as her novel shows, too much interested in human beings to lose faith in them.

1983

Dame Cissie

Rebecca West: A Life, by Victoria Glendinning

There were giant-killers in those days. Storm Jameson, rallying English writers in defense of peace and collective security, had to toss up to decide between Rebecca West and Rose Macaulay for the place of honor. Between these three women enough power should have been generated even for an impossible cause. They were tireless collectors of facts— Rose used to take her newspaper-cuttings everywhere—and what courage they showed, what endurance, what determination to call the world sharply to order, what unanswerable wit, what impatience for justice. They were all prepared to outface the mighty, but they also judged themselves, on occasion, more strictly than anyone else would have dared. "When I come to stand," wrote Storm Jameson, "as they say— used to say—before my Maker, the judgment on me will run: she did not love enough. . . . For such a fault, no forgiveness." "As we grow older," said Rebecca West, "and like ourselves less and less, we apply our critical experience as a basis for criticising our own consciences." It isn't surprising that her son grew up with the "idea that a woman was the thing to be, and that I had somehow done wrong by being a male."

But Rebecca also wrote in her old age: "I was never able to lead the life of a writer because of these two overriding factors, my sexual life, or rather death, and my politics." Here she is both attacking and defending herself, for she felt that the world, on the whole, had treated her basely. From the age of eighteen she made her own life, but she was not altogether satisfied with the results. She would have liked to subsume, perhaps, the lives of both her sisters, Lettie, the correct benevolent professional woman, Winnie, the contented housewife, "living decently in a house with children." She would have liked to live in Rosmersholm without drowning herself, and in the doll's house without letting it defeat her. Her voice, which she found so early, is that of an elder sister, not the youngest. Samuel Hynes has even called it "episcopal"—"praising the righteous, condemning heretics, explaining doctrine." She found it easy to attract, almost as easy to dominate, and "if people do not have the face of the age set clear before them, they begin to imagine it." Authority, then, became a duty, and yet "I could have done it," she believed at times, "if anybody had let me, simply by being a human being."

Some of her first pieces, for the *Freewoman*, the socialist *Clarion*, and the *New Statesman*, were reprinted by Virago in 1982. They were written in her teens, or just out of them, when she first arrived in London, a phenomenon, a marvelous girl, reckless, restless, brilliant, and indignant. All her life she remained pre-eminently a journalist. To the very end, in illness, in fury, in distress, and when almost spent, she continued to react, as a plant does to the light, to new information or even to gossip. She was always on the alert, as Our Correspondent from the moral strongholds of the twentieth century. Her first novel, however, the beautiful *Return of the Soldier* (1918), seemed to class her as what was then called a "psychopathological writer"—with her older friend May Sinclair, who had organized London's first medico-psychological clinic. The *Return* is the case history of an officer invalided home from the trenches. He is an amnesiac who cannot react either to his wife or to the memory of his dead child. His only surviving emotion is for a girl he once loved, who by now is a dreary little straw-hatted woman, "repulsively" faded and poor. This woman courageously shows him the dead son's clothes and toys, which have been locked away. He is cured, but this, of course, means that he will have to return to the Front.

When Rebecca called this novel "rather Conradesque," she was thinking of the unvoiced struggle between good and evil, woman's attempt to
heal, man's invention of war. In 1922, when Freud's *Beyond the Pleasure
Principle* appeared in translation, she related his theory to her own view
of the life-and-death struggle: it became, for her, part of the fierce self-
justification of a natural fighter. She did not hold with Freud's majestic
hypothesis that human beings unconsciously recognized the "sublime
necessity" of the return to the inorganic state. Like many passionately
committed writers, she created a God and then took Him to task for
falling short of her standards. Her case against Him was that He made
sacrifice and suffering a condition of redemption: "pain is the proper
price for any good thing." This was also the basis of her complaint
against Tolstoy and against St. Augustine, whose life she was commissioned to write in 1933: he "intellectualised with all the force of his
genius" the idea of atonement through suffering. Rebecca set herself to
wipe out not guilt but cruelty, by the exercise of reason. *The Harsh Voice*
and the much later *The Birds Fall Down*, the monumental *Black Lamb
and Grey Falcon* and *The Meaning of Treason*, are essentially variations
of the same battle. Blake, she believed, was on her side, so was
Lawrence—though this disconcertingly meant claiming both of them as
champions of the mind. "The mind must walk proudly and always
armed," she wrote, "that it shall not be robbed of its power." What was
her mind like, though—"her splendid disturbed brain," as Wells called
it—and how far did she ever free it, if that was what she wanted to do,
from her emotions? It has been called androgynous, but May Sinclair
came closer to it when she said: "Genius is giving you another sex inside
yourself, and a stronger one, to plague you with."

This plague took the form of an extreme temperament. All her life
Rebecca West was betrayed by the physical, collapsing under stress into
illness and even hallucination. She was a romantic in the highest sense of
demanding universal solutions. "I believe in the Christian conception of
man and the French Revolution's interpretation of his political necessities." But she was also romantic in a much simpler sense. *The Return of
the Soldier* takes place in ancestral Baldry Court, perfect in its "green
pleasantness," except that the post arrives too late to be brought up with
the morning tea. *Parthenope* is set in Currivel Lodge, with its haunted
croquet lawn. The character of Nikolai in *The Birds Fall Down* was
based on a Russian tutor—though he has become a Russian count.

Isabelle, the heroine of *The Thinking Reed*, is young, exceedingly beautiful, "nearly exceedingly rich," tragically widowed. She hunts the wild boar, her underwear is made to measure, her first lover "was not less beautiful as a man than she was as a woman." As a novelist, Rebecca West liked to write about people who were rich or good-looking or high-born or all three, and her public liked to read about them. There was a converse: she found it difficult to forgive ugliness or coarseness—the crowds outside the court in the Stephen Ward case were worse because they had "cheap dentures." All this was part of the great impatient shake with which she left the narrowness and just-respectability of her early life. As her son was to put it, "shabby-genteel life in Edinburgh marked those who had to endure it to the bone." *The Thinking Reed* was said to be about "the effect of riches on people, and the effect of men on women, both forms of slavery," but, like *The Great Gatsby*, it shows that although money produces corruption, it also produces an enviable and civilized way of living, and there is nothing we can do about it. Good writers are seldom honest enough to admit this, but Rebecca West did admit it. With her limitless energy and enthusiasm, she called for harmony, but not for moderation. All that the reader can do, very often, is to trust the driver as her arguments bowl along in splendid sentences or collect themselves for a pause. "Men and women see totally different aspects of reality." "A great deal of what Kafka wrote is not worth studying." "Authentic art never has an explicit religious and moral content." These are sweeping statements—though sweeping, of course, can be a worthwhile activity.

Victoria Glendinning says in the introduction to her new biography of Rebecca West that it is "the story of twentieth-century woman," but that it is a sadder story than she had expected. She has divided her book into episodes: "Cissie," the unstoppable young new arrival in London; "Panther" (this was Wells's name for her), fearlessly launching into questions of history, politics, and morality, and into bed with Wells; "Sunflower," the fiery successful international author and unsuccessful mistress of Beaverbrook; "Mrs. Henry Andrews," the awkwardly married famous writer; "Dame Rebecca." The divisions are helpful, though rather like breakwaters trying to hold back a high tide. It is a fine biography, which for several reasons can't have been easy to write. To start with, Stanley Olson, who became a friend of Dame Rebecca's in 1974, was entrusted with the full-length Life. To conform with this, Victoria Glendinning decided to cut down on the later years. Rebecca lived to be ninety, and the elision somewhat weakens the sense of endurance and of seeing the century through, also of that indestructibility—surely an active rather than a passive quality—which is dear to the British public. Another difficulty must have been the richness of the literary and political background, or battleground, and the sheer number of subsidiary characters. For all of them there was "an overwhelming mass" of material. The only evidence missing seems to have been some diaries and papers which are restricted during the lifetime of Anthony West, and the correspondence with Beaverbrook, which Rebecca and Max burned together at her flat in 1930. With great skill Victoria Glendinning concentrates attention on the story she has been asked to tell. Rebecca was to the end, as one of her housekeepers put it, "black and white and crimson and purple and wild." Victoria Glendinning treats each episode, black or white, with calming, professional good sense. She makes very few direct judgments, only once or twice risking a sad question—"How could she behave so unwisely or so badly?" Some of the story has been paraded almost too often, some not at all. The book is equally successful with the well-known and the unfamiliar aspects, particularly with Rebecca's marriage to Henry Andrews, who is usually thought of, if he is thought of at all, as the wealthy, totally faithful, slightly deaf, typically English banker with whom she found security and a country life. Slightly deaf he certainly was, but he soon ceased, it turns out, to be a banker, was partly Lithuanian, and was unable to resist a long series of tepid affairs with younger women. In Buckinghamshire, where they bought a house and farm, he was quite at a loss. "Rebecca wanted to do everything, having a flair for everything. She took over the management of the greenhouses and the kitchen and flower gardens from Henry . . . complaining that he could not even take the dog for a walk." Henry pottered, and was considered in the village to be a comical old bugger. When he died, in 1968, he left thirty almost identical dark suits from Savile Row, each with money in the waistcoat pocket, ready for giving tips. Yet he lived with Rebecca and traveled with her and drove her about, often losing the way; and he was a man about the house. Victoria Glendinning re-creates him with something like tenderness, and points out that "it was not so different from many marriages." It is only strange as the choice of the brilliant and stormy woman who wrote that "the difference between men and women is the rock on which civilisation will split."

But perhaps "strange" is not the right word, because consistency was never Rebecca West's main concern. In *The Meaning of Treason* (revised in 1962 to include studies of Philby, Burgess, and Maclean), she sometimes confuses treachery with treason and examination with cross-examination, but this doesn't affect the dazzling intelligence of her case histories. As to why she wrote, she gave a number of explanations. She began "without choosing to do so—at home we all wrote and thought nothing of it." "My work," she said, "expresses an infatuation with human beings. I don't believe that to understand is to pardon, but I feel that to understand makes one forget that one cannot pardon." She also said that she wrote her novels to find out how she felt. Victoria Glendinning believes that "she most revealed herself when describing somebody else." She has, therefore, to look even more attentively than most biographers at the correspondence of what Browning called House and Shop. This is a complex matter when it comes to the later work, in particular *Black Lamb and Grey Falcon*. In 1936 Rebecca was sent to Yugoslavia by the British Council (who might have guessed what would happen) as a lecturer, and she went there again in 1937 and 1938. Her book was a testament to the country with which she had fallen in love on a majestic scale. It was not finished until 1942, when the Yugoslav resistance to the German invasion had given it a new intention. The travel book was still there, with Rebecca as the passionate explorer and interpreter and Henry supplying—not always convincingly—the statistics, but it had deepened into a vast meditation on the history, politics, geography, and ethnology of Eastern Europe, following, as she said, "the dark waters" of the Second World War back to their distant source. To do it justice, Victoria Glendinning has had to summarize the troubled history of the southern Slavs (Rebecca was heart and soul with the Serbs), the shifts of British policy, and the devices of the SOE and the Foreign Office. At one extreme, there is the "emotional, curly-haired, Serbian Jew" who acted as Rebecca's official guide and fell in love with her; at the other is her vision of Europe's history as a crime committed by man against himself. The exposition here could not be clearer. When Rebecca declared that she had never made a continuous revelation of herself, she was admitting that she made a discontinuous one. The novels are probably the best place to look for her. "Non-fiction," she said, "always tends to become fiction; only the dream compels honesty." So the biographer arrives, with admiration and caution, at her own view of Rebecca West's view of herself.

1987

Raging Martyr

Jean Rhys: Life and Work, by Carole Angier

A novel has to have a shape, Jean Rhys thought, and life doesn't have any. Hers, however, had a pattern, which disastrously recurred: a cycle of effort, excitement, happiness, collapse, unexpected help, resentment at being helped, black rage, violent scenes, catastrophe.

She spent her life with lovers or husbands, but wrote about loneliness. In choosing these men—or letting herself be chosen, for there was an oddly passive side to her nature she wanted protection (otherwise she was frightened) and also risk (otherwise she was bored). The contradictions were never resolved.

This charming, sun-loving creature, brought up in the West Indies and entitled (as she saw it) to affection, warmth, and spending money, ended up as an abusive, drunken old woman trapped in what for her was a place of terror, a damp Devonshire village. By then she has almost stopped writing. In 1957, when she was nearing seventy, two saviors appeared: the publisher Diana Athill and the most understanding of critics, Francis Wyndham. They cajoled her into finishing what is perhaps the finest of her novels, *The Wide Sargasso Sea*. Her earlier work was republished, she was awarded a CBE. For the first time since the 1920s there was money, and she had at least a short time to spend it in the 1920s style.

Carole Angier is a warm-hearted narrator who allows us to feel for Jean's bewildered victims, especially, perhaps, for the gentle Leslie Tilden Smith, her second husband—she gave him a black eye more than once. This book, however, is, by and large, the life of writer as martyr. In the search for perfection, Jean Rhys drove herself to the edge of madness.

The horrifying ending of *Good Morning, Midnight* was so hard to get right that she tore up both her contract and her manuscript. It took her nine years to finish *The Wide Sargasso Sea* and to release it reluctantly for publication. If she had written in any other way she would not, she explained, have "earned her death."

She also said: "All of a writer that matters is the book or books. It is idiotic to be curious about the person. I have never made that mistake." But she would have to forgive Carole Angier for this truly sympathetic study in depth.

1990

The Near and the Far

An introduction to *The Root and the Flower,*
by L. H. Myers

Leopold Hamilton Myers was born, in 1881, into a distinguished scholarly family. His father, F. W. Myers, was one of the founders of the Society for Psychical Research; their home in Cambridge was a center of hospitality and intellectual discussion, but it was also rather an odd place to be brought up in. Frederic Myers was set upon demonstrating the immortality, or at least the survival, of human personality by acceptable scientific methods, and his children were half frightened and half fascinated by the procession of mediums and "sensitives" who came to the house to give evidence. Leo's mother was passionate and possessive; his father expected rather more of the family than they could give. When he died Leo had to cut short his time at university to take his mother abroad; F. W. Myers had made an appointment to manifest himself after death, and had named a time and place, but the meeting failed. Leo lost faith, but only in his father's methods. He saw now that though reason must always be distinguished from intuition, it should never be separated from it. They must work together.

He was educated at Eton and Cambridge, and although he was always as popular as he would allow himself to be, he bitterly hated both of them. He rejected, in fact, every social structure to which he belonged, including the literary circles that London offered him. To Myers, all of these fell grotesquely short. "Just as an individual cannot live for himself," says the Rajah in *The Near and the Far,* "so society cannot live for itself, but must keep a self-transcendent idea before it." In holding this ideal, and in devoting his writing career to it, Myers was unflinchingly sincere, but his life was not consistent with it. He was neither an ascetic nor a revolutionary. Between his seduction at the age of sixteen and his marriage he had a number of affairs, some, he said, "very squalid." When in 1906 he came into a legacy he moved through society as a generous patron of the arts, but also as a detached and elegant young man, with a taste for racing at Brooklands. Even when, after running through every other political solution, he became a Communist, he still had a part-share in an expensive French restaurant, Boulestin's. Myers, of course, noticed these discrepancies, since he possessed (in the words of his friend L. P. Hart-

ley) "an exquisite wry sense of humour, of which he was half-ashamed."
But Hartley has also described how, with the close of the 1930s and the
threat of war, Myers's self-knowledge darkened into pessimism. A slow
and scrupulous writer, he had always depended greatly on the advice of
his friends. Now he quarreled fiercely with most of them. As a young man
he had asked himself the question: "Why should anyone want to go on
living once they know what the world is like?" On 7 April 1944, he
answered it for himself by taking an overdose of veronal.

Myers left his great trilogy, *The Root and the Flower,* to speak for him.
Like his other books, it has an exotic setting, in this case sixteenth century India under the reign of Akbar. He did not pretend to accuracy and
indeed had never been to India. His motive, as he said in his 1940 preface, is to give us a clearer view of our own social and ethical problems
from the "vantage-point of an imaginary world."

This world, though anything but safe, is a very seductive one. The
slow rhythm of the palace, the desert, and the river are like an audible
pulsation of the Indian heat, but at any moment we may be asked to look
at something as small as a mark in the dust or stretch our ears for a
minute sound. We do not do this for nothing. The descriptive passages
hardly ever stand still, they give the sense of something about to happen:

> At the door he paused again; from the roof there hung down wisps of
> dry, grey moss; ants had built a nest against the threshold and the drop-
> pings of wood-pigeons whitened the window-sills. Contrary to his expec-
> tations the latch came up when he tried it; the door opened and a curious
> smell spread upon the fresh air.

> The absence of the moon and stars made the night intimate and
> earthly; dry leaves, lifted from the ground, were swept across his hands
> and face. It seemed as if the earth's secret energies were working upon
> him, and he yielded to a process which he felt to be beneficent. His spirit
> lay still in a quiet excitement; a sense of expectation gathered; it was like
> that of a woman who is awaiting the first pangs of her first childbed.

> She showed him the place where the young man was buried. There cer-
> tainly were some suspicious marks upon the ground. The soil was
> cracked, having swollen up in a blister, and this seemed to indicate that
> the work was not the work of thugs, for Thugs always drove a stake
> through the body to allow the gases of decomposition to escape without
> a sign.

Myers wants us to look at his world of appearances and beyond it. Appearances cannot be dismissed as an illusion, for no illusion can be created except by reason. On the other hand, the life of the spirit is just as real as the pigeon dung and the bloated corpse. "I am" has no meaning without "There is." How can the two be reconciled? On this problem depend the three great questions of the book. First, how can an individual be sure that he has found himself? "If everyone is pretending to be like others," says Prince Jali, "who is like himself?" Second, if each individual is a solitary heart, how is he to unite with other human beings? Third, if he does so, how can he be sure that the society he lives in acknowledges "the supremacy of the spirit as the guiding principle of life"?

Reading a long book is like living a long life; it needs an adjustment of pace. Myers is asking us to slow down, and so to deepen the consciousness. At the beginning of the trilogy, a story of war, betrayal, torture, and political power, we have to consider what seems a very small incident. The little prince, alone on the palace balcony, sees a snake crawling along the gutter. The wind stirs a twig, and Jali, watching, "entered into the snake's cold, narrow intelligence and shared its angry perplexity." It strikes, loses its balance, and falls to its death on the roof below. The snake shares "the terrible numerousness of living beings, all separate, all alone, all threatened." It could not tell that the twig was not an enemy. It was deceived by appearances. But a little earlier Jali had been gazing at the serene desert horizon, which had looked so different when they made the six days' hot journey across it. "He clung to the truth of appearances as something equal to the truth of what underlay them. Deep in his heart he cherished the belief that some day the near and the far would meet."

The first book of the trilogy gives a sense of the imperial war game that will decide the fate of India. Akbar is the ruinous tyrant or "great man" of history. His dream of uniting India's religions—the Din Ilahi—is folly, and he himself is at heart commonplace. His inheritance is disputed between his two sons, Selim, the brutal soldier, and Daniyal, the perverted intellectual. It is the duty of Rajah Amar, in his small kingdom, to decide where his allegiance lies before he withdraws, as he wishes to do, to a monastery. Almost perversely, he favors Daniyal, because he has always disliked him, and he wants to stand uninfluenced by the affections. Sita, the Rajah's wife, is a Christian who prefers, for good or ill, to stay with the rest of humanity. These two, husband and wife, are far apart, and yet they are both searching for perfection. "The gulf is not between those who affirm and those who deny but between those who affirm and those who ignore." The man whom Sita eventually takes for a lover, Han, is a wild chieftain who relishes life at is comes, but all through the first book we can see him gradually driven, step by step, to concede that he cannot after all live through the senses alone. His love for Sita "seemed to play not upon the nerves of the flesh, not upon the machinery of the brain, but upon the substance of the very soul . . . and he said to himself, 'What is this?'" On the other hand, the Rajah's adviser Gokal, the Brahman philosopher, is caught in sensuality's trap. He is enslaved by a low-caste girl, Gunevati, who in turn is guided by sheer animal instinct.

Myers, of course, saw the danger of all this. "The impression may come into the reader's mind," he wrote, "that what he has before him is a philosophical novel." This, he knew, would mean neither good philosophy, nor a good novel, nor, before long, any readers. But his characters are not representatives of ideas, they are an invitation to think about them, which is a different matter. And in spite of Myers's detached and elegant manner, they are all human beings. Gunevati, for instance, has been taken, I think quite wrongly, as standing for pure evil. Certainly she resorts to poison, and passively accepts the position of fetish to an obscene and forbidden religious sect. But at other times we are asked to pity her, as Hari does, when he realizes what a low price she puts on herself, in spite of her beauty. Beauty has no particular rights in the world as it is. Jali pities her, too, when she turns pale and ill as a captive in Gokal's house. The truth is that she has no way of knowing herself. To destroy her is not justice.

Book Two is a *Bildungsroman,* the education of Prince Jali, the Rajah's son. This, in a sense, is the simplest part of the trilogy, and, in terms of action, the most exciting. Jali's ordeals are of the flesh, the mind, and the spirit. As a young adolescent he finds, under Gunevati's tuition, that women are easy enough and he can get into any bedroom he likes. But he wants to understand life, or at least to see it clearly, and his passion for knowledge leads him to explore the secret cults of the Valley and to discover how they connect with the spying and counter-spying of the court. But Jali—for he is only a learner and a searcher—does not know enough, not enough, at least, to outwit his enemies by himself. And after his escape from the Valley he is in greater danger still, as he approaches the neighborhood of the Camp.

Here, perhaps, Myers let his prejudices run away with him; the Camp, or Plesaunce, is, as he admitted, a monstrous version of the world of Cambridge and Bloomsbury by which he had once been deceived. It is the stronghold of Daniyal, the artificial paradise of the aesthetes, and to Myers the aesthetes were "trivial," a word which for him meant the denial of life. They were the sterile self-regarders and self-indulgers; sterility leads to cruelty, and self-regard to the death of the spirit. The Camp, then the traveling court of Prince Daniyal and his entourage, entices Jali with the most degrading materialism of all. If we are in any doubt as to how dangerous it is—dangerous rather than merely absurd—we have only to follow, as Jali does, the fate of Gunevati. It is at Daniyal's orders that this girl, who can express herself only through her body and her senses, has her tongue cut out; after that she is forced to learn to write. "She opened her mouth wide. Jali found himself looking into a cavern—black, swollen, horrible." It is this that recalls Jali to himself, so that he will never again be mistaken as to the nature of the Camp.

Jali will be the ruler of the future, but for the present power still rests with Rajah Amar. Book Three returns us to the problem we set out with. Is the Rajah justified in giving up the near for the far, or is his longing for detachment only another name for the refusal of responsibility? In the face of Gokal's misgivings, he still prepares to withdraw from earthly concerns. But on the very point of leaving he is summoned to the Camp; there the whole nature of evil is brought home to him by another of the book's apparently unimportant moments, the horrible incident of the white cat. Now Amar has to decide, at his own risk, whether in the face of recognized evil a man can ever be absolved from action. The Rajah does not choose what happens to him, but Myers has shown that though there are strict limits to the human will, there are none to human vision: Amar sees what is to be done.

When Gokal brings his fallen body back across the lake, we do not even know whether Amar is dead, or what effect, if any, he has made on Daniyal. Like the relationships of the characters, which have been, all along, subtle and ambiguous, the story never yields a conclusion. "There is no illusory sense of understanding," Myers said, "only the realisation of what is." But the trilogy unmistakably ends with a return to life. The thought had come to Gokal that if the Rajah were to die without recovering consciousness, it might be as well. "But he condemned that thought," and as he goes up the path toward the house on the farther side of the lake, he hears Han, Sita, and Jali talking together on the verandah. With these quiet everyday sounds Myers concludes his strange masterpiece, which, it has been said, "brought back the aspect of eternity to the English novel."

1985

Betrayed by His Century

Foreign Country: The Life of L. P. Hartley, by Adrian Wright

When I was working on a Life of L. P. Hartley (1895–1972) I went to see Princess Clary, one of the kindest of his hostesses in Venice, who said to me, "My dear, how can you write the life of a writer? If he had entered into politics, if he had commanded an army in warfare, but what life can a writer have?" I felt the force of this, but only gave up when I realized that what I was finding out would be distressing to Hartley's surviving sister, Norah.

In *Foreign Country: The Life of L. P. Hartley*, Adrian Wright says very little about the staff surrounding Hartley in his later years in London "rough trade," young men who amused him more than they amused his visitors; sometimes, apparently, wheedling for fur coats and cars. There is little revealed about the unsavory hangers-on and his unfortunate political views and behavior—he upset his country neighbors by killing swans.

Wright's biography is, however, well written and well constructed; it is elegant and discreet and would have suited Norah exactly. And it is the last opportunity to have written his life with access to the family papers. Norah died in 1994, after giving instructions that all surviving material was to be burned.

Norah and her elder sister, Enid, lived in the Victorian-gothic Fletton Tower, on the outskirts of Peterborough, all their lives. The house had been built from the proceeds of their father's lucky investment in a brickfield. Leslie, the doted-on but ruthlessly ordered-about son, was the only one to leave home. His mother was obsessed with her son's health, and he was sent to Harrow simply because she had heard it was on a hill and thought it would be good for his chest. At Oxford, he realized that it was necessary for him to be a writer, and also that he wanted to breathe a different air—different, that is, from Fletton. He became friends with Eddie Sackville-West and Anthony Asquith, and also with Lord David Cecil, with whom he fell irretrievably in love. As an expert in avoiding disagreeable facts, he perhaps believed that this golden friendship would never suffer mortal change, but in 1932 Cecil married.

Wright had to decide at an early stage in the biography whether or not to call the amiable, sociable Hartley a snob. Hartley was deeply fond of many people who weren't distinguished at all, and he never hesitated to invite his grander friends back to the heavy atmosphere of Fletton. On the other hand, he had a passion for grandes dames. He loved to be given orders by the imperious and to do errands for people who already had everything. One of the first of his patronesses was Lady Ottoline Morrell.

By the end of the 1920s, he was a regular visitor to Venice and its Anglo-American *palazzi*. Wright has been able, therefore, to connect his book with a series of waterscapes the Northamptonshire fens, the glittering Venetian lagoons, and the reaches of the river Avon. After the Second World War, Hartley bought Avondale, a large, old, inconvenient house on the riverbank at Bathford. There he intended, taking Henry James's Lamb House as a model, to live among friends and books. That meant staff and a personal manservant. Hartley always insisted that he was unable even to fill a hot-water bottle.

Charlie Holt, the manservant who was with him from the first at Avondale, massaged him every day (comparing him to a beached whale) and staunchly protected him for twenty years. After Charlie's death, the situation soon deteriorated. Hartley began to revel in the domestic upsets that gave him the precious sensation of having something urgent to do. One of his difficulties as a novelist was to "raise" his material sufficiently for twentieth-century readers, which he managed by killing the characters off, physically or spiritually. Life at Avondale, and later in London, was "raised" by a series of increasingly sinister male factotums. Wright is particularly sympathetic here to Hartley as a frustrated homosexual, knowing himself swindled and insulted but finding it half pleasurable.

Many readers will be grateful for a biography of manageable length, although something surely should have been said about Hartley as a collector. Persian rugs and carpets were his specialty. When, after agonizing indecision, a new one arrived from Bernadout's, some authority would be invited to give gracious advice. He himself had been taught about antiques by his aunt Kathleen, who was a shrewd buyer and seller. But Wright gains a lot from seeing Hartley as a tragic rather than a comic figure. All the lamentable charade of his final years—the gin, the rough trade, the boozy shuffling about in carpet slippers, the ravings against the working class, the Inland Revenue, and the swans who impeded his boat—all these turn into the sad phantasmagoria of a man who outlived so many friends and felt that his country and his century had betrayed him.

Some of Hartley's books are very bad, some are classics, such as *The Go-Between* (1953), which gained an additional large audience after the 1970 film with Alan Bates and Julie Christie. Wright, in search of the "running shadow" that he thinks must have darkened Hartley's life, turns to the fine autobiographical novels and, above all, to *The Go-Between*. There, Wright believes, the author "tells us what we should never be allowed to know about him," and suggests a childhood wounding that shocked him irrecoverably. However, Hamish Hamilton, his long-suffering publisher, said that "Leslie was impotent and that was all there was to it." Dr. Patrick Woodcock, who looked after him untiringly, thought that "Leslie never gave away his emotional life to anyone, not even to himself."

What is certain is that Hartley himself wouldn't have welcomed any investigation that went further than this book. Although he admitted that "Freud was in the air the writer breathes," he objected strongly to the idea of Freudian analysis. This is clear enough from one of his most disturbing short stories, "A Tonic." A tonic is all that the patient, Mr. Amber, wants or needs; but, while Mr. Amber is unconscious, the famous specialist conducts a complete examination, "which in all his waking moments he had so passionately withstood."

1996

The Only Member of His Club

Evelyn Waugh: The Later Years, 1939–1966,
by Martin Stannard

During the second half of his life, Evelyn Waugh became the victim of his own game, not of Let's Pretend, but of Let's Pretend to Pretend. He was impatient when others didn't understand his rules, and impatient with the game itself when it didn't—as games should do—provide a satisfactory alternative to real life. It was played *en travesti*—with embarrassingly loud tweed suits, weird ear trumpets, and a house full of Victorian bric-a-brac, with the tiny Master threateningly aloof in his study, emerging with the message: I am bored, you are frightened. Sometimes he was aghast at the sight of his own bloated face in the mirror. He was asking, it seemed, to be judged severely, and he has been. No one condemns Robert Louis Stevenson for playing king in Samoa, but Evelyn Waugh, it seems, can hardly be forgiven for his nineteen years as the tyrannous squire of Piers Court, his country home.

The game continued while his religious, moral, and aesthetic convictions demanded to be taken with total seriousness. It has often been said that he created a fantasy world out of the England and the Roman Catholic Church he knew because it was useful to him as a novelist. Waugh could never have accepted this for a moment. He saw himself, from the time he wrote *Brideshead Revisited* onward, as a defender of the faith and of the last vestiges of a vanishing civilization.

The second volume of Martin Stannard's biography opens after the outbreak of World War II, with Waugh as a trainee officer with the Royal Marines. There follows a sober account of the six painful years of his war service. He had courageously volunteered, at the age of thirty-six, because (as he told students of the University of Edinburgh in 1951) "I believe a man's chief civic duty consists in fighting for his King when the men in public life have put the realm in danger." But he pictured himself as doing this alongside his aristocratic cronies—a "club of upper-class toughs," Mr. Stannard calls them—who alone would understand him. But they did not want him, and in pursuit of the ideal posting he fell out with so many commanding officers that he was generally considered unemployable. Finally he was sent on a mission of support to

Yugoslavia, where he ended up on a furious and lonely crusade, not on behalf of Tito and his partisans, but of his own fellow Catholics on both sides in the war and the civil strife that followed. This made him such a nuisance to the British Foreign Office that Christopher Sykes (Waugh's official biographer) believed that there was some question of court-martialing him. Mr. Stannard, however, going patiently over the records, concludes that the question was not seriously raised.

By the time Waugh was demobilized in 1945 he had a family of three daughters—Teresa, Harriet, and Margaret—and a son, Auberon. With his gentle, long-suffering, but independent-minded wife, Laura, he moved back into the house he had bought for them, Piers Court, in Gloucestershire. At first, hoping to escape the hated "century of the common man," he had thought of moving to Ireland, but he became reconciled to a country life in England, a little travel, an occasional rampage in London. "If this regime sounds placid," wrote Mark Amory, the editor of Waugh's letters, "it must be remembered that it led to the crisis on which *The Ordeal of Gilbert Pinfold* is based." Gilbert Pinfold hears "voices" that put in words his own worst fears about himself, and they drive him mad.

Meanwhile, during the disastrous, quarrelsome, and drink-sodden war years, Waugh, as always, had protected his breathing space as an author, writing a riotous satire, *Put Out More Flags*, and the enormously successful *Brideshead Revisited*. Charles Ryder, in that novel, during his long love affair with a great and ancient Catholic family, meets the power of the True Faith in action. In the later war trilogy, *Sword of Honor*, Guy Crouchback, like Ryder, is a reserved and decent man, but belonging to an ancient family himself: he is faced with the ruin of all his illusions. Neither of these characters is in the least like their creator, but they justify him—his romanticism, his snobbery, his crusade against the world as it is.

Most novelists, after all, take the opportunity of self-justification. It's the compensation of their profession. Certainly it is too simple to say, as Mr. Stannard does, that Waugh's power to hurt was the mainspring of his comic power. In fact, it might be felt that the mainspring of both his tragedy and his comedy was his experience of being hurt.

The 1950s were the years when the income-tax inspectors, kept at bay until then by his agent and his accountant, closed in on Waugh, and at the same time he lost (deliberately, as it seemed) some of his old friends—though never Graham Greene or Nancy Mitford. At Piers Court, Laura farmed with a particular interest in her cows, and Waugh developed the bizarre persona that he justified by his belief in an independent world of the artist, one that he had the right to defend against all invaders. On visits to the United States he accepted hospitality grudgingly, told Igor Stravinsky that he couldn't stand music, and pretended to believe that if he died there the undertakers would refuse him burial because of what he had said about them in *The Loved One*. On the other hand, he was prodigally generous to Catholic charities. And although he affected to think little of his children (except for his favorite, Meg) he in fact got to know them, as individuals, very well. The family, as so often happens in large country households, formed a conspiracy against the outside world, not feeling the necessity to explain itself.

In 1957 Waugh was working on a book of which he had very great hopes. This was the life of his friend Monsignor Ronald Knox, inadequately described by Mr. Stannard, who teaches English at the University of Leicester, as "a country-house priest with a keen enjoyment of upper-class society." In fact Knox was a brilliant apologist and the translator of the Old and New Testaments. Mr. Stannard seems to have taken against Waugh's *Life of the Right Reverend Ronald Knox*, and speaks of "a certain dishonesty in its tone" and a "thinly disguised rancor." Waugh's aims were certainly very different from Mr. Stannard's. He was not a scrupulous collector of facts but an artist who gave to every book he wrote a strong and elegant pattern. Ronald Knox's family—he was my uncle—knew that the *Life* was inaccurate in places, and that it had proved impossible (for instance) to get Waugh to grasp the deep, wordless affection between Ronald and his brothers. But they admired his courage in criticizing the Catholic hierarchy where he thought fit, and they welcomed the book, which, in its very dryness and melancholy, gave a living likeness of Knox.

When the book appeared in 1959, the Prime Minister was Harold Macmillan, who had been Knox's pupil. Macmillan had been encouraging from the start, and Waugh felt that Knox's biographer might well be rewarded with a knighthood. "That's what one really needs," he told Anthony Powell. Now a letter arrived from Downing Street. It offered to make him only a Commander of the Order of the British Empire. Mr. Stannard says that the creases in the letter show how Waugh crumpled it up in a fury before writing to decline.

Minute attention to detail, perseverance, diligence Mr. Stannard certainly has, and his two volumes will be standard reading for students of Waugh. He has used diaries and letters, published and unpublished, memoirs, reviews, personal interviews. But his researches have not been authorized by the family, and when it comes to analysis of character and motivation he never quite seems to find his feet. Laura, for example, is compared as a mother to Dickens's Mrs. Jellyby, which would mean that she neglected her children. But soon afterward we're told that she "spent much time deflecting his anger away from her brood and on to her own head." Again, Mr. Stannard says that "no one persecuted Evelyn Waugh more relentlessly than himself," but, a few pages later, "his sanity depended on his being right." These discrepancies don't represent changes or new developments. They are the result of Mr. Stannard's day-by-day, pile-'em-high accumulation of details, which makes it hard for him to stand back and see exactly where he is.

At the end of 1956 Waugh left Piers Court for somewhere still more secluded, Combe Florey House, in Somerset. But for how long could the twentieth century be kept at bay? Above all, he felt threatened by the decisions of Vatican II and the changes in Catholic ritual. "The awful prospect is that I may have more than twenty years ahead," he wrote to his daughter Meg. But after he had published the first volume of his autobiography in 1964 he had only two more years left. "The distress caused by the Vatican Council was widespread," Diana Mosley said recently. "It killed Evelyn Waugh."

Boredom can also kill. In fact Waugh collapsed with coronary thrombosis in the downstairs lavatory of his home, and Mr. Stannard concludes that he died, as he lived, alone. How he makes this out I can't tell. In spite of, or because of, his outrageous behavior, Waugh was never without a sympathetic friend, and by his family he was offered more love than he was ever able to accept. I don't call that loneliness.

1992

THE FORTIES AND AFTER

What's Happening in the Engine Room

John Lehmann: A Pagan Adventure, by Adrian White

The first volume of John Lehmann's autobiography, published in 1955, starts:

> When I try to remember where my education in poetry began, the first image that comes to mind is that of my father's library at the old family home of Fieldhead on the Thames. It is an autumn or winter evening after tea, for James the butler has been in to draw the blinds and close the curtains, and my father is reading under a green-shaded lamp.

He has said a good deal already—the little boy who wants to be like his father, the sheltered child who doesn't need to know the time or even the season because James, the always reliable butler, deals with that, the illusion of a dedication to poetry. Adrian Wright, in this new biography, refers several times to Lehmann's half-commitment (in spite of his energy) to the professional life he chose. Fieldhead was the magic enclosure to which, as an adult, he looked back, wishing that it might have been possible to sit there, watching and listening, all his life.

He came of a German-Jewish family, musical, hospitable, successful in business. His grandfather ended up in Scotland, by way of Huddersfield. His father, who built Fieldhead, was called to the Bar, edited the *Daily News*, and was returned as Liberal MP for Market Harborough. He was a dedicated rowing coach, and wrote quantities of light verse, often about rowing, for *Punch*. He married Alice Davis, a strong-minded New Englander twenty years younger than himself. Their family consisted of three girls—Helen, the indulged Rosamond, Beatrix—and, at long last, the boy, John. Their children's talents must have been partly, at least, inherited, but no trace of their father Rude's jolly German *Kameradschaft* seems to have been passed on.

Adrian Wright has been faced with a problem of organization. He has come into all the material collected by John Lehmann's commissioned biographer, Martin Taylor, who died before he could write a word of it. He has seen photocopies of the extensive diaries, and he has interviewed the survivors and their descendants. Lehmann himself wrote three volumes of dignified autobiography about his work, his beliefs, his travels, his dogs, and one, in the unconvincing form of a novel (*In the Purely Pagan Sense*, 1976), on his strenuous life as a homosexual. Wright has the job of combining the two stories, although he gives us fair warning that "when there has had, through reasons of space, to be a choice between discussing the plight of writers in Czechoslovakia or detailing an affair of the heart that made Lehmann's life a misery, the heart has invariably won." There might be a voice of protest from the shades. But Wright is gallant, "attempting"—as he tells us—"to rescue Lehmann from the margins of the literature of which he was once at the heart." Can this truly be done?

John was sent to Summer Fields, and left in 1921 with an Eton scholarship and a report that he was "never likely to do anything dishonourable or mean," a golden lad, as Wright calls him. About Eton he was at best lukewarm. He had wished not to disappoint his father, but he was a rowing failure. The Master in College judged that he had set his ambitions too high, and allowed himself to get depressed. On Cambridge, too, although he went up with the expected scholarship, he came to look back as wasted time.

What next? To a great extent he was conditioned already, having moved effortlessly since birth from one favorable literary atmosphere to another. His father had heard Charles Dickens read when he was six, had helped to found *Granta*, and furiously defended the Liberal cause at the *Punch* table. John himself had been at Eton with Alan Pryce-Jones, Anthony Powell, Eric Blair, and Cyril Connolly, who, we are told, stood at the door of his room in the Sixth Form Passage asking, "Well, Johnny Lehmann, how are you this afternoon?" While he was at Trinity his sister Rosamond published her first novel, *Dusty Answer*, which shed a little of its ambiguous glamour over him, and at the same time he became a friend of Julian Bell, who invited him to Charleston. In 1931 the Woolfs, who had printed his first tentative book of poems, took him on as a dogs-body and part-time commercial traveler at the Hogarth Press. They had already run through two assistants, but, all the same, Wright is perhaps rather too hard on them. In her biography of Virginia Woolf, Hermione Lee describes Lehmann as one of the "ambitious, thwarted, talented young men" who "rubbed up against Leonard's adamantine proprietari-ness and perfectionism. . . . It was a well-known joke among their friends that working at the Hogarth Press drove you mad."

After seven months at the Press, Lehmann made his first appearance as an editor when he commissioned Michael Roberts's *New Signatures* (February 1932), which included contributions from Julian Bell, Richard Eberhart, William Empson, Cecil Day Lewis, Stephen Spender, William Plomer, and Lehmann himself. Through Spender he met Christopher Isherwood. The friendship with Spender from the very first seemed edgy, uncertain, and uneasy, but durable for all that. Isherwood he loved, but he was tolerated, rather than loved, in return.

Spender and Isherwood were spending much of their time in Berlin. Germany was evidently the place to be, the country to be young in, unin-hibited, uncorrupted by the past, electric with political hope for the future:

> We can tell you a secret, offer a tonic; only
> Submit to the visiting angel, the strange new healer.

In August 1932, without giving notice, Lehmann threw up his job with the Woolfs and departed for Vienna.

Though his mother suspected that he was leading a wild revolution-ary life, Lehmann, renting a succession of flats, finally in the Invaliden-strasse, was attempting something much more complex. He wanted the release of his sexuality with the adaptable boys he picked up—Rico, Gustav, Willi, Tiddlywinks (introduced by Isherwood at the Cosy Cor-ner bar), and countless others—to identify with his new Marxist beliefs, felt as freedom and defiance rather than as escape, a mystical as well as a political union with the working class (working, but for the moment unemployed). Lehmann kept them more or less happy with money, clothes, cigarette lighters, and fountain pens.

It was, as he wrote himself, "a contact with earthiness that I needed very badly." He desired wholeness, and believed that destiny offered him the choice of being a poet or an editor. Although he produced eight collections in his lifetime, there was never any evidence that he was able to write good poetry, yet he was convinced that his poetry too gave a dynamic to his existence.

> There have been moments when I have seen the whole of it irradiated by my passion for boys and young men . . . as if I were climbing an Alpine slope, always hoping for and always with blessed luck discovering some rare and hitherto unculled flower that seemed to glow on me with its own internal light; a climb that is not yet over, nor will perhaps be until I reach the highest snows.

This is from *In the Purely Pagan Sense*, which for the most part plods along sedately enough. "Eye signals followed for some minutes, and as the messages seemed of favourable import, I finally ventured on a discreetly beckoning gesture."

The blessed luck was that he settled for editing and publishing, for which he had the gift. He wasn't an intellectual, neither was he original, but he did have an editor's instinct for the latest thing. He worked extremely hard, and although he seems to have been stingy in his daily life—German champagne was served at his parties in small glasses—he had a generous appreciation of his authors and designers.

The first edition of the periodical *New Writing* came out in spring 1936, but by 1938 the new series was appearing under the Hogarth imprint, Lehmann having more or less made up his dispute with the Woolfs and invested some money in the Press. He had thought of calling his magazine *The Bridge*—the bridge, that is, between writers and workers, but also between England and Europe. In *The Whispering Gallery*, the first volume of his autobiography, he describes the planning stages: "I may even have toyed with the idea of starting a new international literature." Taking an "optimistic and Marxist view," he found contributions from France, Spain, Russia, and Poland, and *New Writing* seemed, in its beginnings, the authentic voice of violence and resistance. The voice was to change and grow considerably more mellow with changing times, with Lehmann, as Wright very aptly says, "bringing himself forward bearing his statement on the health of the literary world, like the captain of a ship reporting to his passengers about what is happening in the engine room." But readers could trust him to find for them what was unforgettable. He was the first to print George Orwell's "Shooting an Elephant," Isherwood's Berlin diaries, Rosamond Lehmann's "A Dream of Winter," Auden's "Lay your sleeping head, my love." In 1939 he courageously met the challenge of *Horizon*, edited by Cyril Connolly with what seemed the treacherous help of Stephen Spender. (Connolly, Wright has to admit, "has been perceived as being more fun" than Lehmann.) In 1940, at the suggestion of Allen Lane, who unlike most publishers at that time had a large paper allocation, *New Writing* became *Penguin New Writing*. Wright sympathetically conjures up the blacked-out, hemmed-in Britain where the magazine found an immediate welcome and settled down to sell 75,000 copies a month. He quotes a footnote in issue No. 5: "Leave this book at a Post Office when you have read it, so that men and women in the services may enjoy it too."

For a short time, from 1946 to November 1952, Lehmann reached a near-independence at the head of what was almost his own publishing house. Purnell found the paper for him and retained 51 percent control of the new John Lehmann Ltd. It operated from the basement of his house in Egerton Crescent, and though he began by discreetly poaching some of his old authors from the Hogarth Press, he soon found his own. Probably his favorite enterprise was the Modern European Library. He bought for it Sartre's *Diary of Antoine Roquentin*, Kazantzakis's *Alexis Zorba* (to which he gave the title *Zorba the Greek*), Malraux's *The Walnut Trees of Altenburg*. Among his preferred Neo-Romantic illustrators, Keith Vaughan and John Minton excelled. Minton decorated Elizabeth David's first book, *A Book of Mediterranean Food*, with tipsy Breton sailors, market girls, lobster pots, *fruits de mer*, as a kind of delicious ballet in and out of the dedicated text. As Wright says, when you take up a book published by Lehmann you get the sense of a precious thing, obviously cared for in its creation.

In 1952 Purnell grew tired of losing money, and in spite of a letter to *The Times* signed by the familiar distinguished names, John Lehmann Ltd. was obliged to shut up shop. The BBC offered him a magazine "of the air" and he accepted, and was understandably wounded when he was replaced in the following year by John Wain. His last editorship was the *London Magazine*, financed by Cecil King. Lehmann's heart was perhaps no longer in it when he handed over, in 1961, to Alan Ross.

This distinguished career he described in a letter to David Hughes. "David, my dear, having been *betrayed* by Leonard Woolf—*abandoned* by Allen Lane—*kicked* out, *ruined* by Purnell, *stabbed* in the back and *thrown* out by Cecil King—I think I've had enough." Lehmann seems to have needed an atmosphere of crisis, conflict, parting, and enormous grievances to give him strength for his daily round. This was true of his professional career, even more so of his sex life. In his relationships with his numerous boys there was a schoolmasterish element. He wanted to teach them, to better them, as well as to be cruelly disappointed and to disappoint. With Rosamond, who gave him some of her best short stories for *New Writing*, he showed the same tendency, on the grand scale. So, indeed, did she.

There were two people who remained, through all the storms, ready to serve. One was the immigrant Russian ballet dancer Alexis Lissine, who became Lehmann's lover at the beginning of the war. As his career faded, the "beloved Alyosha" survived as a neglected but tenacious lodger at the lakeside cottage that Lehmann had bought at Three Bridges in West Sussex. He had contributed something to the purchase, but he was not allowed into the drawing room, and did not go into it even after Lehmann's death. The other most faithful follower, who could have been a novelist in her own right, was Barbara Cooper. Arriving in London from the North of England in 1939, she became Lehmann's secretary and the only person apart from him who was allowed to read the contributions and even reject them. She was also "allowed" to do the postage and packing, to pay the office milkman, and to be laughed at by a series of young men for twenty years. "You have been very good to me, dear John," she wrote to him after he resigned from the *London Magazine*.

He ended up, as he said himself, as a "minor cultural monument," a lecturer at American universities, a recipient of the CBE and many European honors. In January 1947 there had been a lunch—to the end of his days he called it a "luncheon"—held in his honor at the Trocadero. T. S. Eliot proposed the toast, but Wright says "the guests seem to have reacted . . . in the way those who knew Lehmann tended to react: with respect, but a feeling, too, of slight absurdity." It had always been so. John Heath-Stubbs, in his *Hindsights*, describes a visit by some young Oxford poets when Lehmann was staying in Cambridge. "At the end of the evening it appeared that an error had been made in booking the guest rooms at King's, and that there was one too few." Lehmann offered his windowseat. "In view of [his] reputation, none of the Oxford party was particularly anxious to avail himself of this kind offer." Dadie

Rylands, who had known him since he was an undergraduate, called him "a romantic old ninny." Isherwood, after a lifetime's friendship, thought of him "basically as a silly old fart."

"Ultimately . . . this is a triumphant life," says Wright, but, as he tells it, it seems (in the noble sense of the word) pathetic, meaning "the moving of the passions in the mournful way, the engaging of them in behalf of merit or worth"—merit, that is, for which recognition falls short. But when have editors, however successful, however perceptive, ever received much recognition?

1999

A Kind of Magician

Louis MacNeice, by Jon Stallworthy

Harold Monro, the gloomy proprietor of the Poetry Bookshop, said that the only thing people really liked to hear about a poet is that he was dead. There is a preference there, too—fallen in battle, suicide in a garret. Then his reputation is left to face the future.

Jon Stallworthy must have had a more difficult job on his hands with Louis MacNeice than he had with Wilfred Owen. But he has created the same confidence in the reader by his elegance, tact, and scholarly patience, explaining unobtrusively as he goes along, and only very occasionally—it is all the more impressive for that—allowing himself a judgment. He was asked to write this book, in the first place, by Professor E. R. Dodds, MacNeice's lifelong friend and literary executor, then by his successor, Dan Davin, and finally by the family. It was to be the first full-length biography, and Dodds wanted it to be a revaluation, feeling that the poet's reputation "still bobbed in the wake of Auden's," calling out for critical rescue.

Louis MacNeice (1901–1963) was Anglo-Irish, giving him, as he said, "a hold on the sentimental English," but starting him off in life as a "jumble of opposites." These seem never to have been political so much as a long-drawn-out difficulty in reconciling himself to his father. The grandfather had been a schoolteacher with the Irish Church Missions, whose aim was conversion and who were felt to be bribing Catholics in hard times by offering meal tickets and a better education. In 1879, the Mac-Neices had to be rescued by the police from stone-throwers. The eldest son, John, Louis's father, took orders, married another mission teacher, and devoted himself fiercely to non-retaliation and peace. They brought up their family in Belfast and later at Carrickfergus Rectory, with fifteen rooms, some with great windows, and an acre of garden and apple trees enclosed by a hawthorn hedge. The railway ran past it and they could listen out for the Larne–Stranraer boat train. They were taken on seaside holidays where the Atlantic "exploded in white and in gulls." They were taken to Belfast Lough to see the *Titanic* on her way to the sea, the "one shining glimpse" Louis remembered forty-five years later, in his elegy for his stepmother. The images, as Stallworthy shows, had already taken up their appointed places. Quite often, in fact, Louis felt the drunkenness of things being various. The garden, the sea, and the house would be there to meet him at every turn.

His mother died when he was just seven. His father, who "made the walls resound," alarmed him. He had an elder sister, Elisabeth, who was of great importance to him and invented with him, in the garden's hiding places, a game called "the Cult of the Old." His brother, William, suffered from Down's syndrome and was sent for a time to a mental home in Scotland. But is Stallworthy right in saying that the loss of Louis's mother to the grave, his brother to an institution, and, later, his wife to another man, "gave him a fellow-feeling for the deprived and suffering"? Certainly, though not a trouble-taker, Louis was compassionate. But were these the reasons? When the Rector remarried in 1917, he was quickly won over by "the comfort and benevolence" his stepmother brought to the house, whereas Willie seemed to him uglier and more monstrous on every visit. His marriage is an altogether different matter.

At the age of nine, he was sent to school—first Sherborne, then Marlborough—and considered himself to be well out of Ireland,

> *Though yet her name keeps ringing like a bell*
> *In an under-water belfry. . .*

At Marlborough, he fell in with Anthony Blunt and with John Betjeman, who were lending a hand with a new school magazine, *The Heretick*. Under Blunt's tuition, as Stallworthy puts it, "the dutiful son of the rectory was fast becoming a sceptical rebel, who wanted cornfields to look like landscapes by van Gogh." A closer friend, the closest of all, was Graham Shepard, the son of E. H. Shepard. He is described here as having "a more conventional Home Counties background" than Louis, but in fact in 1923 his father had not yet done the illustrations for *When We Were Very Young* and the Shepards were living in rustic Shamley Green with a hand-pump over the sink. Louis saw Graham as a "stray from some other place or era," but if so he was a practical stray, liked messing about in boats, and was a good draftsman. Of Louis himself at this time Stallworthy quotes yet another friend's description; he was a kind of magician. "As on a dark clear night, there was a sense of depth without boundaries," and Louis was conscious of this, a showman in control, as most bright sixth-formers are.

He was obsessed with Latin meters, classical and medieval, and recited the *Pervigilium Veneris* "with harsh resonance and a percussive menace in the refrain that was almost a threat," but behind that there were the nursery rhymes and incantations of Carrickfergus, not to speak of "Father O'Flynn" and "Paddy, I Hardly Knew You." He grew up listening to jazz, blues, and ragtime, the Sitwells, Eliot's early poems, and to Yeats, who had declared in 1918 that he was discarding magnificence because there was more enterprise in walking naked. Once he could hear his own music, Louis never really let it go:

> *The same tunes hang on pegs in the cloakrooms of the mind*
> *That fitted us ten or twenty or thirty years ago*
> *On occasions of love or grief.*

Auden, too, cast a long shadow. Louis, having gone up to Merton in 1926, found him already at Oxford. Stallworthy, attentive to what he has been asked to do, points out that, although Louis was impressed by Auden and published in the same magazines, he was never under his spell, and neither of them at this point was interested in politics. It was not until 1932 that Geoffrey Grigson approached both together for the first number of *New Verse*.

Graham (now at Lincoln) and Louis were interested in rugby, long-haired dogs, drink, and women, but both of them liked the idea of marriage and children. Even before he had lurched through his Finals, getting a brilliant First, Louis fell fathoms deep in love with a tiny exotic girl, a don's daughter, Mary, white-skinned but so dark that she was said to have a fine line of hair down the length of her spine. Mary's mother belonged to the Ezra family, and was dissatisfied, while Louis's father, soon to be Bishop of Belfast, wrote that "the thought of an engagement to a Jewess is dreadful." And so, with neither side in favor, the young couple set up house:

> *I loved my love with the wings of angels*
> *Dipped in henna, unearthly red,*
> *With my office hours, with my flowers and sirens,*
> *With my budget, my latchkey, and my daily bread.*

This was in Birmingham, where Louis had got a job as a university lecturer in classics under Professor Dodds. After writing his bitter and nostalgic "Valediction" to Ireland, which has infuriated three generations of Irish readers but which Stallworthy gently describes as "an exorcism," he settled down as a married man in Selly Park. In May 1934, their son Dan was born, and Louis would sit in one of his habitual long silences, contemplating the baby. In September, after several prudent hesitations, T. S. Eliot accepted a volume of poems for Faber. That autumn, they had a long-term guest at Selly Park, a Russian American, Charles Katzman. In November, Mary ran off with Katzman to London.

"Louis was devastated"—these are strong words from Stallworthy, whose clear narrative always keeps its head. Some of his friends expected a nervous breakdown. Little Dan was looked after by relations and hired help, and before long his father saw him only at intervals. There is no evidence that Louis compared Dan's childhood with his own.

He moved back to London to lecture at Bedford College, and with unexpected common sense kept very busy all the time, traveling with Blunt to Spain, with Auden to Iceland, and with Nancy Coldstream to the Western Isles. Being lonely, and since "the lady was gone who stood in the way so long," he had begun a series of good-natured entanglements with the women whose bright determined faces look out of the book's many illustrations. Some of his lyrics during the late 1930s, "Bagpipe Music" in particular, give glimpses of chaos, while others— "Taken for Granted," "The Brandy Glass," "Sunday Morning," "August"—try to fix through recall some golden minute in the past that can never be caged. In "The Sunlight on the Garden," written, we are told, within weeks of his divorce, he is grateful even for the moments of storm with

Mary. This is what he comes back to in the moving Section XIX of *Autumn Journal*: "Thank you, my dear—dear against my judgment." The *Journal*, the best of all his long poems, was, he explained, to be entirely honest. In Spain, he had only noticed what was inefficient, magnificent, smelly, and picturesque; he wouldn't pretend to have predicted the civil war. In Birmingham, he hadn't bothered about the unemployed. Now he was not so much opening his poetry up to the world's concerns as letting them pace beside him, while the ruined idyll is never quite out of earshot.

When war was declared, Louis was lecturing in America, and came back not very willingly to Britain. Auden had already decided what course to take. Graham, married by now, with a small daughter, was in the RNVR and was called up at once. He joined the corvette *Polyanthus*, on the Atlantic run. In bad weather, he said, it was like living in a cottage swinging from the end of a piece of string. Louis might well have ended up, like many other classical scholars, at Bletchley, but the BBC, worried that all the available poets were being filched by the Ministry of Information, asked him to write something for them "that would contribute to the national morale." He accepted, and worked for them for the next twenty-odd years.

In his preface, Stallworthy acknowledges the help he has had from Barbara Coulton's admirable study *Louis MacNeice in the BBC* (1980), but he finds it impossible to sum up how far a poet is affected by writing to order. The work seemed like that, and sometimes was like that, in 1941, for example, when after the German invasion of Russia it was thought necessary to salute our new ally with an epic feature on Alexander Nevsky. The radio feature itself was an awkward form, comparable to the silent film. But there were visionaries in the Corporation, brave spirits, who trusted in it absolutely. In the end, Louis's verdict on his new appointment was that "in spite of the unhealth which goes with a machine that is largely propaganda . . . it has its excitements and (what was less to be expected) its value."

In September 1943, HMS *Polyanthus* was sunk with all hands on the run from Derry to Newfoundland. There were no survivors, and Louis had lost Graham,

> *Than whom I do not expect ever again*
> *To find a more accordant friend, with whom*
> *I could be silent knowledgeably.*

Stallworthy is unexpectedly hard on this elegy, "The Casualty." What is the use of comparing it with *Lycidas* or "In Memory of Major Robert Gregory"? Milton and Yeats had reason for their superb detachment, while Louis had a nightmare (the drowned friend who can't understand that he is too late for the party) to confine into a meter that rocks like the tide with the changing places of the rhymes. In *Autumn Sequel*, he tried again, with even more control, but less effect. But Stallworthy adds that Graham's death was a tragic waste of his potential, "and it may have seemed to MacNeice that he himself had sold his birthright for a mess of propaganda."

"But, on the other hand, there is another hand." By the time Graham was killed, Louis had made a second marriage, with the singer Hedli Anderson. She understood him very well (or perhaps he had grown easier to understand) and was Bohemian in the right way, breast feeding their baby daughter in the saloon bar, which was very unusual in the 1940s, and cooking lavishly for unspecified numbers of people. It was perhaps a mistake for the two of them to appear, as they did, on the same concert and cabaret platforms, Louis reading, Hedli singing (often his lyrics) as she had been trained to do in Berlin. In the end, he refused to go on with it, but Stallworthy emphasizes her warmth and animal vitality and must have regretted reaching the (recurrent) entry in his index: "relationship deteriorates." The marriage lasted, showing increasing signs of wear, until 1960. During these years, the unpractical Louis, who had not even remembered to bring a tent with him to Iceland, became a traveler. The BBC sent him to India, Greece, Egypt, and South Africa, and gave him generous leave of absence to run (though he did not exactly run anything) the British Institute in Athens. It was thought that these new horizons would relieve the poet's black spells of depression.

But Louis drank. The advice given at that time in the Staff Training School was to put a discreet "d" by the name of any employee who might give trouble in this way. (There had to be some allowance for genius.) When Dylan Thomas came to London and spent an evening with Louis at the George, their colleagues had to stand by in dismay as one became deafening and the other sank into a sardonic stupor. Drunk or sober, however, the two of them understood each other very well. Thomas had complete trust, as well he might, in Louis's ear for the sound of words. When he read his "Author's Prologue" aloud to him and found that

Louis couldn't follow the rhyme scheme (who could?) at first hearing, he was bowed down in dejection.

In the "middle stretch," which is hard for poets, and often for biographers, Louis felt that he had lost, not his skill with words, but his sense of his own worth. Like wartime London, he had been "reborn into an anticlimax." Trusting in the power of change, he resigned his full-time job with the BBC, to the relief of those who considered him a dangerous radical, although he had never gone further politically than the visionary ending of *Autumn Journal*. He moved in with the last of his lovers, Mary Wimbush, and at the age of fifty-three returned to what Robin Skelton called "the borderlands between game and ritual, vision and fantasy, fable and history, which are the territory of the poets of the Thirties," and which, more than any other discovery, he had shared with Auden. By this time he had weathered the Apocalyptics of the 1940s, the anti-romantics of the 1950s, and the arrival of Ted Hughes. He knew that his enormous production for radio had lost him the attention of serious critics. But his last poems were not intended to be his last.

He had, as Stallworthy never forgets, unfinished business with his father, who died in 1942, just as he was due for retirement. Frightened of him as a child, at odds with him as he grew up, Louis had come to see him as a great man. "Poems would plot the progress of his grieving and reconciliations," and this, surely, implies a reconciliation with Ireland, his father's house.

> He has gone prodigally astray
> Till through disbeliefs he arrived at a house
> He could not remember seeing before,
> And he walked straight in; it was where he had come from
> And something told him the way to behave.
> He raised his hand and blessed his home.

This, of course, was only something Louis still felt he might do; he knew the way to do it. He went back to Ireland pretty frequently—three times, for example, in 1957—without giving any sign of wanting to live there. But in returning to his childhood's country, his "erstwhile," he could conjure up his father even in the old seaside ritual of emptying the sand out of his shoes at the end of a summer's day on the beach. "The further off people are sometimes the larger." In these memories of Carrickfergus he felt safe, for if he had changed, and even if Ireland had changed, they had not. But there were other experiences that also refused to die. Among these late poems, "The Taxis" has all his old gaiety and his old desolation in an image of total loneliness. The bus passengers in "Charon," unable to hear the rumors of war through the glass, are all put down in a fog on the Thames Embankment to cross the river as best they can. In his "Memoranda," Louis reminds the shade of Horace that they are both of them horrible old fellows, but they are at least poets, to whom the commonplace, even the passing traffic, is always being made new.

In 1963, Louis caught a chill on the Yorkshire moors and developed viral pneumonia, not the worst kind, but it seems that the antibiotics wouldn't take because of the drinking. He asked the doctors, possibly with surprise, "Am I supposed to be dying?" The ferryman in "Charon" might have given him an answer: "If you want to die, you will have to pay for it." Louis might well feel that he had already done so.

1995

The Man from Narnia

C. S. Lewis: A Biography, by A. N. Wilson

My copy of *The Poetical Works of Spenser* once belonged to my mother, who took it with her to Oxford as a student in 1904. On the flyleaf are my own Oxford notes in faded pencil: "CSL says forget courtly Spenser dreamy Spenser—think of rustic Spenser English Spenser homely Spenser, kindled lust, worldly muck, bagpipes, goat-milking."

It calls up the sight and sound of the lecture room with C. S. Lewis (1898–1963), darkly red-faced and black-gowned, advancing toward the platform—talking already, for he saved time by beginning just inside the door. The place was always crowded, often with a row of nuns at the back. His eye was on all of us: "I shall adapt myself to the slowest note-taker among you."

Although Lewis, opening his stores of classical and medieval learning, said that he was only telling us what we could very well find out for ourselves, we were truly thankful for what we received. Connoisseurs may have preferred the scarcely audible lectures of the poet Edmund Blunden, given in a much smaller room. But Lewis was the indispensable teacher, about whom all we personally knew was that he was pipe- and beer-loving, lived outside Oxford, and made a "thing" of disliking the twentieth century. When T. S. Eliot came to read "The Waste Land" to the Poetry Society, Lewis was not there.

As A. N. Wilson says in *C. S. Lewis: A Biography*, Lewis's life was never eventful, "and yet books about him continue to pour from the presses on both sides of the Atlantic." None of them, however, have been as brilliant or as edgily sympathetic as this one.

Jack (christened Clive Staples) Lewis was the son of an Ulster police court solicitor. He was brought up in a villa in the suburbs of Belfast, where he and his elder brother Warnie escaped from the adults into games of high imagination in the attic. For this Little End Room, as they called it, both of them had a profound nostalgia, characteristic of the period, although it suggests not so much Peter Pan, who wanted to grow up and could not, as Alain-Fournier's Meaulnes, who did grow up but could not bear to admit it. Neither the house nor the attic would ordinarily be thought of as romantic, but myth is not answerable to reality.

In 1908 his mother died of cancer; Jack was no more able to accept this than most boys of nine years old. He turned out to be a brilliant scholar, for whom books were not an alternative but an additional life, and in 1921 he was appointed a tutor in English at Magdalen College. (His experiences in the First World War, when he was wounded at the battle of Arras, were, he said, something quite cut off from the rest of his existence.) At Oxford he shared a house with a Mrs. Moore, a woman old enough to be his mother—thought indeed by some people to be his mother—who relied on him to help with the housework.

A "mysterious self-imposed slavery" Warnie called it, for he too had joined the household. Among Jack's friends at the university (not introduced to Mrs. Moore) were the group known as the Inklings, among them the Professor of Anglo-Saxon, J. R. R. Tolkien. Among them they exerted a certain amount of power, and in 1938 they as good as fixed the election for the Professorship of Poetry. A campaign like this showed Lewis in the loud and dominating character that he had adopted for public use. But the Inklings' favorite subjects of discussion were poetry, metaphor, and the transcendent. It was with their help that Lewis "passed on," in his own words, "from believing in God to definitely believing in Christ."

A new readiness to write seemed to be released, and during the Second World War Lewis became, through his books and through radio, one of the most popular and reassuring of apologists for the Christian faith. In the 1950s he began to publish his children's stories, which themselves were Christian allegories. Letters reached him from all over the world, and to all of them he gave a written reply. In 1952 one of his correspondents arrived in England—Joy Davidman from Chicago, separated from her husband and with two growing boys. She and Jack fell in love, and, somewhat to the dismay of his friends, they married. But she had already developed cancer, and in 1960 it killed her. These closing months have been mythologized in Bill Nicholson's play *Shadowlands*, which is running at the moment in London. Mr. Wilson's business, however, is with reality, which, as he boldly says in his preface, is "more interesting than fantasy." No one, surely, could be better qualified for the job. Mr. Wilson, whose previous books include a biography of Tolstoy, knows Oxford very well indeed, and has not been daunted by the huge quantity of material—letters, papers, diaries, an eleven-volume history of the family by Warnie. He can give a proper estimate, and does give a very high one, of Lewis's work on medieval and Renaissance literature. Curious domestic situations and bizarre characters call out his keen sense of comedy, which he keeps just under control.

On the other hand, he has a very real understanding of the difficulties of the spiritual life. What does he make of C.S.L.? A biographer has chosen to be one of God's spies, even if his subject makes it difficult for him. Although Tolkien truly said that, at heart, Lewis was always writing about himself, he was shy of his emotions and adept at self-concealment, particularly perhaps in his autobiography, *Surprised by Joy*. He argued, too, in "The Personal Heresy," that a writer's character should not be deduced from his books. But Mr. Wilson (who never met Lewis) has, with great skill, conjured up a true image. The heavy, red-faced reactionary is there, but Lewis is also shown as a private man of exceptional generosity and humility. Perhaps, indeed, he was a great man. But, in spite of his energy, Mr. Wilson sees him as curiously passive, as if waiting for his life's turning points to arrive.

Lewis was by temperament and belief a Romantic, and, like Wordsworth, he seems to have had his decisions made for him by particular significant moments. Among these were the morning when he was told his mother was dead; the night when, walking and talking with his friends in the starlit college garden, it came to him that the Gospels were not different in kind from other storytelling, except that they were told by God as truth, with human history as material; the debate in 1948 at Oxford's Socratic Club, when his theological arguments were demolished by the philosopher Elizabeth Anscombe. (After that he wrote no more apologetics for ten years. The defeat, Mr. Wilson thinks, "stung" Lewis back into "the world which with the deepest part of himself he never left, that of childhood reading." He pushed open the door of the wardrobe and began to tell the story of Narnia, the world on the other side of the wardrobe, which is redeemed by "a great lion called Aslan.") Lastly, there was the death of Joy. "No one ever told me that grief felt so like fear" is the first sentence of *A Grief Observed*, the most touching and immediate of all Lewis's books, the record of his own bereavement. His own death came three years later.

At the end of his strange and deeply interesting story, A. N. Wilson's attitude is still, I think, a kind of civilized bewilderment. This is especially so when he considers the countless readers and disciples of C.S.L. Lewis has another life, far apart from his biography, in the minds of three generations of children and in the religious experience of millions. "This phenomenon can only be explained," Mr. Wilson suggests, "by the fact that his writings, while being self-consciously and deliberately at variance with the twentieth century, are paradoxically in tune with the needs and concerns of our times. Everything on earth is not rational, and attempts to live by reason have all failed. . . . It is the Lewis who plumbed the irrational depths of childhood and religion who speaks to the present generation." And Mr. Wilson, who has evidently set himself strict rules, feels that a biographer is not qualified to try out those depths. This in no way weakens his detailed portrait of Lewis.

1990

"Not at All Whimsical"

Me Again: Uncollected Writings of Stevie Smith,
edited by Jack Barbera and William McBrien

Stevie Smith (1902–1971) said that she was straightforward but not simple, which is a version of not waving but drowning. She presented to the world the face that is invented when reticence goes over to the attack and becomes mystification. If you visited Blake and were told not to sit on a certain chair because it was for the spirit of Michelangelo, or if Emily Dickinson handed you a single flower, you needed time to find out how far the mystification was meant to keep you at a distance and to give you something to talk about when you got home. Eccentricity can go very well with sincerity, and, in Stevie's case, with shrewdness. She calculated the effect of her collection of queer hats and sticks, her face "pale as sand," pale as her white stockings, and also, I think, of her apparent obsession with death. She was interested in death, and particularly in its willingness to oblige. She had survived a suicide attempt in 1953, she was touched by the silence of the "countless, countless dead," but when in her sixties she felt the current running faster and "all you want to do is to get to the waterfall and over the edge," she still remained Florence Margaret Smith, who enjoyed her life, and, for that matter, her success. Her poetry, she told Anna Kallin, was *not at all whimsical,* as some asses seem to think I am, but serious, yet not aggressive, and fairly cheerful though with melancholy patches." The melancholy was real, of course. For that reason she gave herself, in her novels, the name of Casmilus, a god who is permitted to come and go freely from hell.

Stevie was good company and (what is not the same thing) a good friend. She could be "Comfort Smith." Deep intimacy she drew back from, because she respected it so much. "That troubled stirring world of two" was always strange to her, though love was not.

In the serious process of trying out friendships, Stevie liked to say exactly the same things to a number of different people. There was even a kind of guided tour of Palmer's Green, to Grovelands Park, round the lake, and back to Avondale Road. But if, for her own purposes, Stevie was sometimes repetitive, she was never predictable. Patric Dickinson, in his introduction to *Scorpion and Other Poems,* says that she loathed cruelty, and so she did, but although (for instance) she was fond of children she was not deceived by them, and knew that it could be satisfactory to put them sharply in their place. Again, she was encouraging to beginners, but when she was pressed (probably quite mistakenly) to support Yevtushenko for the Oxford Professorship of Poetry, and was told he would encourage the students to meet and read their poems aloud, she paused for a moment and said: "How terrible!" After her aunt's death she took to plain cookery, and wrote that she loved to feel a slim young parsnip under her knife.

One Avondale Road, the "house of mercy," was, certainly, necessary to Stevie. She tired easily and had never liked going to the office.

> *Dark was the day for Child Rolandine the artist*
> *When she went to work as a secretary-typist.*

It was the privilege of employers, the rich, to waste the time of the poor, and in particular the forty-five minutes or so it took for her to travel back to Palmer's Green. The problem of getting her home as soon as she wanted to go became, in fact, one of the first considerations of her friends. "Riding home one night on a late bus, I saw the reflected world in the dark windows of the top deck and thought I was lost for ever in the swirling streets of that reflected world, with its panic corners and distances that end too soon." Everyone wanted to spare her this. But once she was safely back, the beloved suburb where she had been brought up became a refuge. She was not known as a writer there, and could keep the observer's stance that was precious to her. "Through the laburnums and the net curtains," she said, "you may snuff the quick-witted high-lying life of a suburban community." Her heart went out to all she saw and overheard of the lonely, the peculiar, the poisonously nice, the fatally well-intentioned, and to those misplaced in life who, respectable to all appearances, would prefer to give up and "storm back through the gates of birth." She also liked to sense the warmth of "father's chair, uproar, dogs, babies, and radio," and "yet she would point out that she was really on the edge of the open country," only six stations to the middle of Hertfordshire. The sky was clearer in N13 and she could come to terms with herself there. At the same time she insisted she was driven to write because there was absolutely no company for her in Palmer's Green.

When Kay Dick interviewed her in 1970, Stevie complained about her photographs. "They make me look dead, and as if I'd been dead for a long time. I haven't got a thing about age but I do rather have a thing about looking dead and buried." She made no particular objection, however, to being written about, though her three novels and twelve volumes of poetry seemed to have taken her self-portrait as far as it need go. It might be thought, too, that after the death of her sister in 1975 the truth about Stevie, if hidden, would be hard to find. However, her biography has now been undertaken by two American scholars—a matter of satisfaction in itself, since during her lifetime she was not much appreciated in the States. One can only admire the courage of the joint venture. Not only are they collaborating at long distance (Barbera at the University of Mississippi, McBrien at Hofstra), so that they can only meet to compare notes twice a year, but, as neither of them ever met Stevie, they are getting to know her by running the documentary film about her life over and over again. No investigators can have worked harder. And although she has proved elusive (there is no evidence, for example, that George Orwell was her lover), and has turned out to be a somewhat off-center eccentric, they have remained sweet-tempered and continued to gather, research, and file their discoveries together. The first result of all this is *Me Again,* a handsome selection of uncollected stories, essays, reviews, and poems, and sixty-odd letters, only two of which have been printed before.

For some reason that the two editors don't reveal, nothing, except for the letters, is arranged in chronological order. James MacGibbon, Stevie's literary editor, does not comment on this, but says in his rather cautious preface that their choice is "tantamount to an autobiographical profile." This is not quite so, but he is surely right in saying that the book will give most readers their first authentic idea of her religious convictions. These were self-convictions. She had almost made up her mind that God was one of man's most unfortunate inventions. What needed explanation was not man's failings but his continued demand to love and be loved, even when

> *Beaten, corrupted, dying,*
> *In his own blood lying.*

But that was not enough, and the frail poet hurled herself against Von Hügel, Father D'Arcy, Ronald Knox, and all the propositions of the Catholic and Anglo-Catholic Churches. "Some Impediments to Christian Commitment," which is a talk she gave at St. Cuthbert's, Philbeach Gardens, just over two years before her death, is an account of her own spiritual history, a touching one, with her own particular sense of the sad and the ridiculous. It has never been printed before. "Torn about," as one might expect, by the loss of her childhood faith, she was driven year by year to conclude that "the Redemption seems a Bargain dishonourable to both proposer and accepter." Uncertainty, however, which she finally settled for, proved treacherous, and she had to admit finally that she was a backslider as a non-believer.

Among the ten stories retrieved for us is perhaps the most lyrical of all, "Beside the Seaside," a languorous *fin-de-saison* holiday impression, the pebbles of the beach still warm to the touch but deeply cold underneath, and her friends' tempers just beginning to fray. There is a variable delicate friction between the interests of wives, husbands, and children, and between human beings and nature—one might say between the seaside and the sea. Helena (the Stevie of this story) detaches herself, unable to help doing so, and wanders away inland across the marshes, returning "full of agreeable fancies and spattered with smelly mud" to confront the edginess of the party with her artist's sense of deep interior peace. In "The Story of a Story" she again defends herself as an artist. This wiry situation comedy shows why Stevie sometimes longed, in her character as Lot's wife, to be turned into a pillar of asphalt, since she seemed to give offence so often. Her friends did not want to become her material, as they had in "Sunday at Home" (also reprinted here), and her publisher hesitated, afraid of libel. "The morning, which had been so smiling when her employer first spoke, now showed its teeth." Sitting alone in the rainswept park, the unhappy authoress regrets the loss of friends, but much more the death of her story. She had worked on it with love to make it shining and remote, but also with "cunning and furtiveness and care and ferocity." These were the qualities that went into Stevie's seemingly ingenuous fiction.

About the poems, also industriously tracked down, I am not so sure, since she herself presumably didn't want them included in the collected edition of 1975. Stevie Smith had a remarkable ear ("it's the hymns coming up, I expect"), and when she was manipulated by whatever force poetry is, she knew that all she had to do was listen. She produced then a kind of counterpoint between the "missed-shot tunes" that haunted her and the phrasing and pauses of her own speaking voice. Not all the verses in *Me Again* seem quite to reach this, although you can hear her distinctive note of loneliness—which, as she pointed out, "runs with tiredness"—in "None of the Other Birds" and "Childhood and Interruption."

In the end, one of Stevie's greatest achievements was to be not only a connoisseur of myths, but the creator of one. Out of an unpromisingly respectable suburb at the end of the apparently endless Green Lanes she created a strange Jerusalem.

1981

An Unforgettable Voice

Angus Wilson: A Biography, by Margaret Drabble

"You've better things to do with your time, dear girl," Angus Wilson told Margaret Drabble when, after twenty-four years' friendship, she suggested writing something about him. No, he would do that himself—Angus Wilson on Angus Wilson. He never managed it, and by 1991, when he died, his standing as a novelist had suffered and he had begun to feel like an old trouper or an old queen whose show was no longer wanted. This skillful and sympathetic book, then, is in the first place a matter of rehabilitation, or picking up the pieces, which may not be the very best basis for a biography, but is still an extremely good one.

Throughout she calls him, affectionately, "Angus." She is "Drabble." Angus came from a confusing, shabby-genteel family and a half-world of expatriates and private hotels where he was the precocious, blue-eyed youngest, an eavesdropper on the world. The child's eye view, he came to believe, was crucial to the writer (although one of his schoolfriends thought Angus had never had a real childhood at all). When, at the age of thirty-six, he published his first volume of short stories, *The Wrong Set*, it included the very earliest, "Raspberry Jam": a small boy looks on while two odd village ladies, who don't wish to be spied upon, put out their pet bullfinch's eyes with a pin. Angus liked to say that he had thought of this story, almost that it had thought of him, on a single afternoon. Drabble, however, has found four earlier drafts in the notebooks. You almost regret her thoroughness.

Hemlock and After (1951) and *Anglo-Saxon Attitudes* (1956), his first two novels, were generous in scope but just as deliciously, or frighteningly, acid in flavor. Their success, and that of the much calmer *Middle Age of Mrs. Eliot* (1958), led to an unpredictable result: his commitments expanded enormously and so, in spite of the nervous strain, did his happiness. For the next twenty-five years, as literature entered what Drabble calls "The Age of Conferences," Angus emerged, with only Stephen Spender as a serious rival, as the Indispensable Man. In 1963 he became first Lecturer, then Professor, at the new University of East Anglia as it rose from Norfolk's flat fields. He was on the committee of the Royal Literary Fund and the Arts Council, Chairman of the National Book League and the Society of Authors, eventually a Companion of Literature and a knight. As a distinguished visiting lecturer he patrolled Europe and America, hugely welcomed as a sort of white-haired totem by the world's students. Ceaseless traveling is pretty sure to mean comic mishaps, and Drabble doesn't miss these, but at the same time she skillfully keeps us in mind of the heroism with which Angus (perhaps literally) worked himself to death. He succeeded, not as a born organizer but as someone who was interested in other human beings, a brilliant, malicious man who was still, at heart, a sweet-natured busybody, prodigal with time and effort. Organization was left to his lover, secretary, driver, and cook, Tony Garrett.

All these activities mean that Drabble is faced with a cast of hundreds, but she never lets one slip. Some are famous; others, although their names are listed, are totally obscure; some have their own anecdotes: "Juliet Corke married a Frenchman and Angus spoke at the wedding in fluent French, recalling the little tabby cat she had once given him," Gerard van het Reve "would ask for a plate and some mustard, if conversation at table grew dull; he would then spread the plate with mustard, and lay his penis temptingly upon the plate." Drabble vividly describes the places Angus went to, and even, on occasion, places he might have gone to, but didn't. Drabble assesses the reviews of each book and suggests the originals of the characters (four are given for Rose Lorimer, the sublimely ridiculous lecturer in *Anglo-Saxon Attitudes*). She knows the names of Angus's roses, and makes us interested in his meals. Her sense of period, down to the very year, is, as always, matchless, and you can feel time pass inside and outside the cottage at Felsham Woodside. There is, on the other hand, not much evidence from accountants and it's not quite clear why the money ran out just before Angus and Tony (now acting as a nurse) left England for St. Remy. Readers of *The Independent* will remember the dignified appeal for funds in May 1990 by Rose Tremain, who had been one of his pupils. The end, as Drabble says, was not a happy one. But Dr. Patrick Woodcock, who looked after Angus and many of his friends, once told me that the best provision against old age was "to make sure of your little treats" and these Angus had, in the visitors who brought him his last luxury, gossip.

"He made no secret of the fact that he was a homosexual," Drabble says, "and this volume is in part a history of what we now call gay liberation, and the decreasing need for discretion." Francis King suggested in his memoirs *Yesterday Came Suddenly* that at first Angus Wilson hated his own sexuality, but this does not appear from the biography. He seems to have been admitted to dressing-up games, and perhaps seduced, by his elder brothers. However, although in *Hemlock and After* he wrote, for 1952, quite openly about the subject (Rupert Hart-Davis's *Hugh Walpole*, published in the same year, never mentions it), he still felt obliged in his early novels to restrict himself. Getting rid of the restraints didn't improve him as a writer—when does it ever? Meanwhile in his official capacity as a smiling public man, he felt, although he never denied or compromised, that it was better to proceed with caution. I should add that anyone anxious to read about the details of his personal sex life has come to the wrong counter. Drabble has been guided, as she explains in her preface, by Tony Garrett, to whom the book is dedicated, and who told her that he was prepared to talk about the relationship but not about "actual sexual activity . . . firstly because I cannot ask Angus for his permission."

The truth about his sexual adventures, Angus always insisted, was in his fiction. Everyone is at liberty to look for it there. His real subject, as he explained in his Northcliffe lectures and his self-analytical *The Wild Garden*, was evil, as distinct from right and wrong and their traditional playground of comedy. Margaret Drabble accepts this and says: "He demonstrated that it was still possible to write a great novel." This implies direct competition with the great Victorian classics, and Angus in fact wrote distinctive studies of Dickens and Kipling, but Drabble goes off course, I think, in trying to show that what attracted him to them was that his life-story was like theirs. It wasn't. Their attraction for him, surely, was the lavish, unaccountable nature of their genius— Kipling's daemon, or Dickens's "I thought of Mr. Pickwick." Faced by what seemed almost the duty of greatness, and uncertain of his own daemon, insecurity threatened, and to banish insecurity Angus took to avoiding silence. Nobody who ever knew it could forget his voice— heard from outside in the street, growing louder on the stairs, non-stop into the rooms rising into plaintive arabesques, pausing only for a painfully brilliant imitation. You can hear it, so to speak, through the chinks of this admirable biography, a solid tribute of scholarship and affection.

1995

Joy and Fear

Roald Dahl: A Biography, by Jeremy Treglown

Truth is more important than modesty, Roald Dahl said, but glorious exaggeration seemed to suit him better than either. For example: "It happens to be a fact that nearly every fiction writer in the world drinks more whisky than is good for him. He does it to give himself faith, hope, and courage. A person is a fool to become a writer. His only compensation is absolute freedom." This is the writer as hero, talking to his young readers in their millions in *Boy*—not an autobiography, he tells them, as that would be full of boring things, but a record only of what "made a tremendous impression on me."

What had impressed him most since he was born in 1916 to Norwegian parents were the family's rugged holidays in the fjords, spiffing practical jokes—such as frightening an ugly old sweetshop woman with a dead mouse—savage beatings at school, a confident beginning as a trainee oil salesman in East Africa. In 1939 he trained as a fighter pilot "and I got shot down myself, crashing in a burst of flames . . . but that is another story."

Invalided out of the RAF, he was sent on intelligence work to wartime Washington. At this time he was a handsome young man, with something a little dangerous about him, who was friendly with the rich and famous, and married to the actress Patricia Neal. He also had a ferocious imagination, which he set to work for him. He was fairly well established with *The New Yorker* and *Playboy* long before he began, perhaps more successfully than anyone else in the world, to tell stories to children.

It might be felt that fate had allowed him a good deal, but Dahl knew he deserved more. He felt entitled to dispense with income-tax collectors and quarrel with publishers and, if he was bored, to be exceptionally rude. He was convinced he should have a knighthood, since that was what great writers were given. On the other hand, he was often kind and generous, and met life's worst blows with courage. His favorite daughter, Olivia, died at the age of seven. Dahl nearly went out of his mind, but he said afterward that he had lost all fear of dying. "If Olivia can do it, I can."

Dahl was colorful, noisy, dominating, possibly a genius, certainly an expert in self-publicity. Jeremy Treglown, his biographer, is calm, judicial, accurate, quietly brilliant. The ice man cometh. Treglown is humane, but we would like to know the truth. Was Dahl really shot down, or did he make an ignominious forced landing? Can he be trusted on the subject of his flogging headmasters? How much help did he get from publishers' editors, who patiently toned down the bloody-mindedness of his plots? Treglown never proceeds without evidence, some from documents and from the books themselves, a lot of it from firsthand witnesses. Then he gives his assessment, trying to separate "the detached, scientific, sometimes cruel-seeming Dahl from the kindly magician." This, however, as he must have noticed, means distinguishing one unreality from another.

Roald Dahl's books for children are much less primitive than his stories for adults, which depend on shock endings, Saki-like schemes for revenge, and hateful practical jokes. The much-loved "juveniles" are just as ruthless, but they are life-loving. The eight-year-old Roald was galvanized by the idea of coasting downhill on his bike, no hands. "It made me tremble just to think of it." Joy and fear are indistinguishable here, just as they are when the juice-laden Giant Peach is spiked on the Empire State Building, or the BFG endeavors to please the Queen by farting his loudest. Jeremy Treglown's fine psychological study is the key to these fantasies, which still earn £2 million a year for the Dahl estate. Most writers would tremble just to think of it.

1994

"Really, One Should Burn Everything"

Selected Letters of Philip Larkin, 1940–1985,
edited by Anthony Thwaite

There is no direct train from London to Hull, in Yorkshire. You have to change at Doncaster. Philip Larkin used to claim that he went on working there because literary curiosity-seekers (not to speak of "Jake Balokowsky, my biographer") would be daunted when they discovered that the journey took three to four hours, and might decide on another poet instead.

Certainly Hull seemed like seclusion, almost retreat, with correspondence as a lifeline. "Postmen like doctors go from house to house"—

although Anthony Thwaite is perhaps too optimistic in saying that Larkin thought of both of them as healers. Postmen and doctors make mistakes, and the relief they bring is often only temporary.

Larkin decided early on against marriage, risking loneliness in exchange. He valued jazz, cricket, drink, women (some women), books (some books), poetry, and friendship. "'Friend' can mean three things," he wrote somewhat sourly in 1941, "acquaintance, comrade, or antagonist." Of his three joint literary executors, all were unquestionably his comrades and two are poets—Andrew Motion, whose biography of Larkin comes out this year, and Anthony Thwaite, who edited the *Collected Poems* (criticized for putting in too much) in 1988 and these *Selected Letters* (criticized for leaving out too much) in 1992. The third executor, Monica Jones, a university lecturer, was by far the closest of Larkin's women friends.

The correspondence will only be completely comprehensible when the biography appears. Meanwhile, faced by several thousand letters, Thwaite has had to save space and at the same time do what he could about some awkward gaps. Only a dozen or so letters to Monica Jones have been made available (although Thwaite discreetly says that "apparent losses may later be recovered"), and it seems that those to Bruce Montgomery (the detective writer Edmund Crispin) can't be inspected until 2035. George Hartley, the publisher of Larkin's first important collection, *The Less Deceived* (1955), reserved his letters because he wanted to sell them unexcerpted. And the important correspondence with Kingsley Amis, who first met Larkin when they were students together at Oxford, and to whom the very last letter in this book, dictated just before the final operation, is addressed—this correspondence, too, is rather ragged.

Thwaite's job, or one of them, has been to show the "stages of life" which Larkin himself so dreaded—the inescapable I-told-you-so of mortality. First there's the adolescent, trying out romantic ideas and dirty language. Here the chief correspondent is Jim Sutton, who knew Larkin as an eight-year-old schoolboy at King Henry VIII School, Coventry. Sutton never became a celebrity. He was an unsuccessful painter, an Army driver in the war, later a chemist's dispenser, and evidently a choice spirit. To him Larkin confided not only his early disappointments with publishers and with sex but his concept of poetry itself.

A poem is just a thought of the imagination—not really logical at all. In fact I should like to make it quite clear to my generation and all subsequent generations that I have no ideas about poetry at all. For me, a poem is the crossroads of my thoughts, my feelings, my imaginings, my wishes, and my verbal sense: normally these run parallel . . . often two or more cross . . . but only when all cross at one point does one get a poem.

At this time he was "humanly although perhaps not excusably tired of not getting any money or reviews or any sort of reputation," The only "adventurous" thing in his life, he told the agent Alan Pringle, was to apply and be selected for the public librarianship at Wellington, Shropshire, replacing a man of seventy-six, and "handing out antiquated tripe to the lower levels of the general public" for £175 a year. And yet by the time he was twenty-five he had published two novels and a volume of poetry. The poems had only one reviewer, but that reviewer was D. J. Enright.

From the 1950s his life quite rapidly, if warily, expands. The toad, work, always keeps a precious jewel in its head of self-doubt, misanthropy, and irony. But the nervous beginner becomes what he has to admit is a well-known poet, and the young writer who signed his first book contract for £30 turns out to be an excellent business man. To Patsy Strang (whom he met after moving from Shropshire to Belfast) there is his first series of love letters, or something very like them. "You are the sort of person one can't help feeling (in a carping kind of way) ought to come one's way once in one's life." When she decamps to Paris, he tells her she is like "a rocket, leaving a shower of sparks to fall on the old coal shed as you whoosh upwards." In 1959 he was appointed to the University Library of Hull. In 1961 he was awarded the Queen's Gold Medal for poetry. It was not until the end of the Seventies that he began to feel the wretched approach of dryness, although even then he "would sooner write no poems than bad poems." Thwaite believes that this drying-up or desertion was partly, at least, the result of the unsettling experience of his last move. In 1973 the University of Hull decided to sell off its "worst properties," including the one where he lived, and he became, for the first time, a homeowner, faced with endless practical difficulties, and feeling "like a tortoise that has been taken out of one shell and put in another." But even this experience never stopped him from writing letters.

Two omissions seem strange. There are no letters to Larkin's family, not even to his mother, to whom he wrote regularly until her death at the age of ninety-one. And there are almost none to do with his official career at Hull, and yet the building of the Library Extension, of which he had been in charge since his arrival, was, as he put it, "the daysman of my thought, and hope, and doing." At the same time, he was secretary of the university's publishing committee. Very likely these letters might be considered dull, but dullness is a necessary part of most existences, and certainly of Philip Larkin's.

What was he like, exactly? Having decided, by its usual mysterious processes, that Larkin was one of the very few living poets that anyone (apart from students and teachers) wanted to buy and read, the British public accepted his persona from the poems they knew, and grew attached to it. He was modest and humorous, lived out of tins in rented rooms, was "unchilded and unwifed," worked decently hard without becoming rich, visited churches as a wistful sightseer, had missed the sexual revolution of the Sixties by being born too early, was "nudged from comfort" by the sight of ships and aircraft departing and of the old people's ward. He refused to bother about what didn't interest him. He was the writer who, when asked by the interviewer about the influence of Borges, said: "Who's Borges?" New music, a new generation's language, was not what he wanted. "My mind has stopped at 1945, like some cheap wartime clock," he told Kingsley Amis. In defiance of realism's bad reputation, he continued to write about the recognizable human condition. "I'm not interested in things that aren't true." But with this marvelous talent for the clearest possible everydayness he combined the torment of the romantic conscience and, however embarrassing it might be, the romantic vision. In "The Whitsun Weddings" he is forced to admit—though not until the train is nearly into London—that the absurd honeymoon couples, and not himself, are the source of fertility and future change. The "success or failure of the poem [when read aloud] depends on whether it gets off the ground on the last two lines," he explains to Anthony Thwaite in 1959.

To a considerable extent, the Larkin of these letters is the reader's familiar Larkin. What you paid for is what you get. But there are passages that are not so reassuring. It isn't so much that he sent for girlie magazines and, for long periods, drank too much and got "routinely pissed," or even that he allowed himself to resent the success of others and to hate extensively. His women colleagues in Belfast were "old Sowface" and "old Bagface," Seamus Heaney is "the Gombeen man," R. S. Thomas "Arse Thomas," Ted Hughes a "boring old monolith" and "no good at all" but so are Pope, Shelley, Robert Lowell. Blake is an ass, Byron a bore. "I find old Henry James repulsive sitting there cuddling his ideas, like a butler warming up the undermaids!" Still, these are private letters. Who would want to be answerable for everything they've said, in private letters, to friends they hope to amuse? More distressing by far are his general opinions, forcibly expressed, which leave the whole concept of political incorrectness gasping. If they represent what he really or even sometimes felt, immigration (LETTING THE BUGGERS IN HERE) must be made illegal before every household in the land is overrun, unemployment should be got rid of by stopping national assistance, workingmen are "awful shits marching or picketing," the Labour Party are Communists who would like to see him in a camp for dissidents. In a Hull student's paper he was said to have "Judged it prudent/Never to speak to any student," and if they continue to demonstrate he recommends flogging.

How seriously were his correspondents supposed to take all this? I think quite seriously. When I was working in an unimportant capacity for the British Arts Council Literary Panel, Larkin was asked for advice on the funding of ethnic arts centers. He replied that anyone lucky enough to be allowed to settle here had a duty to forget their own culture and try to understand ours.

Thwaite, it has been suggested, has done his best, through his selection and omission, to sweep things under the carpet and give as favorable a picture as possible. This may be so. And perhaps he was touched by Larkin's mild complaint to a woman friend: "[I am] rather depressed by the remorseless scrutiny of one's private affairs that seems to be the fate of the newly dead. Really, one should burn everything."

It has even been argued that Larkin, a favorite with examiners and educators, shouldn't, after the publication of this book, be allowed any longer onto the school syllabus. But what schoolchildren learn and will continue to learn from his poems is that "what will survive of us is love." And there is some evidence of this too in the *Selected Letters*—in his encouragement of Barbara Pym for example, when she was struggling with unresponsive publishers, a correspondence that became what Thwaite calls "a delightful and moving intimacy." There are the pains he took for his old friend Jim Sutton, who had written an unsaleable book on his war experiences, his loyalty to long-term library colleagues, and his agonizing worry over the health of Monica Jones. His letter to Douglas Dunn, after the death of Dunn's first wife, begins: "Dear Douglas— I don't know whether it is harder to speak or write to you of these last weeks. Whichever I am doing seems the more difficult."

Thwaite makes only the modest claim to have compiled "an interim account of a memorable man, much loved by many people." Meanwhile, I imagine, he must be scanning the horizon for the arrival of Andrew Motion, whose Life, let's hope, will provide him with a much-needed and decisive ally.

1993

Precious Moments Gone

An introduction to *A Month in the Country,* by J. L. Carr

I first heard of J. L. Carr through a passage in Michael Holroyd's *Unreceived Opinions.* Holroyd had had, from George Ellerbeck, a family butcher in Kettering, a letter telling him he had won the Ellerbeck Literary Award, consisting of a non-transferable meat token for one pound of best steak and a copy of Carr's novel *The Harpole Report* (so this must have been in 1972 or 1973). The letter went on: "The prize is only awarded at infrequent intervals and you are only its third recipient. The circumstances are that Mr. Carr, who makes a living by writing, is one of my customers and pays me in part with unsold works known, I understand, as Remainders." Never before or since have I heard of anyone who managed to settle up with a butcher, even in part, with Remainders. It is a rational and beneficial idea, but it took Jim Carr to carry it out.

James Lloyd Carr was born on 20 May 1912, of a Yorkshire Methodist family. His father used to preach in the Wesleyan "tin tabernacle." Jim used occasionally to play truant, but did not and could not forget the old revivalist hymns—"Hold the Fort," "Count Your Many Blessings," "Pull for the Shore, Sailor," and "We Are Out on the Ocean, Sailing."

He went to the village school at Carlton Miniott in the North Riding and to Castleford Grammar School. At Castleford his headmaster was the enthusiastic and progressive "Toddy" Dawes, who, during a miners' strike, took the local brass band across to France to perform in Paris, where it won a competition. "Other schools had ordinary headmasters," said Carr. "We had Toddy." In turn he himself became a teacher and a publisher of historical maps and delightful tiny booklets, *The Little Poets,* a little, that is, of each poet and illustrations of all sizes. These were left by the cash-outs of bookshops to attract last-minute purchasers, and, on occasion, he gave them away like sweets. I only wish I had a complete set now.

In 1968 he retired early to make a living with the pocket books and maps, and to write. He settled not in his native Yorkshire but in Northamptonshire, where he had been a head teacher. He described it as "onion fields, spud and beet fields, mile and mile after mile of hedgeless flatness, dykes and ditches," and he loved it dearly. In 1979 he wrote his masterpiece, *A Month in the Country,* which was published in 1980, shortlisted for the Booker Prize, and won the *Guardian* fiction prize. It was made into a film. "Fine gentlemen from London," as Jim insisted on calling them, arrived at his house in Kettering, and pointed out that the title, of course, would not do, it had already been used by Turgenev. "Is that so?" said Jim. "I don't think I'll change mine, though." He didn't.

A Month in the Country is not quite like any of his other novels. It is 1920, and Tom Birkin is back from the trenches with a facial twitch that the doctors tell him may get better in time. He has been trained by one of the last remaining experts as a restorer of medieval murals, and he has been hired to uncover the whitewashed-over fourteenth-century painting on the wall of a Yorkshire village church. His fee will be twenty-five guineas, and he is told to make the best of what he can find.

He arrives at Oxgodby station in pouring rain and darkness, but receives an offer to come inside and have a cup of tea from the stationmaster, Mr. Ellerbeck. (The name, of course, and the kindness are from Kettering. Carr liked to introduce characters from one book to another, and from real life into books.) But Birkin refuses the offer. He has an appointment to meet the vicar at the church, and in any case he is quite unused to northerners. He feels himself in enemy country.

The rain stops, and the next day brings the cloudless, golden, incomparable summer of 1920. For Tom Birkin, "nerves shot to pieces, wife gone, dead broke," it will be, almost against his will, a healing process. Like Solzhenitsyn in *Matyona's House,* he has wanted to cut himself off and lose himself in the distant innermost heart of the country. "Only time would clean me up," he thinks. But he is brought back to himself first of all by the way things are made—even in the drenching rain he notices that the church masonry is "beautifully cut with only a hint of mortar."

Then there's the way things work—notably the cast-iron Bankdam-Crowther stove in the church itself—"There seemed to be several knobs and toggles for which I could see no purpose: plainly, this damned big monster was going to provide me with several pleasurably instructive hours learning its foibles." Then there is the place. On his very first morning in the bell tower, a vast and magnificent landscape unfolds.

> Day after day, mist rose from the meadow as the sky lightened and hedges, barns and woods took shape until, at last, the long curving back of the hills lifted away from the Plain. . . . Day after day it was like that and each morning I leaned on the yard gate dragging at my first fag and (I'd like to think) marvelling at this splendid backcloth. But it can't have been so; I'm not the marvelling kind. Or was I then?

Next there is the long-dead, unknown wall-painter himself, "a nameless painter reaching from the dark to show me what he could do, saying to me as clear as any words, 'If any part of me survives from time's corruption, let it be this. For this was the sort of man I was.'" (At the very end of the book, Birkin refers to him as "the secret sharer," a reminder that Carr had been given what he called his first stiff dose of Conrad at Castleford Grammar.) Lastly, among his unconscious healers are the natives of Oxgodby, who turn out to be anything but hostile. Carr always dwelt lovingly not only on turns of speech but on details of behavior that separate one region of England from another. He used to describe, for example, a down-and-out traveling show in Yorkshire in which the compère had appealed for someone to "come forward" from the audience. "But," said Jim, "they don't 'come forward' in the North Riding." Certainly they don't need to in Oxgodby, where they are used to speaking out and staying put. Kathy Ellerbeck, yelling her mam's invitation to Sunday dinner up Birkin's ladder, is Carr's heartfelt tribute to the Yorkshire school-leaver.

The epigraphs of his books were important to him. *A Month in the Country* has three. The first is from Johnson's Dictionary—"*A novel:* a small tale, generally of love"—a Carr-like, and indeed Dr. Johnson-like, throwaway. The third, an octet from Trench's "She comes not when Noon is on the roses," was added to the 1991 edition after the death of Carr's wife Sally. The second is from the poems he loved best, Housman's *A Shropshire Lad* (no. XXXII). I am here on earth only for a short time, Housman says. You must trust me.

> *Take my hand quick and tell me,*
> *What have you in your heart.*

Being Housman, he is not likely to expect an answer, and Birkin doesn't get one either.

There are, it turns out, three strangers in Oxgodby besides Birkin himself. One of them, Moon, he meets on his first day in the bell tower. We don't exactly know what Moon does, although he appears to be a professional archaeologist, and had "an RFC pal" to fly him over the site before he began on his commission, which is to make reasonable efforts over a given period to find a lost fourteenth-century grave. We do, however, find out from a chance revelation in a Ripon teashop, the secret of Moon's war record and what was done to him.

Birkin is working at the top of his ladder, Moon has dug himself a hole to live in beneath his bell-tent. Birkin has been accepted from the beginning by the inhabitants of Oxgodby, helps with the "dafties" at the Wesleyan Sunday school, goes on the glorious Sunday school outing, to which Moon is not invited. Moon talks posh. Birkin doesn't, but he and Moon like each other. Are they to be thought of as opposites, or as two marked men, marked, that is, by the war and by their bitter experience of sex, and regarded by old Mossop, the sexton, as (like all southerners) fair cautions?

The other two outsiders (or at least they haven't managed to feel accepted in Oxgodby) are the vicar and his wife, Arthur and Alice Keach. (He is also referred to as the Reverend J. G. Keach, but Carr was a reckless proofreader. He had, he said, a "terrible and inexcusable vice of not reading a proof until after I have published it.") The vicar is businesslike—this seems at first to be his only good quality—disapproving, unyielding, and chilly. He has "a cold, cooped-up look about him," and although he must have got used to the twitch, he continues to talk to someone behind Birkin's left shoulder.. Cold church, warm chapel. Birkin listens through the floor of the belfry to the congregation "bleating away downstairs" and contrasts it with the thick Yorkshire pudding at the Ellerbecks' and the blacksmith's splendid basso profundo. The vicar's wife, Alice, on the other hand, is like a Botticelli—the Primavera, not the Venus—a Primavera, that is, in a straw hat with a rose from the vicarage garden stuck in the ribbon. Birkin's feelings for Alice are what might be expected, and there is a moment when he is very close to asking her Housman's question: What have you in your heart? His attitude to the vicar is also predictable. He and Moon have decided that the marriage is an outrage. "Frankly, if Keach was as awful as he seemed, living with him didn't bear thinking about."

But Birkin runs out of money and finds himself obliged to call round at the vicarage to ask for his first installment of pay. This leads to a passage characteristic of Jim Carr, who likes to beguile us with a story based on his own experience, or something near it, and then allow it to take off, just for a while, into a dazzling, improbable flight. "The house was in a clearing, but what once had been a drive-around for carriages was now blocked by a vast stricken cedar, its torn roots heaving up like a cliff-side and supporting a town-sized garden, its crevices already colonized by wild plants." After a heroic struggle with the bell-pull, Birkin has the door opened to him by Alice Keach herself. She begins a not quite sane story of life in the vicarage where the trees, it seems to her, are closing in on them until mercifully fended off at the last moment by the house walls. She has none of the self-assurance that she shows outside her home. The vicar, too, is different. He has evidently been playing his violin, which is lying by a rickety music stand in one of the vast, chill rooms. Fig leaves, like giant hands, press against the window. The two of them seem huddled together for the comfort of each other's company. And Birkin feels unexpectedly sorry for the Reverend Arthur Keach.

It seems that the only people in the book we are asked thoroughly to disapprove of, even to hate, are the military authorities who sentenced Moon, and the grand new proprietor of the Baines Piano and Organ Warehouse in Ripon, who looks down on the Oxgodby deputation (Mr. Ellerbeck, his daughter Kathy, Mr. Dowthwaite the blacksmith, and Birkin) who have come to replace the Wesleyans' harmonium with a pipe organ. The proprietor thinks he can afford to despise them because they have come to buy secondhand, bringing the cash they have collected with them in a bag. But he is greatly mistaken.

"It is the death of the spirit we must fear" is Carr's epigraph, this time for *The Harpole Report.* The death of the spirit is to lose confidence in one's own independence and to do only what we are expected to do. At the same time, it is a mistake to expect anything specific from life. Life will not conform.

"And it's gone. It's gone. All the excitement and pride of that first job. Oxgodby, Kathy Ellerbeck, Alice Keach, Moon, that season of calm weather   gone as though they'd never been." Early in the book the perspective of time is established. Birkin is looking back, with wonder, at the very last years of a lamp-lit, horse-drawn age. Of course, he and Moon have another set of memories to haunt them, from Passchendaele. But Birkin believes that the future is opening up. "Well, I was young then."

Carr is by no means a lavish writer, but he has the magic touch to reenter the imagined past. Birkin notices, as he walks back down the road, how he first smelled, then saw, the swathes of hay lying in the dusk. At the Sunday school outing, "Afterwards, most of the men took off their jackets, exposing their braces and the tapes of their long woollen underpants, and astonished their children by larking around like great lads." Those tapes! Who would have remembered them except Jim Carr?

From the first Birkin has seen that the wall-painting is a Doom, a Christ in judgment with its saved and its sinners in a great spread of reds and blues. He finishes the restoration according to contract, just as the first breath of autumn comes to Oxgodby. But the moment when the year crosses into another season becomes indistinguishable from his passion, making itself clear as it does quite suddenly, for Alice Keach.

"All this happened so long ago." The tone of *A Month in the Country,* however, isn't one of straightforward remembering or (if there can be such a thing) of straightforward nostalgia, or even an acute sense of the loss of youth. More complex is his state of mind when he thinks of the people—perhaps only a few—who will visit Oxgodby church in its meadows and regret that they missed seeing the master painter himself— "like someone coming to Malvern, bland Malvern, who is halted by the thought that Edward Elgar walked this road on his way to give music lessons." This is a nostalgia for something we have never had, "a tugging of the heart—knowing a precious moment gone and we not there." But even this has to be distinguished from downright pain. "We can ask and ask, but we can't have again what once seemed ours for ever." You can only wait, Carr says, for the pain to pass, but what is it that once seemed ours for ever? Or is this, like the Shropshire Lad's, an unanswerable question?

2000

Writers and Witnesses 1980–2000

WRITERS

A Secret Richness

A Few Green Leaves, by Barbara Pym

In this, the last novel we shall have from Barbara Pym, it is Miss Grundy, a downtrodden elderly church-worker, who says that "a few green leaves can make such a difference." The phrase echoes a poem that the author loved, but found disturbing, George Herbert's "Hope."

> *I gave to Hope a watch of mine: but he*
> *An anchor gave to me.*
> *Then an old prayer book I did present.*
> *And he an optick sent.*
> *With that I gave a viall full of tears:*
> *But he a few green cares:*
> *Ah Loyterer! I'le no more, no more I'le bring:*
> *I did expect a ring.*

The book, in her accustomed manner, is both elegiac and hopeful. It gives a sense of pity for lost opportunities, but at the same time a courageous opening to the future.

High comedy needs a settled world, ready to resent disturbance, and in her nine novels Barbara Pym stuck serenely to the one she knew best: quiet suburbs, obscure office departments, villages where the neighbors could be observed through the curtains, and, above all, Anglican parishes. (Even as a child at school she had written stories about curates.) This meant that the necessary confrontations must take place at cold Sunday suppers, little gatherings, visits, funerals, and so on, which Barbara Pym, supremely observant in her own territory, was able to convert into a battleground. Here, even without intending it, a given character is either advancing or retreating: you have, for instance, an unfair advantage if your mother is dead, "just a silver-framed photograph," over someone whose mother lives in Putney. And in the course of the struggle strange fragments of conversation float to the surface, lyrical moments dear to Barbara Pym.

"An anthropophagist," declared Miss Doggett in an authoritative tone. "He does some kind of scientific work, I believe."

"I thought it meant a cannibal—someone who ate human flesh," said Jane in wonder.

"Well, science has made such strides," said Miss Doggett doubtfully.

Or:

"Well, he is a Roman Catholic priest, and it is not usual for them to marry, is it?"

"No, of course they are forbidden to," Miss Foresight agreed.

"Still, Miss Lydgate is much taller than he is," she added.

In such exchanges the victory is doubtful: indeed, Miss Doggett and Miss Foresight are, in their way, invincible.

As might be expected, however, of such a brilliant comic writer, the issues are not comic at all. Three kinds of conflict recur throughout Barbara Pym's novels: growing old (on which she concentrated in the deeply touching *Quartet in Autumn*); hanging on to some kind of individuality, however crushed, however dim; and adjusting the vexatious distance between men and women. These, indeed, are novels without heroes. The best that can be put forward is the Vicar in *Jane and Prudence*, "beamy and beaky, kindly looks and spectacles," and, as his wife accepts, more than somewhat childish. If men are less than angels, Barbara Pym's men are rather less than men, not wanting much more than constant attention and comfort. Their theses must be typed, surplices washed, endless dinners cooked, remarks listened to "with an expression of strained interest," and the forces of nature and society combine to ensure, even in the 1980s, that they get these things. Women see through them clearly enough, but are drawn toward them by their own need and by a compassion which is taken entirely for granted. Men are allowed, indeed conditioned, to deceive themselves to the end, and are loved as self-deceivers.

Women have their resource—the romantic imagination. This faculty, which Jane Austen (and James Joyce, for that matter) considered so destructive, is the secret "richness" of Barbara Pym's heroines. "Richness" is a favorite word. It means plenty of human behavior to observe, leading to a wildly sympathetic flight of fancy into the past and future. Of course, one must come down to earth, the tea must be made; reason takes over, but the happiness remains. Richness can defeat even loneliness. In *The Sweet Dove Died* pampered Leonora, on a visit to Keats House, looks in astonishment at a faded middle-aged woman with a bag full of library books, "on top of which lay the brightly-colored packet of a frozen dinner for one. . . . And now she caught a glimpse of her [the woman's] face, plain but radiant, as she looked up from one of the glass cases that held the touching relics. There were tears on her cheeks."

Barbara Pym nevertheless guards against sentimentality. She is the writer who points out "the desire to do good without much personal inconvenience that lurks in most of us," the regrettable things said between friends and "the satisfaction which is to be got from saying precisely things of that kind," the irritation we feel "when we have made up our minds to dislike people for no apparent reason and they perform a kind action." But toward her characters she shows a creator's charity. She understands them so well that the least she can do is to forgive them.

For *A Few Green Leaves* she has moved back from the London of her last two novels to the country. Here, too, she has always taken a straight look. Why is it always assumed that English women must "love" the country, and be partial to dead birds and rabbits, and to cruel village gossip? Why are those who dig the garden and keep goats called "splendid"? But, at the same time, this is Oxfordshire, the "softly undulating landscape, mysterious woods, and ancient stone buildings" where Barbara Pym herself spent her last years.

The heroine, Emma Howick, who does not mean to settle there permanently, undertakes some quiet research into her fellow creatures (rather like Dulcie in *No Fond Return of Love*). The original inhabitants of the village have withdrawn to a council estate on the outskirts, leaving the stone cottages to elderly ladies and professional people. Here she begins her field notes. Changes in village life are a gift to the ironist, but Barbara Pym has placed such changes—seen partly through Emma's eyes and partly through her own—in relation to an unexpected point, the human need for healing. The almost empty church confronts the well-attended surgery (Tuesdays and Thursdays). "There was nothing in churchgoing to equal that triumphant moment when you came out of the surgery clutching the ritual scrap of paper." The lazy old senior partner is "beloved," the junior partner's wife schemes to move into the Rectory, far too large and chilly for the widowed Reverend Thomas Dagnall. Even a discarded tweed coat of the young doctor's is handed separately to the Bring and Buy, "as if a touch could heal." But when, in the closing pages, he is obliged to tell a woman patient that her days are numbered—for it's no good trying to hide the truth from an intelligent person—"she had come back at him by asking if he believed in life after death. For a moment he had been stunned into silence, indignant at such a question." In this indignation we get a glimpse, no more than that, of a pattern that Barbara Pym chose to express only in terms of comedy.

The story proceeds from Low Sunday to New Year through delightful set pieces—a Hunger Lunch, a Flower Festival, blackberry picking (but the hedges turn out to have been "done" already). Tom and Emma must draw together, that's clear enough. Both of them feel the unwanted freedom of loneliness. Daphne, Tom's tough-looking elder sister, is yet another romantic:

> "One goes on living in the hope of seeing another spring," Daphne said with a rush of emotion. "And isn't that a patch of violets?" She pointed to a twist of purple on the ground, no rare spring flower or even the humblest violet, but the discarded wrapping of a chocolate bar, as Tom was quick to point out.
>
> "Oh, but there'll soon be bluebells in these woods—another reason for surviving the winter," she went on. Young Dr. Shrubsole moved away from her, hoping she had not noticed his withdrawal.

Who can say which of them, in the satirist's sense, is right? In the same way, the villagers intimidate the gentry, and the old are intimidated by the young, who preserve them and educate them in healthy living and make them carry saccharine "in a little decorated container given by one of the grandchildren"—but in both cases Barbara Pym gently divides her sympathy. We have to keep alert, because she will never say exactly what we expect. The "few green leaves" of the title come from a remark of Miss Grundy's, made to Tom, who reflects how often these elderly women give him quite unconsciously ideas for a sermon: "He made up his mind not to use them."

Through all Barbara Pym's work there is a consistency of texture as well as of background. She has described the texture herself as "pain, amusement, surprise, resignation." This makes it possible for characters to stray out of their own novel into another: in *A Few Green Leaves*, for example, we hear about the funeral of Miss Clovis from *Less Than Angels*. The valedictory note cannot be missed. But once again the ending is an encounter with hope as Emma determines to stay in the village "and even to embark on a love affair which need not necessarily be an unhappy one."

1980

A Character in One of God's Dreams

Reality and Dreams, by Muriel Spark

When Dame Muriel Spark began to write fiction—reluctantly, it seems—the novel was in an interesting condition, very conscious of itself and given to experiments with time and place and to asking the reader to question the whole business of truth and invention. In her first novel, *The Comforters* (1957), the heroine, who is writing her first novel, finds that she and her characters are being written into a first novel by someone else. This pretense (if that is what it is), that the book is a kind of game, suited her exactly, and still does. As she writes it, it is an enthralling game, and deadly serious.

She has pointed out that it wasn't until she became a Roman Catholic, in 1954, that she was able to see human existence as a whole, as a novelist needs to do. Good and evil, and the state of play between them, can be made clear (though not simplified), she found, by looking at a small community. *The Prime of Miss Jean Brodie* takes place in a select Edinburgh girls' school. At the center of *Memento Mori* is a ward (aged patients, female) in a London hospital. *The Abbess of Crewe*, written at the time of the Watergate scandal, takes place in a convent on up-to-date lines, where the bugging system is controlled from a statue of the Infant of Prague in the Abbess's parlor. *The Girls of Slender Means* presents young women living in a respectable hostel as World War II comes to an end. They will not escape violence, however. An unexploded bomb is buried in the garden.

This is the kind of apparently gross injustice, in the form of brutal interruptions to the smooth-running narrative, that you expect from

Evelyn Waugh and still more from E. M. Forster. In Dame Muriel's stories these interruptions are a reminder of the vast unseen presences on which our lives are dependent or contingent. In *Memento Mori*, eighty-one-year-old Bettie, who has been a distinguished penal reformer, is battered to death by a casual thief. Dull, blameless Mavis, in *The Ballad of Peckham Rye*, gets stabbed to death with a corkscrew. It's not for us to distinguish between the tragic and the ridiculous.

"He often wondered if we were all characters in one of God's dreams." That is how Dame Muriel begins her latest novel, her twentieth, *Reality and Dreams*. We're in yet another closed area, the movies. "He" is Tom, a successful if somewhat old-fashioned film director—an auteur, really, who writes his own screenplays. It sounds as if he might be in search of spiritual truth, but the author soon disillusions us. He has just recovered consciousness in an expensive clinic after a nasty accident on the set. He has fallen off a giant crane, breaking twelve ribs and a hip. Cranes, as his assistant pointed out, are quite unnecessary these days, but Tom had wanted to feel godlike. From the marvelously written, half delirious opening sequence we get the impression of a man who has been hopelessly spoiled. Like both Miss Jean Brodie and the Abbess of Crewe, he is fond of poetry, and this may redeem him a little—not much, though.

Tom's wife is Claire, easygoing and rich. (Dame Muriel has always faced unflinchingly the difference money makes.) He has two daughters, the beautiful Cora, from his first marriage, and, with Claire, the plain, hostile, alarming Marigold. Marigold is a mean-minded sociologist, without warmth, without "magnificence," in Aristotle's sense. Such people are not tolerated by Dame Muriel, who has demolished them in earlier books.

Marigold appears early on in *Reality and Dreams* as Tom's bedside visitor: "'Don't wear yourself out,' she said, 'with too much conversation. I bought you some grapes.' She said 'bought' not 'brought.' She dumped a plastic bag on the side table. 'This is a wonderful clinic,' she said. 'I suppose it costs a fortune. Of course nothing should be spared in a case like yours.'"

You must not imagine Marigold was particularly deprived. Her last remark should remind Tom, if he could hear it, that he is in the hands of an all-knowing narrator, sometimes gentle, sometimes cutting, sometimes even malicious, but always elegant. But Tom thinks that he himself is a creator. About his fellow human beings his question is always: What could I cast them as? How can I make them less real? The film he is making is about a nobody, a girl he had once seen on a trip through France as she was serving out hamburgers at a campsite. In the film she becomes a millionairess overnight. "Do you think," he asks Dave, his private cab-driver, "that she would know what to do with that sort of money? Would she ever learn?" Dave replies that that would depend on what kind of person she was, but this means nothing to Tom. She will only exist as part of his work of art. Then she will be irreplaceable.

Will Tom's egocentricity—his pride, to give his sin a name—lead him to another fall? It proves ruinous, not to him, but to others. As a result of the hostility he stirs up around him   "'It's so very difficult,' said Tom, 'to realize that one makes enemies, especially in one's family'"—Dave gets shot at and wounded, and there is another hideous accident with the giant crane. But Tom himself flourishes. *The Hamburger Girl* does quite well, and he has an idea for another film, about a Celt in Roman Britain who foresees the future. Admittedly it sounds terrible; however, he finds the money to make it. In the meantime, many of the other characters have lost their jobs—so many that they form a group, like the old or the sick. Tom's brother has been laid off in a company downsizing campaign, so has his day nurse's husband, so have both his daughters, both his sons-in-law, Marigold's brother-in-law (from an international electronics firm), and Dave's brother-in-law (let go from a pizza bar). We live in a world where millions find themselves unwanted overnight, expended, like casualties of the century's wars.

This is the dispiriting fact. But the ironic quotation that accompanies Tom throughout the book is the first line of "The Love Song of J. Alfred Prufrock": "Let us go then, you and I." In the Eliot poem Prufrock ends up in a sea dream, where if human voices wake him, he will drown. Tom knows that at best he inhabits a "tract of no man's land between dreams and reality." About redundancy in the work force, all that he can say is "Nobody fires a man if he is exceptionally good." It is as if he couldn't risk too much sympathy, or even too much good sense. His profession, as he admits, is not ordinary life. "But let me tell you that for people in the film business, yes, it is life."

His comment on the second disaster with the crane—a death, this time—is "I'm glad the film is coming to an end. We're just about ready to wrap it up." But we're made to feel that he is considerably shaken. What's more, he is left with a consoler. This Dame Muriel rarely does in her fiction. (Job's unsatisfactory comforters are the metaphor of a whole novel, *The Only Problem.*) But Tom is left with his wife, Claire, who is calm and affectionate, quite unmoved by his infidelities and indeed by her own. He can feel her strength and courage sustaining him as the story closes, leaving nothing more to be said.

Dame Muriel is as enigmatic in this novel, as distinct, as relentlessly observant of human habits and unguarded moments as she has ever been. *Reality and Dreams* is very short but, as she pointed out twenty years ago in an interview with Frank Kermode, it's no good putting a pint of beer in a small glass. "I think the best thing is to be conscious of everything that one writes," she told him, "and let the unconscious take care of itself, if it exists, which we don't know. . . . The best thing is to know what you are doing, I think."

1997

The Great Importance of Small Things

The Collected Stories of John McGahern

Perhaps John McGahern's classic short stories should be read as nearly as possible at one sitting. In that way you could watch the images and the characters recur and echo one another. In "Wheels," the first story in this collection, the speaker (who never gives his name) goes back home from Dublin on his yearly leave from the office to help on the farm. "I knew the wheel," he says—that is, the turning wheel of Time and Nature. "Fathers become children to their sons," and his own father, aggressively swallowing his food at the kitchen table, has turned into "a huge old child" to his stepmother Rose. Meanwhile, he himself has drifted away from the shining upper reaches of childhood without ever reaching the destination he hoped for. He can evoke past summers only by putting on his old work clothes, kept ready for him, and helping to bring in the hay. His weak bully of a father nags at him to take over the land. But in "Gold Watch," when he comes back with the young woman he wants to marry, the old couple have rented out the meadows and there is no haymaking to be done. And in "Sierra Leone," Rose dies and we are faced with yet another possible ending.

In "Wheels," the battle within the family (fought almost in silence), the balance of power between men and women, the nostalgia for a cheerless country childhood, all put us straight into McGahern's Ireland. Life on the land (oats and potatoes) or in the sawmill or the creamery is tedious enough. At the day's end there is scarcely anything to relate, except "the shape of a story that had as much reason to go on as to stop." No one conceals his excitement when a cow falls on its back or a neighbor tries (unsuccessfully) to hang himself from a branch. But "all of all of life turns away from its eventual hopelessness and finds refuge in the importance of small things," and of these McGahern is a connoisseur. Take his description of the barman who helps himself to a whiskey only when his wife, at the other end of the room, isn't looking. The way he watches her is "beautiful in its concentration, reflecting each move or noise she made as clearly as water will drifting clouds." McGahern has every respect for these "small acts of ceremony." Repetition makes them almost sacred, memory gives them a second life. In "A Slip-up," an old farmer, left by his wife to wait outside a supermarket, remembers minute by minute the work he would have been doing if he'd been allowed to keep the land—clearing, draining, fencing. "The hard way is the only way."

This is "the solid world." The Korean War and the Cuban missile crisis are seen as a background only. McGahern has recorded the changes, certainly, in Ireland since the 1950s. The old poorhouse has become the Rest Home for Senior Citizens, the teacher is no longer paid at the back door once a week by the priest's housekeeper, the "strange living light of television" has replaced, in most homes, the red lamp in front of the Sacred Heart. After the war, when Britain had to be rebuilt, "the countryside emptied towards London and Luton." Later, the site-workers mostly came back, and headed for overcrowded Dublin. But the problems of education, opportunity, "the narrow rule of church and custom"—how far have they been solved? They are all, as McGahern sees them, aspects of the idea of home, which has to be left behind, but can never be got away from.

This, of course, is one of Stephen Dedalus's most intractable difficulties in *A Portrait of the Artist as a Young Man*. He escapes painfully from the nets of home, as his destiny requires, and McGahern pays a tribute to Joyce in "The Recruiting Officer," where the Christian Brothers going down to the beach might well be the same ones that Stephen sees, on the same strand at Dollymount. In this story, too, the narrator suffers, like Joyce's Dubliners, from a paralysis of the will, and (all the more perhaps because he is a teacher) "a feeling that any one thing in this life is almost as worth while as any other."

McGahern's women, and, above all, his young women, are more enterprising by far than the men and have modernized much more readily. Love between the sexes, however, is more awkwardly treated than the long-standing, sometimes reluctant affection between friend and friend, brother and brother, fathers and sons, and even old dogs and their masters. When we love, McGahern says, we know nothing about each other even if we are able to go through the "low door" of submission to each other's wishes. We assemble love and become absorbed in it, and then "wake in terror in the knowledge that all we have built is terminal, that, in our pain, we must undo it again."

McGahern is a realist who counts every clean shirt and every pint of Guinness but who writes at times, without hesitation, as a poet. This is only possible because of his magnificently courteous attention to English as it is spoken in Ireland. There are no characters in these stories as sinister as the child-beating father in McGahern's novel *The Dark* (1965), who sleeps in his son's bed, or as tragic as the dying mother in *The Leave-taking* (1974). He has deliberately set himself the task of showing, in everyday incidents, the grief and tension they only just conceal.

1992

Fried Nappy

The Van, by Roddy Doyle

This is the third and last of Roddy Doyle's novels about the Rabbitte family of Barrymount, an unprepossessing council-estate suburb of North Dublin much like Kilbarrack, where Doyle was born himself. Barrymount, although by no means a foul rag-and-bone shop, is a place for dreams to start. In *The Commitments* young Jimmy Rabbitte decides that Ireland is ready for soul music and gets his group together. Just as there seems to be a chance with a recording company, they desert him one by one. In *The Snapper* Sharon Rabbitte, drunk in the car park at the Soccer Club Christmas do, gets pregnant by that fucking old eejit Mr. Burgess—the father, what's more, of a friend of hers. Still, the family will help to look after her snapper, and she can always pretend she's had a night out with a sailor. In *The Van* Jimmy Rabbitte Sr. is helping to run a fish-and-chip van. It ends up a wreck. All these could be called success stories. What matters is the strength to believe in possibilities. There is hardly any of the bitterness here that the past generates. Barrymount, as Doyle shows it, is not much interested in the What Happened Shite.

The Van is Jimmy Sr.'s book, but since *The Snapper* he has become a much weaker figure. He is a skilled plasterer, but his firm has let him go. He no longer has a car, hangs about the public library (where they've run out of Action Packs for the Unemployed), and fixes things about the house—one at a time, though, to make them last. His relationship with Darren, the youngest son, the clever one, has deteriorated. When he tells the argumentative Darren not to forget who paid for the dinner that's in front of him, Darren answers: "I know who paid for it. The State." But Darren wishes he had not said this.

Jimmy Sr.'s tools are not likely to be needed again.

> Jimmy Sr. had a mug for work that he'd had for years; he still had it. It was a big plain white one, no cracks, no stupid slogans. He put two teabags in it; used to. My God he'd never forget the taste of the first cup of tea in the morning, usually in a bare room in a new house with muck and dirt everywhere, freezing; fuck me, it was great; it scalded him on the way down; he could feel it all the way. And the taste it left; brilliant; brilliant. He always used two bags, squeezed the bejesus out of them. . . . After a few gulps he'd sip at it and turn around and look at his work. . . . Then he'd gulp down the rest of the tea and get back to it. The mug was outside in the shed, in a bag with his other work stuff. He'd wrapped toilet paper around it.

Jimmy Sr. would normally say "jacks paper," but not in this passage, where we need to feel his respect for the mug. This surely is what Doyle means when he says he wants to show his characters thinking, rather than himself writing.

He prefers, however, to write largely in dialogue. As a teacher in a Dublin Community School he knows how people talk, but a teacher's viewpoint is not what he wants. The dialogue is heard in concerted passages, and Doyle has a range of dashes, longer dashes, and exclamation marks that act as a kind of musical notation. The language itself, like James Kelman's Glaswegian, has its repetitions and limitations, but is subtle when you get to know it. Jimmy Sr. notices at their dinner, when they're talking about what's happening these days, that "the twins called Thatcher Thatcher and Bush Bush but they called Gorbachev Mr. Gorbachev: that said something." Tom Paulin has said that Doyle "pushes Irish English to wonderful imaginative extremes," but doesn't mean by this quite what you might expect. Doyle is a wordmaster and you have to trust him, and do trust him, as to when the right word is "Jaysis" and when "Jesus" or "Good Jayesus," and the distinction between Hiyeh, Hiyis, and Howyeh. "Fucking" (which is usually taken to have lost any meaning at all) is an indicator in this novel of character and situation. Veronica, the mother, never uses it, and there is a swearbox on the kitchen table in consideration of Gina, Sharon's snapper. All agree with this on principle. "Bitches," says Sharon to her young sisters, "if Gina starts usin' dirty language I'll kill yiz." Jimmy's great friend Bimbo, a bakery worker, "hardly ever said Fuck," and this establishes him as what he is, a mild nature, a sensitive. His doorbell plays the first bars of "Strangers in the Night," although there doesn't seem much point to it when his house is the "exact same" of all the others in the street and you could hear a knock on the door anywhere in the house.

Bimbo, then, dispenses with Barrymount's metalanguage, and Jimmy Sr. himself knows there is a time and place for it. On Christmas morning, for instance, he is stuck making conversation with Bimbo's old mother-in-law.

> Maybe she hadn't said anything. Maybe she couldn't help it; she couldn't control her muscles, the ones that held her mouth up.
>
>   He heard feet on the path.
>   —Thank fuck!
>   It was out before he knew it. And she nodded; she did; she'd heard him; oh Christ!
>   She couldn't have. No, she just nodded at the same time, that was all. He hoped.

Doyle takes a risk with the structure of his new book, which is more complex than the other two. It starts in a low key, reflecting Jimmy Sr.'s empty days. About a quarter of the way through, Bimbo, too, is let go by his bakery firm and puts part of his redundancy money into a fish-and-chip van. With no wheels, no brakes, no engine, no water, no electricity, filthy, too, almost beyond purification, the van might stand for the valiant illusions of Barrymount. Neither Bimbo nor Jimmy Sr. knows even how to peel a potato. But they open up for business, and the book's action gets into gear with demonic scenes of frying and spilling and beating the frozen cod, hard as chipboard, against the rusty freezer. The family lend a hand as the van becomes a kind of fortress under siege. The fellow from the Environmental Health is on their track. Kids try to disconnect the gas canisters. One of Gina's nappies gets fried in batter ("it'd look like a piece of cod, folded up," says Bimbo to the raving customer). All these splendors and miseries keep pace (the year is 1990) with Ireland's successes in the World Cup.

> The country had gone soccer mad. Oul' ones were explaining offside to each other.... There were no proper dinners being made at all. Half the mammies in Barrymount were watching the afternoon matches.... The whole place was living on chips.

Parked outside the Hikers' Nest for the quarterfinals, the reeking van reaches the height of its earthly glory and Jimmy Sr. takes home £160 on top of the dole. "And then they got beaten by the Italians and that was the end of that."

After this dramatic check comes the third movement of the book. The publishers have accurately described *The Van* as "a tender tale of male friendship, swimming in grease and stained with ketchup." With the decline of the chipper trade comes a falling-out that we wouldn't have thought possible. Bimbo—or perhaps it was his wife Maggie, one of those destructive women with a grand head on her shoulders—comes to believe that he'd do better with the van on his own. Jimmy Sr., once again, is let go. Roddy Doyle, however, has an impeccable sense of endings. We last see the two of them by night on the strand at Dollymount, the place where Stephen Dedalus recognized his destiny. They're knee-deep in the freezing water ("Jeeesus!!"), shoving drunkenly at the poxy van that has come between them and that, Bimbo confusedly knows, must be committed as a sacrifice to the sea. Even so, "You'll be able to get it when the tide goes out again," says Jimmy Sr.

The Commitments has been filmed and the film rights of *The Snapper* are sold. When they get round to *The Van*, let's hope they can find a way of conveying the delicacy of human feeling in this book, and, above all, in its last scene.

1991

To Remember Is to Forgive

Excursions in the Real World: Memoirs, by William Trevor

What is the real world in which William Trevor is making excursions? Is it County Cork, "sunshine and weeds in a garden at Mitchelstown, Civic Guards in the barracks next door, a tarred gate . . . dark limestone steps in Youghal, and a backyard tap in Skibbereen"? Or (which is not the same thing) is it his memory of these places? And is his fiction more or less unreal than what he calls "the bits and pieces of experience" that lie behind it? Never let it be thought that Mr. Trevor, to all appearances the most crystal clear of writers, will make the answers to these questions easy. As he notes in these memoirs, he became aware very early "that black and white are densities of more complicated grays."

He was born William Trevor Cox, in Mitchelstown, in 1928. His family belonged to a minority: the small-town, not-well-off Protestants who were without much of a place in de Valera's new Catholic Ireland. His father was a bank clerk, so too was his mother, the first "lady clerk" to be employed by the Ulster Bank. The love and hatred between the two are described to their bitter end in the essay called "Field of Battle." She, perhaps, expected too much from life; he was too undemanding. The father's job took the family from place to place. "Behind the lace curtains that had been altered to fit windows all over the south of Ireland life stumbled on, until it stumbled to a halt." The mixture of tenderness and detachment here is entirely characteristic of Mr. Trevor.

Cork was the first city he knew and his first idea of an earthly paradise. He writes lyrically about "the waitresses with silver-plated teapots and buttered bread and cakes" at Thompson's and the Savoy, and above all of his twice yearly visits to the cinema—"Clark Gable and Myrna Loy in *Too Hot to Handle. Mr. Deeds Goes to Town*." There is irony here, of course, even if it's of an indulgent kind, but with it comes the recognition of the human need to escape through the imagination: "The Gentlemen's lavatory in the Victoria Hotel had to be seen to be believed, the Munster Arcade left you gasping." In much the same way, the dispossessed in Mr. Trevor's fiction (for example, in his recent pair of novellas, *Two Lives*) console themselves with what they know must be always out of reach.

The essays are more or less in chronological order, though they are memoirs only, not a full-fledged autobiography. After the childhood in County Cork came boarding school in Dublin, a school of which young William and his brother had hoped great things, but which turned out to be "a part of hell in which everyone was someone else's victim." In describing a stomach-turning school dinner, Mr. Trevor keeps, as always, strictly to the date and period (1941): the greasy, yellowish soup has to be swallowed from tumblers made of Bakelite.

Unassumingly, almost apologetically, he is revisiting his past. His years at Trinity College, for which he makes no great claim, are followed by his first jobs as an assistant teacher in Armagh and as a copywriter in the seedier West End of London. On the whole, he laments change, although we can't tell quite how seriously, and searches, as most of us do, for evidence that what was once part of him has not perished entirely from the earth. We last see him taking a walk up Ireland's Nire valley, between the Monavullagh Mountains and the Comeraghs. There he finds, "in the chilly air and sheep scratching for nourishment," a defiant Nature. "You would swear that this Ireland all around you has never been different."

Mr. Trevor also, of course, remembers people. In these marvelous sketches from the life, he feels it necessary to suppress, or at least to keep in order, his genius as a writer of short stories. But, as in the stories, there is a magical sense of time passing, and his own life passing with it, as his perspective alters. His first teachers are preserved as they seemed to him as a little boy. Miss Willoughby, pedaling against the wind on her huge black bicycle, was severe, Evangelical, and unapproachable. Young William was not one of her chosen few. Miss Quirke, a pink-cheeked farm girl from Oola, had a seemingly endless store of knowledge, perhaps from an encyclopedia, and a calm voice. "Mathematical subjects were less distasteful than they had been. Even geography had its moments, though admittedly not many." But even though he once took the valves out of Miss Willoughby's bicycle, and tried (quite unsuccessfully) a practical joke on Miss Quirke, he recognized them as beings not quite of this earth. During his time at St. Columba's (the last of his schools) he observed, as a puzzled adolescent, the headmaster's wife: shy, awkward, and academic, "fingers tightly interlocked behind her back when she crept, crablike, into Dining Hall or Chapel." Some secret was guessed at, but not discovered until many years later.

In the essay called "A Public-House Man" he is a bewildered trainee copywriter, still somewhat in awe of Marchant Smith, his formidably heavy-drinking boss. "Sarzy" (an essay about Frances Sarzano, a middle-aged, half-Italian waif) takes us on to London's Soho and Fitzrovia in the late 1950s. In all these re-creations, Mr. Trevor shows an exceptional power of forgiveness. Henry O'Reilly, the farmer who once taught him to snare a rabbit, was known as the laziest man in Ireland, but seemed to him the nicest. Marchant Smith was a ruinous bully, but at least he employed the otherwise unemployable. Sarzy soon became impossible, but she was an innocent, and innocence is a quality Mr. Trevor highly prizes.

He tells us in his introduction that from the very beginning he has used anything in his writing that was useful. What has been especially useful to him has been his empathy with the defiantly eccentric, the non-communicators, the old—sometimes left alone while their houses fall to pieces about them—and with all who despair but do not care to admit it. There are moments, too—his greatest to my mind—when (in the novel *The Old Boys*, for instance, and the story "In at the Birth") he lets himself leave the earth altogether, but these are not the concern of *Excursions in the Real World*.

This delightful book, which seems so relaxed as to be almost casual, is in fact a serious confrontation between Mr. Trevor and his memory. A writer, he says, must be able to separate himself from his identity as a human being. He must stand back, and that means exile. This is the most important lesson that Stephen Dedalus has to learn in *A Portrait of the Artist as a Young Man*, but Mr. Trevor goes even farther than Joyce. Stories derive from memories, but they can equally well be memories of anywhere and anyone. "Real people and real places," he writes of Samuel Beckett, "got him going." "The likeness of Thomas Farrell, stationmaster of that time, is not forgotten. . . . But there is hardly any doubt that in some other place, with different recollections, Beckett would have succeeded as well." Here, in his well-mannered, entirely persuasive way, William Trevor is claiming sovereignty for the writer over his source.

1994

Luck Dispensers

The Kitchen God's Wife, by Amy Tan

Amy Tan was born in San Francisco soon after her parents emigrated from Communist China. A few years ago she joined a Writers' Circle, which told her, as Writers' Circles always do, to write what she had seen herself. She wrote about what she had seen herself and what she hadn't—her own experience and her mother's. She produced a long, complex, and seductive narrative, *The Joy Luck Club*, which was one of the bestsellers of 1989. The Joy Luck Club itself is a group of young wives, stuck in Kweilin during the Japanese invasion, who keep up their spirits by playing mah jongg with paper money that has become worthless. All four of them escape to California, and one of them, as an old woman, wants to tell her Americanized daughter, who has "swallowed more Coca-Colas than sorrows," what happened to them, then and afterward. But the story at best will be no more than a fragment of the whole memory—like a single feather from a swan that has flown.

In *The Kitchen God's Wife* Amy Tan returns to more or less the same material, seen in a more comic but at the same time a sadder light. The Kitchen God, surely one of the most irritating minor deities ever conceived, was once a rich farmer called Zhang, with a kind and patient wife. But he chased her out of the house, spent all his substance on another woman, and reduced himself to beggary. Nearly at death's door, he was carried into the kitchen of a charitable lady who took pity on the unfortunate. *Ay-ya!* The lady was none other than his wife! Ashamed, Zhang tried to hide in the fireplace, and was burned to ashes. But when he reached the other world, the Jade Emperor rewarded him, because he had admitted his fault, by making him the Kitchen God and entrusting him with the task of watching over human behavior and deciding who deserved good luck, who bad. He must always be placated, therefore, with gifts of cigarettes, tea, and whiskey.

No problem in buying a porcelain image of Zhang at any good China Trading Company. It is impossible, of course, to get a statue of his wife. She is not an Immortal, although she tried with her tears to put out the fire that burned Zhang. Time and history may bring her into her own, though if she were to be translated, she would be the goddess, not of independence, but of consolation and compassion.

As a writer, and as a second-generation immigrant, Amy Tan wants to provide a fair hearing for the past, the present, and the future. The novel is told from the viewpoint of Winnie Louie, formerly Jyang Weili. At the beginning and end we hear the voice of her daughter, Pearl. Winnie's oldest friend, Helen—once Hulan—who followed Winnie to America, has decided (quite mistakenly) that she must soon leave this world, and in order to free herself from the burden of lies, proposes to tell everyone the never-referred-to story of their earlier life. Fear and embarrassment drive Winnie to do the telling herself. "I will call Pearl long, long distance. Cost doesn't matter, I will say. . . . And then I will start to tell her, not what happened, but why it happened, how it could not be any other way."

It could not be any other way, not only because of human weakness and "the mistakes that are mine," but because of the universal rule of luck. Chance determines your birth, luck decides your life, although it can be deflected at any moment by an unhappy word. "According to my mother, *nothing* is an accident," thinks Pearl. "She's like a Chinese version of Freud or worse." Winnie's luck has been bad. Her mother deserted her father and she was brought up on an island upriver from Shanghai by an uncle and his two wives, Old Aunt and New Aunt. She is married off to Wen Fu, a brute for whom no excuses are made. "He would roll me over, unbend my arm, unbend my legs as if I were a folding chair." It is a feudal marriage and her in-laws measure her worth by her husband's belch. In 1937 when the Japanese invade, Wen Fu begins training as a pilot in Hanchow with the three-hundred-strong Chinese Air Force. But his unit, with their wives, have to retreat across the mountains, first to Chungking, then to Kunming. In 1949 Winnie makes her way to Shanghai, only five days before the Communist flags go up over the city. Her little son dies of a rat-borne plague, she is arrested for deserting her husband, and after a year in jail begins the painful process of bribing her way out of China. At the last moment, Wen Fu turns up, rapes her, and threatens to tear up her visa. But the Luck Dispensers cause her old friend Helen to come into the room at that moment, and between them they are able to down Wen Fu.

Evidently this could make, and does make, a long, large, engrossing, colorful, comforting, first-and-second-generation saga—comforting because Winnie marries a Baptist minister and later opens the Ding Ho flower shop in San Francisco. You expect, and get, heroic mothers, bewildered sons-in-law, bizarre relations, crowded weddings, open-casket funerals where the generations join battle, and a confusion of cultures—what to keep, what to throw away. When Helen turns out her purse she finds two short candles, her American naturalization papers in a plastic case, her old Chinese passport, one small motel soap, knee-high nylons, "her *pochai* stomach pills, her potion for coughs, her tiger-bone pads for aches, her good-luck Goddess of Mercy charm if her other remedies do not work." Corresponding to this mix up are the beguiling variations of spoken English. (Timothy Mo has said that his Hong Kong novel, *An Insular Possession*, is essentially about language.) Amy Tan indicates particularly well the differences between Chinese speaking Chinese to each other, Chinese speaking fluent American and broken Chinese, and Chinese speaking a version of the "funny English" that has been the novelist's standby ever since Defoe created it for Man Friday.

What gives *The Kitchen God's Wife* its distinction is the refreshingly sweet-sour and practical attitude of the older generation. Winnie admires her preacher husband, but she feels she ought to have got him to take a different job, because swallowing other people's troubles has changed his own luck. She herself finds forgiveness difficult. "When Jesus suffered, everyone worshiped him. Nobody worshiped me for living with Wen Fu." On the subject of Communism, she says she would have joined the Party if it were the best way out of her marriage. "If I had had to change the whole world to change my own life, I would have done that." Helen is her friend, but they tell each other lies and exasperate each other. It's true that Pearl perceives that the lies are a form of loyalty, "a devotion beyond anything that ever can be spoken, anything that I will ever understand." But there is no way for Winnie to express it, or even what she feels for her daughter.

In this tale of survival the future should rest with Pearl. She is the traditional carrier-on. But Pearl also has a secret to tell: she is in the early stages of multiple sclerosis. At the end of the book Helen and Winnie are preparing to take her on a visit to China, a journey of memory and forgetting and, they believe, of miraculous healing—all at cut-price through a Chinatown travel agency. But we are not encouraged to think that Pearl will be cured.

1991

Watchers and Waiters

Cold Spring Harbor, by Richard Yates

In the fiction of Richard Yates (*Eleven Kinds of Loneliness*, *Young Hearts Crying*) we are down among the half-lives: New Yorkers who are hopeful as kids, humiliated as adolescents, uncommunicative as adults, although drink helps a little there. If each drink leaves you feeling it hasn't quite done the job there will always be more where it came from. There is "an aching, crying need for will and purpose in your life—anybody's life," but to have a need is no guarantee that it will be met. Women, in Yates's earlier books, are more practical than men and get off more lightly, but not in this one, where they are dreamers, and are therefore likely to end up discarded, or not quite right in the head.

Cold Spring Harbor takes place during the Second World War, on Long Island and along Route 7. Chance and misunderstanding are stronger than human good will, or even human ill will. Charles Shepard is heart and soul in his mediocre army career, but his eyesight begins to fail. His son Evan, whose only gift is messing about with engines, marries his first wife at eighteen because she gets pregnant after only a few evenings in the back of the car. Charles and Evan meet Gloria Drake because their car happens to break down near her apartment. Evan has been driving his father to an appointment at the eye clinic, but they never get there. Evan makes a second marriage with Gloria's daughter Rachel, but by chance her kid brother, Phil, destroys it. There is nothing that any of them can do to help themselves. "Maybe all you could ever do, beyond suffering, was wait and see what might be going to happen next." Or you can watch life, with a kind of double self-consciousness, as though it was a movie. Phil, in particular, does this. He sees Evan as a man who holds a slice of bread "the way working-class heroes ate in the movies." He refuses (at first) to accept a bike paid for by a rich friend's family "because it wouldn't be right—and Phil could dimly hear, in his own voice, a tone of righteous, stubborn pride that he guessed he must have learned from movies about the Depression." Thus second thoughts leave Phil without moral values.

Yates has a kind of weary tenderness for his characters. Indeed, to know as much and forgive as much as Yates, or Salinger (whom he particularly admires), or Updike, or John Cheever, must be a tiring business. In Yates's story "Builders" there is a writer, Bob Prentice, who knows that too much sensitivity is a mistake, and upsets the readers. Prentice, however, is an unsuccessful writer. Yates, an expert in painful details and sad, inconclusive dialogue, is not.

1987

What Daisy Knew

The Stone Diaries, by Carol Shields

The Stone Diaries (though there are in fact no diaries, they are said to have been lost) because everyone raised in the Orphans' Home in Stonewall Township, Manitoba, is given the name of Stone; because Mercy Stone's husband, Cuyler Goodwill, works in the limestone quarries; because her neighbor, the dour Magnus Flett, comes from the stony Orkneys; because Mrs. Flett is killed when she falls against the sharp stone corner of the Bank; because for all of us the living cells will be replaced in death by "the insentience of mineral deposition." A train of imagery, then, which recalls the mermaid metaphors "giving off the fishy perfume of ambiguity" in Shields's last novel, *The Republic of Love*. The present book is just as readable, but more disconcerting.

The section headings—Birth, 1905; Childhood, 1916; Marriage, 1927; Love, 1936; Motherhood, 1947; Work, 1955–64; Sorrow, 1965; Ease, 1977; Illness and Decline, 1985; Death—cover all the grand old topics of *McCall's*, *Good Housekeeping*, and the *Canadian Home Companion* (which for so many decades gave social and moral counsel and explained how to turn out a jellied veal loaf). The protagonist is Daisy Goodwill. Her mother, Mercy Stone, dies in childbirth. Clarentine Flett, the next-door neighbor's fed-up wife, takes the baby and flees to Winnipeg "with a dollar bill taken the night before from her husband's collar-box." Reclaimed by her father, Daisy goes to Bloomington, Indiana, where in the Twenties stone-carvers are still needed. She marries a rich young gold-hatted lover who throws himself out of a window; in 1936 she becomes the wife of Barker Flett, twenty-two years older than herself, an expert on hybrid grains. When her three children are grown she launches for the first time on a career—"working outside the home," as people said in those days; she becomes Mrs. Green Thumb, the gardening consultant on the *Ottawa Recorder*. But the editor—who has taken fright at the idea that he might be expected to marry Daisy—gives her column back to a staffer. She takes a while to get over the resultant depression, but emerges in old age as a "wearer of turquoise pants suits" in a condo in Sarasota, Florida. During her terminal illness she is moved to the Canary Palms Care Facility. Her last words (unspoken) are "I am not at peace."

I have summarized this plot to show how faultlessly Carol Shields has devised Daisy's story. It would in fact have been readily accepted, with a trivial change of ending, by the dear old *Canadian Home Companion*. Daisy is precisely what her son Warren calls her, "a middle-class woman, a woman of moderate intelligence and medium-sized ego and average good luck," and Shields herself has said: "I am interested in reality, in the texture of ordinary life, and the way people appear and relate." *The Stone Diaries* could only have been written by an expert in sensuous detail, from the blood-drenched kitchen sofa where poor Mercy dies to Daisy's longing, as she recovers her nerve, for "the feel of a new toothbrush against her gums, for instance. Such a little thing." Shields also likes, she says, to write about survivors. Daisy Goodwill Flett surely survives for eighty years thanks to the overwhelming force of her ordinariness.

This, however, brings us to the most interesting though perhaps not the most successful element in the book. Daisy, member of the Mother's Union, the Arrowroots, Ottawa Horticultural Society, Bay Ladies' Craft Group (she even has a diploma in Liberal Arts somewhere, but can't remember which drawer she put it in), is also a closet Post-Modernist. Aware that her life is drifting harmlessly past her, she is determined to acquire power over it by standing apart and reporting on it as an independent witness. She begins with her birth. "Why am I unable to look at it calmly? Because I long to bring symmetry to the various discordant elements, though I know before I begin that my efforts will seem a form of pleading." She is aware, too, that "the recording of life is a cheat" and that she will never be able to recount the whole truth. "She understood that if she was going to hold onto her life at all, she would have to rescue it by a primary act of imagination, supplementing, modifying, summoning up the necessary connections, conjuring the pastoral or heroic or whatever . . . getting the details wrong occasionally, exaggerating or lying outright, inventing letters or conversations of impossible generality, or casting conjecture in a pretty light." Very well, then, Daisy knows that she will have to do this, but now a narrator appears, in corrective mode, to tell us that she is often wider of the mark than she thinks. She has translated (for instance) her uncle's "long brooding sexual state" into an attack of indigestion. Later, this same narrator tells us that Daisy's is the only account there is, "written on air, written with imagination's invisible ink." But we cannot trust her, since she insists on showing herself in a sunny light, "hardly ever giving us a glimpse of those dark premonitions we all experience." Indeed, after the loss of her gardening column Daisy's consciousness seems to disintegrate altogether, for a time leaving her friends and family to interpret the situation as best they can. (This is reminiscent of the method of Shields's brilliant literary mystery story, *Mary Swann*.)

The Stone Diaries, it seems, is a novel, among other things, about the limitations of autobiography. As far as Daisy is concerned, it never gets away from them, even when the narration changes from the first person in 1905 ("My mother's name was Mercy Stone Goodman. She was only thirty years old when she took sick") to the third person in 1916 ("the infant—a little girl of placid disposition—was clothed in a white tucked nainsook day slip"). All the change really does is to mark the last point when she can truly establish her identity, before her mother dies and she herself, new-hatched, begins to live. This failure to find a language—as she realizes at the very end—frustrates heaven knows how many. Her eyes "stare icy as marbles, wide open but seeing nothing, nothing, that is, but the deep, shared, common distress of men and women, and how little, finally, they are allowed to say." Carol Shields, however, believes that women have been much harder done by, in this matter of silence, than men. It is of their limitations that she is thinking.

Daisy has something important in common with Mrs. Morel in *Sons and Lovers*. "Sometimes life takes hold of one, carries the body along, accomplishes one's history, and yet is not real, but leaves oneself as it were slurred over." Mrs. Morel sets herself to live through her sons, but Daisy does not even contemplate doing this. She makes her own sortie into the world of earning money and respect, is unkindly rejected, recovers, and maintains a certain dignity without asking help from anybody, "and yet a kind of rancor underlies her existence still: the recognition that she belongs to no one." Her children are moderately fond of her, her great-niece Victoria very fond. Victoria, in fact, bids fair to bring the whole book to a happy resolution. She is the daughter of a gone-astray niece whom Daisy has taken in, with her baby, out of pure good nature, and this baby has grown up to become a paleobotanist, classifying traces of fossil plants in the rock. In other words, Victoria combines Shields's stone and her plant imagery, just as Daisy Stone does when she becomes the well-liked gardening correspondent Mrs. Green Thumb. But here Daisy does not deceive herself. She is certain that none of her descendants will do more than look back on her with forbearance. This gives her a frightening feeling of inauthenticity.

In the process of growing up, of becoming a middle-aged woman and an old woman, Daisy has failed either to understand or to explain herself. If you were to ask her the story of her life, says the narrator, and one can hear the exasperated sigh, "she would stutter out an edited hybrid version, handing it to you somewhat shyly, but without apology, without equivocation, that is: this is what happened, she would say from the unreachable recesses of her seventy-two years, and this is what happened next." She is accustomed to her own version, and so, sadly enough, are we, all of us, accustomed to ours.

An exception, of course, is the witty, cautious, sometimes lyrical narrator, who knows all the words, all the versions, and all the weak places. For fear we might doubt the reality of her characters, convincing though they are, Shields supplies a section of attractive-looking, faded photographs of five generations. Daisy herself, as might be expected, doesn't appear, but by comparing the family snaps with the portrait on the back dust jacket we can make out that Carol Shields must be the mother of Alice, the most difficult of Daisy's children. (Alice becomes an academic, whose first novel is everywhere unfavorably reviewed. But she is able to rise above this, because she knows she is making up her own life as she goes along.)

Talking recently at Edinburgh about her books and her motivation for writing them, Carol Shields spoke of her care to establish the narrator's credentials and said that Daisy's inability to express herself was the true subject of *The Stone Diaries*. This would make it the tragedy of someone incapable of being tragic. But the novel as it stands suggests something more complex. The publishers tell us that Daisy's signal achievement is to write herself out of her own story. "Somewhere along the line she made the decision to live outside of events"—that is, to accept her own insignificance. But the reader is also asked to decide whether this is "a triumphant act of resistance or a surrendering to circumstances." In novelist's terms, did she do right or wrong? Daisy is described as summoning up her "stone self" so that even her brain becomes transparent— "you can hold it up to the window and the light shines through. Empty, though, there's the catch." She is shown as breathing her own death and contriving it, taking charge of it, in fact, as though in exasperation with what has so far been suppressed in her. If she is capable of this, there was no need, perhaps, for the narrator to pity her quite so much.

Carol Shields is asking us to play a game—a game for adults—but she is also playing it against herself. The epigraph, attributed to Alice's daughter, says that nothing Grandma Daisy did was quite what she meant to do,

> but still her life
> could be called a monument

and that, in the end, is what the novel makes her.

1993

WITNESSES

Grandmother's Footsteps

Wild Swans: Three Daughters of China, by Jung Chang

Jung Chang's grandmother, Yu Fang, walked "like a tender young willow in a spring breeze," meaning that she could only totter because her feet had been bound and the arches crushed with a stone. If this was not done, a girl would be exposed to the contempt of her husband's family and she would blame her mother for weakness. Fifty years later, Jung Chang herself was fourteen when the Red Guards were organized in her school. "It went without saying that I should join, and I immediately submitted my application to the Red Guard leader in my form."

Those in authority could take for granted the habit of obedience and the habit of fear. Jung Chang points out that China never had any need of an equivalent to the KGB. People could always be induced to destroy each other. In an epilogue to her book, she comments on the demonstrations of 1989, not only in Peking but in Sichuan. "It struck me that fear had been forgotten to such an extent that few of the millions of demonstrators perceived danger. Most seemed to be taken by surprise when the army opened fire." It was this that in fact most impressed Jung Chang. In a country that has no tradition of political opposition except raising a rebel army, the old fear seemed to her to have lost its hold. "Yet Mao's face still stares down on Tiananmen Square."

This is a quite exceptional book, whose origins are pity and indignation. In 1988 Jung Chang, living in England, first learned the whole truth about her family, and realized it was necessary to write *Wild Swans*. It is a woman's story, told in confidence by one generation to another, by mothers and daughters who acquired the patience and strength to outwit history. It is also, of course, the story of China over the last hundred years, since the country emerged from humiliation by foreign powers anxious to help themselves to territory, to face the Japanese invasion and the civil war. The People's Republic was created out of poverty and weakness, on the world's most disastrous model, and worked out in a long series of crazy experiments. The withdrawal of Soviet experts in 1960 meant, as it had to, the Smile Policy Toward the West, "winning friends from all over the world," and the Middle Kingdom, after two thousand self-regarding years, unsteadily began to look for foreign friends. In 1978 even the Class War was abandoned, but by then Mao (two years dead) had created a moral wasteland. Loyalty and compassion, where they survived, shone by contrast like the pearls that were formerly put in the mouths of corpses.

Yu Fang, Jung Chang's grandmother, was the daughter of an ambitious small-town policeman, who sold her as a concubine to a warlord, General Hue. (He arranged that the General should have a glimpse, as she knelt in the temple, of her bound feet.) When Hue died, Yu Fang bribed two horsemen to help her escape with her baby daughter, otherwise she would have been at the mercy of his widow, who might have sold her into a brothel. Later she became the wife of the kindly, elderly Dr. Xia, and lived with him in Manchuria under the shadow of the Japanese occupation. The daughter, Jung Chang's mother, Bao Quin, grew up under the Kuomintang. She became a Communist agent, smuggling out messages hidden in green peppers, for the sufficient reason that the Communists were the only party who promised to put an end to injustices against women. She married a high-minded, incorruptible civil servant called Wang, and after the Communist victory she was appointed herself (without any consultation) to the Public Affairs Department. Both of Jung Chang's parents, then, had joined the "high official" class, which, more than any other, suffered from the incomprehensible campaigns, purges, rehabilitations, and persecutions of the People's Republic.

Bao Quin worked ceaselessly, although in forty years she never qualified for a "soft seat" on the railway—these could be bought only by officials of Grade 14 and above. In the "January Storm" of 1966, when Mao decided to disrupt the party structure, she was denounced and made to kneel on broken glass. Three years later she was arrested and imprisoned in the local cinema, where she could hear her children's voices in the street but never see them. Meanwhile Wang, after years of irreproachable service to the Party, had come to the conclusion that the Chairman could not know what was happening. He carefully composed and wrote a letter to Mao. As a result he was taken into custody, and came back to his family insane. These two were only cleared of guilt at the end of the Seventies, when the old incriminating records were taken out and burned. "In every organization across China, bonfires were lit to consume these flimsy pieces of paper that had ruined countless lives."

Jung Chang, born "a high official's child," writes of herself with an irony that she never uses about her parents. As small children, she remembers, called upon to do good deeds like the hero Lei Feng, "we went down to the railway station to try and help old ladies with their luggage as Lei Feng had done. We sometimes had to grab their bundles from them forcibly, because some countrywomen thought we were thieves." In 1968, sent with the fifty million "down-to-the-country" contingent to learn from peasants, she found talking to them, after a hard day in the rice fields, "almost unbearable." She was taken on as a barefoot doctor, or rather as a barefoot receptionist, in a clinic in Deyang, without any training whatsoever, and worked as an electrician although she had never even changed a fuse. When the universities reopened after the Cultural Revolution, she was entitled to enter as a former peasant and worker, to study English. She can look at these discrepancies with a certain dryness. But she never sees her country's history in the twentieth century as anything less than a tragedy.

Wild Swans is a book of a thousand stories about men and women, some of them unimaginably powerful, some of them so unimportant that they are commemorated here and nowhere else. In 1941, when the Japanese had reserved the rice supplies for themselves and their collaborators, Dr. Xia was treating a railway coolie for emaciation and stomach pains.

> Most of the local population had to subsist on a diet of acorn meal and sorghum, which was difficult to digest. Dr. Xia gave the man some medicine free of charge and asked my grandmother to give him a small bag of rice which she had bought illegally on the black market.
>
> Not long afterward, Dr. Xia heard that the man had died in a forced labor camp. After leaving the surgery he had eaten the rice, gone back to work, and then vomited at the railway yard. A Japanese guard had spotted rice in his vomit and he had been arrested as an "economic criminal" and hauled off to camp. In his weakened state he survived only a few days. When his wife heard what had happened to him, she drowned herself with her baby.
>
> The incident plunged Dr. Xia and my grandmother into deep grief.

Even this one passage shows the calm and rational style of *Wild Swans*, and the absence of "speak-bitterness." Jung Chang is the classic storyteller, describing in measured tones the almost unbelievable. As a historian explaining the political and economic background, she uses the same voice.

Although she had been disillusioned with the regime ever since her days as a Red Guard, Jung Chang never felt, or permitted herself to feel, critical of the Chairman himself until the autumn of 1974, when she read her first foreign magazine (a copy of *Newsweek*) and experienced "the thrill of challenging Mao openly in my mind." This book is not a record of heroic dissidence but of endurance and the gradual opening of the eyes. And while it is a personal record, she is not calling for sympathy, or even for attention, on her own behalf. Her book is dedicated to the grandmother and the father who did not live to see it, while the mother's undemanding presence is felt on every page. She came, in 1978, to see her daughter off at Chengdu airport, perhaps for ever, "almost casually," Jung Chang writes, "with no trace of tears, as though my going half a globe away was just one more episode in our eventful lives."

1992

A Fortunate Man

I Will Bear Witness: The Diaries of Victor Klemperer,
translated from the German by Martin Chalmers

Volume I: 1933–1941

These diaries begin eight days after the Reichstag fire, with Hitler elected as Chancellor "and all opposition forces as if banished from the face of the earth."

Victor Klemperer has set himself to bear witness, however, not so much to history on the grand scale—"I am not writing a history of the times here"—but to its impact on himself, a middle-aged Jew, Professor of Romance Languages at Dresden Technical University (not a very distinguished job), married to an Aryan, Eva Schlemmer, a musician who hasn't fulfilled her ambitions.

They are childless, and their illnesses, together with their cherished cats (also frequently ill), seem almost an occupation in themselves. But it is a story of true devotion. Klemperer's story of his eight days in prison for a blackout offence ends: "I stepped out to the street. The sun was shining. My wife was waiting." This is the quiet language of the heart.

Klemperer's status depended largely on his certificate of service as a volunteer with the Bavarian field artillery in 1915. On 2 May 1935 he was dismissed from his post, not, however, as a Jew, but because Romance languages were no longer to be studied. This meant he could at least claim a pension, although it was only four hundred marks per month, "a quite undignified lack of money."

He made applications to London, New York, and Switzerland. All failed and time was running out. His friends were departing yet one gets the impression Klemperer did not really want to leave. He was no Zionist, regarding himself, sincerely and unquestionably, as a German European, and it took him a long time to realize the nightmare would never end of its own accord. "Weariness of life and fear of death." However, there were also moments of obstinate happiness. The Klemperers had a plot of land at Dölzschen, southwest of Dresden, and, after excruciating negotiations for a loan, they built themselves a small wooden house and planted seven cherry trees and ten gooseberry bushes.

Klemperer learned to drive, if not well, and bought an old unreliable car in which they ventured out to see their relations.

His great resource (after he had cleaned the stoves and the cat boxes) was his work: first, on his history of eighteenth-century French literature, then, when as a Jew he was no longer allowed to borrow books from the college, on his autobiography. To risk writing these journals and to keep them hidden was heroic—a scholar's heroism.

Meantime, by 1936, his own books were removed from the Dresden lending libraries and French was relegated to a school subject. Who would want to publish a history of French literature? Rejected by his publishers, Klemperer toiled on, a decent, faulty human being, irritable, embittered, harassed, keeping a flame alight in the surrounding disgraceful darkness: "27 March 1937. My suit is fraying, our home is thick with dirt, neither house nor garden is finished and I count every penny." But when visitors came to stay he gallantly kept up appearances and even in the hottest weather put on his worn collar and boots.

In August 1937 the persecution was stepped up. The important date— as Martin Chalmers, the translator, points out in his introduction—was not the declaration of war but Kristallnacht, 9 November 1938, the first step toward the Final Solution.

Jewish doctors were struck off the medical register, Jewish driving licenses were withdrawn, Jews were not allowed to enter libraries or cinemas or the passenger steamers on the Elbe. They were not allowed tobacco coupons, typewriters, or pets.

The Klemperers lost the little house they had built at Dölzschen and had to move to a "Jews' house" in the city. There they had two rooms— "tangled chaos in both—Muschel's box, garden peat, crockery, beds, suit-cases, furniture"—and the torment of over helpful next-door neighbors. But "how can it be compared with what is experienced by thousands upon thousands?" Klemperer asked himself. "We two have got so used to our poverty and troubles." And he turned to his journal of witness: "No half measure, a fearfully whole thing I think I called it at the beginning."

And that is what it is—a frighteningly absorbing book to read, a difficult one to review because it depends on the patient record of detail from day to day, from the moment when Klemperer first noticed a swastika on a tube of toothpaste at the chemists to the day (19 September 1941) when he was issued with the compulsory yellow star. Every Jew had to pay ten pfennig for his yellow star. This, however, is only the first volume. The title of the complete diaries, published in Germany in 1995, was *Ich will Zeugnis ablegen bis zum letzten*—"I will bear witness unto the last."

1998

Volume II: 1942–1945

Victor Klemperer was born in 1881 in East Prussia, the son of a rabbi, and in 1921 became Professor of Romance Languages at Dresden's Technical University. In 1906 he had married a Protestant, Eva Schlemmer, a pianist. In 1935 he was dismissed from his post, not (officially at least) because he was a Jew but because French literature was considered a waste of time at a technical university. Some concessions were made for his service in World War I and the fact that he was married to an "Aryan." For example, he received a pension. He even bought a car and learned to drive it, although not very well. Eva and he could make little Sunday expeditions. He might even consider himself lucky. That is one of the most frightening things about these diaries—that they are, in a sense, the records of a fortunate man.

All this we learned from the first volume of Klemperer's diaries, which took us up to 1941. This second volume covers the remaining war years, as Klemperer dutifully continues to keep a day-to-day record of his life in Dresden as the Nazi regime grows ever more malignant toward its Jewish citizens.

For the three years following Kristallnacht, the Nazis had put pressure on the Jewish community to emigrate. Klemperer, perhaps thinking himself too old to make a new life, did not take the opportunity to leave. We see him now, in 1942, cooped up with Eva in one of the crowded communal "Jews' houses." In June, he lists thirty-one emergency decrees, including a ban on Jews using the telephone, going to concerts, buying newspapers or cigarettes, possessing a car, a typewriter, a radio, a blanket, a fur coat—or any kind of pet.

Thus the Klemperers take their beloved little tom cat to the vet, who disposes of him. "But all together they [i.e., the decrees] are as nothing against the constant threat of house searches, of ill-treatment, of prison, concentration camp, and violent death." A few days later, he writes: "Of the five men in the house, Ernst Kreidl, Paul Kreidl, Dr. Friedmann, Richard Katz, myself, I am now the only one left: Katz dead of cancer, Ernst Kreidl shot, Paul Kreidl deported, Friedmann imprisoned without hope." Klemperer himself has to wear the yellow star, which he tries to conceal under his coat. "No animal can be so hounded, so timid." The Final Solution has begun.

One of a thousand incidents is the death of Frau Pick. She was a "great lady," defying her seventy-eight years, who, after hearing she was to be deported to Theresienstadt, killed herself with a dose of veronal. She left a letter of thanks to the inmates of the "Jews' house" for their courtesy. But Klemperer also registers his own coldness of heart. His first thought was: We shall come into her store of potatoes.

In April 1943, he is conscripted as an herbal-tea packer and later as a worker in an envelope factory. He is, he admits, not at all handy at either job, nor can he find any philosophical consolation. "It is only a matter of maintaining one's dignity until the very end." After fourteen months he is released on a medical certificate, but he knows he is marked out for deportation, probably in a matter of weeks.

Then, in February 1943, comes, as a kind of miracle, the first Allied bombing of Dresden. The diary opens out in terror, bewilderment, and relief as, in the confusion, the Klemperers escape onto the crowded roads and make their way, mostly on foot, to the south. As Martin

Chalmers points out in his preface, there is an indescribable atmosphere about this spring and summer flight, in spite of all its hardships. It is, for a few weeks, a kind of idyll.

By keeping these records, of course, Klemperer risks his own safety and that of Eva, who takes the manuscript, page by page, to be hidden in the house of a friend. He has other projects, one of them a dictionary, in the spirit of the Enlightenment, of Nazi rhetoric. But the diary is his obsession. If a day passes without an entry he notes down "catchwords" that he will be able to pick up later. The point is not to write history but to provide evidence: "I will bear witness unto the last."

That, of necessity, means confession. If he is worried (and he nearly always is) about his heart, if he feels bitter over the success of some colleague, if he is reduced to stealing his landlady's sugar, down it all goes in the diary. On the other hand, Klemperer is a true liberal, believing that liberalism means standing by the sentence in St. John's gospel: "In my Father's house there are many mansions." He is also a deeply patriotic German who had come to see Nazism as a nightmarish aberration. "I am a German and I am waiting for the Germans to come back. They have gone to ground somewhere."

I Will Bear Witness is of great value to historians in their present debate as to how far ordinary Germans collaborated in the death of six million Jews. But, in a sense, it is even more precious as a story of love between two sixty-year-olds, neither of them a great success in life, both hypochondriacs who try each other's nerves almost to breaking point but who know—this is the entry for 18 March 1945—"the main point after all is that for forty years we have so much loved one another."

Then there is the question of Dölzschen. In 1934 they had bought a plot of land in this village to the west of Dresden and built themselves a small house. It was Eva who really wanted it, longing to make a garden, while Victor worried himself sick over the expense. Yet when it was finished both of them felt something like happiness. Dölzschen was their home.

In January 1942, the little house is taken away from them for "Aryanization." For years they hear about it only at secondhand: There is to be a "forced auction"; it is being used as a grocer's store; it is hopelessly lost to them. Only in June 1945, after they have struggled back to Dresden, do they get the good news. And *am späteren Nachmittag stiegen wir nach Dölzschen hinauf*—"In the late afternoon we walked up to Dölzschen."

2000

Places

THE GRANGE

Nothing (with one small but important exception) remains of The Grange, where the Burne-Jones family lived for more than thirty years. It was in North End, Fulham, and consisted, from the eighteenth century on, of two red brick houses, standing back a little from the road, with iron gates and a short flagged path. Samuel Richardson had lived there from 1738 to 1754 (when his rent was put up to £40 p.a.), but there is no evidence that either Burne-Jones or Morris took any interest in Richardson. I'm writing not about the architectural history of the house, not even about the pictures that were painted there, but from the point of view of a biographer.

The Burne-Joneses went there in 1867, eleven years before Morris discovered Kelmscott House, but why did they go there at all? Certainly, they had to move. After the death of their second baby, Christopher, they went to 41 Kensington Square, where Margaret was born. But in 1867, when they came back from their summer holiday in Oxford with the Morrises, they found that their landlord had sold the lease and they had to be out by Christmas. Still, there were always plenty of houses to let in London. Why The Grange?

North End contained two brewers, a horse-dealer, and a private asylum for ladies. This in itself shows how remote the place was, since (as readers of *The Woman in White* will remember) private asylums had to be as far as possible from any form of transport, and although the Thames Junction Railway ran through the fields below The Grange, trains didn't stop there. Milk was still delivered in pails and there were briar roses in the lanes (but Burne-Jones was never a countryman anyway—the country, he complained, was so noisy). The north house, which was the one they chose of the two, had the advantage of a good

---

Based on a lecture given at the Annual General Meeting of the William Morris Society, at Fulham Library, London, 21 May 1994.

north light and an indoor studio, but even with two children it was too big for them, and the rates were high in Fulham. They had in fact to share it at first with an old Birmingham friend, Wilfred Heeley, and his wife, who were waiting to go out to India, or they could never have managed the rent at all.

The Grange, then, had almost nothing to recommend it to Georgie except inaccessibility. The directions were said to be "Go down the Cromwell Road till your cab horse drops dead, and then ask someone." But, as it turned out almost immediately, it was not inaccessible enough.

The two menaces from whom Georgie was in strategic retreat in 1867 were Charles Augustus Howell and Mary Zambaco. Howell was a kind of dubious confidential agent, a sparkling, gossipy Anglo-Portuguese who amused Rossetti, was ignored by Morris, and proved much too worldly and slippery for Burne-Jones. "Mr. Howell was a stranger," Georgie wrote, "to all that our life meant." He lived in Brixton, and she must have thought that North End was far enough away. What can she have felt when, not long after the move, Howell suddenly appeared in Fulham? He gave it out that Ruskin, for whom he had done some charity work, was paying for him to live in North End Grove "in order to keep Jones in health and spirits." There is no record of Howell in the Fulham rate-books.

With Mary Zambaco, that wild and wealthy Greek beauty, the trouble was not that she came down to The Grange, but rather that Burne-Jones himself kept making a dash for it, "running up" to London in a cab to Mary's house in Porchester Terrace, knowing that in his absence—as Rossetti put it—she "beat up the quarters of all his friends for him." Georgie remained steadfast at The Grange, seeing to the decorating, which she calls "a veil of green paint and Morris paper," all, of course, from the Firm. She was the source of energy, taking charge of everything. When, in 1868, her sister Alice Kipling arrived from India and had her second baby in the study, Georgie wrapped it in a rug and carried on unperturbed.

I can't say how it was that Howell eventually overstepped the mark, but he made some total miscalculation, so that after 1870 neither Ruskin, nor the Ionides family, nor the Burne-Joneses ever saw him again. Mary Zambaco went off to Paris, though not for good, in 1872. This was a time of crisis, when Georgie went away with the children sometimes to stay with her family, and once to Whitby to seek advice from George Eliot.

Burne-Jones would be left moping at The Grange, living, like all Victorian husbands left to themselves, on bread and mutton chops, very lonely, and sometimes doing unexpected things. On one occasion he gave notice to the cook, because—although larger than himself and twelve times larger than Georgie—she was so ugly. The Grange, which was to have been a retreat, begins to sound like a place of desolation.

And yet it's the early 1870s that Rudyard Kipling, Georgie's nephew, is describing in *Something of Myself*. His parents went back to India, leaving him with childminders in Southsea, where he was miserable, but the Christmas holidays he spent at The Grange. Here he had love and affection, he says, "as much as the greediest could desire"—and he was not very greedy—the smell of paint and turpentine, and in the rooms "chairs and cupboards such as the world had not yet seen, for our Deputy Uncle Topsy was just beginning to fabricate these things." And once when little Ruddie and Margaret were eating bread and dripping in the nursery, Morris came in and sat on the rocking-horse and "slowly surging back and forth while the poor beast creaked, he told us a tale full of fascinating horrors, about a man who was condemned to dream bad dreams. . . . He went away as abruptly as he had come. Long afterwards, when I was old enough to know a maker's pains, it dawned on me that we must have heard the Saga of Burnt Njal."

This doesn't sound at all like what Burne-Jones himself called them— "the desolate years." He had quite rightly resigned from the Old Watercolour Society because they had wanted him to alter his *Phyllis and Demophöon*, one of the most beautiful likenesses of all of Mary Zambaco. As a result he had nowhere to exhibit his work. He lay low, sometimes when he was alone not even answering the door. But he did have the incomparable support of Morris, who had moved his family to Chiswick and began, in 1872, to come to breakfast on Sunday mornings. (This is always referred to as "an easy walk," but it is not so very easy.) The breakfasts were partly a delightful interlude, where the two of them sat reading the comic *Ally Sloper*, partly a working conference. Burne-Jones depended for an income at this time on glass designing, and was nearly always in debt to the Firm.

In 1871 a new picture—a very small but beautiful rose pink and brown picture—appeared at The Grange, where it was hung in the dining room. (It was later in the drawing room at the house of Lance Thirkell, Burne-Jones's great-grandson, rather awkwardly hung behind the piano.) It had been given to Ned by the American scholar, Professor Norton, and when it had been cleaned it turned out to be *Europa and the Bull*, perhaps by Giorgione. As Graham Robertson said, "Giorgione was a painter and must have painted something, so why not this *Europa*?" It seems to have provided the impulse to make Burne-Jones start off on a rather crazy three-week tour of Northern Italy, leaving the studio in charge of his assistant, Thomas Rooke, while Georgie and the children went to stay with her sister, Louisa Baldwin. He came back penniless and dazed, having seen Pieros, Mantegnas, Botticellis, Michelangelos, and started work on some of his loveliest things, *The Hesperides*, *The Mill*, *The Beguiling of Merlin*. He was still not exhibiting, but his friends increasingly thought that he should. The determining factor, predictably, was another young woman. This was Frances Graham, the younger daughter of the Liberal M.P. and generous patron of the arts William Graham. She saw Burne-Jones as a dreamer like herself. "Mrs. Burne-Jones was otherwise," she wrote. "She was rather daunting."

Her gentle pressure on Burne-Jones to exhibit coincided with the opening of the Grosvenor Galleries in April 1877, where he did show, with enormous success. His *Golden Stairs* was the Grosvenor's great sensation of 1880. The Grange, therefore, opened up in the 1880s, by which time, as Georgie complained, the respectable old name of Fulham had been taken away and replaced by West Kensington. There had been a good deal more building, including a hotel, the Cedars, which seems to have been a kind of landmark for people who got lost on the way to The Grange. But the place was easier by now to get to—a bus came from Kensington to the top of North End Lane, and The Grange was now only a few minutes from the District Railway's West Kensington station. Meanwhile, W. A. S. Benson had been called in to design a new studio in the garden. Here the huge canvases could be passed in and out through slits in the walls, there were hot-water pipes, and a skylight so that it could be used for painting with scaffolding. The garden continued to be lovely, with white lilies, stock, lavender, acacias, and a great mulberry tree. Inside, Graham Robertson says in *Time Was*, the house seemed to be holding its breath.

> The hall was dark and the little dining-room opening out of it even more shadowy with its deep-green leaf-patterned walls; and it is strange to remember that the Brotherhood of Artists who loved beauty did not love

light, but lived in a tinted gloom through which clear spots of colour shone jewel-like. At the end of the dining-room stood a dark green cabinet [now in the V&A]. Above it hung a small painting, a little figure in magical red [the Giorgione].

This was Graham Robertson's first visit, so that he didn't notice the doing-up The Grange had had since Burne-Jones's success at the Grosvenor—the Firm had redecorated, providing Bird & Vine bed-hangings and yellow velvet chair-covers. Everything was modest compared with the homes of the princely artists of the 1880s, and there was only one sofa that, under its Morris chintz, actually had springs. However, Burne-Jones was now expected to keep open house on Sunday afternoons. Georgie disliked presiding over so many people, but Margaret, who was now growing up, "dispensed," as Burne-Jones put it, "lower middle-class hospitality with finish and charm." There was plenty for the visitors to see, as there had been a considerable expansion of work in the studio—silversmithing, gesso work, designs for pianos, needlework, and jewelry, as well as studies for the great canvases of the 1880s.

Everything, of course, had to be cleaned. To Georgie the domestic-help situation was "either a bloody feud or a hellish compact." One of her staff, familiar from Burne-Jones's comic drawings, was Mrs. Wilkinson, said to carry so much equipment—brooms, buckets, and soap—that she had to come into the studio sideways. After Burne-Jones had resigned from the Academy—he joined as an Associate in 1885 but realized at once that he had made a mistake—he said that he felt "cleaner than even Mrs. Wilkinson could make me."

As well as the Sunday visitors, and often at the same time, friends arrived, from the very earliest to the much later ones—Sarah Bernhardt, Robert Louis Stevenson, Henry James. But there was, of course, a deeply dissonant note in these prosperous years, the imperfect sympathy with Morris. In the January of 1883 he joined the Democratic Federation, and as Burne-Jones put it, "we are silent now about many things, and we used to be silent about none." He came much less often to The Grange, and if he did come, had to leave early to "preach." Burne-Jones felt that Morris was surrounding himself with the unworthy, but he also felt that he himself had failed his friend. Fellowship is heaven, and lack of fellowship is hell.

After Margaret married Jack Mackail in 1888—Burne-Jones was fifty-five that year but after the wedding said he felt ninety-seven—The Grange was no longer open to visitors on Sundays. They did sometimes appear—Aubrey Beardsley, for example, with his portfolio and his sister Mabel, or Julia Cartwright, the art historian. "I got into a bus which stopped short of North End Road and lost my way into the bargain," she wrote in her diary, "but when I got to The Grange, all my troubles were forgotten. Philip opened the door, Lady Burne-Jones rushed to welcome me and took my coat to dry, and Sir Edward came running down the stairs saying. . . what could he do for me! . . . Later, just as I was going he said I must let him give me one of his little finished drawings and he would send it after me in a case." Such was the courtesy of The Grange.

Although Burne-Jones frequently gave out that he would finish up in the Fulham workhouse, if they would allow him to go on painting there, the question of their leaving The Grange was raised only once. A new lease—the old one was due to run out in 1902—was rapidly arranged by that prince of solicitors, George Lewis, who was a great friend and admirer. If the family wanted fresh air, they had by now a small, white-washed house at Rottingdean, although Burne-Jones sometimes couldn't face the icy cold there. This came second only to Kelmscott Manor, where the water jugs in the bedrooms were frozen solid by morning.

For the 1890s there are detailed accounts of life at The Grange, in par-ticular Rooke's studio diary, which was certainly edited by "the Mistress" (as Rooke calls Georgie), and perhaps started at her request. We're told these notes were made while Rooke and "the Master" were working at different levels of the huge canvases (although if there was one thing Burne-Jones disliked above all it was having his conversations taken down). Then there is *Three Houses*, by Angela Thirkell, who had been the little Angela Mackail, born in May 1890. In *Three Houses* The Grange appears as a children's paradise even more paradisal than it had been to Rudyard Kipling in the 1870s, partly because while Kipling was understood and most kindly treated, Angela was grossly spoiled. When she was born Burne-Jones entered on yet another term of hopeless slav-ery. He was in a state of open rivalry with Gladstone as to which of them could spoil their granddaughters the most. Angela always sat next to him at lunch, blew the froth off his beer, had her bread buttered on both sides, rushed into the kitchen to talk to Robert the parrot. The children were free to roam the whole house, except the studio, and yet she saw

William Morris only once, in Georgie's sitting room. She saw him as "an old man (or so I thought him) with the aggressive mop of white hair who was talking, between fits of coughing, to my grandmother."

And yet Morris was often in the house. Having become a printer, he assumed that Burne-Jones would be the chief illustrator for the Kelmscott Press. The Sunday-morning breakfasts returned and seem to have been times of heroic and unwise eating on Morris's part—sausages, haddock, tongue, and plover's eggs, according to Rooke, "and then he would go to the side-table and wish he had had something else." And then, in the February of 1896, Morris suddenly leaned his forehead on his hand in a way that Ned and Georgie had never seen before—never, in all the time they had known him.

If we take into account Morris's illness and the fact (which Burne-Jones faced perfectly honestly) that during the 1890s his large pictures were beginning not to sell, and that the height of his great reputation was past, we might see The Grange during these last years as reverting to what Georgie had wanted in the first place, a dignified retreat. A place, too, Burne-Jones felt, since Margaret left, "of echoes and silence," but still it had become, or should have become, a spiritual stronghold where he could paint undistracted, as he had always wanted to, in a world "more true than real." However, not long after he had started work on the Chaucer illustrations he fell in love again, this time with Mrs. Helen Gaskell, a delicate-looking creature twenty-five years younger than himself, one of the Souls. He got behind with the drawings—"you know why," he wrote to Mrs. Gaskell—"I must lock myself into a room, but I can't lock my soul up—but Morris never fails, nothing disturbs the tranquil stream of his life . . . he looked so disappointed that I had done nothing since last year—and I couldn't tell him why." Often he wrote to Mrs. Gaskell, who seems to have been a sensitive and tactful woman, by every post (and there were five deliveries in those days). "Such strength as his [Morris's] I see nowhere—I suppose he minds for me more than anyone, yet the day I go he will lose nothing, only he will have to think to himself, instead of thinking aloud." And then in the evening at The Grange he would sit down with Georgie for a game of checkers, or they often had some music. Georgie had a grand piano by now, and Margaret's clavichord was still in the drawing room.

Burne-Jones survived Morris's death by only two years. At the end of a visit in May 1898 Julia Cartwright wished him good health (he was only too liable to catch influenza). He only replied "I hope, I hope, I hope." During the night of the 16th of June, he died in his bedroom at The Grange.

The Grange is now "a house of air." But when Georgie went to live permanently in Rottingdean, it must in any case have lost its character. Kipling certainly thought so when he wrote about "the open-work iron bell-pull on the wonderful gate that let me into all felicity. When I had a house of my own, and The Grange was emptied of meaning, I begged for and was given the bell-pull for my entrance, in the hope that other children might also feel happy when they rang it." It is all that is left, but it means that anyone who goes to Batemans can feel they have at least been in touch with The Grange.

1998

THE MOORS

It can't be a favorite place unless you have been happy there. The place I want to describe is the village of Milton Abbot—but at this point there's an interruption. Everyone says they know it well, but it turns out they mean Milton Abbas, in Dorset. Milton Abbot, in west Devon, six miles northwest of Tavistock and just next to Cornwall, is a village that guidebooks neglect. It is a village built on a slope—the south side draws its water from the mains, the north side gets it from springs—and sheltering round a noble fifteenth-century church, St. Constantine's. This church is built of the beautiful local Hurdwick stone, green in color— "underwater green," it has been called.

At the end of the churchyard there is a steep drop, with a flight of stone steps, down to the Green, the center of all things for Milton Abbot's not very many young children. This is an echoing green, as in Blake's vision, and when it darkens the last game of three-a-side football trails into silence.

In fact, Milton Abbot is never a noisy place, though I should perhaps make an exception of the rooks, whose voices are much louder than the children's. The village has been lucky enough to keep all its English elms, and the rookery with them. The lane at the bottom crosses a stream which until a year ago used to run over it, and for a hundred yards or so after that, from spring until autumn, there is a display of wildflowers, not rare, but spectacular even for Devon: primroses, violets, stitchwort, red campion. To the west, beyond the elms, the view opens toward the Cornish moors, scattered with rocks.

I go there to visit my daughter, my son-in-law, and their three young children. They live in a cottage with honeysuckle at one side of the front door and a rose at the other (although this is not really good soil for roses). The kitchen, built out at the back, looks out over green pastures.

The new tiles on the kitchen roof have been known to leak, the old ones are stalwart. As the children get taller, the cottage gets smaller, and it's agreed, and has been agreed for some time, that the family is on the verge of moving. Meanwhile, they are not only prepared to sleep on the floor when visitors arrive, but give the impression that they prefer it. The garden, by a legal compromise made too long ago to be disentangled, is 150 yards away from the cottage. It is large enough to accommodate a precarious shed and an apple tree—glorious apples that foam more meltingly than any Bramley when they are cooked (though 1993 was not a good year). What kind they are I don't know, perhaps Grenadiers. There are hundreds of anonymous kinds of apple planted, mostly in Victorian days, in the numberless orchards of Devon.

It doesn't take long to walk around Milton Abbot—much longer, though, if you're interested, as I am, in Edwardian architecture. To the north side of the Green (not our side) it has the distinction of being largely designed by Lutyens. Seven centuries ago, the village and its surrounding cow-pastures belonged to the Abbey of Tavistock. It was transferred by Henry VIII, with the rest of the monks' property, to the Earls and Dukes of Bedford. In 1908–09—by which time the village had still not changed hands—the then Duke of Bedford commissioned Lutyens to lay out new estate cottages. At this period, nearly everyone in Milton Abbot except the baker and the undertaker worked at Endsleigh, another of the Bedford properties. They walked the two miles to work every morning across the fields.

Lutyens, at that date, had not reached his grand manner. He was still thought of as a sound Arts and Crafts man who a couple of years earlier had done a row of model thatched cottages for laborers at Ashby St. Ledgers, near Daventry. The early twentieth century was in fact the end of two hundred years of English model-village building, undertaken, as John Betjeman put it, "with the best intentions, and a conscious effort to provide better living conditions."

Meanwhile, Lutyens had established for himself a Ruskinian moral truth in architecture that implied natural, local materials and a responsibility to the site itself. Elsewhere in Devon this might have meant cob and thatch, but here the material to hand was the familiar green Hurdwick stone, with slate roofing. In the early 1900s Devon produced plenty of graded slates (they have to be imported now from Wales) and, since Tavistock had three times in its history burned to the ground, a number of the farmers had already begun to prefer slate.

If you look round the village you will see at once how Lutyens's favorite hipped roofs are exactly suited to the plunging sweep of the

Green, while the square chimney stacks—reasonably low for an Arts and Crafts man—stand out against the open sky like a modest echo of the church tower itself. The cottages are not all on the same plan. They varied not only with the levels of the ground, but the status of the tenants. But estate workers could count on two to four bedrooms, parlor, kitchen, scullery, fuel store, covered access to the lavatories, and a good bit of garden. "I hate squalid houses and mean gardens," Lutyens wrote to his wife in 1909, and here he has certainly solved his problems without meanness. Milton Abbot, however, is a Devon village without cream teas, without a pottery, and without bed-and-breakfast. There is one pub, the Edgcumbe Arms (Lutyens wanted to add an inn in keeping with his cottages, but the duke turned down the idea). Here they welcome visitors, but can't put them up.

They may well suggest that you try Tavistock. To Milton Abbot, Tavistock is the metropolis. Plymouth and Exeter are for major expeditions, but Tavistock is, for example, where the schools are. Probably the boys and girls at St. Peter's Primary School never notice, while they're there, that every time they go in and out they can see Dartmoor stretching away to the horizon under a changing sky. But I would think that they will remember it for life.

Tavistock lies on the banks of the river Tavy, more on the north bank than the south. The valley is so steep that some of the houses have an iron staircase to connect them with their gardens. In the 1840s, the then Duke of Bedford had the town remodeled into open, airy, sturdy, mild-Victorian gothic—an impressive, greenish, gothic Guildhall; a fine, greenish, gothic Bedford Hotel; a covered market. (Hurdwick stone, incidentally, weathers well, but if restoration is necessary the citizens watch narrowly to see that the builders are working faithfully and not, for instance, using green-tinted cement.)

The duke was building over the site of the old abbey, but bits of it were left as picturesque ruins, as they still are. The porch of the misericord is at the back of the Bedford Hotel; the main gateway of the abbey—considerably patched up—is in Guildhall Square; part of the ancient walls still run along the banks of the river. The Tavy, which means so much to the town, was brimming and foaming over its weir when I last saw it in December.

Charles I is supposed to have said that whatever else was uncertain in this world, it was sure to be raining in Tavistock. In this he was ungrateful to his loyal supporters in the West Country. Tavistock has an average seventy-five inches, but Princetown, fourteen hundred feet up on the moors, has over one hundred inches, with wind and fog.

Even so, there are people who make their way there precisely in the hope of fog. I am thinking of the Poor Folk Upon the Moors, a society based in the southwest and entirely devoted to studying the stories of Sherlock Holmes. They were up there last Christmas, in the *Hound of the Baskervilles* country, wearing deerstalkers and gaiters, to offer dinner to the prison governor. They saw nothing but beauty in what poor Watson called in his diary "the dreary curves of the moor, with thin silver veins upon the sides of the hills, and the distant boulders gleaming where the light strikes upon their wet sides." But then, Watson had an altogether unfortunate experience of Devon.

To return to welcoming Tavistock—the whole town seems to stand under the protection of its two bronze statues, of the Duke and of Francis Drake, its favorite son. Drake, with his compasses, is on the Plymouth road—the statue on Plymouth Hoe is a replica. (For some reason both statues have recently been given a coating of what looks like chocolate, but it seems that this will weather down.)

Behind the main square, in a building paved with granite setts from Pew Tor, the Pannier Market takes place on Fridays and sometimes on other days. Permission to hold it was granted in 1105, and I suppose it was a great place then as now for cheese, gingerbread, bacon, and dress lengths. These days it deals not only in craftwork and handmade jewelry but a profusion of little glass and china and silver-plated or even silver objects which make you feel, in the teeth of experience, that today you are going to pick up a bargain. Occasionally you do. But the Pannier Market's specialty is half-price must-haves—Ghostbusters, Visionaries (remember them?), Thundercats, Subbuteo, Gladiators—secondhand, but in good condition, the antique toys of the future. Tavistock, then, is the place where we make good the distressing losses and gaps in my grandchildren's collections. Where else do we take them, bearing in mind that they are too young as yet for the superb walks and trails across the moors? The National Park Authority provides all the information needed to cross Dartmoor's granite back, but there are a few much shorter and much more modest expeditions.

Wellingtons, however, and a complete change of pretty well everything will probably be needed, as there is almost always water to get wet in. Endsleigh, the estate where the population of Milton Abbot used to work, is about two miles out of the village. The elaborate "cottage"—in fact a large villa—was an indulgence of Georgina, wife of the (sixth) Duke of Bedford. Sir Jeffry Wyatville designed it, with ornamental gables and its own Swiss Cottage, in 1810, while Humphry Repton was given a free hand with the gardens. These two had a site in a thousand on a steep hillside overlooking the Tamar, which divides Devon from Cornwall. Repton, who aimed at creating an earthly paradise, combined nature and art, intertwining real branches and trunks with branches of stone. Endsleigh is now a fishing hotel. But when, in 1955, the Bedford family had to sell their paradise, the Endsleigh Trust ensured that the grounds should be open to the public on summer Sundays. Once a year, too, the right of way is open beside the riverbank. You walk from beautiful Greystone Bridge as far as Endsleigh.

You can stop for a picnic, or go on to Horsebridge. If the children want to see the Dartmoor ponies close up, a good place is Pennycome-quick, just outside Tavistock on the Princetown road, where you can park off the road on the edge of the moor.

If the sight of the tors gives them an uncontrollable desire to run downhill, we go to Double Waters. Take the Plymouth road out of Tavistock and, opposite the cemetery, turn down an unpromising lane which looks as though it leads to an industrial estate. It ends at a cattle grid, and beyond that is open moor where everyone can run straight down the valley where the Walkham and the Tavy meet. Persuading them to walk up the hill again is, of course, a different matter.

The place to go if the children want to climb is Pew Tor. Drive out of Tavistock on the Princetown road as far as Moortown and you will see it on the other side of a stream. Anyone can go up it without difficulty and stand at the top in the great washes of air, looking for miles across the two counties. Apart from the climb, there is a chance of finding among the boulders, half hidden in cotton grass and heather, one of the curious objects that I stumbled across on a recent visit. They are tin canisters, each with its own seal; what they are for, who puts them there and moves them secretly around West Dartmoor, is a mystery. A ritual is, however, growing up around them: if you have been careful to bring an ink pad and notebook, you can take an impression of the seal and record the date and place, then put the canister back in its hiding place.

Sometimes we take the Tavistock-to-Okehampton road and turn left at Mary Tavy. Between Peter Tavy and Mary Tavy—both once copper-mining villages, now silent—there is a track leading down through oak trees to a bridge across the Tavy.

You can sit here by the golden-brown water, watching it divide round the granite rocks in its bed, or you can paddle or go a little way across on the stepping stones. There is no particular need to cross the bridge. This must be one of Devon's most undemanding expeditions, but it's the one I remember most clearly of all, between summer and summer.

1994

CANALETTO'S VENICE

Most of us see Italian landscapes for the first time over somebody else's shoulders the valley of the Arno, for example, behind Pollaiuolo's martyred St. Sebastian, or the lakes of Mantua through the back windows in Mantegna's strange *Death of the Virgin*. After a time it seems natural to want to move the all-important central figures for a while and to walk into the picture, in particular the part that they necessarily hide from you.

On my bedroom wall, from as early as I can remember, there hung a colored Arundel print, in what I thought of as a gold frame, of the Mona Lisa. (Parents were less enterprising then about what they put on the walls.) There she sat, and beyond her in the distance heaven knows what mists and shining waters, a bridge that seemed to have very little support, and a road that led from the water margin, with extravagant bends and twists, apparently to nowhere. I have been told since that the magic landscape is a fantasy on Leonardo's studies for public works, the project, that is, for diverting the course of the Arno and flooding the Valdichiana. Several people have been able to identify the place exactly, but no two of them have ever agreed. In any case, it was my first Italy.

With Canaletto, two and a half centuries later, the cityscape and waterscape have moved to the foreground. He was painting for visitors and cognoscenti who wanted to take away with them first-class pictures of manageable size that would also be a noble memento of Venice. He succeeded to such an extent that even today, the mental image we have of Venice derives from the pictures he painted. We are reminded of this in "Canaletto," the exhibition of eighty-five paintings and sixteen drawings at the Metropolitan Museum of Art. Even more than Arles belongs to van Gogh and Provence to Cézanne, Venice belongs to Canaletto.

A review of "Canaletto," an exhibition organized by Katherine Baetjer and J. G. Links, on view at the Metropolitan Museum of Art, New York City, 2 November 1989–21 January 1990.

In the middle of a city stranger than the imagination could devise, Giovanni Antonio Canal—Canaletto—worked with professional calm and industry, and presumably with an increasing number of assistants. It was his business to adapt Venice to his patrons, and his patrons to Venice. His work, perhaps as a natural consequence, can be found all over the world except in Venice itself—until quite recently, only two of his pictures hung in the Accademia. (His eleven views of London and England in the present exhibition came about because his patrons invited him to London, where he painted Venice-like views of the River Thames, among other things. But the English are more inclined to get their view of London and the Thames from Whistler.)

"Most people," wrote Hugh Honour, "derive their first impression of Venice from Canaletto." This should mean, and does mean, a superb display of palaces, churches, and campanili, patterned with sun and shadow, between a scarcely clouded sky and the reflecting water.

But for a good many British picture fanciers their first Canaletto is not like this. It is *The Stonemason's Yard*, lent to this exhibition by London's National Gallery. The setting here is the Campo San Vidal, or Vitale—not a showplace—looking across the Grand Canal toward what was then the Scuola and church of Santa Maria dell Carita. The smoke in the distance might be from the boatyard that is still in the Fondamenti Nani, and where somebody always seems to be burning old paint or tar off the hull of some vessel or other. Apart from that, there is not much left today to recognize in this beautiful picture. Santa Maria della Carita's campanile fell in the 1740s, the Accademia's bridge has been built across the canal, and there is no stonemason's yard. Indeed, it seems doubtful whether there ever was one, although it may have been opened up temporarily for the repair of the Church of San Vidal. The Grand Canal appears only as a gleam of dark blue, with just-discernible ferryboats waiting to cross.

In the left foreground there is a daily (or more likely hourly) moment of drama. A child has fallen over (there are lumps of stone lying about everywhere). The mother drops her broom and holds out her arms in dismay. Another woman leans, rather dangerously, from the drying balcony of her house. This is the women's world, although one of them has crossed over to do some washing to the men's world of work on the right. There are boulders of white stone, hewn and unhewn, and the masons can be seen in their rickety wooden shelters, which appear to be made out of driftwood.

The picture, then, is divided into what is made and who does the making, somewhat like Velázquez's *Hilanderas*, where the barefoot weavers are in the foreground, with the tapestries and important personages at the back. (There is no way of telling whether either Velázquez or Canaletto had any social comment to make. Tapestries have to be woven and buildings have to be built and repaired, and no one is likely to understand this better than a practicing painter.)

J. G. Links, an organizer of the show and the world's leading authority on Canaletto, comments in the catalogue that the picture is "Canaletto at his finest, the Canaletto that might have been perpetuated but for the pressures of the English dukes and their representatives in Venice." He is thinking in particular of the Duke of Bedford, who commissioned, through his agent, twenty-two views and two festival scenes.

However this may be, Canaletto seems not have resented the pressure of money, and continued for forty years to paint the majestic Venice that we (although not dukes) expect to see and want to have seen. The effect of these paintings, Ruskin said, was that "we fancy we are in our beloved Venice again, with one foot, by mistake, in the clear, invisible film of water lapping over the marble steps in the foreground. Every house has its proper relief against the sky, every brick and stone its proper tone of retiring air."

Ruskin, of course, wanted much more than this, and denounced Canaletto (although he admitted that his materials were good and his colors lasted) for material-mindedness. "Let me count—five-and-fifty, no; six-and-fifty, no; I was right at first—five-and-fifty bricks." Here he was mistaken, for Canaletto did not aim at that kind of accuracy. He combined different viewpoints to include everything that he wanted, altered the bend of the Grand Canal, and even moved, if necessary, the column of St. Mark. This makes his work more, rather than less, delightful to topographers.

But in the main, the just-likeness, the unfailing control, even the five-and-sixty (no, five-and-fifty) bricks are some of the great pleasures of looking at these pictures, and so they were meant to be. Canaletto is meticulous, too, about which roof is being retiled, which façade is being patched up, and which pavement is being laid, and although it is hard to tell what season it is you can judge the time, not by the unreliable clock towers but by the length and angle of the shadows.

Venice is often said to have changed less since the eighteenth century than any other city in Europe. The current exhibition, although it hasn't been arranged with this in mind, will take you on a majestic journey up the Grand Canal. You will, however, have spent a good deal of time over the early stages since Canaletto, naturally, had to concentrate on the most splendid, popular, and often-commissioned *vedute*, or views.

After an entry from the sea along the Molo, the quay at the foot of the Ducal Palace, with a heartening display of shipping from many nations on the sparkling water, you land at the Riva del Schiavoni and then pause while Canaletto shows view after view of the Piazza San Marco. Trained as a stage painter, he is presenting the Piazza as a vast theater. It is said to be never quite empty, not even in the cold Venetian winters, not even in the early hours of the morning. Canaletto (whether Tiepolo painted the figures in for him or not) has arranged it with groups of substantial-looking citizens in wigs and tricornes, together with Moors, Turks, and beggar boys approaching likely customers who are obliged, perhaps, to give something in order to avoid losing face in this most public of places. There are women, too, with baskets and in black clothes, who may or may not be selling something, and a number of small curly dogs of a breed that can still be seen in the Piazza.

In this Venice without vaporetti, without aerials, without pigeons except for an occasional flight across the limpid sky, you are not exactly at home, for you are always watching from the outside and usually slightly from above, but if you have a little time to spend you become a deeply concerned spectator. Then you will notice the sweep attending to the trumpet-shaped Venetian chimneys from the outside, a puppet show raised high above the spectators, friars arriving by boat at the landing stage, knife grinders, street vendors protected by unwieldy umbrellas, men urinating in quiet corners or stretched out in the sun. Above all, these people, if they possibly can, are conversing with one another, for that is what they came out into the streets to do. You can feel the human pace of life necessary to the city that, after all, is still like no other on earth or water.

It you leave the Piazza with Canaletto's patrons and embark, at last, up the Grand Canal you pass on your left the little Dogana—still in business as a customs house—and the great plague church, Santa Maria della Salute, the Virgin of Health and Salvation. The architect was commissioned, in 1631, to give it "presence," as a mark of thankfulness for the city's deliverance from the plague, without incurring too much expense. His solution was the vast dome, gray as the passing clouds, and apparently out of proportion with the rest of the Venetian churches; it seems almost to have hypnotized Canaletto, who includes a view of it, near or far, in as many of his pictures as possible.

After the Salute you have to trace your course to the Rialto, the only bridge at that time across the Grand Canal. Here Canaletto pauses again, to take views from different positions on the steps and in different directions—north, northwest, southwest. The next great reach ends where the Cannaregio Canal joins the Grand Canal, leading away toward the mainland.

There is a great deal that Canaletto could not, and in any case would not have wanted to, tell us about Venice. To many addicts it seems an autumnal, twilight city, melancholy with the weight of its past. There is not much trace of this in Canaletto, or (this is Ruskin again) of "what there is of mystery or death." Perhaps this is only to say that Canaletto, who died in 1768, before the final ruin of the Republic, was not a romantic. He doesn't—as Francisco Guardi does—show us the restlessness of the light, the uneasiness when a squall blows up, the slip and slop of the water or the strange weathers when the buildings seem to be disappearing or even taking off into the mist.

There is a darker side, too, to what D. H. Lawrence called the "abhorrent green slippery city." When one of the oddest residents of all, Frederick Rolfe (Baron Corvo), found himself at the end of his resources, he rowed a *sandalo* out to one of the empty islands. "I'll be quite plain about it. If I stay out on the lagoon, the boat will sink, I shall swim perhaps for a few hours, and then I shall be eaten alive by crabs. At low water every mudbank swarms with them." The scandalous novel the unhappy Rolfe wrote in Venice was called *The Desire and Pursuit of the Whole*, and the hopeless search is another powerful image of the maze-like city.

Henry James's American visitor never gets possession of the Aspern papers. He is left drifting among the small canals and backwaters "to the continued stupefaction of my gondolier, who had never seen me so restless and devoid of a purpose and could extract from me no order but 'Go anywhere—everywhere—all over the place.'" In Thomas Mann's "Death in Venice," Aschenbach, staying on and on in humiliating pursuit of Tadzio, falls in love with his own corruption. "The atmosphere of the city, the faintly rotten scent of swamp and sea—in what deep, tender, almost painful draughts he breathed it in!"

These are seasons of the mind when the gondolas look—as they have done to so many people—like swimming coffins. To Canaletto, it is surely safe to say, they never did. It was his business—in every way his business—to leave us with only the serene aspects of the Serenissima.

1989

THE HOLY LAND

If you go to the Holy Land as a pilgrim, you are hoping for (which, of course, is not the same as expecting) an experience not like any other.

Someone gave me a pocket guide "prepared by the Polyglott Editorial Office" that says that the visitor to Jerusalem does not expect sights of the usual kind; "he wants above all to visit the Holy Places." More blood is said to have been spilled over Jerusalem than over any other city on Earth. You are going there, however, to walk where Christ walked, and you hope for the gift of tranquility.

Probably you ought to do what you can to guard against disappointment. You have to take yourself to one side and remind yourself that you know, or have been warned, that almost all the churches have been rebuilt, that there is scarcely any proof that anything's what it's traditionally said to be, that Jerusalem itself has moved northward over the centuries so that the walls are in a different place. The Inn of the Good Samaritan is a police post, where you can be photographed sitting on a camel. The Holy Sepulchre is a nightmare, divided up between every Eastern church that reunited with Rome from the twelfth to the nineteenth century. Possibly you particularly wanted, as I did, to see Emmaus, where, three days after the crucifixion, Christ sat down with two of the disciples "and was known to them in the breaking of the bread." But you won't see Emmaus, because nobody has any idea where it was.

Then there is the question of the lilies of the field. Polunin and Huxley, in their *Flowers of the Mediterranean*, say there are a thousand different flowering plants within a five-mile radius of Jerusalem. I hesitated to ring up the travel agency to ask them how many would be out at the beginning of April, because I didn't want to sound like what I was, an elderly English female traveler. In the end, I did ring up. It turned out that everyone else had asked the same thing. And although it had been snowing the day before we arrived, the lilies of the field were out in their myriads.

The bulbs and seeds lie dormant in the unpromising-looking *batha*— the dry heath between patches of rock. Now it was their season—the corn gladiolus, dark red corn poppy, field marigold, star of Bethlehem, scilla, dwarf iris, anemones in drifts, and the pale pink *Cyclamen persicum*, a reminder that cyclamen, like budgerigars, should be seen wild, and in flocks.

The native flora mustn't of course be dug up or picked. The New Zealand couple in our party, a retired chemist and his wife, said that this was a good thing in ways you mightn't expect. A few years back they had taken home some packets of English wildflower seeds from the Chelsea Flower Show and planted them and they had grown out of all proportion—giant feverfew, overwhelming cowslips. Both husband and wife seemed almost to welcome each day's difficulties, as something to be got round and put right. Their tolerance was a miracle in itself.

Equally calm, and almost equally skilled with photographic equipment, were two good-looking Australian women near retiring age. They were nuns, belonging to an Australian teaching order which had quite recently given up the habit, so that they had been faced with the situation other women can only dream of: they had been given a reasonable sum of money and told to buy everything new from scratch. Sister Paula's great-grandfather had been an Irish convict—he had been transported for setting fire to a house—and it amused her to think that this "sin" had turned out to be a great help to her.

The Franciscans have been caring for the holy sites and their excavations since the fifteenth century. Like other custodians, they have closing times during the day, but if Sister Paula was at the gate there seemed to be none.

In charge of all of us was a Methodist minister who knew every stone of the way. It's impossible to calculate how many religious groups are circulating through Palestine in the weeks before Easter, but all of them have to welcome each other in fellowship, yet avoid crowding each other in practice. As he negotiated this, without apparent effort, it struck me that the minister might have been the right man to bargain for hostages. On April 3rd we went into Jerusalem through the Damascus gate. All new buildings in the old city must now by law be faced with the local limestone, so as soon as the sun falls on it, it is Jerusalem the Golden.

In the morning, the Western Wall, the Temple Mount, the Dome of the Rock.

In the afternoon, the Shepherds' Fields, the old night pasture a few miles to the east of Bethlehem.

The driver was unwilling to go, because not long before there had been some bus stoning. He was persuaded. There were anemones in the fields, and poppies, mustard, cyclamen, yarrow, chamomile, thistles. At the Franciscan chapel, built to the north of the fields in 1954, the brother in charge spoke only Spanish. Responsibility for the Holy Places is supposed to be shared between the nationalities, but it's difficult to get enough Franciscans from Britain and the United States, and the Spanish and Italians do much more than their share. You can rest here before going down to Bethlehem and the bewildering Church of the Nativity.

On Wednesday, along the old Roman road via the Wadi Quelt, with the rock-built monastery of St. George high up on the other side of the divide, to the mud-colored ruins of Jericho which lie along the wadi's banks as it opens into the Jordan valley; then to the high plateau of Masada, where the Jewish rebels, the Sicarii, held out for three years against the Roman armies; then a bathe in the Dead Sea, and back through Bethany to the house of Lazarus, a rock-cut tomb in the cellars. No one pretends to know whose house it is—but it dates, at least, from the first century. Lazarus, perhaps, was buried there twice, since after being raised from the dead he must have died again.

On Thursday, the Mount of Olives. The most beautiful of the gardens is not Gethsemane, but the garden of the Russian Orthodox church of Mary Magdalene, built by Alexander III in memory of his mother. But it is not always open.

On Friday, north to Caesarea, lunch, in a stiff breeze, at Herod's Palace overlooking the lake of Galilee, a coach (with the driver shouting "Hallelujah!" as he rounded the corners) up Mount Tabor, in the evening the Ganei Hamat Hotel at Tiberias, warm, prosperous, palms, mangoes, orange groves, storks, white-tailed fish-eagles. From the hotel's drying-roof at night you could watch the lights of the fishing boats moving like sparks on the dark blue water of the lake.

Saturday was left for northern Galilee. We took off our shoes and stood in one of the streams that are the sources of the Jordan, a clear shallow edged with thick rushes. On the way back we crossed the Golan Heights down to the eastern shore of the lake. At the kibbutz at Ein Gev, like everyone else, native or stranger, since the Feeding of the Five Thousand, we were given St. Peter's fish for lunch. Further round the lake, a Byzantine mosaic at the Church of the Loaves and Fishes, which has been moved now to a place near the high altar, shows the basket with five miraculous loaves and two of these fish. They are lake mullet, ornate, deep-finned, fried deep brown, with a reproachful eye and many bones, succulent but strongly flavored. We took the ferry back, six miles or so across the lake, and bathed in the natural hot springs at Tiberias. (This is expensive, but if you stay for two nights the hotel gives you one free ticket for the baths.)

Meanwhile Sister Paula went to dine with yet another Franciscan friend of her brother's, this one from Sydney, at a waterfront restaurant; St. Peter's fish again, she told us. On Palm Sunday we were at Cana, where Christ, at the wedding feast, turned water into wine. Sweet wine was already poured out for us to try in the brilliant sunshine. After Cana there was only one place left for us to visit before Tel Aviv airport, and that was Nazareth.

I must have left out a quarter of what we saw and did. After a few days, I began to think I had been wrong to ask for the precious experience of tranquility, or rather an idea of what tranquility was like. I changed my mind, or rather my mind was changed for me, on the northwest shore of Galilee. Very early on Palm Sunday we went to the chapel of St. Peter's Primacy, which commemorates the place where Christ gave the charge to Peter, "Feed my sheep." The air was still cold and the sky, from end to end, was the color of an opal. The minister stood in the open air, under an evergreen oak, to celebrate Communion. Outside the lakeside chapel the rock projects a little and the clear water of the lake washes over the stones, grinding them down, so much more slowly than the sea, into pebbles.

Some may have traveled down from as far as the snows of Mount Hermon. I took one of these pebbles from the edge of the lake and kept it. It is a pale red conglomerate, perfectly flat and smooth and almost a perfect oval. I think it may have some jasper in it, and it shines a little in a good light.

1992

Life and Letters

CURRICULUM VITAE

I consider myself lucky, because when I was four years old I lived in a house with a garden, and in the garden was a double rose hedge—two hedges, that is, planted close to each other, but with enough space between them, even now they'd grown thick, for a person of my size to sit there without difficulty. Into this space the briar roses shed pale pink petals and heavy drops of rainwater or dew, so that it never quite dried out. I collected the petals into small heaps, each heap representing one of the dozen or so other regular inhabitants of the rose-hedge space. I knew their names then, but now can remember only a few. (One of them was Fatty Arbuckle, which gives you the date but not the circumstances. I am sure nobody in the village knew anything then about the misfortunes of Arbuckle. It was simply a name for anyone fat, whether male or female.)

Every day, of course, one or more of the piles of rose leaves perished, withered at the top, moldering underneath. They had no fragrance while they were alive, but a curious smell when they were dead. I buried them where the ground was soft, at the foot of the hedge. Prayers and a hymn had to be said over them, but that was no problem to me; we were churchgoers and I knew plenty of both. After they were decently laid to rest, however, a new anxiety began. No empty spaces must be left by the time I was called back into the house. More fallen petals to collect, more piling up. And so Fatty and his companions rose again from the earth.

All this talk about hedges may suggest that we lived in a big place, but that we certainly didn't. When my father came back from the First World War, wounded through the shoulder, houses to rent were so scarce in London that he began to think he would have to live, with his family, in a furniture van. His job was on the staff of *Punch* (of which he eventually became the editor). Making your living by being funny is always hard work, and, in the 1920s, not well paid. So my mother, a quietly spoken woman whom nothing defeated, found a house in the village of Balcombe, in Sussex, an hour by train from London and a walk from the station.

I had a brother, much loved and admired, but three-and-a-half years older, at that time an unbridgeable gap. He was not a rose-heap builder, but, to his credit, not a destroyer of rose heaps either. While I was conducting toy funerals he would have been down at the village carpenters, where I wasn't wanted, or at the blacksmith's (which by then was a garage, hiring out two Citroëns), or competing with his friends to see who could pee farthest out of the window, disturbing the hens as they pecked about the grass. He was Rawle, a family name on my mother's side. It seemed to me that in the conversation that went on (quite literally) above my head, in church and at home, his name was mentioned frequently. "We thank Thee, Lord, for Rawle Thy mercies," "after Rawle," "they're Rawle as bad as each other . . ." And this struck me as quite natural, for he was very important to me.

Twenty years or so later, Rawle came out of a Japanese prisoner-of-war camp to become a journalist and a distinguished Far Eastern correspondent, so that in the end we both of us finished up as writers.

The truth is that we came of a writing family, and I suppose some people might think an eccentric one. When I was young I took my father and my three uncles for granted, and it never occurred to me that everyone else wasn't like them. Later on I found that this was a mistake, but after all these years I've never quite managed to adapt myself to it. I suppose they were unusual, but I still think that they were right, and in so far as the world disagrees with them, I disagree with the world.

They were a vicarage family, and vicarages were the intellectual powerhouses of nineteenth-century England. Their father, Edmund Knox, left his country parish for industrial Birmingham, crowded and thick with soot, because he thought there was more important work to do there, and the Knoxes grew up in an immensely hard-working Evangelical household where comfort and beauty counted for very little and money for almost nothing—there was always good reason to give it away. They remained faithful to their upbringing—I say this because I count a violent reaction against an upbringing a kind of faithfulness. My Uncle Dillwyn, for example, who came next after my father, was an extreme agnostic, referring to Jesus Christ as "that deluded individual, J.C." He was a brilliant scholar of ancient Greek texts, and using, I suppose, the same part of his mind, a great cryptographer; in the First

World War he broke the German flag code, and his work on the "spy" variation of the Enigma cipher shortened the Second World War by roughly six months. One would expect from him clarity and coldness, but in point of fact nobody could understand his working methods, and although he could be ruthless if you made a foolish remark he was tenderhearted to a fault when anybody was in real trouble. The same was true of my second and third uncles, Wilfred and Ronnie, but they, on the other hand, were two of the most convincing Christians it would be possible to meet, and both became priests. All of them, including of course my father, were distinguished by courage and a frightening honesty. (My Uncle Wilfred never told a lie in his entire life—he never saw the necessity.) But I won't write more about this, because, as they would have said themselves, what's the use of courage and honesty if you can't take them for granted? I should like, however, to mention their wit. Some of it lay in their fondness for quiet understatement. "One gets so little practice at this," said my father gently when, in 1971, he lay dying. Indeed all of them (although Ronnie published so many books that he lost all count of the titles) had a horror of talking too much. Wilfred said that no congregation ought to have to listen to a sermon for more than ten minutes, and any priest or minister who went on longer than that ought to have his income cut down proportionately every thirty seconds. I, too, feel drawn to whatever is spare, subtle, and economical.

My mother's family were called Hicks. She too came from a vicarage, and from a "long family," so musical that they could give an entire parish concert between them. Both my grandfathers became bishops, and both of them started out with next to nothing. Edward Hicks, in fact, had even less than that—his father was a small tradesman in Oxford who went bankrupt, and Edward had to set himself, in the old way, to free his family from debt. This may have been the reason why, during his ministry, he never refused to see anyone who came to his door for help. He was a great enemy of poverty and injustice, having come, while he was at Oxford, under the influence of John Ruskin. Ruskin he admired, not only for his teaching but also for his delight in even the smallest details of life. Ruskin, he said, would describe "with the keenest relish" the joy of shelling peas—"the pop which assures one of a successful start, the fresh colour and scent of the juicy row within, and the pleasure of skillfully scooping the bouncing peas with one's thumb into the vessel by one's side." I can honestly say that I never shell peas in summer without thinking of Ruskin and of my grandfather.

Well, those were my ancestors, and I can only say once again that I should like to have lived up to them. I should like to have been musical, I should like to be mathematical, and above all I should like never to have told a lie.

We left Sussex, the village, the hens, and the rose hedges, in 1922. Commuting had become impossible, since my father had been asked to act as theatre critic for *Punch*, as well as deputy assistant editor. We went to No. 34 Well Walk, a small eighteenth-century house in Hampstead, to the northwest of London. The rent at that time was £40 a year. If I may be allowed to quote from what I wrote about it some years ago, Hampstead at that time was a place of "high thinking, plain living, and small economies. The steep, charming old streets were full of ham-and-beef shops, old bookstalls, and an amazing number of clothes-repairers, all helpful to shabby refugees and literary men. There was even a jeweler's where one bead could be bought at a time, for all the Hampstead ladies wore long necklaces."

Poets, conspicuous in their wide-brimmed black hats, roamed the streets, as indeed they always had done. At one end of Well Walk, under the lime trees, was the wooden seat where John Keats was supposed to have sat down to rest. Certainly he had lived just round the corner. At dusk the lamplighters came round and, one by one, the gas lamps flickered into brightness. Muffin men appeared on the streets in winter, and in summer the lavender sellers. To go down into London was an expedition. I was taken, for example, to the Poetry Bookshop, where you could buy, for sixpence, colored rhyme sheets illustrated by fine artists—new ones every month or so. We traveled by underground railway, because Hampstead's hill was too steep for a bus to get up it.

I hadn't expected to be happy in Hampstead, but I was. Then, partly because of my mother' illness, I had to be sent away to boarding schools. I got a very good education, leading to an Oxford scholarship, but I learned only too quickly that homesickness is a real illness and that reason has no power against it. I still believe this is true, even though while I'm writing it down I realize what a small thing my wretchedness must sound, in view of the partings that were to come and the haunting faces that television now shows us day by day of the displaced, the rejected, the bewildered, and the totally lost. "Even before they set out on life's journey they seem weary already of the way." There are children now who are homesick without ever having had a home to remember.

I've never been able to write short stories. In my whole life I've only written three, and then only because I was asked to. It took me almost as long to finish one as to write a novel. Biographies and novels are the forms that I feel I can just about manage. They are the outcome of intense curiosity about other people and about oneself. I think that the best way to continue with these notes about my life would be to look back through the novels I have written.

I left Oxford with an honors degree and might perhaps have stayed there, but it was 1938 and it hardly seemed to be the right thing to do at the time. In 1939 I took a job at Broadcasting House, the London head-quarters of the wartime BBC. Broadcasting House was designed to look, and does look, like a great ship headed south, and in 1939, "with the best engineers in the world, and a crew varying between the intensely respectable and the barely sane, it looked ready to scorn any disaster of less than *Titanic* scale. At night, with all its blazing portholes blacked out, it towered over a flotilla of taxis, each dropping off a spectator or two." Reading that I can see that I was impressed, almost in spite of myself, by the seven-decked building, the sole source of news and wartime instructions for the British public over the next six years. But I myself was only a Recorded Programs Assistant—almost, I think, the lowest of the low. We were not even junior program engineers, who were allowed to turn knobs that we were forbidden to touch and had the right to join a union. We were busy all day, and (since the BBC was on twenty-four-hour shifts) often all the night, and yet I have to think hard now to remember exactly what it was we did. To a large extent we were beasts of burden—very young ones. We had to make sure that things were in the right place at the right time by actually carrying them there. There were some tapes in existence, but the enormous everyday traffic in recorded sound was all carried on aluminum 78-RPM discs coated with acetate. The acetate smelled very strong, particularly as the whole build-ing was now sealed off, its entrance packed with sandbags, its windows (so we believed) not to be opened until peace was declared. Quantities of these discs seemed to be needed for every transmission—speeches, interviews, messages, broadcasts from enemy countries patiently tran-scribed by refugee scholars who toiled quietly in a department of their own. Some of them were standbys—there had to be an alternative recording ready, for instance, when King George VI was speaking to the nation, because his stammer was unpredictable, and for the chimes of Big Ben, because in very cold weather there was a chance that the mechanism might slow down.

I dream, sometimes, of those many thousands of discs. All of them were perishable. They melted easily—a cup of tea put down on top of them would do that—and in winter the teams on the mobile recording vans found that they also froze. They had a tendency, also, to disappear. There is, I think, a strong human instinct that prompts anyone who sees a neat stack of anything to move it somewhere else, and this (not only at the BBC) defeats all that filing systems and catalogues can do. But even when the discs were in their expected place they were distinguished from each other only by handwritten labels, and these labels were not always filled in correctly, or filled in at all. Or they were illegible—was it "Church bells" (which were to be rung only in case of invasion) or "Churchill"? In the basement transmission studios the announcers, whose familiar voices, during the wartime years, brought reassurance to millions, were waiting. As part of a system of finders, fetchers, and carriers in a building where the lifts had been halted, for security reasons, at the third floor, leaving four more flights of stairs to be struggled up and down, I can't claim to have been the strongest link in the chain, but I can say that I was willing.

The novel that I wrote about my years at Broadcasting House was called *Human Voices* (1980). The reviewers called it "light," and I suppose it is, although novelists never like to be called light. All I can say is that I never went far away from the truth. Broadcasting House in wartime was a life within a life. We so often had to sleep, when we were on night shift, in the concert hall, rigged up as a dormitory with a line of gray blankets supposed to separate male from female. It was a fitful sleep, disturbed by the anxious torchlights and muffled alarm clocks of those going on and off duty. Twice in the concert hall I had to help out when someone had an epileptic fit. In my novel I changed this to the birth of a baby, but that wouldn't have surprised me either. Broadcasting House had become the capacious, all-providing shelter for us all.

I remember, too, that I learned to listen there. From room after room, if the patent self-sealing rooms were open for the moment, bursts of music from replays and editing sessions beguiled the passersby. I had never heard anything by Satie before, or by Fauré, or by Kurt Weill, except for the *Dreigroschenoper*. The program editors considered me a little savage, but they kindly let me stay and listen. I have said that my mother's family was born, as birds are born, musical. I wasn't, so I am all the more grateful for the education in hearing that the BBC gave me. I also fell in love, with someone very much older and more important, without the least glimmer of a hope of any return. This was quite common in those days, but I suggested in *Human Voices* that we were the last generation to behave like this and that after the Second World War the human species no longer found it biologically useful. Certainly, toward the end of the war or just after it, we all of us married, had children, and forgot why and even how we'd managed to love without return. In 1943 I married an Irish soldier, and my three children are now respectively a professor of economics, a teacher of Spanish, and a research physiologist enquiring into the nature of pain. With my youngest grandchildren I can gain a little credit by telling them that I can remember a time when there was no television, and I carried recordings about, like Jill and her pail of water.

In the late 1950s we were living in Southwold, which is on the east coast of England, a flat, sandy, Holland-like coast with wide skies and bright clouds, beloved of painters and a temptation to those who think they can paint but can't. Southwold at that time was largely cut off from public transport. The branch railway had been closed for thirty years, the river had silted up in the nineteenth century, and the car ferry had collapsed during the great floods of 1953. We had no car, and hardly any money; we lived down by the harbor, which was no longer a harbor since the seawall caved in sometime in 1910. The house we got had once been an oyster warehouse, and had been plastered with sea salt, which meant that it was never quite dry. Underneath the living room there was a flood cellar, where the water slopped about at very high tides. The children lived like aquatic animals, taking no harm.

While they were at the local primary school, just across the marshes, I took a job in what was then the only bookshop in Southwold, and the novel I wrote about those years was called *The Bookshop* (1978). I still miss, and shall always miss, the wide shining horizons of East Suffolk, and the sight of the rooks and the seabirds balancing themselves on boundless currents of air. The human community of Southwold, however, was divided into friends and enemies. In my story I called the town

Hardborough. (In the matter of "calling names" writers have an advantage.) The novel is really the report of a battle, a very minor engagement, of course, but important to the wounded.

My employer, however, Mrs. Neame, was kindness itself, and it seemed unjust that the shop (admittedly the building was three hundred years old) should be haunted—haunted, too, by that most mindless form of the supernatural, a poltergeist. It manifested itself, on what you might call its days on, by first tapping, then knocking, then drumming furiously. At first I thought the noise must have come from next door, which was a shoe store, part of a large chain. I didn't reflect that the assistants in shoe stores don't, nowadays, spend their time hammering, like goblins in fairy tales, at the cobbler's last. "They're a noisy lot," I said to Mrs. Neame, who turned pale, and told me not to talk about it to the customers, or we'd soon lose them all. It was a rapper—that was what they were called in East Suffolk. They were known, too, to "bring a chill with them," and unquestionably the temperature dropped during the uproar and the shop (although it was summer) became almost cold. But it would have seemed odd to light the paraffin heater in June. As we shut up shop there was a silence, then came a tremendous battering, more like a series of small explosions, not on the wall this time, but on the locked back door—the rapper triumphant. I recognized that afternoon something I had never met with before—malignancy.

This was my first novel—before that I had only published a biography and a mystery story—and not long after it came out the publisher rang up to tell me that it was on the shortlist for the Booker Prize, which is the best known of Britain's fiction prizes. That raised the problem of evening dress, because the Booker dinner is a formal occasion. Still, it isn't difficult to make a long skirt, and I was advised to wear earrings and not to take off my shoes under the table, because at some point each writer would have to go up separately and shake hands with the chairman. For the same reason, I ought to make sure that I looked all right from behind. This advice has taken me through three Booker dinners.

At the beginning of the Sixties we had to go back to London, and not being able to find a house that we could afford, we settled for a boat. It was moored on Chelsea Reach, between Battersea Bridge and Albert Bridge, so that we were in one of the very grandest parts of London. On the other hand, we were living on an old wooden barge that for many years had carried cargoes up and down the east coast under sail, but was now a battered, patched, caulked, tar-blackened hulk, heaving up with difficulty on every rising tide. Her name was *Grace*, and she had never been fitted with an engine, so that there was plenty of room for us in the huge belly of the hold. There was a very old stove, in which we burned driftwood. Driftwood will light only when it has paint or tar on it, and we knew its bitter fragrance well from the foreshore at Southwold, just as we were used to a more or less permanent state of damp and to the voices, at first light, of the seagulls. Now we had to get used to the movement of *Grace*, rocking on the high tide, and the echoing wail of the hooters from the passing colliers on their way to the Port of London.

Grace was anchored next to the wharf, so that she was the first of a long line of lived-in craft—barges, landing craft, and even one minesweeper. They were connected by a series of gangplanks that were anything but safe, so that the postman and the milkman had, very sensibly, refused to go on delivering. There were other drawbacks, too—the boat owners were only allowed to let out wastewater, and to use the lavatories, on a falling tide. Our great consolation was that a Thames barge, because of the camber of the deck, never sinks completely. On this point I could give evidence, because we went down twice, and on both occasions the deck stayed just above water. We were taken off the first time by a kindly Swede in a dinghy, and the second time by the river police in their patrol launch. Among our drenched and floating possessions I saw a bottle of champagne that had been intended for a party. I was glad to be able to retrieve the champagne so as to have something to give, in gratitude, to the police, who reminded me that they were not allowed to drink on duty but agreed to put it aside for later. Poor *Grace*, much loved, was towed away to the Essex marshes to be broken up. I dedicated my novel *Offshore* (1979) to "*Grace* and all who sailed in her."

It was a pity that the title was translated into various European languages with words meaning "far away" or "far from the shore," which meant the exact opposite of what I intended. By "offshore" I meant to suggest the boats at anchor, still in touch with the land, and also the emotional restlessness of my characters, halfway between the need for security and the doubtful attraction of danger. Their indecision is a kind of reflection of the rising and falling tide, which the craft at anchor must, of course, follow. This novel did win the Booker Prize, and I knew then that some of the people who read it must have understood it.

Why don't you teach? people used to ask me, for women are supposed to be able to do this. I did teach while we were on *Grace*, and one of the places where I taught was a theatrical school, Italia Conti's. It has moved premises since, but at that time it was in the depths of South London. The large front room was used on Sundays by a Christian community who practiced adult baptism, so that there was a large bath on the raised stage. The Conti children (who seemed to be much wilder than ordinary children, as though they were giving a performance of wildness) knew how to unlock the cold tap, and, if they didn't care for their classes, flooded the hall.

Freddie, the school's owner in *At Freddie's* (1982), was not at all like Italia Conti. I transferred her, or rather she appeared to transfer herself, from another school where I worked later. She was a freakish tyrant, kindhearted by fits and starts, a natural grande dame of a species that, allowed to flourish unchecked, becomes in time uncontrollable. My job at Conti's, on the other hand, I have described pretty nearly exactly as it was. I had to help give the pupils what was called their "education," and they did not disguise their lack of interest in it. I don't mean that they were bored—it was much more positive than that, a fierce electric thrill of rejection that ran from one end of the class to the other. They wanted not education but "work." Work was largely in TV commercials and small movie roles, but there were those, especially around Christmastime, who actually got a stage part, and this gave them a certain dignity, the almost-vanished magic of belonging to a venerable profession. The authorities allowed them to stay in one show for six months at a time, and to make up for their lost schooling I had to go round backstage and attempt, as they came back to their dressing room in a state of pitiable excitement, to calm them down and give them their lessons. A little arithmetic (we still taught arithmetic then), a little spelling. They were brilliant with confidence. "How was I, Miss? Why don't you go and see it from the front?" But after a certain age—say ten or eleven—these children, particularly the dancers, were never likely to get another part. That was why I was being paid to teach them to spell. They might, in the future, need a tedious everyday job, such as I had. And under their bravado, they knew this, and even knew that I knew it.

I have tried, in describing these books of mine, to say something about my life. In my last two novels I have taken a journey outside of myself. *Innocence* takes place in Italy in the late 1950s, *The Beginning of*

Spring in Moscow in 1913. Most writers, including the greatest, feel the need to do something like this sooner or later. The temptation comes to take what seems almost like a vacation in another country and above all in another time. V. S. Pritchett, however, has pointed out that "a professional writer who spends his time becoming other people and places, real or imaginary, finds he has written his life away and become almost nothing." This is a warning that has to be taken seriously. I can only say that however close I've come, by this time, to nothingness, I have remained true to my deepest convictions—I mean to the courage of those who are born to be defeated, the weaknesses of the strong, and the tragedy of misunderstandings and missed opportunities, which I have done my best to treat as a comedy, for otherwise how can we manage to bear it?

1989

SCENES OF CHILDHOOD

Thinking of Balcombe

When my father was demobilized from the army in 1919 he had no job to go to and nowhere to live. He was supporting his wife and two small children by writing a poem every week for *Punch*. Before the war he had taken the lease (or so he thought) of a small house looking on to Hampstead Heath, in London. But now it turned out that the writer Katherine Mansfield was living in it, and although she disliked the place it seems to have been impossible to ask her to leave. So, when I was two years old, we went to live in Balcombe, in East Sussex.

That meant I had my own room, looking out over a lawn with a cherry tree, splendid with white blossom in spring and splendid, too, in the cherry season—but then the birds more or less lived in it, and I can't think there was ever much fruit left for us. With the walnut tree we did better. Mrs. Ticehurst, who came in once a week to help out, knew the best (she said the only) recipe for walnut ketchup. Unfortunately, it was unaffordable: a hundred very young green walnuts, half a pint of best port wine, anchovies, brandy, horseradish, nutmeg, wine vinegar. Mrs. Ticehurst herself admitted she had never made it. She pickled the walnuts, and so did we.

The garden was small, I suppose, for the country. I have been back to look at it since, but only once. I prefer to think of it as it was then, when I knew it was enormous. A large garden is one that a tame rabbit can get lost in, and my brother's rabbit was lost most of the time. I, too, had my hiding place. This was between the bushes of a double rose hedge that ran along one side of the lawn. They must, I think, have been *Rosa gallica*; they certainly grew too tall for a tidy-looking hedge. Where I used to sit, beneath the level of the crowded leaves and the pink flowers, the ground was never quite dry, and the light fell only in patches. You could sit in a patch of sunlight and move along with it gradually as it shifted.

After a while I would be called back into the house to help. I couldn't be of help, but someone stood me on a chair at the kitchen table to see what was going on. I remember the business of "going through" the raisins, bought from the grocer's by the shovelful—you had to sort out the small pieces of gravel. How did they get there in the first place? The rice, too, had to be "picked over." There were so many long, slow processes, but I knew (because I had heard people say so) that we were lucky to be living in modern, labor-saving times. We had no refrigerator and no telephone, but we had a clotheswasher, worked by turning a handle, and colored tablecloths (that needed no bleaching) and stainless-steel knives (that needed no cleaning). And however much there was to do there was a time, on hot summer afternoons, when everything seemed to run down almost to a stopping point. The garden was silent, not a murmur even from the hens in their run behind the rose hedge, and inside the house the only sound, apart from the kitchen clock, was the red-currant juice dripping slowly through the strainer into the jelly pan.

We walked long distances, my mother and I, and so did most of Balcombe's inhabitants. Often we were delivering messages, or returning borrowed objects, or telling the baker and the grocer, who delivered three times a week, that what they had sent was not quite what had been asked for. On the way there and back, across the fields and by the roadside, I had my collecting to do. Feathers, pheasant feathers in particular, were needed for Red Indian headdresses. My brother, when he was at home, was a warrior brave and I was Minnehaha. Then there were horseshoe nails, cast horseshoes, snail shells, beechnuts, pignuts, flints, and wayside flowers. When I got home, everything was laid out on my bedroom windowsill to be counted and recounted, one of the most reassuring activities of all for a small child. Cataloguing easily becomes poetry. My mother read to me from Walter de la Mare's *Peacock Pie* about the poor widow who planted her garden with weeds:

> *And now all summer she sits and sews*
> *Where willow-herb, comfrey and bugloss blows,*
> *Teasel and tansy, meadowsweet,*
> *Campion, toadflax and rough hawksbit;*
> *Brown-bee orchis, and Peals of Bells;*
> *Clover, burnet, and thyme she smells . . .*

The naming of names, as de la Mare very well understood, is halfway to having magical power over things.

From time to time Lady Denman, the most important benefactress in the neighborhood, took me out for what was then called a joy ride in her chauffeur-driven motorcar. My brother was nearly four years older than I was and had started school, so the treat was for myself and one or two other children of the same age, sitting stiffly and wordlessly beside the chauffeur or next to Lady Denman herself in the leather-and-petrol-reeking (though sumptuous) interior. To me it was bitterly disappointing. You could see so much from a trap, where you sat high up above the fields and hedges, which seemed to be snatched away from each side of the road as the horse pounded forward. Not quite as good as a trap, but better than kind Lady Denman's Daimler, was a ride home on the last cow when they were brought in for afternoon milking. You had to sit sideways because a cow's backbone is as sharp as a rail and the view was limited, but the movement was delightful. The cow took not the slightest notice of me, but continued to chew as she walked. Ahead of us the majestic stomachs and udders of her companions swayed gently from side to side, and as they idled down the lane they left a trail of sweet grass-eater's breath.

We returned to London when I was five and a half. When I look back to my years in Sussex I have to tell myself that not everything was perfect. I was frightened of chained farm dogs, and still more of ganders. I didn't like Sussex bacon-and-suet pudding, which Mrs. Ticehurst praised because it would stick to our ribs. Sometimes I was overwhelmed, standing in a field under an open blue sky, by a kind of terror at the enormity of the turning earth. I never remember feeling anything like that in London. But Balcombe was the place where for three years I had no real anxieties, and looked forward every night, as I fell asleep, to waking up the next day. My father was one of a large family, and he used to tell me that they were so happy in one of their homes (Kibworth Rectory in Leicestershire) that in later years they could always cure themselves of sleeplessness by thinking about it. I, too, if I can't sleep, think of Balcombe.

1999

Well Walk

Hampstead Village, London NW3, is now such a desirable residential area that you can't find anywhere to buy a reel of cotton or a stick of licorice. When I was a small girl in Hampstead in the Twenties, there were sheep grazing on Hampstead Heath, chair menders, knife grinders, and muffin men in the streets (the muffin men, like the sheep, were seasonal), lamplighters who walked at dusk from gas lamp to gas lamp, and small shops that sold pennyworths of licorice and Phillips soles, with which you repaired your own shoes. Milk came round in a pony cart. There were still plenty of horse-drawn vans.

At 11 A.M. on Armistice Day, no matter what day of the week it was, the traffic stopped dead for two minutes. That was hard on the horses if they were on one of Hampstead's steep hills, and the drivers sometimes threw out a drag, like a kind of anchor, to keep from slipping. But during those two minutes, you really listened to the silence. Not that Hampstead, in those days, was in any way a noisy place. Today, it is very different, full of cars and bustling shoppers.

Our home was No. 34 Well Walk. The Well is still there, on the north side of the street, although it no longer connects with the Hampstead spa water, which was the right thing to drink in the eighteenth century and apparently contained enough iron to make it the color of dark sherry. The spa itself lost favor, but the rows of small houses like ours, built for the visitors, remained. No. 34 was a Queen Anne house with two rooms on each floor, which my father rented for £40 a year.

He was a journalist, and at that time had to write a weekly humorous article for *Punch*. A messenger boy cycled up from the printers in Mount Pleasant to collect the copy. Being funny is a very hard way to earn a living, and as my brother and I listened to my father pacing to and fro in the study overhead, our hearts ached for him. Usually, the boy sat whistling cheerfully in the hall until past the last possible moment. Nothing had to be typed, however—printers, in those days, still worked, if necessary, straight from handwriting.

Meanwhile, like so many other children, we produced our own weekly, humorous article and all, on an almost unmanageable device, a John Bull toy printing set. Why our mag was called *IF, or Howl Ye Bloodhounds*, I can't remember now.

Well Walk has always been a place for writers and painters. No. 40 was No. 6 when the great English landscape painter Constable lived there with his two motherless daughters (who, at times, got out of hand and put a broomstick through one of his canvases). D. H. Lawrence lived at No. 32, and eloped from No. 40. I don't pretend that as a small girl I had heard of him, but because poetry was read to us at the earliest possible age, I did hear of John Keats. He and his brother Tom lodged, in 1817–18, at No. 46, just past the pub on the corner—once the Green Man, now, rather more grandly, the Wells Hotel. Their landlord was a Mr. Bentley, at that time the only postman in Hampstead. He was kindness itself when poor Tom died of TB, and helped John to move his books out, carrying them in a clothesbasket.

In my Well Walk days, No. 46 had long since been knocked down. The trouble was Keats's ghost. Two doors from us lived a quiet, well-established actor, Leslie Banks. His life was made intolerable by taps (gas and water) being turned on and off by unseen hands and a rich, mysterious smell of cigar smoke in the garden. Why Keats, who didn't smoke and could never have seen a house with gas and water laid on, should have been blamed for the haunting, I don't know. A priest was called in to exorcise the unwelcome presence, but the cigar smoke continued to drift.

Before I went away to school I had lessons in the afternoons with Miss Lucas, a retired infant teacher who lived in a discreet room within walking distance. Miss Lucas was devoted to her ginger tomcat, Bubbles, a rapist and pillager who ranged the neighborhood, springing through unwisely opened kitchen windows and helping himself to large pieces of fish from the slate shelves of other people's larders. Bubbles was almost as broad as he was long.

One day Miss Lucas confided something in a low tone to my mother. "You will think me very foolish, but I have engaged myself to be married." Before long a coughing, grumbling, sodden-looking man—"this is Mr. Green, my husband"—was seen occupying Bubbles's favorite armchair by the front window. "Work of any kind makes him feel dizzy," Miss Lucas explained. My mother worried. Surely he was after her savings? But, in fact, Miss Lucas had a strange need for arrant, repulsive selfishness in her companions. Bubbles (now sulky) had done pretty well at this, but he couldn't compare with Mr. Green.

By autumn, Mr. Green had moved away from the window and must certainly have been close to the fire, which was the only place in any room in those days, except possibly the kitchen, where you could get properly warm. There was no heating at No. 34, and it needed real resolution to face the chilly climb upstairs to bed.

Our beloved coal fires, of course, polluted London and clouded its skies, but they made incomparable toast, and on late-winter afternoons (when the fifth post of the day arrived through the letterbox) they created a glowing illusion of security and peace that can never be recovered. And if you were thought to be poorly, you might have the fire lit in your bedroom. Then, as you dropped off to sleep, it would throw a changing shadow play across the reflection of its broad golden light on the ceiling. By morning, it had died down, but there was still a breath of warmth left in the room. I used to get dressed under the bedclothes and make (like a seal under ice) a small clear patch to look through on the frosty window. Our neighbors, a husband and wife who were retired missionaries, might be venturing out onto the glassy pavement with their knitted socks over their boots. This was the way they had managed, I was told, in Tibet.

The Queen Anne houses on Well Walk have fared very well, through time. They are all still there just as I remember them. In later years, I passed No. 34 quite often. The knocker looked wrong because it seemed much lower than it once had, but the front door was painted the same green.

Then, a few years ago, I had a telephone call from the owner of the house. She was someone I had known as a little girl and hadn't seen since she married. Now she was moving, with her small daughter, to a new home in Dorset. Everything was packed up, they were going that very afternoon, would I like to see the house once again before she locked up? She meant, would I like to see my childhood once again? Yes, all things considered, I would.

Because so much had been crated up, I could easily imagine our furniture back in the empty spaces. The little boiler (though surely it can't have been the same one) was in the same place in the dark basement kitchen. The built-in solid shelves were still there, and with no effort at all I could conjure up the old standbys—arrowroot, suet, sago, black-lead, starch, Rickitt's Blue, Monkey Brand soap, Borwick's Baking Powder. I'm not sure I'd know what to do with sago or blacklead now.

A passage led from the kitchen, past the small dining room and out into the garden. In my time, the back of the house had been covered with a vine. The sooty grapes had ripened, I think, only in one year—the heat wave of 1926. The vines were gone, but the indestructible fig tree, usually figless, still offered its shade.

On the ground floor of the house, I looked into the room where my brother had laid out endless war games on the worn-out Turkey rug. I was allowed to run the field hospital, wearing my nurse's outfit. My brother disposed of the toy troops, which included Serbian light infantry, the King's African Rifles, and Generals, with their staff, on horseback. When all the forces were drawn up, we opened the door and let the dog in. He rushed toward us with a furiously wagging tail, and everything he knocked over counted as a casualty. Then he was banished once again, protesting, to the garden.

At the top of two more flights of steep, narrow stairs was, and is, the bathroom, dear to me, as it is to most children. The window had a tremendous view to the southwest. On a clear day you could see the Houses of Parliament, and the flag on top of the building that showed that they were sitting. Miss Lucas had told me that they were all hard at work there to keep us safe and at peace, since the last war (in which my father had been wounded) had been the war to end wars. Although the bathroom window is still there, just as it was in my youth, the view has definitely changed. Today, hundreds of new buildings fill the skyline, and you can no longer see Westminster from Well Walk.

Nowadays, the chair menders, knife grinders, and muffin men have vanished from Hampstead. Up and down the High Street, it seems that the only way for shopkeepers to pay the rent is to regularly open and close restaurants and boutiques. During my childhood, there were none of these in Hampstead. People did go out to dinner in restaurants, of course, but that meant dressing up and making an expedition into London. As for boutiques, Gazes the drapers sold all that you were likely to want in the button, woolens, stocking, and knicker line. But you had to know what you wanted: the stock was not on display, but was kept in deep wooden drawers behind the counter. There was a bead shop where beads were sold separately; in those days, Hampstead women wore long necklaces ending in a tassel. I used to be allowed to help to sort out the beads: amber, ivory, jet, cornelian, jade, and the cheaper ones made of sealing wax, china, and glass. In the windows of Knowles Brown, the clock-maker, there was a wonderful sight—a silver clock in the shape of a panting spaniel whose tongue moved up and down with every tick.

A few years ago, Knowles Brown closed down. He was last of the old Hampstead tradesmen, I think, and now there is hardly anyone who remembers the way it used to be.

1994

Schooldays

Twice in your life you know that you are approved of by everyone: when you learn to walk, and when you learn to read. I began to read just after I was four. The letters on the page suddenly gave in and admitted what they stood for. They obliged me completely and all at once, in whole sentences, so that I opened a book in my lair under the dining-room table and read aloud, without hesitation: "My hoop can only run by my side, and I often wish it was a dog and could bark." I was praised, and since then have never been praised so much.

In 1924, therefore, when we left Sussex and came to live in Hampstead, I went to kindergarten as a reader. The teacher gave me credit for this, but she also recognized that a six-year-old child wants to know not just some things but everything, immediately. When we sat down to draw one morning and she found that none of us could do a cow—didn't, in fact, know whether it got up with its front legs or its hind legs first—she walked us straight across the Heath to Highgate, where there was a farm in those days, and told us to watch the cows for ourselves. In this way I learned in London what I had never noticed in the country. Afterwards, in the dairy, we had glasses of milk, one between two, and these, I am sure, she paid for herself.

I was perfectly happy at this school. Hampstead is a hill village and I walked to school up flights of steps with my sandals in my shoe bag and my exercise books, which had on the back of them calculations in gallons, pecks, troy weight, furlongs, and farthings. These were for "sums," which were then thought to have something to do with mathematics. I had a red tam o'shanter and a Liberty smock. The smock was embroidered in chain stitch, as was my shoe bag, which bore the words SHOE BAG. At home, at teatime, the hot-water jug was under a flannel cover marked HOT WATER. My mother seemed always to be at home, and by six o'clock my father was back from his work at the *Punch* office. I felt secure. The terms passed reassuringly, from springs to the yellow fogs of autumn, when we brought fresh skeleton leaves from the pavements to show to teacher. But at eight years old I was sent, like my brother before me, into exile and imprisonment. No one doubted that it would be best for me to go to a preparatory boarding school at Eastbourne.

They looked after us very well. The South Coast air was good for us. When we were sent out for a walk Matron told us to breathe deeply, because our parents had made great sacrifices to give us the benefit of the air. We paraded up and down the Front, strictly forbidden to put a foot on the white line at the edge, and back to the Meads between clumps of tansy and veronica. All the flowers had the curious quality of looking as though they were pressed dry, even when they first came out. As for the lessons, I came from an Evangelical background and never expected to gain anything of value without hardship. You couldn't hope for poetry, English, music, and painting every day of the week. Wednesday (ballroom dancing, gym, geometry) was, admittedly, so terrible to me that simply to reach bedtime and know that it was over seemed an achievement in itself. But often I didn't begin worrying about next Wednesday until quite late on Sunday evening. It was nobody's fault, therefore, that I felt as wretched as I did. But homesickness, though I suppose it has never been clinically diagnosed, is a real illness. Indeed, many of the little girls were in worse condition than me, because they came from families in the Colonial Service. In our atlases many areas of the world were colored pink; their parents lived there, and only came on leave at rare intervals. These were the children who cried longest at night in the dormitories. Again, the town itself, a bland resort dedicated to morning coffee and tennis, could in no way be blamed if I associated it with horror. That came about quite by chance.

In my first winter term, when, as a treat, we were taken to the skating rink, a small boy, also from one of Eastbourne's myriad prep schools, said to me confidentially, "Will you help me find it?" A skate had passed over his finger as he lay on the ice and if we could only find it, some grown-up would put it together again. But so many people flashed by, and so confusingly. A little later, I saw him being led away.

My consolations at school were the three sweets we were given after lunch, the poetry I knew by heart, and the sea. Anyone who sleeps within earshot of the sea must be considered lucky. And Debussy, after all, was sitting in one of Eastbourne's deck chairs when he first heard the sounds of *La Mer*. The English Channel whispered in the darkness, above the snuffling of the homesick. In winter we were allowed to watch, at a safe distance, the white and greenish heads of foam crashing over the rails and flinging pebbles broadside across the Front.

My fondness for reading persisted and after four years I won a scholarship to Wycombe Abbey, but for me this was quite overshadowed by my failure to become a Girl Guide. To "get your wings" and fly up from the Brownies to the Guides, you had to pass in General Information, knitting, and rice pudding. Our puddings, each in a small white dish rimmed with blue, were put into the kitchen range and were supposed to be cooked by inspection time. I don't know why my pudding came out almost raw. It must have been jostled into the coolest place, at the bottom of the oven, I suppose. When I saw it I braced myself for failure but not for being called, as I was, a disgrace to the ideals of Baden-Powell. I still think that was putting things too strongly.

Six years later, safely at Oxford, I thought the whole process was over, but, of course, I was wrong. When my children began their education— although my daughters never went to boarding school—my memory opened its register and through them I lived my experiences again. It isn't until their last report card that we are truly free. Their schooldays are over then, and so are ours.

1980

ASPECTS OF FICTION

Following the Plot

Suppose I were to try to write a story which began with a journey I made to the north of Mexico twenty-seven years ago, taking with me my son, then aged five. We were going to pay a winter visit to two old ladies called Delaney who lived comfortably, in spite of recent economic reforms, on the proceeds of the family silver mine. They had lived in Fonseca ever since they were girls—one was sister-in-law to the other. Their relations in Ireland had died, they were alone in the world, and it was hoped that because of some distant friendship they might take kindly to my son and leave him all their money. Indeed, if I had understood their letters correctly, they had suggested the idea themselves.

The old ladies lived in a shuttered mansion in the French style, surrounded with pecan trees; the house was always cool because of the double height of the rooms. In the half-darkness of these rooms, as I discovered the very first evening I arrived, they were drinking themselves steadily to death. For two hours or so every morning there was a lucid period, and that was the time for callers. The manager of the mine came then, and so did everyone in Fonseca who was interested in the Delaneys' wealth and therefore wanted to get rid of me and my son as soon as possible.

If I got as far as this, I should have to stop. The details are accurate, these things happened in Fonseca, and many more were to follow. I take it that the novel proceeds from truth and re-creates truth, but my story, even at this stage, gives me the impression of turning fiction into fiction. Is it the legacy, or the silver, or the Latin American background, testing ground of so many twentieth-century writers? I know that in any case I could never make it respectable (by which I mean probable) enough to be believed as a novel. Reality has proved treacherous. "Unfortunate are the adventures which are never narrated." And I am sorry to let it go, because of what seemed to me the natural energy of the plot.

Watching a good plot is like watching something alive, or if it is adroit and sinuous enough, something struggling for life. Between the once-born and the twice-born plot (which makes the reader, even if he is reading it for the twentieth time, want to interfere at every stage), the difference, of course, is great. But I am easily satisfied in this respect. The test lies in the plot's independence of characters, and even of names: only relationships are necessary, as in rhythm without music. I would place very high—irrespective of whether they were borrowed or not—the plots of Chaucer's "Clerk's Tale," Godwin's *Caleb Williams*, Galdós's *Miau*, W. W. Jacobs's short story "Head of the Family," and Somerset Maugham's still shorter one, the servant who went to Samarra. Thinking of these, I can remember how I became an addict.

I was brought up in a journalist's home and in a family where everyone was publishing, or about to publish, something. We children also tried to write, and our elders were resigned to this. Being dipped in ink began for us, I suppose, at about six or seven when we were first allowed to use it, and we were given the back of old galley proofs to write on. What was more, although my father once pointed out that there was no difference between journalism and literature except that journalism is paid and literature isn't, we expected to become rich by writing novels, or, if not novels, then short stories, for it was still the heyday of the railway magazines—*The Strand, Nash's, Pearson's, The Windsor*.

For these stories, which were also called "tales" and even "yarns," the author had to find a plot, rather as the academic painter once had to look for his annual subject. It was the main thing. But writers, temperamentally less hopeful than painters, have always suspected that the supply is not inexhaustible. Gérard de Nerval put the entire number of dramatic situations at twenty-four; his calculations were based on the seven deadly sins, ruling out Sloth and Lust as not likely to produce significant action. Goethe, quoting the author of *Turandot*, suggested thirty-six, but added that Schiller, who set to work methodically on the problem, hadn't managed even to get as far as that. All this looks unpromising, but the "yarn" business was so important in the late Twenties that the magazines offered, so to speak, their own remedy. Among the back pages there were advertisements for Plotfinders. They could be ordered by mail and sent in plain envelopes, presumably because writers in those days were thought to live in boarding houses where they would not want their affairs known.

The Plotfinders consisted of revolving cardboard circles with three concentric rings of slots. Through these, you could read off characters and actions and vary and recombine them until the *donnée* made its appearance. Seaside landlady, landlady's daughter, hero, hero's friend, jealous rival or enemy, vicar, elderly lady or aunt, practical joker (the influence of Kipling here), comedy foreigner, censorious neighbor, returning husband or foreigner, mysterious lodger. All, of course, were interchangeable, ready both to act and to be acted upon. Many years later, when I heard Lévi-Strauss lecture on his *Mythologies*, he told us to do what amounted to the same thing—*plier et replier le mythe*—with King, Queen, Mother, Father, Brother, Sister, Sister-in-Law, and, among the Pueblo and Algonquin Indians, the Ceremonial Clown and the Ancestor of Owls.

Since our Plotfinder was for "sunshine stories," the action suggested was largely romantic, but the main object, in every case, was the "turn," introduced by the linking words *after all, suddenly, to the general astonishment/consternation, unexpectedly, little realizing that, through an absurd misunderstanding.* More expensive models, I suppose, would have produced a double or multiple effect. I have sometimes wondered since who should be considered the presiding genius of the "turn"—perhaps Mark Twain, who wrote a sixty-thousand-word novel to lead up to the surprise in the last sentence. But even the greatest novelists, those who stand in the way of all subsequent comers and threaten them with bankruptcy, use it at times. *Ulysses* ends with the returning husband climbing into his house, only to find that the door, after all, is open; he introduces a mysterious lodger/son into the home, little realizing that his wife has taken a fancy to him. This is quite within the capacities of the Plotfinder, and I am sure Joyce meant it to be.

The short stories I wrote at the age of eight and nine did not bring me the success I hoped for, and years of formal education in English literature gradually taught me the uneasy moral status of plots. If they were of the extravagantly ingenious kind, they had to be "forgiven" or "overlooked" on behalf of the writer. They were "strained," and, worse still, they strained the reader, or "made demands" on him. Dickens and Hardy were overlooked in this way. Clearly, the acceptable story was imposed by life upon fiction without hope of appeal. By the time I reached university the final "turn" was not much in favor either. Indeed, the novels I admired most at that time—*Afternoon Men, The Root and the Flower, Confessions of Zeno, A Passage to India*—all avoided it, although for Forster this must surely have been a considerable sacrifice.

When at last I tried to write fiction again, I was more cautious. Everyone has a point to which the mind reverts naturally when it is left on its own. I recalled closed situations that created their own story out of the twofold need to take refuge and to escape, and which provided their own limitations. These limitations were also mine. I knew that I hadn't the capacity to relate the wide-spreading complications of the Mexican legacy, however well I remembered them. As time went on, more pretenders had arrived, even one who claimed to be a Delancy, and moved into the house. On the other hand, the manager was eliminated. Seeking to extend his sphere of influence, he began to drink level with the old ladies, slipped on the polished French Provincial staircase, and cracked his skull. My son and I were blamed for these and other disasters, and we left on the long-distance bus without a legacy, but knowing what it was to be hated. We had been characters in a yarn, and I am only sorry not to be a yarn-spinner.

In the novel's domain, plots were the earliest and the poorest relations to arrive. For the last two hundred years there have been repeated attempts to get them to leave, or at least to confine themselves to satire, fantasy, and dream. Picaresque novels, however, both old and new, are a kind of gesture toward them, acknowledging that although you can easily spend your whole life wandering about, you can't do so in a book without recurrent coincidences and, after all, a return. And the readers of books like plots. That, too, is worth consideration.

1980

Hearing Them Speak

Of course you want to hear their voices. Having summoned up these human beings, you want to know what they sound like. In the novels I used to read, and still do for that matter, people spoke "sharply," "reluctantly," "with unaffected warmth," "with a touch of bitterness." They spoke of "taking her hand in his," or "whipping out a gun." These last two, of course, are actions, and must be described if anything is going to be understood at all, but when I'm writing myself I have a slight sense of failure every time I put in a "sharply" or a "reluctantly." The characters and the situation between them ought to have made it clear already how sharp or how reluctant they are.

When the dialogue begins, the tempo slows down to the pace of the story itself. The reader understands very well that he is being drawn close in. He, too, is relieved to hear what the voices are like.

What is the first thing he is going to hear? The first novel I did was called *The Bookshop*. In the opening paragraph Florence Green, who is worried about whether she should open a bookshop in a small town on England's East Coast, dreams of a heron she once saw

> flying across the estuary and trying, while it was on the wing, to swallow an eel which it had caught. The eel, in turn, was struggling to escape from the gullet of the heron and appeared a quarter, a half, or occasionally three-quarters of the way out. The indecision expressed by both creatures was pitiable. They had taken on too much.

I now think this was a mistake, because dreams in fiction are just as tedious as people's dreams in real life. I should have done better to start straight away with Florence Green courageously asking the bank manager for a loan, so that the first speaking voice would be the manager's, suggesting in itself the strength of the sluggish opposition ranged against her.

At the beginning of *The Gate of Angels* Fred Fairly, a lecturer in physics, is biking into Cambridge on a stormy day. Acquaintances catch up with him one by one.

> He was shouting. It was like sea-bathing. . . . A whole group went by, then one of them detached himself and was riding alongside.
> "Skippey!"
> He couldn't hear what Skippey said, so dropped back and came up on the other side, the lee side.
> "You were saying?"
> "Thought is blood," Skippey replied.

Fred speaks for the first time in public, so that there is likely to be a difference between what he is saying and what he would like to say. In this way I hoped to get the words to work twice for me.

You can, of course, write a novel entirely in dialogue. One writer who did this was a late-nineteenth-century woman of the world called (or calling herself) "Gyp." Henry James admired her, and thought of doing the same thing in *The Awkward Age*, but fortunately didn't. And you can manage without dialogue, as Swift did in *Gulliver's Travels*, where all the conversations are reported (except, I think, the Lilliputian words "Hekina degul" and "Borach mivola"). This is all the more remarkable because *Gulliver*, as a traveler's tale, is necessarily a monologue, and in a monologue above all you feel the need of another voice breaking in, a very different one if possible—like, for instance, Mr. Antolini, the corrupt schoolmaster in *The Catcher in the Rye*.

But exactly when ought speech to be reported, and when ought it to be out loud? One of the few advantages the novelist has over the dramatist (and they are getting fewer all the time) is that his passages of dialogue last for a limited time only. The storyteller's instinct, or perhaps his judgment, tells him when they have gone on long enough to make their greatest impact, and when to let the voices fall silent. Kafka's *The Trial* (as translated by Willa and Edwin Muir) opens with the famous incident of K.'s arrest at his lodgings.

> "I'd better get Frau Grubach—" said K., as if wrenching himself away from the two men (though they were standing at quite a distance from him) and making as if to go out. "No," said the man at the window, flinging a book down on the table and getting up. "You can't go out, you are arrested." "So it seems," said K. "But what for?" he added. "We are not authorized to tell you that. Go to your rooms and wait there. Proceedings have been instituted against you, and you will be informed of everything in due course.". . . "You'll soon discover that we're telling the truth," said Franz, advancing on him simultaneously with the other man. They both examined his nightshirt and said he would have to wear a less fancy shirt now, but that they would take charge of this one and the rest of his underwear and, if his case turned out well, restore them later.

The change to reported speech distances you from K.'s visitors, and makes any hope of understanding them, or of the case "turning out well," seem less and less likely.

While the talking is going on, the novelist has a welcome feeling of relaxation and freedom. There are so many possible variations in dialogue, the most musical of all the novelist's techniques. Confrontation is, of course, only one of them. TV probably conditions us too much to disagreement and insults, the staple of the comedy script. A novelist can allow time, if he wants to, for conversations that just tick over, the dialogue of contentment. Nothing is more extraordinary in *War and Peace* than the last chapters, where the happy (but not perfect) marriages are, as John Bayley has said, "the equivalent of the Russian victory over Napoleon." At the Bolkonskys' country home, when Pierre comes back from the wars, the children are in ecstasy because the governess has finished a pair of stockings, and, by a secret known only to herself, has knitted both of them at once. "Two of them, two of them," the children shout. Tolstoy doesn't suggest that this happiness can last. The French invasion lies behind these people, the December revolution is just ahead, but through the children's voices he shows what the nature of happiness is.

Kazuo Ishiguro, the most restrained of contemporary novelists, uses a high proportion of dialogue. His narrators, although apparently as clear as daylight, are ambiguous because they are always self-deceiving. In *A Pale View of Hills* the narrator, Etsuko, is a Japanese woman living in England. She has to come to terms with the present (her daughter has committed suicide) but also with her past. She recalls the 1950s, when she was living in the muddy wasteland outside Nagasaki, and the people who mattered to her then—her irritable husband, her bewildered father-in-law, her friend Mrs. Fujiwara who had lost everything and was reduced to keeping a noodle shop, her strange new acquaintance Sachiko who declared or pretended that her American lover was going to pay for her passage back to the States. These are all unsensational people who talk in a quite unsensational way, but with a certain formality and repetitiveness that is understood as Japanese convention.

"In any case, Etsuko, why would he have gone to all this trouble if he wasn't absolutely sincere? Why would he have gone to all this trouble on my behalf? Sometimes, Etsuko, you seem so doubting. You should be happy for me."

"Yes, of course, I'm very happy for you."

"But really, Etsuko, it would be unfair to start doubting him after he's gone to all this trouble. It would be quite unfair."

Gradually these repetitions begin to sound like a ritual whose meaning we are afraid to understand. None of the speakers ever raises their voices. Ishiguro has the chance, at any point, to change the whole tone of his book and to introduce shock or violence, but he never does. Behind everything, however, that is said or done there are recurrent images of hanging and drowning, rope and water. The sinister enigma of Etsuko's daily life is never quite solved. Nor is the nightmare of Japanese history.

Ishiguro excels at one-to-one dialogue, and it has to be admitted that this is the easiest kind to write. I used to find that after I had got quite a long way with a book I hadn't managed a single scene where more than two people were talking to each other. I still have this difficulty.

In D. H. Lawrence's *Sons and Lovers*, William, the collier's eldest son, who has been working in London as a clerk, brings his smart fiancée back to meet the family at Christmas.

She glanced round the kitchen. It was small and curious to her, with its glittering kissing-bunch, its evergreens behind the pictures, its wooden chairs and little deal table. At that moment Morel came in.

"Hello, dad!"

"Hello, my son! Tha's let on me!"

The two shook hands, and William presented the lady. She gave the same smile that showed her teeth.

"How do you do, Mr. Morel?"

Morel bowed obsequiously.

"I'm very well, and I hope so are you. You must make yourself very welcome."

"Oh, thank you," she said, rather amused.

"You will like to go upstairs," said Mrs. Morel.

"If you don't mind; but not if it is any trouble to you."

"It is no trouble. Annie will take you. Walter, carry up this box."

"And don't be an hour dressing yourself up," said William to his betrothed.

Annie took a brass candlestick, and, too shy almost to speak, preceded the young lady to the front bedroom, which Mr. and Mrs. Morel had vacated for her. It, too, was small and cold by candle-light. The colliers' wives only lit fires in bedrooms in case of extreme illness.

"Shall I unstrap the box?" asked Annie.

"Oh, thank you very much!"

It isn't only the cross-currents of feeling here that Lawrence does so well, but the integration of five voices and five distinct points of view to make the whole complex family-kitchen situation. He worked hard on his dialogue, as his manuscript corrections show, and yet it was so much a natural element to him that he could risk all kinds of bizarre effects. In *Kan-*

garoo the speakers can hardly hear each other over the roar of the sea, and in *The Captain's Doll* the lovers' voices are carried away by the noise of the car, so that the Captain has to shout in Hannele's ear: "When my wife died I knew I couldn't love any more." *Women in Love*, which begins with dialogue, also ends with it. Ursula tells Birkin that it's out of the question for him to have "eternal union" with one man, as well as one woman:

> "You can't have it, because it's false, impossible," she said.
> "I don't believe that," he answered.

Lawrence is also, when he wants to be, a faultless impersonator. He can "do" voices, tones, accents and dialects, although this is something a lot of writers are good at; it may have been why they started to write in the first place. Joyce, I suppose, took impersonation about as far as it can go, imitating even the cab horse. Novelists, however, quite often prefer to heighten the dialogue and, in general, to make the speakers more acute and knowing and more articulate than they are likely to be in real life. Henry James did this, Ivy Compton Burnett did, so did Samuel Beckett in his novels:

> What a joy it is to laugh from time to time, [Father Ambrose] said. Is it not? I said. It is peculiar to man, he said. So I have noticed, I said. . . . Animals never laugh, he said. It takes us to find that funny, I said. What? he said. It takes us to find that funny, I said loudly. He mused. Christ never laughed either, he said, as far as we know. He looked at me. Can you wonder? I said.

This kind of dialogue shows us what we could say if we had our wits about us, and gives us its own peculiar satisfaction.

I ought perhaps to try to say something about the great high points, but I should like to end instead with one of dialogue's special effects which, as far as I know, has never had a name given to it.

> Before they separated, however . . . Mr. Bob Sawyer, thrusting his forefinger between two of Mr. Pickwick's ribs, and thereby displaying his native drollery, and his knowledge of the anatomy of the human frame, at one and the same time, inquired, "I say, old boy, where do you hang out?"
> Mr. Pickwick replied that he was at present suspended at the George and Vulture.

If Dickens had made Pickwick say "I am at present suspended &c &c" the effect would be gone, vanished into the vast limbo of failed ironies.

In Jane Austen's *Persuasion*, kindly Mrs. Musgrove has to think what to say to Mrs. Croft, who is an Admiral's wife.

> "What a great traveler you must have been, ma'am!" said Mrs. Musgrove to Mrs. Croft.
>
> "Pretty well, ma'm, in the fifteen years of my marriage, although many women have done more. I have crossed the Atlantic four times, and have been once to the East Indies, and back again; and only once, besides being in different places about home—Cork, and Lisbon, and Gibraltar. But I never went beyond the Straits—and never was in the West Indies. We do not call Bermuda or Bahamas, you know, the West Indies."
>
> Mrs. Musgrove had not a word to say in dissent; she could not accuse herself of ever having called them anything in the whole course of her life.

Does Mrs. Musgrove in fact say anything at all? Again, in Christine Brooke-Rose's *Amalgamemnon*, the speaker is Cassandra, a teacher of classical languages who has been made redundant by the cuts. She is also doomed, like her Greek prototype, to foretell the future, but in vain.

> Tomorrow he'll say Sandra my love when shall I see you again I'll be free tomorrow, I'll be free Friday Saturday Sunday. Friday Saturday Sunday I must prepare my classes correct papers no I must weed the vegetable garden clean the pigsties wash my hair meet Orion invent Andromeda from time to time unheeded and unhinged discover the grammar of the universe.

What has been said so far? Nothing. "If he were someone in a nineteenth-century novel I might ironically detach him," Cassandra thinks, but *Amalgamemnon* is a post-modernist novel and Christine Brooke-Rose uses "non-realized tenses" to conjure up spoken voices. However, like Dickens and Jane Austen, she can remind us that one of the privileges of dialogue is silence.

1993

WHY I WRITE

1. First, because something inside me compels me to tell stories. I mean that I get great satisfaction out of making people believe that this event happened at that time. Unlike history, fiction can proceed with confidence.

   For example: a few years ago we were living on a Thames barge, and on the boat next door lived an elegant young male model. He saw that I was rather down in the dumps, a middle-aged woman shabbily dressed and tired, and he took me on a day-out to the sea, to Brighton. We went on all the rides and played all the slot machines. We walked for a while on the beach, then caught an open-top bus along the front. What happiness!

   A few days later he went back to Brighton, by himself, and walked into the sea until it had closed over his head and he drowned. But when I made him a character in one of my books, I couldn't bear to let him kill himself. That would have meant that he had failed in life, whereas, really, his kindness made him the very symbol of success in my eyes.

2. I am drawn to people who seem to have been born defeated, or even profoundly lost. They are ready to assume the conditions the world imposes on them, but they don't manage to submit to them, despite their courage and their best efforts. They are not envious, simply compassless. When I write it is to give these people a voice.

3. I write to make money. I think that, even today, the most widely held view of the writer is of one who creates something, and even makes money out of it, starting from almost nothing, using memory, imagination, time, making marks on paper. He begins by dying of starvation in a garret, then he buys himself a word processor and soon he finds himself needing an accountant. In the eyes of the public he must be either a magician or a fraud. But this unfounded reputation does not upset the writer unduly. In a world full of dangers it is comforting to be considered, even wrongly, a crafty so-and-so.

1989

HOW I WRITE:
DAISY'S INTERVIEW

How Do Novelists Write?

If the subject is how, rather than why, then I think you have to distinguish between male and female novelists. I believe that most women will always be kitchen-table writers and worse still that they become irreversibly conditioned to it. Just as Napoleon, if he had ten minutes to spare, allowed himself to go to sleep for ten minutes exactly, so a woman, in my experience, can pick up her draft novel and go on with it, precisely until the telephone, the doorbell, the egg timer, or the alarm clock rings. Women adapt in a peculiar way to the battle against Time and Nature. I started writing during my free periods as a teacher in a small, noisy staff room, full of undercurrents of exhaustion, worry, and reproach, and for a long time after I gave up my day job I missed the staff room, and, sitting in peace and quiet, could scarcely get anything written. I had thought of both of them—peace and quiet—as the absence of certain things. That's not so, they are positive, but to my dismay I found they worked against each other. In the tranquility of my own room, overlooking a garden with a large pear tree, I found I was waiting obsessively for an interruption and even ready to welcome it.

The patron saint of all kitchen-table novelists must be Margaret Oliphant (1828–1897)—Mrs. Oliphant, as she always called herself. I once wrote the introductions for five of her novels for Virago, and in that way got to know her. She married an invalid artist cousin, for whom, if we read about him, we feel distinctly sorry—but, however that may be, he died of TB, leaving Margaret Oliphant pregnant, with nothing much beyond his debts. She paid these off, raised her children, saw every one of them die, and made herself responsible for her alcoholic brother and numerous other relations. In consequence she had to write at night, usually to pay off money that had already been spent. She wrote 98 novels, 25 biographies, about 50 short stories, some of them strikingly good.

When her friend James Barrie said that "she was of an intellect so alert that one wondered she ever fell asleep," he was poeticizing an almost frightening way of life.

Mrs. Oliphant, of course, had no mechanical help of any kind, only keeping a small container of prepared ink into which she put a few drops of water, enough for each night's work. On the other hand, she took for granted one great advantage of the nineteenth-century writer—that is, a constant supply of listeners. These were nieces, second cousins, friends' daughters, some of them apparently living in the house and all of them ready to give their opinion when she wanted to read what she had just written aloud. That, I've always felt, would be of considerable help. But I can't tell, it's an experience I've never had.

Daisy's Interview

Before I start on a novel I don't need a synopsis of what is going to happen, but I do need the title, the opening paragraph, and the last one. Once I've got these, I can start.

In 1990 a book of mine came out called *The Gate of Angels*. It was one of those novels that start from a persistent, even obsessive, idea or image (the famous example would be George Eliot's *Silas Marner*—she called it "a story which came across my other plans by a sudden inspiration, a sort of legendary tale, suggested to me by having once, in early childhood, seen a linen weaver with a bag on his back"). The image that stayed with me wasn't—though they so often are—from childhood. It was something I saw on a visit to Cambridge, through the window of a bus, somewhere near Newnham. It was a tremendously windy day, and on one of Cambridge's unexpected patches of green land there were cows moving about under the willow trees. The wind had torn great wreaths and branches off the willows and thrown them down to the ground, and the cows were ecstatic—they were prancing, almost dancing; they'd hoped all their lives to get at the trees and now at last they could. It struck me that in this orderly University city, the headquarters of rational and scientific thinking, things had suddenly turned upside down, reason had given way to imagination.

It happened that I had been wondering what exactly was meant by the term "Mach 2." I knew that it was a measure of supersonic speed and I thought it was named after a distinguished scientist, but I didn't know who Mach was, and certainly didn't realize that he was an opponent of Rutherford and the early atomic physicists because he considered that atoms were only a provisional idea; they were unobservables, and science shouldn't be based on the unobservable, otherwise it was no better off than metaphysics, which asks us to speculate about the unseeable. While I was trying to think about this, with the image of the cows and the willow trees intervening, a novel suggested itself, turning on the problem of body and soul. The title would be *The Unobservables*. But the publishers, or rather their sales department, rejected this immediately as lacking not only in sex but also in human appeal of any kind. I changed it to *Mistakes Made by Scientists*, which I liked almost as much, but I was told, quite correctly, that it wouldn't fit on the jacket and didn't sound like a novel anyway.

On this one occasion, then, I had to work without a title. Still, my attempts to find out more about Ernst Mach (1838–1916) had put me into the right period—that is, the time just before the First World War when (in Cambridge in particular) there was a fierce debate between scientists and metaphysicians. I imagined Fred—representing the mind and reason, though only partly—as a young physicist during the glorious early experimental years at the Cavendish, and Daisy as a strong young woman training to be a hospital nurse. Of course, they wouldn't be anything like precise opposites. To start with, both of them would be young and poor, though Fred's would be the poverty of a shabby country vicarage and Daisy would come from teeming South London.

Daisy is a fearless survivor, a favorite type with the late-Victorian and Edwardian light novelists—W. W. Jacobs, for instance, or Barry Pain in *Eliza*. Men don't disconcert these girls, nor do the regulations and prohibitions men make. In the following bit of dialogue Daisy is waiting her turn for an interview with the matron of a great London hospital, the Blackfriars. A notice painted on the inner door reads: "This hospital turns away more than a thousand applications a year from persons desiring to train as nurses. Every year perhaps 4 or 5 are accepted."

Daisy was the last to be called. She looked with respect at the woman sitting on the other side of the desk. You had to struggle, perhaps fight and bleed, to get a position like that. Matron was short, pale and pale-haired, as straight as though suspended from a hook.

"You may sit down."

She repeated from the application paper in front of her Daisy's name and address.

"You are nearly eighteen. Are you a single woman or a widow? If you are a widow, have you children? If children, how are they provided for?"

"I'm single."

"And have you anyone dependent on you for support?"

"Not now."

"You may call me Matron."

"Not now, Matron."

"But recently?"

"There was my mother. She died in March."

"And that left you free to apply to enter the nursing profession, which of course would entail your living away from home."

"I suppose it did."

"So that her death has been a release for you."

"No, I won't say that, and I don't say that. It wasn't a release for her either."

The matron appeared not to listen to this, but fixed her attention on the papers on her desk. "Your birth certificate. You're too young, but the Governors have changed their policy about that to some extent. Vaccination certificate. Height?" Daisy said she thought five foot six, without heels. "It's not a matter of thinking," the matron said. "Educated at the Victuallers' School, certificate of good conduct and application. Did you study Latin? Do you understand what I mean by enemata?"

Daisy did not, but said that she was prepared to learn.

"I don't expect the girls who come to us to know anything. Now, are you strong and healthy, and have you always been so? Let me explain, in order to save time, that several of the applications today mentioned, apparently only as an afterthought, that they had rheumatic fever as children, which meant that if they were accepted here they might collapse and become a nuisance and an expense at any given moment."

"I've always been strong and healthy," said Daisy and beneath her put-on clothes she felt her physical self-respect extend and stretch itself, like a cat in the sun.

"And your sight and hearing are perfect?"

"Yes, I think so. I've never thought about them."

"You notice that I wear reading-glasses myself. I need them now, but as a probationer I did not need them. Have you any physical defects?"

"What kind of defects?" Daisy asked, a little troubled.

"Any I can't see at a cursory glance. You may be subject to very heavy periods. You may be marked and scarred. Your spine may be crooked. . . .

Have you any tendency to pulmonary complaints?" She looked up sharply. "Do you know what I mean by 'pulmonary'?"

"Yes, it means to do with the lungs."

"Pertaining to the lungs. A sickly nurse is of no use to the profession. One might call her an enemy of the profession. Above all, though, we don't want a weakly habit of constant complaint. As a rough guide, remember that while the average man is ill for four days a year, a grown woman must expect to spend one fourth of her life in actual pain."

Daisy felt a rush of admiration. So far she herself had done nothing like her fair share.

This is the "catechism type" of dialogue, on which Joyce declared he based his *Portrait of the Artist as a Young Man*, where one side has the right answers and the other sometimes knows them and sometimes has to guess them. It's also a confrontation where the reader is asked to have some sympathy at least with both sides.

A Few Remarks on the First Draft

At the beginning I see that I hadn't really settled Daisy's age (or even her height). The qualifying age for probationers at that time was over twenty, but that was too old for Daisy, who is going to act with the rashness and curiosity of a very young girl, so in the text I've made the hospital (not very probably) alter its admission policy. I've done this as unobtrusively as possible, as readers are very quick to notice this kind of mistake.

20 The distinction between "lady nurses" and ordinary probationers is characteristic of the early 1900s and I wanted to get it in somewhere, but this wasn't the place to do it. The matron would have seen immediately that Daisy was "of the domestic servant class."

28 "This was not quite true." The concept of absolute scientific truth—Fred, the physicist, holds it, and so does the matron—is totally different from Daisy's. Her idea of truth is relative, and largely depends on her own convenience and the wish not to hurt other people's feelings. This is important to the story, but it's not the moment to hold up the dialogue.

41 "You should call me Matron." The matron ought to have said this much earlier. She detects the independent streak in Daisy and must make

FIRST DRAFT

1   Daisy's turn came; she was the last to be
2   called; the last of the 1000, perhaps. She
3   looked with respect at the woman, ~~neither~~
4   ~~young nor old~~ sitting at the other side of
5   the desk who could scarcely have got there
6   without a ~~tough~~ prolonged struggle. [The]
7   Matron was small and sandy-haired and sat
8   up as straight as though suspended from a hook.
9   [You may sit down] she repeated from the piece
10 of paper in front of her Daisy's name and address
11   Are you a single woman or a widow? If
12 you are a widow, have you children? If children
13 how are they provided for?
14   I'm single, Daisy said.
15 ~~You are twenty-two.~~
16 And have you anyone dependent on you for
17 support?
18   Not now—
19   What was your last occupation? You under-
20 stand that ~~we have a number of gentlewomen~~
21 ~~applying here for training. There seems to~~
22 ~~be a certain fashionable craze in that respect.~~
23 ~~Of course they would not be asked to undertake~~
24 ~~any disagreeable tasks. Our staff nurses are~~
25 ~~drawn mainly from the domestic service class~~
26 ~~I'm not a gentlewoman~~ Daisy said But I've
27 ~~never been in service either~~
28 ~~That was not quite true There had been the~~
29 ~~washing-up job at seven shillings a week with~~
30 ~~threepence held back for breakages~~
31   Your age last birthday? You are still only
32 ~~to 22~~ 17? Your vaccination certificate? Your
33 height? Daisy said she thought five foot four,
34 without heels. It's not a matter of thinking the
35 Matron said. Where were you educated? —
36 I went to the elementary, ~~then I had the~~
37 ~~council scholarship~~ then I went to the Victuallers
38 school. — And you have a certificate of good
39 conduct and application?
40 Yes ma'am
41 You should call me Matron. That is something
42 that you might have learned, if you went to High Schoo
43 Did you ~~learn any~~ study Latin? Do you understand
44 what I mean by enemata?
45 Daisy did not, but said she was prepared to lear

46 Her ignorance, however, didn't seem to displease
47 the matron.
48 Are you strong and healthy, and have you always
49 been so? Let me explain in order to save time,
50 that two of the applicants today had had
51 rheumatic fever and yet they only mentioned it as
52 an afterthought [while still at school which mean
53 that if they were employed here they might ~~be~~
54 collapse and become a nuisance] at any given
55 moment] [and an expense].
56 Ive always been strong & healthy. [Underneath   Matron
57 her put-on clothes, the costume and the inked [?]
58 straw hat, she felt ~~the~~ her ~~proper~~ physical pride
59 ~~of her twenty-17 years~~ collect & extend itself like
60 a cat in the sun.
61 And your sight & hearing are perfect?
62 Yes, they're very good. [TEST here Matron to ask
63 her about something in sight not much in sight
64 bring out austerity of the room]
65 You notice that I wear ~~glasses myself~~ ~~spectacles~~ reading glasses. [I need them
66 now, but as a probationer I did not need them]
67 I've never had ~~any~~ ~~glasses~~ spectacles
68 Have you any physical defects?
69 What kind of defect? Daisy asked in a low voice.
70 Any that I can't see, Miss Saunders, at a ~~rapid~~
71 cursory glance. You may be marked or scarred.
72 Your spine may be crooked... Have you any tendency
73 to pulmonary complaint she looked up sharply. Do
74 you understand what I mean by 'pulmonary'? - Yes it
75 means to do with the lungs. - Pertaining to the lungs,
76 the Matron said. - ~~chest troubles phthisis we're~~
77 ~~not consumptive in my family~~ At the same time,
78 I don't mean a weakly habit of complaint &
79 ~~fancied~~ imaginary aches or fancied weariness. You
80 realise perhaps that a grown woman must expect
81 to spend one fourth of her ~~life~~ in actual pain?
82 I suppose that's true considering your stays always
83 hurt a bit, where the laces come Daisy said.
84 [Real pain I am referring to]
85 To resume, have you ever been present at a death
86 or a birth? (Daisy shakes head.) Finally my dear
87 (me my dear startled Daisy) why do you want to
88 be a hospital nurse? - I wasn't there when my
89 mother died, but I wish I had been.
90

it as clear as possible from the beginning that there is no place for it in the running of a great hospital.

63   "(TEST here)." A mistake. Quite out of place for Matron to make a random test at an interview, or indeed at any time.

65   "I need them now." I left this in because it's not meant as a sentimental reflection, only as a warning to an ignorant girl.

At the end, however, as I saw as soon as I read it over, the dialogue goes completely to pieces. I got the question "Have you ever been present at a death or a birth?" out of one of the numerous handbooks published around 1912–14 on the nursing profession. It has a certain force, but it's wrong here, and so is Matron's "my dear" at line 86. The two women must end, as they began, as adversaries who feel respect for each other, but nothing more (or less) than that. Daisy finishes "down," but not down and out. No one ever gets the better of Daisy except herself, or rather her own weaknesses.

All this seems like paying far too much attention to an unimportant passage. But as I'm a hopelessly addicted writer of short books I have to try to see to it that every confrontation and every dialogue has some reference to what I hope will be understood as the heart of the novel. As I've tried to explain, it's about body, mind, and spirit.

2000

Coda

LAST WORDS

"Old end-game lost of old," Beckett calls it, "play and lose and have done with losing." A human being is old when he has survived long enough to name, with absolute confidence, a year, one of the next thirty, which he won't be there to see. Clinically speaking, during these last stages he is likely to lose his memory for recent events, his skill at problem solving, his power of abstract reasoning, and his ability to work with new and unfamiliar systems. (This will be partly because he can't adapt to them, but just as much because he doesn't admit the need for them.) What survives, if his body doesn't let him down completely, will be word fluency, understanding, enthusiasm, memory of long-passed events.

This looks like a special providence for old writers. Story time can continue to the very end, even if they are reduced (as Shakespeare surely was) to playing the last games against themselves. The memory of distant events and atmospheres, in particular, will stand by them. "My mind," George Eliot found, "works with the most freedom and the keenest sense of poetry in my remote past." *Middlemarch* followed. But the writer's memory is of a special kind. The opening of L. P. Hartley's *The Go-Between*—"The past is a foreign country: they do things differently there"—suggests that the return to childhood may not be consoling or even safe. At the age of fifty-eight Hartley felt himself compelled to go back there, putting it, however, a few years earlier than it really was, partly so that there would be no telephones and the small boy would be absolutely necessary to the lovers at the great house as a go-between, partly because the date 1900 would show Edwardian England at its deceptive "new dawn." There the narrator, as an aging man, re-enters the old domain of half-guilty, half-innocent emotions, "ignorant of the language but compelled to listen."

An old writer is even less likely than any other old person to be serene, mellow, and so forth. More probable are a vast irritation with human perversity, sometimes with fame itself, and an obstinate sense, against all odds, of the right direction for the future. "I detest the hardness of old age," Virginia Woolf wrote in her diary, the year before her death. "I feel it. I rasp. I'm tart." But she added, "I walk over the marsh saying, I am I: and must follow that furrow, not copy another." This certainty, even if it makes the readers uneasy, acts as a call to order, even as an unintentional reproach.

Tolstoy wrote *Resurrection* at the age of seventy-two, ferociously and without warning, to raise money for a charitable appeal. By this time he treated all fiction, and his own in particular, with reckless injustice. He was, he said, simply the clown in front of the ticket office, grimacing in order to get the crowd inside, where they would learn the truth. They would learn from *Resurrection* that man-made law and punishment— but also man-made revolution—is useless and evil. The resurrection takes place now and on this earth in the individual soul of every man and woman, as soon as they begin to pity each other. Prince Nekhlyudov is serving on a jury when a prostitute is brought into the dock, accused of murdering her drunken client. He recognizes her as his aunts' "half servant, half ward, the black-eyed, light-footed Katusha." Ten years earlier he had seduced her and left her pregnant. Now, when she is sentenced to exile, he follows her, trying to make reparation, from one convict camp to another across the breadth of Russia to Siberia. As readers we struggle alongside, knowing very well that Tolstoy cares nothing for our difficulties. The pages are crowded with characters whose names we can't remember, some introduced almost at the last moment. We are lectured unmercifully, and there is nowhere to hide from Tolstoy's indignation. But the old storyteller's art still beguiles at one moment and then, at another, strikes like a blow in the face.

To finish it, Tolstoy worked day and night, violently resentful of interruptions. Boris Pasternak, whose father did the illustrations, remembered the glue sizzling on the range ready to mount the drawings while a uniformed guard waited outside to take them to the Petersburg train. Such was the urgency of the old man and his book. The fact that the secretary of the charity committee had second thoughts, feeling that they ought not have accepted the profits from *Resurrection* because it aroused lust, shows that moral giants were in conflict here. Tolstoy replied with forbearance, but could have done so in the terms Joyce used about *Ulysses*— "If *Ulysses* isn't fit to read then life isn't fit to live." So, too, could Thomas Hardy, meeting the attacks on *Jude the Obscure* ("Jude the Obscene,"

Joyce's brother, Stanislaus, called it, when sent out to buy it in Dublin).
This powerful novel was the last of Hardy's "ventures into sincerity." He
had meant to call it *The Simpletons*—Jude being a simpleton to dream of
a university education when he was born a stonemason's son, and Sue, the
"slight, pale, bachelor girl," "the intellectualized, emancipated bundle of
nerves," being even more of a simpleton in trying to defy nature. For the
first and only time (he was fifty-five) Hardy was writing about his exact
contemporaries (when Sue leaves Jude she takes a steam tram). He had
direct reforms, in education and in the marriage laws, to press for. But the
book's subject, as he made clear, was the "deadly war between flesh and
spirit," which Jude is drawn into against his will, and which no reform is
ever likely to alter. It was this, in 1895, which caused outcry. Hardy must
have expected it, but he knew how to pretend to be astonished. Criticism
of *Jude*, he said, completely cured him of any interest in novel writing. He
had thirty-three more years to comment on the ironic and self-defeating
business of living and dying, but he preferred to make his farewells in
poetry.

Some late novels, however, have a note of leave-taking. *News from
Nowhere* was one of the last books William Morris wrote, publishing it
as a serial in *The Commonweal* in 1890. The subtitle is "An Epoch of
Rest," and although the rest is for the future inhabitants of England, the
"Once Poor," I don't think Morris would have chosen it if he hadn't
been getting on for sixty. He begins by looking at himself with kindly
detachment as he comes back one night on the Hammersmith Underground, disgusted at having lost his temper at a socialist meeting. The
party work is for equality, peace, and fellowship, but "if I could but see
a day of it! if I could but see it!" When he wakes next morning, into the
London of the twenty-first century, the builders and haymakers also see
a day of William Morris. It is this that gives the story its pathos and tension. Morris is the guest of the future. He is treated with overwhelming
hospitality, but, as he sees from the first, he is "other." His intellectual
curiosity and interest in history make him an odd man out, and at times
he gives the bright, contented people a touch of uneasiness, "making us
feel as if we were longing for something we cannot have." The interac-
tion between past and present follows him like a shadow. His journey up
the Thames leads him to his own house at Kelmscott. It stands
unchanged by the water meadows, but the garret bedrooms belong now
to little boys, the sons Morris never had. And at Kelmscott, the journey's

end, he finds not that the vision fades but that the people of Nowhere can no longer see him. "I noticed that none of the company looked at me. A pang shot through me, as of some disaster long expected and suddenly realized."

At the head of the last section of his *James Joyce*, Richard Ellmann printed a line from *Finnegans Wake*: "Quiet takes back her folded fields. Tranquille thanks. Adew." For Finnegan, the giant presence who sleeps beneath the city of Dublin, the wake is a resurrection as well as a funeral party, but Joyce, as he made an end of his book, felt exhausted, as though all the blood had run out of his brain. He calculated that the last passage, where Anna Livia runs out, "seasilt saltsick," into the Irish Sea, fading into a murmur at the last, had cost him sixteen hundred hours of work since he started on his book. It had taken him fifteen years to find the words for the journey of the night mind, asleep and dreaming, which we all share between us. Two years after publication he was dead. He referred to the *Wake* as a monster and believed that in the course of it words had gone as far as he could take them. They had become "pure music." It may be for this reason that composers—John Cage, John Butler, Stephen Albert—have paid the *Wake* so much attention. But Joyce certainly never ceased to believe that speech is the distinguishing mark of human beings, and that things, too, have their language. Language and speech can both be reassembled, in Joyce's own phrase, as a scissors-and-paste job, cut out and reassembled from everything he had heard and read, "engraved and retouched and edgewiped and puddenpadded" to represent the truth even of the unconscious. The boldness of such an attempt at the end of a career, Gide thought, was more beautiful than the boldness of a young man. But Joyce, as always, was surprised that his readers didn't laugh more at what, for him, had been comedy on the grand scale. Even in the final passage, where the river's voice confounds sleep and death, he had not intended to be bitter. One might say, no more bitter than is necessary for a good Irish joke.

While Tolstoy and William Morris both came to doubt art's power to change society—and if it failed in that it failed for them in everything—James Joyce and Virginia Woolf entrusted themselves to it, for its own sake, entirely. "Now they're bombing Spain," said Joyce in 1936. "Isn't it better to make a great joke instead, as I have done?" Virginia Woolf's Miss La Trobe, in *Between the Acts*, is her last version, perhaps consciously her last, of the artist in relation to society. Finishing the book, as always, was a strain on her perilous mental balance. It was written, but not revised for the press, when she walked out of her garden gate and down to the river to drown herself.

From 1938 onwards Leonard and Virginia Woolf were living for longer and longer periods in the country, at Rodmell in Sussex. *Between the Acts* is contained in a day and a night, and in one country house with its barn, pastures, and gardens. Poyntz Hall is old but middle-sized and ordinary—as far as anything described by Virginia Woolf is ordinary. There is no mention of it in the guidebooks, but "driving past, people said to each other, 'I wonder if that'll ever come into the market?'" But although its beauty is real, its suggestion of a settled contentment is not. A closer look shows "vast vacancies" of body and spirit. Children are divided from adults, husband from wife, servants from employers, and Poyntz Hall itself seems cut off from the war and almost unconcerned, although at any moment "guns might rake the ancient land into furrows." Miss La Trobe is the unlikely force that will make for wholeness. She is a bizarre, disconsolate figure, a lesbian deserted by her lover, fond of drink and known to the villagers as Bossy. Her art is as a presenter of pageants. She "gets them up," composing everything herself, words, music, and passing shows. A setting is required—Poyntz Hall itself— and an acceptable cause, in this case a collection for the repair of the parish church, but these are not the things that matter to Miss La Trobe. A heap of old clothes and a cast of amateur actors who don't always know their parts are all that she has to work with, and she despairs, or almost despairs, of making her audience "see." What she had had in mind to show them had been the whole history of their island, back to the "night before roads were made, or houses," through to the present moment when they would be asked to see their own reflections in great mirrors and looking glasses, borrowed from the Hall and held up to their view. All this had been her intention, but in her own judgment she has failed. She needs company, she needs a drink, but in the village she is an outcast and she knows that when she goes into the public bar, the customers will fall silent. This, however, is not important to her (just as Virginia Woolf tried to persuade herself, time after time, that what her critics said was unimportant). For her the failure—worse than death—is failure as an artist. But when the pageant is over and the audience has drifted away, leaving the park to the cows and the roosting swallows, Miss La Trobe is already possessed by a new idea. She has "heard the first words." These are words that other characters in the book will speak, but have not yet spoken. In fact, we never know what they are. But Miss La Trobe does know.

She strode off across the lawn. The house was dormant: one thread of smoke thickened against the trees. . . . From the earth green waters seemed to rise over her. She took her voyage away from the shore, and, raising her hand, fumbled for the latch of the iron entrance gate.

1988

INDEX